For Alan Spitzer,
with thanks for suggesting
this subject in the fall
of 1972 and for your
encouragement and support
ever since.

January 1, 1984

# Drink, Temperance and the Working Class in Nineteenth-Century Germany

# Drink, Temperance and the Working Class in Nineteenth-Century Germany

JAMES S. ROBERTS

Boston
GEORGE ALLEN & UNWIN
London        Sydney

**Allen & Unwin, Inc.,**
**9 Winchester Terrace, Winchester, Mass. 01890, USA**

George Allen & Unwin (Publishers) Ltd,
40 Museum Street, London WC1A 1LU, UK

George Allen & Unwin (Publishers) Ltd,
Park Lane, Hemel Hempstead, Herts HP2 4TE, UK

George Allen & Unwin Australia Pty Ltd,
8 Napier Street, North Sydney, NSW 2060, Australia


First published in 1984

---

**Library of Congress Cataloging in Publication Data**

Roberts, James S.
   Drink, temperance, and the working class in
nineteenth-century Germant.
Bibliography: p.
Includes index.
1. Liquor problem—Germany—History—19th century.
2. Temperance—History—19th century.
3. Labour and laboring classes—Germany—Social conditions. I. Title.
HV5476.R6      1983      394.1'3'0943      83-15449
ISBN 0-04-943029-7

---

**British Library Cataloguing in Publication Data**

Roberts, James S.
   Drink, temperance and the working class in
nineteenth-century Germany.
1. Liqor problem—Germany—History
I. Title
178'.1'0943      HV5447
ISBN 0-04-943029-7

---

Set in 10 on 11 point Plantin by Grove Graphics, Tring, Hertfordshire
and printed in Great Britain
by Biddles Ltd., Guildford, Surrey

# Contents

# List of Tables

# List of Figures

For
Deborah

# Preface

In Germany, as in the other industrializing countries of Europe and North America, the Drink Question – the discussion of the causes, consequences, and control of popular drinking behaviour – was a matter of persistent public concern throughout the nineteenth century. In this book, I attempt to explain why by examining both the realities of popular drinking behavior and the perceptions and activities of those influential Germans who made the Drink Question an enduring public issue. My discussion has three fundamental goals and in pursuing them develops three interrelated arguments. In the first place, I attempt to define the nineteenth-century alcohol problem. I argue that alcohol was not so much psychologically as physiologically rooted in the everyday experience of working-class life. The primary characteristic of popular drinking behavior was not widespread drunkenness but the use, day in and day out, of relatively small quantities of alcohol in a variety of everyday settings. To the extent that drinking was a problem, not for the guardians of social order but for the people consuming the alcohol, the problem was the result of this everyday drinking, deeply rooted in larger patterns of work, diet and sociability. Secondly, I chart the main contours of public concern with the Drink Question in the context of Germany's social, economic, and political development. The Drink Question was taken up both by the educated middle classes and the socialist labor movement. I argue that the temperance reform was more than a reaction to modernity or an effort to manipulate the lower classes, as some commentators have suggested. Instead I try to show how the temperance movement was part of Germany's liberal tradition, sharing both its strengths and its weaknesses. Finally, by drawing on the growing literature on the Drink Question in other nineteenth-century societies, I seek to put Germany's answer to the Drink Question into comparative historical perspective. I argue that social, economic, and political circumstances peculiar to Germany both shaped the terms in which the Drink Question was framed and limited the range of tactical options open to the temperance movement. Unlike its British and American counterparts, the German temperance movement eschewed electoral politics and a direct confrontation with the drink trade. A national consensus about drinking behavior was thus preserved that spared German society the divisive conflicts over alcohol that characterized England and the United States.

In proportion to its length, the chronological and geographical sweep of this book is large. What it lacks in local detail, however, I hope it makes up in historical perspective. Although the periodization employed here may seem at first sight to derive only from the landmarks of conventional political history, it is only tangentially related to them. The year 1815 marked the final reckoning with Napoleon and the political restoration effected by the Congress of Vienna, but in terminating years of warfare, it also brought new market conditions to German agriculture that hastened the spread of rural distilleries and thus established the material foundation of the nineteenth-century alcohol problem. And in 1914, when Germany went to war with most of the rest of Europe ranged against her, legal restrictions on the production and consumption of beverage alcohol were put into effect that set the seal on more than a decade of declining per capita consumption. As in so many other ways, the First World War marked the end of an era in Germany's confrontation with the Drink Question as well. The per capita consumption of alcoholic beverages in Germany did not again reach prewar levels until the mid-1960s.

The geographical assumptions of political history may be even less appropriate for social history than the temporal ones. Nonetheless, the locus of study in this book is the Germany defined by the *kleindeutsche* nation state of 1871. After mid-century the German temperance movement became increasingly national in scope and increasingly political in tactics. In attempting to shape the many aspects of the Imperial Commercial Code that affected the drink trade, for example, the temperance movement had perforce to operate on the national level. The movement was therefore shaped by national institutions, and it was these that it most wanted to influence. This national focus may obscure the subtleties of regional variation and local custom, especially in the discussion of drinking behaviour itself. I have done my best to acknowledge these nuances, but I have not been able to explore them in any detail.

This is also the place to express my gratitude to the teachers, scholars and friends who have helped make the time and effort put into this book worthwhile. Two superlative undergraduate teachers at Northwestern University, Robert J. Bezucha, now at Amherst College, and James J. Sheehan, now at Stanford, set me on my professional course. David Schoenbaum and Alan B. Spitzer continued their tradition in different ways at the University of Iowa, allowing me to develop my rather novel interests in an atmosphere both challenging and supportive. During two years as a DAAD research fellow in Germany, historians at the University of Freiburg provided patient criticism as well as consistent stimulation. I am especially indebted to Professor Heinrich A. Winkler, Dr Ulrich Kluge, Andreas Kunz, and Rudolf Muhs, not only for sharing with me their vast knowledge of German history but also for their practical introductions to the beers and wines of the Upper Rhine. Archivists and librarians throughout Germany generously shared with me their time and resources but none more graciously than Frau Maria-Dina Mähler, Librarian of the *Deutsche Hauptstelle gegen die Suchtgefahren* in Hamm and Herr Reinhardt Strecker, Archivist of the *Deutsche Caritas Verband* in Freiburg. I am also grateful to Professor Jürgen Kocka and Professor Hans-Ulrich Wehler of the University of Bielefeld for their invitation to present the preliminary results of my research to the Fourth Bielefeld Social History Workshop in the summer of 1977.

I have spent the last three years as a Lecturer in the History Department at Stanford University, where I have been privileged to call Gordon Craig, Peter Paret and James Sheehan my colleagues. Their interest and encouragement have buoyed my spirits more often than they know. I would also like to thank my colleague J. R. Bailey, who has read every conceivable form and fragment of this book and who has never given up the task of trying to make me a better historian. The Alcohol Research Group in the School of Public Health, University of California, Berkeley, has provided my intellectual home this year. Robin Room, Ron Roizen, Harry Levine and Susanna Barrows, all affiliated in one way or another with the ARG, have provided invaluable stimulation as this project has been brought to a close. All of these people have contributed to the strengths of this book; responsibility for its weaknesses is all my own.

I wish also to acknowledge the financial assistance of the *Deutscher Akademischer Austauschdienst* for research support during 1975–7, the University of Iowa, Stanford University, and the Alcohol Research Group, which awarded me a post-doctoral fellowship for 1982–3 under its National Institute on Alcohol Abuse and Alcoholism Grant No. 2 732 AA07240-05 for Graduate Research Training in Alcohol Problems. Portions of Chapter 5 originally appeared in my essay 'Drink and the Labour Movement: The *Schnaps* Boycott of 1909' (in *The German Working Class, 1888–1933*, ed. Richard J. Evans [London: Croom Helm, 1982]) and are reprinted here with the permission of the publisher.

Finally, I would like to thank the members of what is becoming a very extended family – Jakubs, Ellis, Dion and most of all Roberts – for years of patience, love, understanding, intellectual stimulation, and plain good humor. To my wonderful father, who in having two children grow up to be historians has borne nearly all that a father can bear, I pay special homage. And to my fraternal colleague, David D. Roberts, who first introduced me to the life of the mind, I express both gratitude and the admiration that, although I remain seven years his junior, is no longer a little brother's.

# Drink, Temperance and the Working Class in Nineteenth-Century Germany

# Chapter 1

# Introduction: Temperance History in Comparative Perspective

> No other vice has . . . such power over man as drunkenness;
> it brutalizes him, degrades him, and reduces him to an animal.
> (Böttcher, 1839c, p. 107)[1]

Men drink for an extraordinary variety of reasons. They use alcohol to lend dignity to the rituals of human life, from the most profound religious ceremonies to the most elementary forms of hospitality. They drink to quench their thirsts, to enliven their diets, to enhance their sexual pleasure, to endure the heat, the cold and the rain. They drink to relax, and they drink to call forth extraordinary exertions. They use alcohol to celebrate their triumphs and to drown their sorrows.

Alcohol's effects on human behavior and on human society are just as contradictory as the motives that lead men to drink in the first place. Alcohol enlivens but it also enervates. It helps to reinforce social ties but it also destroys them. It lends solemnity and dignity to man's activities but it also brings shame and degradation. It fosters happiness, contentment and contemplation, but it also spawns aggression, violence and destruction.

Anthropologists have been among the keenest students of the ambivalent relationship between man and alcohol. (Pittman and Snyder, 1962; Heath, 1975, 1976; Marshall, 1979a) The metabolism of alcohol and its effects on sensory-motor functions do not vary, but how men use alcohol and how they behave under its influence are attributes of culture that are socially learned. (MacAndrew and Edgerton, 1969; Marshall, 1979b, pp. 451–7) Both formal and informal rules govern the consumption of alcohol in every society, and these vary markedly from place to place and over time. As one anthropologist has written,

> when a man lifts a cup, it is not only the kind of drink that is in it, the amount he is likely to take, the circumstances under which he will do the drinking that are specified in advance for him, but also whether the

---

[1] The Harvard (author/date) system has been used for the references, except for anonymous periodical articles which are cited in full in the text.

contents of the cup will stupefy or cheer, whether they will induce affection or aggression, guilt or unalloyed pleasure. These and many other cultural definitions attach to the drink even before it touches the lips. (Mandlebaum, 1979, p. 17)

The rules that govern drinking and not drinking are thus the historical and cultural artefacts of human experience. In complex, highly stratified societies, where formal and informal sumptuary codes denote social standing, these rules often become the subject of social and political controversy. In such situations, styles of alcohol consumption, drinking and not drinking, can become an integral part of individual and group identity and thus one of the focal points around which social and cultural conflict revolve. (Gusfield, 1962, 1963; Honnigmann, 1979)

## Origins of the Drink Question

The rules that governed drinking behavior were severely strained in the industrializing societies of Western Europe and North America in the course of the eighteenth and nineteenth centuries. Innovations in popular drinking behavior coincided with the fundamental social changes that have created the modern world. Among these fundamental transformations were the emergence of an urban-industrial social order, the consolidation of modern nation states with increasingly democratic forms of government, and the rise to social, economic and political prominence of the middle classes.

The Drink Question – the discussion of the causes, consequences and control of popular drinking behavior – was born out of this convergence. The traditional norms that had governed alcohol consumption were undermined in two ways. On the one hand, a sudden and altogether unprecedented increase in the availability of distilled alcohol made new and potentially disruptive patterns of alcohol consumption feasible. And on the other, the champions of the larger processes of social change called traditional habits of consumption into question as they undertook the enormous task of remaking popular traditions to suit their own values and interests. Changes in popular consumption patterns would have been sufficient to make the Drink Question an important public issue. The energy and zeal of new social forces made it a crusade.

Changes in popular drinking behavior were rooted in the development of agrarian capitalism. Within the context of the emerging money economy, the capacity to produce agricultural products outstripped the available opportunities for profitably marketing them. (Rorabaugh, 1979, pp. 87–9) In this situation, landowners began to convert their surpluses of staple crops into alcohol. The product that flowed out of their simple but rapidly improving stills was more easily stored and transported than the raw materials from which it was made and found a ready and almost infinitely elastic market. The production of alcohol thus became a typical feature of the development of agrarian capitalism on the eve of the Industrial Revolution and an integral part of the cycle of agricultural production. The use of strong drink, once a luxury of the affluent, was now readily within the financial grasp of the common man. (Webb, 1963, pp. 24–8; Engels, 1962c; Teuteberg and Wiegelmann, 1972, pp. 234, 238, 247–50, 329–30; Rorabaugh, 1979, pp. 6–92)

This revolution in the production of distilled alcohol coincided with other fundamental social processes that were bound in their own right to provoke attacks on traditional habits of consumption. Men from social groups which had previously indulged themselves with strong drink came to disdain it, and what once had been the proper man's pleasure now became the poor man's vice. (Rorabaugh, 1979, p. 57) As the middle classes adopted coffee and tea, beverages that fostered sobriety and concentration, they worried all the more about the alcohol consumption of their social inferiors. (Schivelbusch, 1980, pp. 25–95 passim)

In the first place, industrialization and urbanization altered the context in which alcohol was consumed. As Brian Harrison has observed, the development of industrial capitalism had contradictory consequences for popular drinking behavior, but in the main, the new system of production and social relations exerted a pressure towards sobriety. (Harrison, 1971, pp. 40–1; cf. Lambert, 1975; Roberts, 1981a) Industrialization and urbanization thickened the web of human interdependence, enhancing the potential dangers alcohol could pose to the social order while making its control by customary means more difficult. At the same time, the new system of production increased the number of people with a material stake in sobriety. All those concerned with economic efficiency and social discipline insisted that popular alcohol consumption had to be curtailed.

As the material foundations of Western European and American life changed, so too did its fundamental forms of political organization. With the political enfranchisement of ever wider sectors of the population, both champions and critics of popular democracy insisted on the need for sobriety. A political system intended to allow rational men to find rational solutions to their problems had to encourage – and for some, even enforce – popular sobriety. Drunkenness, on the other hand, could only pervert the political process, liberating the beast in man and corrupting his rational faculties. (Levine, 1978, p. 124; Rorabaugh, 1979, pp. 194–5) Patriotic Europeans and Americans saw the heavy drinker as a threat to the common good, and they frequently appealed, whether to their fellow citizens or to the state, for ameliorative action on patriotic grounds.

These changes in the way men governed themselves and satisfied their material needs were bound up with important shifts in individual and social values whose tendency was also to call traditional habits of consumption into question. In the broadest sense, these changes can be described as the emergence of a middle-class ethos. The elements of this ethos are broadly familiar – a self-reliant individualism, a self-conscious work ethic and a glorification of hearth and home. Its glue was the ideal of self-control. As Max Weber wrote in his classic study of the Protestant ethic, the individual was expected to put himself under 'the supremacy of a purposeful will, to bring his actions under constant self-control.' This new personality type required 'a systematic method of rational conduct with the purpose of overcoming the *status naturae*, to free man from the power of irrational impulses.' (1958, pp. 118–19; Levine, 1978, p. 141) Frugality, punctuality and sobriety were among the cardinal virtues of this ethos, and the suppression of blood sports, immorality and, not least, popular drunkenness were among its principal goals. Self-confident and aggressive, the middle classes impressed this bundle of values and aspirations on more and more political and social territory in the course of the late eighteenth and nineteenth centuries.

One of the intellectual underpinnings of the middle-class ethos was the thought of the Enlightenment. The Enlightenment tradition affected perceptions of popular drinking behavior in several ways. Alcohol created a dependence and servility that was antithetical to the Enlightenment ideal of the rational individual and thus clouded the prospect for social improvement. More immediately, the tradition of scientific medicine nourished by the Enlightenment was one of the first authoritative intellectual traditions to call the habitual use of alcohol into question. (For an overview: Hirsch, 1949; Bynum, 1968) In the American colonies, the works of the Quaker physician Benjamin Rush were path-breaking. His *An Inquiry Into The Effects of Ardent Spirits Upon The Human Body* was published in 1785. Other important works followed. The leading figure in Great Britain was Thomas Trotter, whose 1788 dissertation at Edinburgh (*De ebrietate, ejusque effectibus in corpus humanum*) was expanded and published for a more general readership, appearing in 1804 as *An Essay, Medical, Philosophical, and Chemical, on Drunkenness*. The most important German physician to write on the subject during this period was Christoph Wilhelm Hufeland, the court physician in Berlin, whose world-famous *Makrobiotik* condemned the non-medicinal use of spirits on both medical and moral grounds in 1796. (pp. 190–2, 305–7) Hufeland published a shorter broadside, *Ueber die Vergiftung durch Branntwein* in 1802. (Bergman, 1907, pp. 100–5) All of these works, the first signs of a changing perception of alcohol and its individual and social consequences, reflect an increasing preoccupation with self-control and alcohol's apparent ability to destroy it.

A second major source of the middle-class ethos was Protestant religion. Despite the rationalism of the Enlightenment and its ultimately secular and anti-clerical implications, the middle classes, in Eric Hobsbawm's words, 'needed the discipline and organization of a strong and single-minded morality' in their efforts to remake the world in their own image. (1962, p. 260) The late eighteenth and early nineteenth centuries brought Protestant religious revivals to societies not only strained by decades of war and revolution but also feeling the first consequences of the transition to industrial capitalism. For the middle classes, evangelical religion justified and encouraged the austerity and hard work necessary for success in a generation of rising entrepreneurs and competitive small businessmen. It sanctioned their profits and their social position against the suspicions of traditional elites and provided a measure of emotional gratification in a life otherwise given over to the pursuit of material gain. It encouraged the individual and social discipline − the subjugation of the flesh − required in the new society.

At the same time, evangelical religion promoted a tradition of social activism and responsibility that was anything but conservative. It was the bedrock of middle-class concern with a wide variety of humanitarian reforms and social issues, from anti-slavery to feminism. Rejecting the Calvinist insistence on the inadequacy and even irrelevance of human effort to attain salvation, evangelical religion fostered a commitment to social amelioration that made the reformer's zeal a sign of salvation and grace. (Timberlake, 1966, pp. 4–38; Walters, 1978, pp. 21–38) The evangelicals' emphasis on brotherly love and making the world a Christian place was a principal means by which the tension between rationalism and religion was resolved. (Smith, 1955) The fruits of modern science and industry could be legitimately enjoyed only in a just society, and this required positive social action in addition to personal piety and rectitude. As William Rorabaugh has written of the American scene, 'men who believed that salvation required faith, that good deeds could be signs of holiness, and that man was God's agent on earth turned to a religion that preached social reform.' (Rorabaugh, 1979, pp. 213–14). This was one of the ways the virtues of self-control were propagated throughout modern society.

Religion and Enlightenment fused in the temperance reform, a middle-class creation that expressed − even anticipated − the needs of the emerging social order. As Harry G. Levine has written, 'the alcohol problem, as it came to be defined in the 19th century, centered on the grand social issues of developing capitalist society: poverty, crime, violence, family problems, health, business efficiency, individual mobility, and financial success.' (1978, p. 87) Control, both of self and of others, was the underlying theme of these concerns. (Levine, 1978; Dannenbaum, 1981) Alcohol was perceived as a threat to the most basic assumptions of bourgeois society because it appeared to dissolve the barriers that held man's darker instincts in check. In an emerging social order whose economic and political systems assumed the rationality, freedom, and essential equality of the individual, these barriers had to be constantly created and maintained.

The men whose principal task it was to erect and repair these inner barriers, physicians and clergymen above all, made alcohol, only recently available to the great mass of the population as an everyday beverage, the focal point of their concern about the ultimate efficacy of these internalized social controls. They developed a new conception of alcohol and its individual and social consequences. In Early Modern Europe and Colonial North America, alcohol had been accepted as one of God's gifts. (Levine, 1978, pp. 67–75; Stolleis, 1981; cf. the article 'Saufen' in Zedler, 1714/63) Man was believed to possess the moral freedom either to use it rationally or to abuse it. What replaced this earlier view was an almost Manichean vision which ascribed independent, demonic powers to alcohol. Alcohol was removed from the arena of man's moral discretion; instead of serving man, alcohol now threatened to master him. It was no longer assumed that alcohol was used and abused according to the other predispositons of the individual drinker. The new view had it that alcohol itself could control human behavior, destroy the rational will, and thus lead man, his moral defenses shattered and his bestial instincts given free rein, to self-destruction and social evil.

The scientific and medical veneer of this moral theory, which shows unmistakable affinities to Protestant ethics, was provided by the concept of addiction, a creation of the late eighteenth and early nineteenth centuries, which, as Levine has written, 'can best be understood not as an independent medical or scientific discovery, but as part of a transformation in social thought' characteristic of the Western world in the late eighteenth and early nineteenth centuries. (1978, p. 46) The concept of addiction was the mirror image and hence the symbolic affirmation of the ideal of rational self-control. Temperance reformers propagated a view of alcohol akin to contemporary views of heroin. Whoever used it would eventually become addicted; their degradation and ruin would inevitably follow. The only way to prevent this disaster was to abstain completely from spiritous liquor, that is, to make a positive act of self-control, and to encourage others to do the same. This was the governing conception with which the nineteenth-century temperance reform began. Religion and science could now march hand-in-hand in eradicating – or at least reforming – the use of Western man's traditional drug of preference: beverage alcohol. (cf. Schivelbusch, 1980, p. 215)

Traditional assumptions about the use of alcoholic beverages were thus undermined from two separate directions. A revolution in the production of spirits made strong drink more accessible and traditional methods of control more difficult. At the same time, the social, economic, and political context in which alcohol was produced, marketed and consumed was being transformed. In the process, new social forces came to the fore with both a moral and a material stake in sobriety. The relationship between alcohol, man and society was rethought, and men and women began to mobilize their energies and resources for what historian Jed Dannenbaum has rightly called 'the most popular, influential and long-lived social reform movement in the Western world' (1981, p. 3).

## Voluntary Association and Temperance Reform

The late eighteenth and early nineteenth centuries saw a massive proliferation of voluntary associations of all kinds as the free association of free men became an increasingly important part of the social order. Association was the catchword of an age distrustful of government and confident in man's capacity for moral and social improvement. (Nipperdey, 1976, pp. 174–205) As Alexis de Tocqueville observed, no society was as densely covered by voluntary associations as America, and it is not surprising that the first modern associations for the promotion of temperance developed on American soil. (1945, Vol. 1, pp. 198–205; Vol. 2, pp. 114–18) But from its American home, the temperance movement eventually had an impact of global proportions.

The temperance movement was created by men concerned about the fragility of the social order in a period of rapid economic and political change. Many of the movement's basic features were similar wherever the reform took root. Its leadership and impetus came from the Protestant middle classes; its grass roots support was found among self-respecting farmers and workingmen. Its religious leitmotifs were sin and salvation, human frailty and the power of brotherly love. Its secular goals, seldom divorced from their Christian inspiration, were social harmony, earthly justice and the amelioration of human suffering. Its initial methods were those of evangelical revivalism – camp meetings, emotion-laden rhetoric, and the mass distribution of hortatory tracts. Its weapons, at least at first, were moral suasion and the temperance pledge. Its ultimate aim was to promote the individual and social discipline essential to a self-governing industrial society.

The Drink Question, then, was on the social and political agenda all over Western Europe and North America in the nineteenth century. Voluntary associations for the promotion of sobriety were created to counter the threat that popular drinking behavior seemed to pose for a rapidly changing social order, but these associations quickly proved inadequate to the tasks they had set themselves. The temperance Utopia was not in sight. Once initial hopes for quick success were dashed, temperance history became intertwined with the other features of each nation's social, economic, and political development. At this point, the interesting differences in temperance history begin to arise, for the temperance movement ultimately took different forms, adopted different tactics and pursued different goals in each of the countries where it struck root. In contrast to its British and American counterparts, the German temperance movement never embraced teetotalism and prohibitionism and never entered the arena of electoral politics. As we shall see, the fact that the German temperance movement had little to do with politics in the narrow sense had a great deal to do with politics in the wider sense – with the political culture and political institutions of nineteenth-century Germany.

## Social Reform or Social Control?

In the past two decades, the temperance movements in England and the United States have attracted a great deal of historical attention. New directions in social and labor history have encouraged this line of research by directing attention to the process by which the institutions of industrial capitalism were created and maintained in Western Europe and North America and to the ways in which specific social groups participated in and experienced this great transformation. Research on the conditions of working-class life and the patterns of working-class culture has focused attention on the important roles – and the positive and negative consequences – of drink and the tavern for working-class populations. (e.g. Conzen, 1976, pp. 119–20, 156–7; Cumbler, 1979) At the same time, investigations of the way old and new elites responded to the problems of an industrializing society have focused attention on a variety of middle-class reform movements, both enriching and going beyond traditional political perspectives. (Harrison, 1965/6, 1971; Chickering, 1975; Blocker, 1976; Evans, 1976) The temperance movement has been one of the strands of middle-class reform frequently mentioned in this literature. Finally, recent interest in local history and community studies has revealed some of the specific contexts and concerns out of which the temperance reform was generated and the patterns of class relations it expressed. (Faler, 1974; Dawly, 1976, pp. 36–7; Bodnar, 1977; Dodd, 1978; Hirsch, 1978, pp. 104–5; Johnson, 1978; Walkowitz, 1978; Laurie, 1980)

Two rather different interpretations of temperance history have emerged in the recent literature, one sympathetic, the other more critical. The most favorable interpretations have come from historians and other scholars who have either assumed or sought to demonstrate that intemperance was no mere figment of the bourgeois imagination but a serious social problem that demanded remedial action. Historians of English temperance like Brian Harrison and A. E. Dingle as well as students of the American scene like James H. Timberlake and Ian R. Tyrrell have not only only seen the temperance reform as necessary and desirable, they have also linked the temperance movement to the other major currents of progressive, humanitarian social reform. (Timberlake, 1966; Burnham, 1968; Harrison, 1971; Blocker, 1976; Clark, 1976; Tyrrell, 1979; Dingle, 1980) In the process, they have challenged the older notion, advanced by an earlier generation of American historians like Ray Allen Billington and Richard Hofstadter, that the men and women who supported the temperance cause were essentially reactionary, anti-modern and self-serving. (Billington, 1964, pp. 195, 323; Hofstadter, 1955, pp. 288–93, 298–9; cf. Gusfield, 1963) This sympathetic perspective has received at least tangential support from recent studies of labor history which suggest that many workingmen embraced the temperance cause on their own initiative, realizing that drink could be a major obstacle to both personal improvement and collective advance. (Harrison, 1973b; Faler, 1974; Dodd, 1978; Walkowitz, 1978, pp. 126–7; Laurie, 1980, pp. 71–2)

A more critical perspective on temperance history has been developed by historians who view the alcohol problem as a mere epiphenomenon of nineteenth-century history and who see the fundamental problems of that (and this) era in the basic economic and political structures of industrial capitalism. They too assert the middle-class character of the reform, but for them middle-class reform is a contradiction in terms. According to this interpretation, advanced for example by John J. Rubarger's study of the influence of big business in American temperance history, Levine's examination of temperance ideology, and Paul E. Johnson's study of early-nineteenth-century Rochester, New York, the temperance reform was an expression of narrow class interests often intertwined with the worst kinds of American middle-class activism, including nativism, racism, and the suppression of labor. (Rumbarger, 1968; Johnson, 1978; Levine, 1978) In this view, temperance was a coercive reform, designed above all to create and control a stable labor force and to discipline, at least in the American case, an unruly immigrant population. It was a means to defend middle-class values and thus the social and political pre-eminence of the middle class against the increasingly threatening forces of plutocracy and big business, on the one hand, and an increasingly restless working class, on the other. For these writers, the key term in the study of temperance history is not social reform but social control.

At first sight, these views appear mutually exclusive, but in fact there is a measure of validity in both of them. This is not to say that the truth lies somewhere in between but rather to suggest that the social and political import of the temperance reform could vary from one context to another. Just as the consumption of alcoholic beverages has different consequences in different cultural settings, so the temperance movement could take on different meanings, and appeal to different constituencies at different times and places. (Dannenbaum, 1981) Concern with the Drink Question could be combined with any number of political and economic positions. It was the kind of issue that could appeal alternately or even simultaneously to labor leaders and businessmen, to farmers and workers, to Protestants and Catholics. But neither the underlying motives of their concerns nor the forms through which they expressed them were ever precisely the same.

The historiographical conclusion to be drawn from the recent literature on the temperance movement would seem to be that few unqualified generalizations about the movement's composition, appeal, purposes or methods can be made. Despite the common developments that put the Drink Question on the social and political agenda all over Western Europe and North America in the nineteenth century, the concerns it evoked and the responses it elicited were historically contingent, specific products of specific historical circumstances, and thus subject to local variation and change over time. The growing literature on England and the United States suggests important interpretive possibilities and provides useful opportunities for comparison, but an analysis of the German temperance movement must begin with German conditions, focusing on particular organizations in specific historical settings.

# Chapter 2

# Volkserhebung Wider Den Branntwein: The Early German Temperance Movement

This is a war of Reason against insanity, of Christian culture against bestial brutality, of freedom against the most disgraceful slavery. It is a sacred war, a struggle for the most cherished values of humanity. ('Aufruf an edle deutsche Frauen und Jungfrauen,' *Monatsblatt für die Enthaltsamkeitssache*, vol. 2, no. 8 (May 1846), pp. 58–9)

In 1815 peace was restored to the German states as to the rest of Europe. The immediate goals of the Wars of Liberation had been accomplished; Napoleon had twice been defeated, and Germans could now go back to ordering their own affairs. But for those Germans who had participated in the Wars of Liberation in the hopes of not only defeating the French intruder but also bringing about a renewal of their own national life, the aftermath of victory proved profoundly disappointing. Their aspirations for a liberal and united Germany clashed head-on with the realities of dynastic interests and a strong ideological and cultural reaction against the principles of the French Revolution. Their hopes never had the remotest chance of fulfillment at the peace conference convened in Vienna to reorder the affairs of Europe. Old principles of legitimacy were reaffirmed, and despite some territorial reorganization, the dynastic principles of the past were preserved. The loose and nearly meaningless bonds of the German Confederation succeeded the equally inconsequential Holy Roman Empire, a victim of Napoleon's hegemony in the German states after 1806, and the dualism of Austria and Prussia was perpetuated.

## Society and Politics in the German States, 1815–48

With the sovereignty of the territorial princes upheld, German domestic politics took on old particularistic forms. Only in the south German states of Baden, Bavaria, and Württemberg were constitutional governments established with representative assemblies. In Prussia, the country in which the idealistic younger generation had invested its hopes, Frederick William

III never granted the constitution he had promised under the influence of the great reformers Stein and Hardenburg. Prince Metternich, the Austrian prime minister and the architect of political reaction in Central Europe, carried the other German states with him in an effort to eradicate liberalism and nationalism as effective political forces. In this he could not fully succeed, but for nearly three decades after 1819, when the famous Carlsbad Decrees put an end to the radical student movement known as the *Burschenschaften*, German political life remained in a straitjacket. The universities were purged and Enlightment ideals discredited. A neo-pietist religious revival brought theological rationalism into disrepute while strengthening the ties between Throne and Altar. In Prussia the Protestant church emerged as one of the most steadfast supporters of the Hohenzollern monarchy, insisting on absolute loyalty and obedience to what it proclaimed to be a God-willed social and political order.

In this atmosphere, the liberal movement that developed all over Germany in opposition to this Restoration was forced to take subterranean forms. (Sheehan, 1978, pp. 7–50) A loose 'family' of men and ideas, this liberal political opposition, with its demands for constitutional self-government and its hopes for national unification, aimed to create a new political organization for the German people that would allow them to participate more directly in shaping their collective destiny and to take their rightful place among nations. Their ideals found a home in the hearts and minds of that broad *Mittelstand* of German society that lay between the economically dependent and still largely apolitical masses of rural and urban wage earners and the overwhelmingly conservative nobility. The *Mittelstand* thus included a broad spectrum of German society, from master craftsmen and industrialists to independent professional men and higher civil servants. Their dissatisfaction, prodding and scolding provided the political dynamic of the years between the Restoration of 1815 and the Revolution of 1848, the years known in German historiography as the *Vormärz*.

German politics were played out in an atmosphere of economic crisis. Germany remained an overwhelmingly rural and agrarian society in the first half of the nineteenth century. In 1816, about three-quarters of Prussia's inhabitants lived in the countryside; a half century later this figure had scarcely changed (the shift was from 73.5 per cent in 1816 to 71.5 per cent in 1872: Borchardt, 1972, p. 581). Those who worked the land could take little comfort in this apparent stability. Despite the legal emancipation of the peasantry in the first half of the nineteenth century, the economic condition of the rural masses declined in many areas. In the Prussian East the number of independent peasant farms decreased by 50,000 in the aftermath of the emancipation, and an additional 70,000 small-holdings were absorbed by the large estates. (Holborn, 1964, p. 409) In the South and West, where partible inheritance was the rule, the land was divided and subdivided so many times that even a bare subsistence was nearly impossible. (Hamerow, 1958, p. 53)

If most Germans were engaged in agriculture, there were still about 2.9 million Germans, or 20 per cent of the working population, employed in industry and handicrafts by the end of the 1840s. (Kaufhold, 1976, p. 354) But compared to England, Germany remained an economic backwater. German steam engines could muster only about 6 per cent of the power generated by British machines at mid-century. (Borchardt, 1972, p. 53) As late as 1846, only about 4 per cent of the work-force was employed in the modern industrial sector (Engelsing, 1973, p. 149)

Yet any view that this was a stagnant society would be misleading. Population growth, agricultural reform and industrial innovation were shaping German society just as they were the other nations of Western Europe. Though the 1820s were dominated by a long-lasting agricultural depression, the 1830s and early 1840s were years of economic expansion. The Prussian-German Customs Union was inaugurated in 1834 and soon linked 18 states and 23.5 million people. The first German railway line opened a year later. By 1850, 3,660 miles of track had been laid, more than twice the total mileage of France. (Henderson, 1975, p. 49) There was a substantial increase in the number of people involved in industry and handicrafts. Whereas an estimated 1.6 million Germans had been employed in crafts, textiles, mining, and factory production (*Großgewerbe*) in 1800, by 1846/8 the total had reached 2.9 million. The German population had grown 45 per cent in this period, but the number of people employed in industry and handicrafts had increased by 80 per cent. Most of the gains occurred after 1830. (Kaufhold, 1976, p. 354) This period of rapid expansion came to an end only after the disastrous harvest failures of the mid 1840s.

Yet despite the expansion of output and the quickening pace of economic activity that began in the early 1830s, Germany was caught in a structural crisis that confined hundreds of thousands of its citizens to a life of misery. (Abel, 1972; Köllmann, 1974a) The 1846 edition of the *Brockhaus Real-Enzyklopädie* noted with alarm that a new term had entered the German language: *Pauperismus*.

> Pauperism is present [the article explained] where a numerous class of the population can earn only the scantiest livelihood despite the most strenuous efforts, is not certain even of this, is sacrificed to this condition as a rule for life at birth, has no prospects for improvement, sinks ever deeper into apathy and brutality, provides recruits for the epidemic *Branntwein* plague, for bestial depravity of all kinds, and for the poor houses, work houses and prisons, and is still increasing and reproducing itself with growing rapidity. (Quoted in Bosl and Weis, 1976, pp. 257–8)

Population growth was at the root of the problem. By mid-century there were 10 million more Germans to be fed, clothed, sheltered, and employed than there had been when the Napoleonic Wars ended.[1] This rapid population growth far outstripped the ability of German society to absorb it and produced a period of endemic social crisis. Almost 800,000 Germans were forced to leave their homelands, most of them for the New World, between 1815 and 1849. (Köllmann, 1974b, p. 36; 1976, pp. 27–30) The standard of living of those who remained deteriorated markedly, and the number of people in both town and country who lived on the very edge of subsistence, unable to find secure employment or an adequate income, increased at a pace that shocked and alarmed contemporaries. Something on the order of 50–60 per cent of the German population lived in these conditions. (Conze, 1954; Fischer, 1963) All those who contributed to the wide-ranging *Pauperismus* discussion that developed in the 1830s and 1840s agreed on the threat this situation posed to the social order. (Mombert, 1921; Jantke and Hilger, 1965) The uprising of hard-pressed handloom weavers in Silesia in 1844 was only the most dramatic and alarming revelation of this potential. As the German economy adjusted slowly and painfully to these population pressures, the shock of successive harvest failures in 1845, 1846 and 1847 and an attendant commercial depression made the latent crisis manifest, pushing thousands of families below the level of subsistence and preparing the way for the revolutionary disturbances of 1848/9.

## The Schnaps Revolution

These processes of social and economic change naturally affected the production, distribution and consumption of alcoholic beverages. Indeed, one of the important innovations in German agriculture during the period of the *Bauernbefreiung* was the establishment of commercial distilleries on the landed estates. (Laves, 1887; Ritter, 1955, pp. 783–805; Herlemann, 1952, pp. 3–7) This was made possible in part by the capital accumulated by peasant redemption payments and highly desirable by the depressed prices for agricultural produce in the 1820s. After a half-century of buoyant prices for its products, German agriculture entered a period of crisis in the first years of the nineteenth century that was particularly acute in the grain-exporting Prussian East. Foreign markets were closed to German exporters and prices fell precipitously. (Franz, 1976, pp. 314–15) One widespread response to this decades-long structural crisis was to convert excess produce to alcohol. Unlike the raw materials from which it was made, alcohol kept indefinitely and was easily stored and transported. The mash left at the end of the distillation process could be fed to livestock herds, thus substantially reducing the cost of fertilizer. Distilleries were widely recommended by agricultural improvers for just these reasons (von Recum,

1827; Engel, 1853), and they were actually established at a phenomenal rate in the first two decades of the century. In Prussia and other German states agricultural distilleries were accorded tax benefits that put them on a favorable footing *vis-à-vis* the traditional, commercially oriented urban establishments. In 1831 there were 22,988 stills in Prussia alone. (Dieterici, Vol. 1, 1838, pp. 299–302)

Hand in hand with the rapid diffusion of agricultural distilleries in the German countryside went a shift in the basic raw material used in the production of alcohol. When disastrous harvests in the years 1816–19 produced severe grain shortages, distillers discovered that the potato provided an attractive substitute. Indeed, it was the substitution of potatoes for traditional grains as the basic raw material of spirits production that brought the real revolution to German distilling. By substituting the more versatile potato for grain, distillers could increase their yield of alcohol per acre planted nearly fivefold. (Ferber, 1829, p. 174) The remaining potato mash could also be fed to livestock, and thus the cheap source of fertilizer was preserved. In 1842, when production reached its highest point before mid-century, there were 2,327 urban and 7,994 rural distilleries operating in Prussia. They consumed 3.2 million bushels of grain and 20.8 million bushels of potatoes. (Dieterici, Vol. 3, 1844, pp. 331–4) Altogether some 265.1 million Prussian quarts of *Branntwein* were produced in the Customs Union that year, and virtually all of it was consumed domestically. (Dieterici, Vol. 3, 1844, p. 334) Just over 75 per cent of this total, or about 200 million quarts, was produced in Prussia. The provinces Brandenburg, Saxony and Silesia accounted for more than half of the Prussian total. At the same time, the consumption of beer was in decline. Dieterici's figures suggest that per capita consumption fell during the first half of the nineteenth century in every Prussian province but the Rhineland. (cited in Baer, 1878, p. 253) Except in Bavaria, this was the general trend throughout the German states. (Struve, 1893)

Thus Germany experienced a revolution in the production of beverage alcohol in the first half of the nineteenth century. This revolution had three essential features: the much cheaper potato replaced grain as the basic raw material of spirits production; distilling moved from the towns to the countryside and became an integral part of agricultural production; and finally, the geographical center of production shifted from Hanover and Brunswick to the eastern provinces of Prussia, where large-scale distillation became a permanent feature of the *Junker* estates. This was a fateful connection, for in no other state in Western Europe or North America were the interests of such a politically powerful social elite permanently tied to the production, and hence also the widespread consumption, of strong drink.

The immediate consequences of this transformation of the social, economic, and technological bases of alcohol production were profound.

Distilleries of various sizes proliferated throughout the German countryside, the price of the now readily available *Kartoffelschnaps* plummeted, and a large and often powerful group of producers emerged with a material interest in marketing their product. ('Der Branntweingenuß und die Gesetzgebung,' *Central-Blatt für die Rheinisch-Westphälischen Enthaltsamkeitsvereine*, no. 18, 27 August 1847, n.p.; cf. Herkner, 1906, p. 8) The distilled beverages that had once been reserved for the well-to-do and for a few festive occasions of the common man now became staples of even the very poor. At a time when beer, even in Bavaria, was of low quality and too expensive for the laboring poor (Mayhew, 1865, p. 339; cf. Bayerisches Hauptstaatsarchiv, Abt. 1/MInn 62572), the now readily available *Kartoffelschnaps* entered labor relations as an element of the truck system in manufacturing, as part of the board served to agricultural laborers, and as a valuable stimulus to hard work provided by employers to their workers. (Böttcher, 1841, p. 27; LaRoche, 1845, pp. 110–13; Anton, 1891, p. 25) For the people who consumed it, the new and almost wondrous beverage seemed a panacea. It provided a dietary supplement, a source of stimulation and refreshment on the job, and a welcome source of diversion from a life of unremitting toil, material hardship and perpetual anxiety.

According to Friedrich Engels, who witnessed this revolution in the Wuppertal, a hogshead of *Schnaps* had cost 39 Thaler in 1813. Four years later, after a miserable harvest, the price had jumped to 70 Thaler. At this point, distillers began to use potatoes as their raw material, and by 1823 the price had sunk to as low as 14 Thalers per barrel. The results of this rapid fall in prices, Engels reported, were truly unprecedented. 'The drunkenness that had once cost three or four times as much was now readily available every day, even to the very poor.' (Engels, 1962a, 1962b; cf. Engel, 1853, p. 164) The economist and statistician Ernst Engel estimated that the consumption of spirits had nearly tripled between 1806 and 1831, increasing from three to eight Prussian quarts per capita. (Engel, 1864, p. 129)

## The Nineteenth-Century Alcohol Problem

Thus, by the 1830s and 1840s, the contours of the classic nineteenth-century alcohol problem were clearly visible. Alcohol, in the form of cheap, low-quality *Kartoffelschnaps*, had entered the daily life of the laboring poor in new and often pernicious ways – as a dietary substitute and supplement, as a thirst-quencher on and off the job, and as a means of sociability and escape. The laboring poor used alcohol in ways significantly different from their more well-to-do countrymen, for whom alcoholic beverages, whether beer, wine or the finer sorts of brandies, were a mere refinement. For the laboring poor, on the contrary, alcohol filled much more vital roles and was consumed not as a matter of choice but as a physiological necessity. Though nineteenth-century critics of popular drinking behavior were not always fully aware of the fact, alcohol could make a significant contribution to the energy needs of workers whose intake of calories was otherwise inadequate. (Forsander, 1963; Goldberg, 1963; Kendis, 1967; cf. the well-informed contemporary discussion in Grotjahn, 1898, pp. 119–25) The metabolism of one gram of alcohol provides seven calories of energy. Only fats provide energy more efficiently, at nine calories per gram, while a gram of either protein or carbohydrate provides only four. An adult male can metabolize seven grams of alcohol per hour, or up to about three centiliters of distilled liquor. Taken in small quantities and spread over the whole day, as much as half a liter of spirits could be metabolized per day, enough to provide 30–40 per cent of an adult male's energy needs without inducing intoxication. This was precisely the pattern that many workers followed in their mealtime and on-the-job drinking.

Throughout the nineteenth century distinguished observers like Jacob Moleschott, Rudolf Virchow, Fridolin Schüler, Max Weber, Alfred Grotjahn, and Max Rübner continued to stress the close connection between dietary insufficiency and heavy drinking. (Moleschott, 1853, pp. 161–2; Virchow, 1879, Vol. 2, p. 323; Schüler, 1884; Weber, 1892, p. 777; Grotjahn, 1902, p. 61) This was the nub of the nineteenth-century alcohol problem. Workers were forced to rely on alcohol to meet their basic physiological needs which financially more secure Germans could meet with higher quality and generally more costly alternatives. Given popular beliefs about alcohol's nutritive and medicinal properties, the abysmal dietary standard of the laboring poor, and the dearth of suitable alternative beverages, this pattern of alcohol consumption, rooted in the social conditions of the *Vormärz*, was bound to persist into the industrial era. A revolution in supply had made new habits of consumption possible; these factors affecting demand sustained them. The laboring poor was thus trapped in a vicious circle of dietary insufficiency and heavy alcohol use whose consequences were best described by the contemporary chemist and physiologist Justus von Liebig:

When . . . a worker earns less by his labor than he needs to buy sufficient food to replenish his strength, he is forced by an unyielding, inexorable natural law to resort to *Branntwein*. He is supposed to work, but the strength he needs each day fails him because of his poor diet. *Branntwein* allows him . . . to use a portion [of his strength] today that should really only be consumed tomorrow. This is a loan, drawn against his health, which has to be perpetually extended because the means to redeem it are lacking. The worker consumes the capital instead of the interest; hence the unavoidable bankruptcy of his body. (1851, pp. 558–9)

But if in reality the alcohol problem had more to do with diet than drunkenness and if its solution thus depended more on improving the economic conditions of the laboring poor than on altering their drinking habits, it was drunkenness that was indelibly impressed upon the middle-class consciousness. The spectacle of public drunkenness prompted an almost visceral abhorrence of that portion of mankind unable or unwilling to live according to the internalized standards of self-control required of bourgeois society. Drunkenness could be passed over as a harmless diversion when university students or officer cadets were doing the drinking, but when the lower classes were involved, it was viewed through different lenses and took on a more threatening aspect. The drunkenness of the lower classes was a constant reminder of the fragility of the social order and of the need for persuasion, indoctrination, and coercion to hold it together. Thus, behind all the specific arguments raised in the nineteenth century about the individual and social costs of alcohol consumption lay the dim perception that beneath the facade of a civilization based on Christianity, reason, and increasing social and economic interdependence, the beast in man lay waiting. Alcohol, it was feared, allowed this beast to slip out of the social straitjacket; it thus threatened the social order of which it was becoming an everyday part. By crippling man's reason and destroying his moral sense, alcohol destroyed precisely those faculties that set man above the animals. The temperance reform was necessary above all to shore up these moral barriers, to educate the lower classes in the virtues of self-control. (cf. Böttcher, 1839c, pp. 104-6)

## Origins of the Nineteenth-Century Temperance Reform

By the beginning of the nineteenth century, attempts to control the use of alcohol from the pulpit, by government edict and by way of the gendarme were centuries old. But as the consumption of alcohol increased and became more visible, these approaches began to appear bankrupt to many contemporaries. New solutions were sought to the perennial problem of controlling the use of alcoholic beverages and limiting their destructive potential. As restraints on economic activity were lifted and the production and distribution of strong drink expanded, alcohol's potential threat to both community and individual well-being seemed to grow. The revolution in the production and distribution of alcoholic beverages, making them ever more accessible to the mass of the population, coincided with other, more fundamental changes in the social fabric that produced an anxious searching after explanations and solutions to a myriad of unprecedented and often confusing social problems, ranging from crime and poverty to religious indifference and political insubordination. (cf. Blasius, 1976) The real origins of these problems lay in long-term demographic and economic changes, but to many contemporaries in both Europe and America, the growing use of alcohol appeared a plausible explanation and temperance reform a logical solution. Applying the widely discussed principle of association to the drink problem was their innovation.

Temperance association was an American invention (Krout, 1925; Rorabaugh, 1979; Tyrrell, 1979), originating among Boston businessmen and clergymen in 1813. Against a background of economic uncertainty and declining Federalist political fortunes, the Boston Brahmins who founded the Massachusetts Society for the Suppression of Intemperance (MSSI) created an organization of limited social appeal and even more limited aims. The MSSI eschewed popular agitation, appealing instead to their social peers to set a worthy example to the lower orders, whose drunkenness was the ultimate target of their reform. Organizationally moribund almost from its inception, the MSSI had all but vanished by the mid-1820s. Its legacy, the idea of voluntary association for temperance reform, nevertheless had far-reaching consequences.

The MSSI's successor, the American Temperance Society (ATS), founded in 1826, brought significant innovation to the goals and tactics of the temperance movement. This, in turn, led to a considerable broadening of its public support. No longer the preserve of backward-looking Brahmins, the temperance reform, now fueled by evangelical revivalism, found increasing support among the most progressive elements in American society, successful entrepreneurs and respectable mechanics, men aiming not to reverse the tide of change around them but to profit from it. On the basis of total abstinence from spirits and through the device of the signed temperance pledge, the ATS took its cause to the people, sending paid agents across the country and inundating America with temperance tracts. By 1835, the ATS claimed 8,000 local organizations and 1.5 million members, making it far and away the largest ante-bellum reform movement.

Under American influence and via Scotland, the anti-spirits movement had also taken root in England by 1831, when the London-based British and Foreign Temperance Society was launched. English temperance reformers soon provided a decisive innovation: teetotalism. (Harrison, 1971) Beginning in Preston, teetotal societies spread from the early 1830s and profoundly altered the basis of the temperance movement's appeal. Under the teetotal banner the temperance movement turned its attention directly to the drunkard, to the secular redemption of the victims of alcohol. Its appeal to the workingman was enhanced by the more absolute teetotal standard, which proscribed the drinks of the well-to-do as well as those of the laboring poor. The now more radical movement was a source of anxiety for its former patrons. As the temperance mainstream turned away from the established church and began to emphasize temporal rather than spiritual salvation, the self-improving workingman began to dominate the affairs of local temperance organizations. The alarming secular and radical ends to which the temperance ideal might be put were revealed most clearly in the Teetotal Chartism of men like William Lovett and Henry Vincent. (Harrison, 1973b)

Teetotalism also came to dominate the American temperance movement in the 1830s and 1840s and had similar effects. The patronage of old elites declined and the movement's popularity with ordinary workingmen increased. By the 1850s, as the movement's initial faith in the power of its own example faded, prohibitionism had emerged as a major force in British and as the dominant force in American temperance. (Krout, 1925; Clark, 1979; Tyrrell, 1979; Timberlake, 1966; Harrison, 1971; Hamar, 1977; Dingle, 1980) Though their histories throughout the rest of the century and into the twentieth would be markedly different, British and American prohibition had similar origins as a reaction to state licensing systems which sanctioned the harmful and immoral liquor trade. Prohibitionists intended to alter decisively the environment that produced generation after generation of inebriates. The German anti-alcohol movement would undergo a similar tactical shift from moral suasion to efforts to secure the intervention of the state in the Drink Question. The goals and methods of German temperance reformers, however, would remain markedly different from those of their Anglo-American counterparts.

## The Temperance Reform in the German States

The temperance reform spread to Protestant Europe in the 1830s. (For an overview: Bergman, 1907, pp. 133–49) The Reverend Robert Baird, representing the American Temperance Society and other evangelical causes, arrived in Paris in 1835. At the behest of the American ambassador, who faced a mounting number of inquiries about the reform, Baird composed his *Histoire des sociétés de tempérance des États-Unis d'Amérique* in 1836. (1836; cf. H. M. Baird, 1886; Smith, 1955) Translated into the major languages of Europe, Baird's work would introduce the continent to the wonders of American temperance.

The early German temperance movement was a product of American influence. (Martius, 1891, pp. 6–9) Concern about Germany's rapidly rising spirits consumption had become widespread by the 1820s and 1830s. As early as 1830, a temperance association had been founded under British influence by the Hamburg Baptist J. G. Onken, an agent of the Edinburgh Bible Association, but it was only with the translation of Baird's book in 1837 that the temperance reform attracted any significant public interest in Germany. (Baird, 1837) The American evangelist had been received enthusiastically at the Prussian court in 1835. When Baird's *Histoire* appeared, Frederick William III had it translated and distributed 30,000 copies at his own expense to Prussia's clergymen. The book's success was assured by its royal patronage and by favorable reviews in such influential clerical-conservative journals as the *Evangelische Kirchenzeitung*. (15, 19, 22 and 26 April 1837, nos 30–3) Baird's book, J. H. Böttcher later recalled, 'produced wonderment wherever it was received; . . . it worked like a stroke of magic on Germany' (quoted in LaRoche, 1845, p. vii). In the same year that the translation of Baird's work appeared, the Prussian Minister of the Interior and of Police, von Rochow, ordered provincial authorities to promote and support temperance associations in the areas under their jurisdiction. (Hitzig, 1837, pp. 46–8) The rulers of other North German states likewise lent the new movement their active support.

The reform from above fell on fertile ground. German temperance was nourished not only by royal patronage and bureaucratic support but also by the social, religious and political currents of the *Vormärz*. The efforts of the state to minimise the potential social costs inherent in the use of alcohol no longer seemed adequate as pauperization threatened social stability and the *Schnapspest* coursed through town and country alike, wherever the poor and undernourished were gathered. The funds apparently squandered on alcohol consumption seemed to many observers to explain the massive poverty of the *Vormärz*. 'And is it any wonder,' Böttcher asked in view of the rapid rise of consumption, 'that now, after 25 blessed years of peace, so many complaints are heard, especially from the lowest classes of society, about the 'bad times' and 'lack of funds?' (Böttcher, 1840, p. 47; cf. 1839a) 'One need not be a prophet,' another temperance enthusiast insisted, 'to know that all efforts to combat the widespread and rapidly spreading *Pauperismus* will be unsuccessful as long as the common man fails to realize that the principal source of his degradation and misery is his fondness for drink' (Der Mäßigkeits-Verein zu Posen und seine Widersacher,' *Der Mäßigkeits-Herold für die Preußischen Staaten*, vol. 5, no. 4, 1845, p. 30).

In the face of the pressing social and economic problems of the post-Napoleonic era, men of widely differing political and theological persuasions lent their support to a movement whose message was one upon which all respectable society could agree: *'Der Mensch mus sich bessern'* (Martius, 1901, p. 22). Temperance arrived on the German scene in time to provide a convenient explanation of this widespread suffering and to offer the hope of both material and spiritual salvation to the masses of small holders and artisans, both Protestant and Catholic, who took the anti-spirits pledge before 1848.

The religious Awakening (*Erweckung*) that began during the War of Liberation also helped to prepare the ground for Baird's message. (Martius, 1901, pp. 16–33; Tiesmeyer, 1902/12; Schnabel, 1951, pp. 379–492; Shanahan, 1954; Beyreuther, 1963; Holborn, 1964, pp. 485–96; Bigler, 1972; Sagarra, 1977) The German temperance movement was part of a broader movement of Christian renewal which arose in the late eighteenth century in reaction to the formalism and rationalism of orthodox German Protestantism. This popular religious 'Awakening' gathered force during the period of Napoleon's domination of German affairs and the ensuing War of Liberation. At the theological level, the Awakening drew on older pietist traditions and the inspiration of contemporaneous religious movements in England and the United States. In its more popular manifestations, the Awakening produced a number of efforts to spread the gospel to the rural and urban poor and to establish institutions of 'rettende Liebe.' By the late 1830s, awakened clergymen, with their concern for good works and the salvation of individual souls, had already created a network of charitable schools, orphanages and hospitals that would culminate in Johann Hinrich Wichern's *Innere Mission*. Attention to the drunkard's salvation and the protection of the rest of the community from his fate was a natural sequel to these concerns.

The connection between neo-pietism and the temperance reform was especially close in Prussia, and this connection shaped the temperance movement in several ways. 'The temperance associations in the Prussian monarchy,' Albert Freiherr von Seld observed in 1848, 'have been founded for the most part by believing clergymen (gläubige Prediger); the men of reason (die Geistreichen), the Friends of Light, the so-called men of progress have played no part' ('Baron von Seld in Ostpreußen,' *Central-Blatt der Vereine gegen das Branntweintrinken für die Provinzen Brandenburg, Sachsen, Pommern und die Insel Rügen*, vol. 3, no. 3, March 1848). In contrast to the evangelical revivals in England and the United States, which remained at odds with orthodoxy and hierarchy and provided the moral underpinnings of movements of social and political dissent, Prussian neo-pietism became the orthodoxy of the established state church. (Beyreuther, 1963, p. 28; cf. Sagarra, 1977, p. 218) The spirit of the awakening pervaded the ruling house and its closest advisors. Under the influence of the leading Prussian theologian of the Restoration, Ernst Wilhelm Hengstenberg (1802–69), a professor at the University of Berlin and editor of the influential *Evangelische Kirchenzeitung*, the religious awakening was given a conservative political cast that made it a bulwark of the absolute monarchy. As the spirit of the Awakening hardened into a new confessional orthodoxy cast more or less explicitly as a defense of the status quo, those members of the middle classes who in England and the United States found in evangelical religion both a justification for their private ambitions and an inspiration to social action were forced to look for theological and philosophical alternatives. In Prussia, these groups by and large remained rationalists and deists, aloof from the neo-pietists' personal religion. In the 1840s they rallied to the support of the so-called *Lichtfreunde*, or Friends of Light, whose rational religion came under increasing attack by Hengstenberg and the official church. (Bigler, 1972, pp. 187–230 and passim; Rosenberg, 1972, pp. 41–4)

In Prussia, at least, the temperance reform clearly belonged to this politically and religiously conservative camp. This close identification with the ascendent powers in church and state was a source both of strength and of weakness, for the vast majority of Prussia's local pastors had been educated in the rationalist tradition that was now under attack. (Bigler, 1972, pp. 49–50) Many of them were reluctant to support the temperance cause both because it seemed the tool of a clerical faction whose goals they opposed and because its demand for total abstinence from strong drink seemed a restriction on Christian liberty. They rejected the neo-pietist tendency to narrow the realm of individual moral choice and espoused instead the ideal of true moderation. (cf. Scharfe, 1980) At the same time, the temperance movement was vulnerable to attack from a more orthodox, confessional direction. The temperance movement seemed to put an emphasis on good works and individual perfectability whose Arminian implications some traditionalists found repugnant. This was especially true in confessionally mixed areas. Supporters of the reform in Lower Silesia, for example, complained in 1847 that only about one-twentieth of the Protestant clergy had taken an active interest in the movement. ('Gegenwärtiger Stand der Enthaltsamkeitssache in den evangelischen Theile von Nieder-Schlesien,' *Monatsblatt für die Enthaltsamkeitssache*, vol. 3, no. 5, May 1847, pp. 68–73) This was an area of intense resistance to official church policy and to the Prussian king's efforts to fuse Lutherans and Calvinists into a single Evangelical church. (Kantzenbach, 1969, pp. 118–26)

The temperance movement was also nourished by another, more novel current in German public life, expressed in the educational and self-help organizations founded and led by the liberal *Bürgertum*. (Nipperdey, 1976; Stein, 1936) Here temperance fits into a different tradition, based less on the religious impulse to save souls or establish the Kingdom of God on earth than the desire to spread enlightenment and encourage the self-reliance fundamental to the liberal conception of civil society. The temperance movement could help to preserve and broaden the middle strata of society upon which liberals hoped to rely in transforming German public life while at the same time reinforcing the boundary between themselves and the rabble they both loathed and feared. (Sheehan, 1978, pp. 47–8) Not surprisingly, therefore, German liberals were also instrumental in the temperance reform; it was the *sine qua non* of their other self-help reforming efforts. Johannes Fallati discussed the liberal associational network just after the Silesian weavers' uprising in 1844. In the hopes of integrating the increasingly threatening proletariat into the existing social order, he encouraged the further development of self-help institutions under middle-class patronage. But for savings schemes, burial clubs, mutual aid societies and similar undertakings to succeed, Fallati argued, it would also be essential to pursue the temperance reform to a successful conclusion. (1844, pp. 776–7, 781–3)

What was at stake for Fallati and other liberals was not simply economic self-help but the personal discipline and social virtues essential to the liberal vision of political order. The temperance reform promised to bring a new sense of human dignity and individual worth even to the poor and degraded. It would help them accumulate property, giving them a stake in the existing order and a foundation for responsible political participation. Once the reform succeeded, one contemporary promised, 'the wall dividing the lower from the upper classes must and will fall, *Bildung* will become the common property of all, and the poor, who now imagine only the policeman and the taxman at the mention of the word 'state', will be uplifted to the great ideal of the *Vaterland*' (loose leaves in Archiv des deutschen Caritas Verbandes, XIV, 6A).

Finally, though Germany's was hardly yet an industrial economy, the temperance movement promised to improve work discipline at a time when the naked cash nexus was beginning to erode older patriarchal relations between the buyers and sellers of labor. This was as true on the landed estates as it was in the handicrafts, where overcrowding was destroying the personal ties that had once bound masters and journeymen in a single community of interests. (Conze, 1954; Hamerow, 1958; Fischer, 1963; Koselleck, 1962, pp. 97–8; Marquandt, 1975; Henning, 1977) The temperance movement was meant to be one of the agencies that would reshape the habits and mentality of the laboring classes, instilling the virtues of sobriety, frugality, and punctuality and encouraging obedience to established authority. Employers who took the temperance pledge promised to break with the custom of providing their workers with a daily ration of *Schnaps*. They concluded, according to one account, 'that as a general rule the journeymen, workers, day laborers etc. who do not consume *Branntwein* are preferable and more serviceable [than those who do]: more honest, more punctual, more accurate and safer on the job, obedient and humble; consequently altogether more human [menschlicher] and more useful' (Vincas, 1847, n.p.). The results were similarly favorable on the landed estates when owners or their managers put temperance principles into practice. By curtailing their customary *Branntwein* ration, they not only found that they could save money, they also got more efficient and more tractable workers. (Böttcher, 1841, pp. 169–71) Temperance reformers believed there were lessons here for all employers.

The temperance movement flourished in the decade following the publication of the German edition of Baird's book in 1837. In its fight against drink, the movement's principal weapons were the temperance oath and the association of abstainers. The reform was based on what the British and Americans called the 'short pledge': total abstinence from spirits and moderation in the use of milder beverages. (Examples of statutes: Hitzig, 1837; Böttcher, 1841; Stubbe, 1911, pp. 49–50; Niedersächsisches

Hauptstaatsarchiv, Hann Des 74, Hann VIII, H5, Nr. 5) Teetotalism, making substantial inroads in both the American and British movements, found little support in Germany, where beer and wine continued to be promoted as temperance beverages.

More important than the pledge was the power of association. If those not yet lost to drink could find the courage to renounce the use of spirits, they could be saved from ultimate degradation, and the society of the future would be protected from the scourge of intemperance. The example of relatively few dedicated men could convince the multitude that it was possible – and in many ways beneficial – to live without hard liquor, and the ranks of the temperance army would then swell. Those drunkards of the present who could not be saved by the temperance movement would soon enough die out, and the Drink Question would have found its solution. Apart from its moral and financial support, government intervention was neither expected nor desired by the early German temperance reformers. Neither the state nor the individual was adequate to the task at hand. As for so many other contemporary problems, association appeared to be the only answer. (On attitudes to the state: Liebetrut, 1844.)

Whether under the influence of the American temperance movement or in imitation of native evangelists, the temperance movement in Germany adopted the methods of religious revivalism. Preceded by temperance tracts, usually Böttcher's *Hauskreuz* (1839b), the movement's agents combed the countryside, taking their message to village after village and into the towns, accepting the anti-spirits pledge (*Gelubde*) as they went. The maverick philanthropist Albert Freiherr von Seld spoke extensively in Prussia's Eastern provinces and was the most popular German temperance orator. (von Seld, 1865; *Allgemeine Deutsche Biographie*, vol. 33, pp. 671–3) Pastors Huchzermeier and Steffan worked the villages and the towns of Westphalia and the Rhineland. J. Mathias Seling of Osnabrück, one of the most energetic Catholics involved in the reform, spoke in 80 different places in one 18-month period in the years 1843 and 1844 and took the pledge from nearly 20,000 men and another 40,000 women and children. But not all were friendly to the reformers' message. A major riot broke out at a large public meeting in Hamburg in 1841, and similar scenes were repeated in at least ten other German cities. (Böttcher, 1841, p. xv; Stubbe, 1911, pp. 34–6) Such incidents of mob action, fueled by alcohol supplied by self-interested drink sellers, only confirmed the movement's darkest images of the destructive potential of the lower orders and made the reform seem all the more necessary.

The high point of the temperance year was the celebration of the anniversary of each local association's founding. The movement's patrons and beneficiaries came together in a pageant of social harmony and a celebration of the possibilities and rewards of virtue. These events were almost invariably celebrated as religious services, with lengthy sermons and rousing temperance hymns. Dynamic temperance orators from all over North Germany were often featured on such occasions, which served to renew the membership's dedication to sobriety and awaken public interest in the reform. But it was difficult to maintain a high level of interest throughout the year, and there were frequent complaints about slack attendance at the weekly or monthly meetings many associations attempted. Nevertheless, some local and regional associations launched a wide range of activities. An impressive temperance press developed all over North Germany. Leaflets and pamphlets were printed in untold numbers, and there were at least 22 monthly and bi-weekly newspapers. The editor of the *Central-Blatt für die Rheinisch-Westphälischen Enthaltsamkeitsvereine* claimed that 100,000 pieces of temperance literature had been distributed in the two provinces in 1846. Other associations, like the one in Hamburg, made serious efforts to reclaim drunkards and to protect them from the temptations of the larger social world. Elsewhere, temperance reformers broadened their application of the self-help principle and established their own mutual aid societies.

## The Social and Geographical Contours of the German Temperance Movement

Despite the limited means at its disposal and the immensity of the task it set itself, the temperance movement made remarkable progress. By 1846, an estimated 600,000 adult men had taken the temperance pledge and more than 1,250 local organizations had been founded (see Table 2.1). Böttcher reckoned that, including dependents, a total of 1.65 million German men, women and children had been directly affected by the reform. (Martius, 1901, pp. 9–10) These figures include Catholic *Kirchspielvereine* established in Posen and Silesia in 1844 and 1845, where whole congregations took the pledge under the sway of local clergymen. (Liese, 1922, Vol. 2, pp. 167–73; Roßnick, 1915, pp. 54–62; Martius, 1901, pp. 23–6) By 1846, there were 348 of these *Kirchspielvereine* with some 420,000 members. In the remainder of North Germany, therefore, there were some 900 associations with 180,000 adult male members. There is no way to verify Böttcher's figures, but he was undoubtedly the best-informed man in Germany about the progress of the temperance reform. Even if we take his estimates with a grain of salt, it seems certain that, as in England and the United States, the temperance movement was the single most popular vehicle of social reform in the decades before mid-century.

Geographically, the movement's strength lay in predominantly Protestant North Germany, especially in the kingdoms of Hanover and Prussia (see Table 2.2). The geographical contours of temperance activity thus seem to correspond to the religious divisions among the German states, with the

Table 2.1 *Membership in Temperance Organizations, 1837–46*

|  | Members (Adult males) | Associations |  |
|---|---|---|---|
| 1837 | 500 | 17 | |
| 1838 | 2,800 | 76 | |
| 1839 | 5,280 | 129 | |
| 1840 | 17,080 | 262 | |
| 1841 | 20,000 | 303 | |
| 1842 | 27,000 | 391 | |
| 1843 | 40,000 | 537 | |
| 1844 | 66,000 | 754 | |
|  | 150,000 | 226 | in *Kirchspielvereine* |
| 1845 | 160,000 | 854 | |
|  | 420,000 | 348 | in *Kirchspielvereine* |
| 1846 | 180,000 | 902 | |
|  | 420,000 | 348 | in *Kirchspielvereine* |

Source: *Tagesblatt der dritten Generalversammlung der Deutschen Vereine gegen das Branntweintrinken*, p. 42 (in Staatsarchiv Münster, Oberpäsidium 703).

Protestant North actively involved and the Catholic South indifferent. This is a misleading interpretation, however, since there were Catholic areas *within* the predominantly Protestant territories where the temperance movement, under the local leadership of Catholic clergymen, made truly remarkable gains. This was true, for example, in religiously mixed Westphalia as well as in predominantly Catholic Posen and Upper Silesia. Just as important, there were predominantly Protestant areas south of the Main – Hessen and Würrtemberg, for example – where the movement had little impact. If the South was indifferent to the temperance reform, it was not because its population was predominantly Catholic but because beer, wine and cider rather than spirits were its principal beverages. The geography of German temperance thus seems to be explicable principally in terms of the patterns of alcohol production and consumption outlined earlier. The German temperance movement was an anti-spirits movement that actively encouraged the consumption of beer and wine. It struck root in those areas of North Germany where spirits were produced and consumed in greatest volume.

Because these areas were heavily Protestant, Protestant clergymen provided the leadership of the German temperance movement. They were supported by an assortment of other men from the middle strata of German society. Of the sixty-two men gathered at the Third General Assembly of German Associations against Spirits Drinking [*Dritte Generalversammlung*

Table 2.2 *The Geography of the German Temperance Movement in 1847*

| Name of Central Association | No. of Affiliated Associations | Name of Central Association | No. of Affiliated Associations |
|---|---|---|---|
| **PRUSSIA** | | Bentheim | 8 |
| Märkische (Berlin) | 50 | Lingen | 12 |
| Uckermarck | 6 | Ostfriesland | 48 |
| East and West Prussia | 80 | | 351 |
| Posen (including Catholic *Kirchspielvereine)* | 217 | **OTHER NORTH GERMAN STATES** | |
| Lower Silesia | 50 | Oldenburg | 64 |
| Upper Lusatice | 14 | Cutin | 2 |
| Upper Silesia | 142 | Schleswig-Holstein | 41 |
| Pommerania | 15 | Hamburg | 3 |
| Saxony | 30 | Bremen | 2 |
| Westphalia | 52 | Lübeck | 1 |
| Ravensberg | 20 | Mecklenburg-Schwerin | 2 |
| Rhineland | 36 | Brunswick | 15 |
| Other | 6 | Hesse-Cassel | 10 |
| | 718 | Hesse-Darmstadt | 2 |
| | | Nassau | 10 |
| **HANOVER** | | Lippe Detmold | 7 |
| Calenberg | 50 | Lippe-Schaumberg | 6 |
| Hoya and Diepholz | 24 | Waldeck | 4 |
| Hildesheim | 32 | | 169 |
| Göttingen and Grubenhagen | 20 | | |
| Lüneburg | 44 | **OTHER GERMAN STATES** | |
| Bremen and Verden | 48 | Württemberg | 2 |
| Osnabrück | 42 | Weimar | 1 |
| Meppen | 23 | Kingdom of Saxony | 1 |
| | | **GRAND TOTAL** | 1243 |

Source: *Tagesblatt,* pp. 40–1.

*der deutschen Vereine gegen das Branntweintrinken*] held in Brunswick in 1847, twenty-nine (46.8 per cent) were clergymen, including at least one Catholic, J. Mathias Seling of Osnabrück, and one Rabbi, Dr Frankfurter from Hamburg. The remaining delegates included six teachers and rectors, six lawyers and judicial officials, five merchants and manufacturers, five master artisans, and four physicians and surgeons. (*Tagesblatt*, pp. 1–3, 19, 30) There was only one member of the nobility present, Freiherr von Seld. Apart from the preponderance of clergymen, this was the social profile of German liberalism. (Sheehan, 1978, p. 24)

But this conclusion masks important differences between the social characteristics of the temperance reform's leaders in Prussia and in the other North German states. The Prussian delegation was composed almost exclusively of clergymen and teachers directly dependent on the state while the representatives from other areas came from much more diverse social backgrounds. More than 75 per cent of the Prussian delegates were preachers or teachers and less than 20 per cent were members of the professional and commercial *Mittelstand*. Clergymen also predominated in the non-Prussian states of North Germany, but the proportion of men from professional and commercial backgrounds was more than twice that in Prussia, amounting to more than 40 per cent.[2] (Computed from *Tagesblatt*) This finding may simply be a result of where the meeting was held, but the patterns revealed in local membership lists suggest otherwise.

In Prussia the temperance movement bore the marks of a reform from above. The Prussian court had initiated the movement and mobilized the state bureaucracy in its support. Local leadership typically lay in the hands of theologically and politically conservative clergymen. They were supported by local school teachers and, in some rural areas, by substantial landowners. In the association for Danzig, for example, 23.4 per cent of the 363 members in 1839 were teachers (69) and clergymen (16). They were joined by 60 landowners (Guts- und Hofbesitzer, 16.5 per cent) and seven government officials (1.9 per cent). There were only two members of the professional and commercial *Mittelstand* – a physician and a veterinarian. No full membership list is available for the association in Breslau, one of the centers of Prussian liberalism, but a list of those present at a meeting in August 1844 reveals a similar pattern. Of the thirty-five men present, seven were clergymen and only two were members of the professional and commercial *Mittelstand*. ('Der Breslauer Verein gegen das Branntweintrinken,' *Monatsblatt für die Enthaltsamkeitssache*, vol. 1, no. 4, January 1845, p. 37)

Representatives of the *Mittelstand* were conspicuously absent in these Prussian associations, in part because they were unrepresented in the village social structure out of which many of the associations emerged. But this was not the only reason. Because of its origin as a reform from above, the temperance movement in Prussia was bound to seem a tool of reactionary political and clerical interests to members of the liberal *Bürgertum*. This suspicion is confirmed in the surviving traces of the temperance movement's social, political, and theological polemics, which suggest that the politically conscious middle strata of Prussian society viewed the temperance reform with grave misgivings. 'The real tendency of the so-called temperance associations,' an editor of the liberal *Barmer Zeitung* charged in 1843, 'is to turn the eye of the people away from the important questions of the day and to restore the control over their minds which in the past few years has been slipping.' 'As bad as the tyranny of *Branntwein* is,' he went on, 'the tyranny of government ministers, the tyranny of priests is certainly much worse.' (Quoted in 'Eine Stimme vom freien deutschen Rhein,' *Mäßigkeits-Zeitung*, vol. 5, no. 12, 1 December 1844, pp. 89–93) It is also significant that supporters of the persecuted *Lichtfreunde*, members of the liberal middle strata of Prussian society, were notoriously hostile to the temperance reform. ('Briefe von Andres,' *Central-Blatt für die Rheinisch-Westphälischen Enthaltsamkeitsvereine,* vol. 1, no. 3, February 1846; 'Miscellenen,' *Monatsblatt für die Enthaltsamkeitssache,* vol. 3, no. 7, July 1847. On the *Lichtfreunde,* see page 22 above).

Elsewhere, the social bases of the temperance movement's leadership were much different, drawing much more heavily on the urban and predominantly liberal middle classes. In the kingdom of Hanover and the *Hansestädte* in particular, the temperance movement enjoyed broad-based popular support. These areas would provide the movement's principal recruiting grounds throughout the nineteenth century. Of the 2,268 men who had taken the temperance pledge in Hamburg by 1844, for example, 8.4 per cent came from the city's commercial sector and 6.2 per cent from its educated elite of preachers, physicians, university professors, and school teachers. (Stubbe, 1911, pp. 69–71) The situation was similar in Osnabrück, where 8.4 per cent of the associations 1,751 members in 1840 were recruited from the upper reaches of the *Mittelstand.* Side by side with the clergymen and school teachers who provided the movement's leadership in Prussia were men from the liberal professions, the civil service, and commerce and industry. (Niedersächsisches Hauptstaatsarchiv, Hann Des 80, Hildesheim I, E18) The openness of these areas to English influence may help to account for their support of the temperance cause, but a more important consideration would seem to be that in these areas the religious Awakening of the early nineteenth century ultimately took different forms than in Prussia. The evangelical impulse was not transformed into a politically conservative orthodoxy but continued to stress the common core of inner religious experience, the transforming power of the Gospel, and the duty of Christian charity. The desire once also evident in the Prussian Awakening to overcome confessional boundaries remained alive in these areas so that it was possible for Protestants and Catholics of all persuasions to co-operate in a common project of Christian social renewal. This ecumenical approach was dramatically symbolized in February 1845 when J. H. Böttcher and the Catholic temperance apostle J. Mathias Seling mounted the same platform in Hildesheim and publicly embraced, addressing each other with the familiar 'Du' amidst a cheering throng of temperance enthusiasts. (Wilhelm Martius, 'Vor fünfzig Jahrens, *Mäßigkeits-Blätter,* vol. 12, no. 4, April 1895, pp. 60–1) Indeed, the philosophical foundations of the movement in these areas was generally sufficiently broad to harness purely humanitarian motives. In contrast to the preoccupation with sin and salvation typical of Prussian temperance periodicals, those in places like Hanover and Hamburg emphasized broader ethical and social concerns, basing their claims more on enlightened self-interest and common sense than on the Gospel. It was essentially a question of exchanging what had proved to be socially and individually pernicious habits for new and better ones. (See for example, 'Der Mäßigkeits-Verein in Hamburg und dessen ersten öffentlichen Versammlung,' *Mäßigkeits-Zeitung*, vol. 2, no. 3, 1841, pp. 20–3; 'Zweiter Jahresbericht über der Stader Mäßigkeits-Verein,' *Mäßigkeits-Zeitung*, vol. 2, no. 6, 1841, pp. 41–5.)

The initial vitality of the German temperance movement thus depended on the ability of liberals and conservatives to co-operate in a common endeavor. This was possible because they shared a moral vision that saw poverty as an individual moral failing. Similarly, they saw individual self-discipline as its only possible remedy. But if both liberals and conservatives hoped to reform the behavior of the lower classes, they ultimately had different ends in view. For the theological and political conservatives who dominated the movement in Prussia, the temperance reform was a means to preserve an increasingly threatened social order. The liberals who were the principal supporters of the reform elsewhere had something else in mind, however, for no matter how patronizing their view of the lower classes, their ultimate intention was to develop the self-reliance and independence essential to a political order of self-governing citizens. Just as the bonds of political and theological tutelage would have to be broken for their ideals to be realized, subservience to alcohol would also have to be overcome. This liberal conception of the temperance reform was marred by fundamental contradictions. It was a movement that promised to ensure the dignity of the common man, but it was also a movement that defended existing property relations and a hierarchical social order that was bound to relegate masses of men to the bottom of the social heap. Nevertheless, it is important to keep in mind that if the temperance movement was meant to be an agency of social control, its sponsors would not have agreed on whether the reform was intended to preserve the status quo or to transform it.

But if the temperance reform was spearheaded by old and new elites who shared a common moral vision, it was also a grass roots movement of artisans, journeymen and small-holders. Why did tens of thousands of them take the temperance pledge in the 1830s and 1840s? There is virtually no direct evidence that can be brought to bear on this point. Apart from occasional biographical sketches of reformed drunkards, the temperance press does not contain the voices of the rank and file but of the preachers, teachers and bureaucrats we encountered earlier. The stories of reformed drunkards, highly stylized accounts of degradation and salvation, are not much use either, since the vast majority of those who took the temperance pledge were not themselves drunkards. This, indeed, may be the main point.

Whatever the composition of the temperance movement's leadership, its rank and file was recruited overwhelmingly from artisans and small-holders, that is, from the lower end of the *traditional* rural and urban social structure. Artisans and agricultural laborers accounted for 68.1 per cent of the movement's membership of 1,751 in Osnabrück and surrounding areas in 1840. (Niedersächsisches Hauptstaatsarchiv, Hann Des 80, Hildesheim I, E18) Master craftsmen and their journeymen made up 45 per cent of the total membership of 2,268 in Hamburg in 1844. Dockers, day laborers and others outside the handicraft system accounted for another 14.9 per cent. (Stubbe, 1911, pp. 69–71) In the Rhenish village of Röthgen, near Aachen, 64.3 per cent of the 28-member association was composed of weavers and other artisans in 1846. (Hauptstaatsarchiv Düsseldorf, Reg. Aachen, 4793) Small-holders, their sons and agricultural servants accounted for 95.1 per cent of the membership of 61 in the Hanoverian village of Altenzelle. (Böttcher, 1841, p. 289) The rank and file of the 366-member Danzig county association was made up of artisans (27 per cent), small-holders (13 per cent) and domestic servants (6.1 per cent). (Böttcher, 1841, pp. 171–2)

Temperance organizations were thus not recruited from the emerging industrial proletariat or from the growing mass of landless agricultural laborers who constituted the very bottom of the social hierarchy but from those who occupied a once-respected but now increasingly threatened place in the traditional social order. These were not the people most likely to have had the greatest problems with alcohol but those most intent on demonstrating their sobriety and preserving their place in a rapidly changing social order. Membership in temperance associations was a badge of respectability that could help distance them socially from the emerging proletariat. But at the same time, temperance ideology held out the more practical promise that self-discipline and hard work would be rewarded in an increasingly fluid social order. These were men who still aspired to property ownership and the security and status it provided, but in fact their chances of realizing these aspirations were every day being undermined. The Revolution of 1848 did not destroy the ideal of the small property-holder to which these men clung – industrialization did – but it did open up new ways to defend it that were bound to undermine the temperance movement's appeal.

## Notes to Chapter 2

1 Hoffmann and his associates estimate an increase from 25 million in 1817 to 35 million in 1850 in the territory of the future *Kaiserreich*.
2 Exact figures are as follows: Prussia: Teachers/Preachers 76.5 percent, Mittelstand 17.6 per cent. Non-Prussia: Teachers/Preachers 57.8 per cent, Mittelstand 42.2 per cent.

## Chapter 3

# Decline and Renewal: 1848 and Beyond

A part of the bourgeoisie is desirous of redressing social grievances, in order to secure the continued existence of bourgeois society. To this section belong economists, philanthropists, humanitarians, improvers of the condition of the working class, organisers of charity, members of societies for the prevention of cruelty to animals, temperance fanatics, hole-and-corner reformers of every imaginable kind. . . . [They] want all the advantages of modern social conditions without the struggles and dangers necessarily resulting therefrom. They desire the existing state of society minus its revolutionary and disintegrating elements. They wish for a bourgeoisie without a proletariat. (Marx and Engels, 1978, p. 496)

The year 1848 was a momentous one in German politics, and it affected the temperance movement no less profoundly. News of the successful Parisian revolution against Louis Philippe hit the German tinder-box of the late 1840s like a lightning bolt. Harvest failures and an attendant trade depression had aggravated long-term economic problems and now produced an acute social crisis. At the same time, liberal political opposition mounted. In Prussia, for example, Frederick William IV was forced to summon his provincial estates in a United Diet, which then refused to grant the king the fiscal authority he wanted without constitutional concessions. These tensions remained unresolved in the winter and spring of 1848, and when news of the February revolution in Paris reached Germany, mass meetings were held in the streets of major German cities to demand constitutional reform. By the middle of March, it appeared that the political opposition would succeed. Prominent liberals were called to office by frightened rulers, new constitutions were drafted on liberal principles, and a national representative body took up its work in Frankfurt. Though many of the revolution's early gains proved ephemeral, its consequences for the temperance movement were not. The movement lost its support in the maelstrom of political events and new sociopolitical programs. J. H. Böttcher's lament reflected the bitter disappointment of the movement's leaders: ' "Freedom and Equality," ' he wrote, 'was the byword of those days; the most insolent license reigned among the lower classes in both

town and country; discipline, order and moderation had completely vanished
[and] the promising reform of popular life we hoped to achieve through
the introduction of sobriety and thriftiness, through diligence and order,
was destroyed in mid-course.' (1896, p. 31)

## Temperance and Politics in the Revolution of 1848

The contrasting temper of the movement in Prussia and the other North
German states was clearly revealed in the local associations' responses to
the Revolution. In both areas, the leaders of the reform faced hard times
– declining membership, public apathy and popular derision. To the
movement's supporters, however, the Revolution seemed to make the
temperance reform more necessary than ever before. In Prussia, this new
sense of urgency was linked to a wholesale condemnation of the Revolution
itself, which was seen by at least some of the movement's spokesmen as
a divine warning to the German people to return to religious piety.

One of the sins in question was the continued consumption of *Branntwein*.
Drink was held responsible for the manifestations of popular revolt that
accompanied the Revolution. 'Everywhere riot and revolt against the
spiritual and temporal order broke out,' concluded Pastor Kutta in Breslau,
'spiritous beverages were the true, necessary and indispensible instigator.'
('Vorwort,' *Der Volksfreund. Monatsblatt des Breslauer Vereines gegen das
Branntweintrinken*, vol. 3, no. 1, January 1849, p. 1) Under the influence
of alcohol, the people had fallen all the more readily under the sway of
unscrupulous agitators whose fantastic promises had set the poor against
the rich and turned them away from the only path that could guarantee
their ultimate happiness, the path of true religion. This happiness could
never be achieved through politics. The deluded masses would soon discover
that their

> welfare cannot flourish on the road of limitless freedom, whether
> manifested in politics or in socialism, but only over the narrow path of
> spiritual improvement and moral purity, persevering and diligent labor,
> prudent housekeeping, and sensible thrift and sobriety. This is the
> healthiest and most beneficial politics, and it would also produce a healthy
> politics in the state. ('Vorwort,' *Der Volksfreund. Monatsblatt des Breslauer
> Vereins gegen das Branntweintrinken*, vol. 3, no. 1, January 1849, p. 1)

In Prussia, then, the Revolution made the temperance reform more pressing
than ever before because it promised to bring the people back from politics
to piety and thus to restore prosperity and political order.

Temperance reformers outside of Prussia seem to have responded somewhat differently to the revolutionary events of 1848. Like their Prussian counterparts, they too believed that the Revolution demanded renewed dedication at a time when public support was dwindling. But contrary to the case in Prussia, the men who made this argument in Hamburg, Hanover and other North German states were seeking not to negate the middle-class revolution but to complete and preserve it. Rather than fighting the liberal movement, temperance reformers claimed to be a part of it. ('An die Freunde und Theilnehmer in der Enthaltsamkeitssache,' *Mäßigkeits-Zeitung*, vol. 10, no. 1, 1 January 1849, pp. 1–3) 'We too joyously enter the ranks of freedom fighters,' the *Mäßigkeits-Zeitung* of Stade proudly proclaimed. ('Der Mäßigkeitsverein inmitten der politischen Bewegung,' *Mäßigkeits-Zeitung*, vol. 9, no. 5, 1 May 1848, p. 35)

Several of the movement's liberal supporters distinguished themselves politically in 1848. Maximilian Heinrich Rüder and Johann Ludwig Mösle of Oldenburg, Gabriel Riesser and C. F. Wurm from Hamburg, Karl Heinrich Jürgens of Brunswick and Hermann Adolf Lüntzel of Hildesheim, were sent to the Frankfurt Parliament, while Johann Carl Bertram Stüve, Alexander Levin Graf von Bennigsen and Johann Heinrich Wilhelm Lehzen joined the liberal cabinet formed in Hanover. (Böttcher, n.d. (in Hauptstaatsarchiv Düsseldorf, Reg. Aachen 4793); Bode, 1896, p. 74; Stubbe, 1911, p. 129; Valentin, 1930/31) For men of this persuasion, the temperance movement's contribution to the liberal movement reached deep into the past and would extend well into the future. They were proud of their contribution to German liberty, for they had founded 'the first truly *popular* associations' in Germany. They had promoted the new social order, encouraging 'everyone, regardless of birth, rank, station or financial contribution' to speak freely and publicly about important public issues. ('An die Freunde und Theilnehmer in der Enthaltsamkeitssache,' *Mäßigkeits-Zeitung*, vol. 10, no. 1, 1 January 1849, p. 2) Temperance associations had long demonstrated the public spiritness and concern for the common good that had now begun to enter German political life.

Temperance associations, liberals claimed, had helped educate the common man to the use of reason, and what he learned with regard to his drinking behavior, they confidently predicted, he would also apply to the rest of his personal and social existence.

Just as the temperance man repudiates *Branntwein*, he also rejects everything else which contradicts his Reason. Just as he breaks the chains of sensual pleasure, he rebels against every other form of bondage. Strengthened by the fight against *Branntwein*, he has learned to rise above prejudice, to endure scurrilous criticism for the sake of a lofty ideal, and to maintain courage and conviction amidst a struggle. All this he will carry over into every other aspect of his life; for freedom is a precious treasure, and he who has obtained even a portion of it will not rest until he possesses the whole. ('Der Mäßigkeitsverein inmitten der politischen Bewegung,' *Mäßigkeits-Zeitung*, vol. 9, no. 5, 1 May 1848, p. 34)

Temperance was an education in virtue: not only personal virtue, but also the virtue of citizens newly in possession of their liberty. The two were inextricably intertwined, for no matter how secular their orientation, liberals believed that the quality of Germany's public life would ultimately depend on the self-discipline and moral sense of each of its individual citizens. 'The more insistent the striving for the political freedom of the whole people,' therefore, 'the more indispensable the efforts to provide its moral foundation in each individual.' ('An die Freunde und Theilnehmer in der Enthaltsamkeitssache,' *Mäßigkeits-Zeitung*, vol. 10, no. 1, 1 January 1849, p. 3) Political liberty was impossible without individual self-control.

This view of the temperance movement's ethical and ultimately political importance was shared, for example, by Carl Bertram Stüve, one of the most prominent liberal supporters of the temperance reform. As we have seen, Stüve was one of the leading liberals of his day. He had invested a heavy burden of hopes in the temperance movement all along, seeing in individual virtue the only foundation for social progress. For Stüve, self-help was not only the best solution to the economic and social ills besetting Germany: it was the surest defense of the *Bürgertum* against the growing threat of communism. His appeals were intended at least as much to convince the propertied classes of the necessity of this line of defense as to win adherents of the lower classes to his cause.

Stüve was born in Osnabrück in 1789 to one of the city's leading families. (G. Stüve, 1900; Ott, 1933; Vogel, 1959/60; Graf, 1970) He attended the universities of Berlin and Göttingen and was a founding member of the German *Burschenschaft* movement. At the death of his father, Stüve abandoned his plan to pursue a university career and instead returned home with a law degree to care for his aging mother. He was soon involved in the politics of both his native city and his country. He entered the *Landtag* in 1824 and quickly became an expert on agrarian reform. Stüve drafted the legislation that emancipated the Hanoverian peasantry in 1833. Several years later, Stüve gained even greater fame during his tenacious but ultimately unsuccessful defense of the kingdom's first constitution. At the death of William IV in 1837, the English crown passed to Victoria, while William's brother Ernst August, the Duke of Cumberland, became King of Hanover. The new ruler almost immediately abrogated the constitution of 1833 and thus opened up a bitter struggle which found Stüve at the head of the opposition. By 1840, the conflict had been decided in the king's favor − the pliant *Stände* accepted a new constitution of the king's making.

Stüve refused to acknowledge the new constitution and remained banned from public life on the national plane for most of the 1840s. Prevented by the government from taking up the *Landtag* mandates to which he was repeatedly elected, Stüve intensified his involvement in municipal affairs. It was in these years that Stüve helped launch the temperance movement in Osnabrück, where it was to achieve some of its most striking successes.

The Revolution of 1848 brought Stüve's return to national political life. Shaken by events in Paris, Vienna and Berlin, Ernst August dismissed his aristocratic ministers and promised constitutional reforms. Stüve was the man he called upon to restore order and guide this process of internal renewal. Agreeing now to accept the constitution of 1840 as his point of departure, Stüve served as Minister of the Interior from March 1848 until September 1850, when the March ministry resigned *en masse* in the face of reactionary pressures from the king. Stüve inaugurated an imposing series of reforms in administration, the judicial system, and in city government. The fulfillment of his domestic program, which had the support of both the political clubs in the capital and the *Landtag*, was slowed by Stüve's extremely unpopular opposition to the tactics and claims of the Frankfurt Parliament, which had set itself up *de facto* as the supreme political authority in Germany. Because of these complications, many of the reforms he inaugurated were completed only after his departure. The period of reaction beginning in 1855 saw much of his work undone. In 1850 Stüve again departed the national political stage, and again he returned to Osnabrück – to the office of mayor, to his work in social welfare organizations, and to his activities as political publicist and amateur historian. Stüve died in 1872, crushed by the Prussian annexation of Hanover in 1866, contemptuous of Bismarck, and pessimistic about the future of the *Kaiserreich*.

Stüve's active support for the temperance movement followed naturally from his broader social and political views. Stüve was a liberal in the Burkean rather than the French Enlightenment mold. His profound distrust of the centralized state and modern bureaucracy, his hatred of aristocratic pretension and prerogative, and his disdain of abstract principle motivated his search for ways to adapt traditional corporate institutions to modern needs and to preserve and even broaden the realm of individual and local initiative. Stüve's fundamentally conservative orientation was also evident in his approach to contemporary social problems. He was a decided critic of economic individualism and the symptoms of nascent industrial capitalism which were destroying the old guild system. Here as in other areas, Stüve sought to reform and improve rather than to abolish and create *de novo*. But as he sought to modernize and shore up the legal foundations of the guild system, he also hoped to strengthen its moral foundations. Stüve was a pious man concerned less with dogma than with ethics and moral action. He saw morality as the foundation of public life and private virtue as the key to individual happiness. For those in need, there was fundamentally only one solution: self-improvement.

For Stüve and others like him, the temperance movement was one way to address the social ills of the day in accordance with this overall conception. It looked not to the state but to p.ivate initiative. It aimed not to transform the social order but to foster self-discipline, self-reliance and self-help. It fostered moral improvement and thus promised to strengthen the foundations of the state. The temperance movement, finally, reinforced precisely the kind of patriarchal social ties that Stüve hoped to see generalized throughout the society. Just as Stüve and other leading citizens of the community joined forces with respectable craftsmen, so masters could join their journeymen and apprentices, and farmers their servants and laborers in a moral compact that testified to a common view of the social and political world.

In attempting in the fall of 1848 to rekindle dormant temperance enthusiasms, Stüve's *Osnabrücker Mäßigkeits-und Enthaltsamkeitsverein* issued an urgent 'Weckruf und die Kämpfer wider den Branntwein', which captures the spirit of *Vormärz* liberalism and the precariousness of the liberals' position in 1848. (Staatsarchiv Osnabrück, Erw A16, Familie Stüve, no. 152 Drucksachen, 1848/50) The more confident side of this appeal presupposed the victory of liberal principles. The *Volk* had acquired its freedom, but freedom without order and obedience, the manifesto warned, could only amount to tyranny. The goals and opportunities of the moment could be pursued to a happy conclusion only by a population truly free in mind and spirit. This desideratum made the fight against *Branntwein* a political necessity. Like many other temperance enthusiasts, the Osnabrückers pointed to the Americans, 'the freest of all people,' who had also done the most to curtail the use of spirits, to prove their point.

But there was a darker side to this argument. Like other men of education and property, these temperance reformers feared the lower classes. The massive demonstrations and occasional violent conflicts that were part and parcel of the revolution from which the liberals hoped to profit had heightened these fears, and they assumed almost automatically that it was *Branntwein* that had fueled the revolutionary crowds. The popular disturbances of the recent past, they insisted, should be a warning to all men of property and friends of order who had hitherto turned their backs on the temperance cause, for the 'fight against *Branntwein* [is] also a political struggle.'

It was a political struggle not just in the sense of controlling the revolutionary crowd but also in contributing to the solution of the Social Question, 'the question, what is to become of the lowest classes of human society, of the so-called proletariat!' The Osnabrück association warned against the organization of labor and the destruction of private property, for 'it remains once and for all God's order that the poor must live from the wealthy and that only through skill, diligence, and parsimony . . . can they make a living. Any other way is simply impossible.' As long as the lower classes continued to drink *Branntwein*, therefore, no solution to the Social Question could be found. 'If the deeply felt misery of the lower classes is not to become so great that it threatens the security, even the very existence, of bourgeois society, . . . then it is only by banning *Branntwein*, if not alone by banning it, that this outcome can be prevented.' But this was no call for prohibition, for most temperance reformers continued to believe that association and moral suasion were the only ways to meet the evil.

## The Crisis of the Temperance Movement

Despite the dedication of the movement's leaders, only a few local temperance associations survived the Revolution. The vast majority simply vanished. But the Revolution was only the *coup de grâce*, for even before the spring of 1848 many local reports had complained of stagnation and even decline.

In large part, the movement's problems stemmed from the deepening social and economic crisis of the *Vormärz*. The temperance movement faced three interrelated problems. Most important was the rapid erosion of the movement's popular support. The movement's rapid growth during the early 1840s had come to an abrupt end by 1847. (Tagesblatt, 1847, p. 42) Organizations that had grown rapidly now found it impossible to maintain the loyalty of their rank and file. The social, economic and political crisis of the immediate pre-revolutionary years undermined the appeal of a movement which promised so much but could do so little to offset the hardships faced by small farmers and urban craftsmen. The promise that the individual could control his own destiny and that virtue would be rewarded was belied by the course of events. Many of the small farmers, masters and journeymen who had taken the temperance pledge must now have sought other solutions to their problems. The proliferation of popular associations concerned with advancing the economic and political demands of urban craftsmen opened up new avenues of social action that now seemed more promising to the temperance movement's clientele. (Noyes, 1966; Hamerow, 1958) Indeed, as in the genesis of the Berlin *Handwerkerverein*, where Stephan Born gathered the political and organizational experience that would propel him into national prominence as the leader of the *Allgemeine deutsche Arbeiterverbrüderung*, temperance associations sometimes provided a bridge to more far-reaching social and political concerns. (Balser, 1959, pp. 91–2) Finally, of course, the emergence of independent workers' organizations, like much else in the Revolution, strained the relationship between the movement's middle- and upper-class patrons and its rank and file. The bonds of deference had begun to snap. The temperance movement was one of the early victims of this long-term social process.

The movement also faced new organizational challenges. If the period of growth and confidence had ended, what was to become of the existing organizations? The response seems to have been surprisingly uniform. Those local associations that managed to keep afloat did so by erecting barriers between themselves and the outside world. The line between the virtuous and the depraved was now drawn more tightly, and a self-righteous conventicle spirit that had previously been visible only sporadically came to predominate in the remaining organizations. This may have been the best way to survive a time of crisis, but the price ultimately paid was high. All the worst suspicions of the movement's critics now seemed to be confirmed, and the associations lost all public influence. In the end, the temperance landscape was abandoned to scattered local organizations, tightly knit and highly sectarian, whose audience was the already converted.

Finally, the erosion of grass roots support in turn created new problems for those who hung on. How could the movement achieve its goals when the people it most wanted to help were deserting it? In a sense this was a problem faced in every country where popular movements to reform drinking behavior emerged in the early nineteenth century. They had all begun from the naive assumption that once the truth was proclaimed, a new era in human history would be inaugurated. But when this approach failed to produce the temperance Utopia, as it always did, new and often more radical tactics were developed. Persuasion gave way to coercion, and self-help gave way to increasingly insistent appeals to the state. The *ne plus ultra* of this tendency was the demand for the legal prohibition of the production, sale and/or consumption of alcoholic beverages. The turning point in the United States was the passage of the so-called 'Maine Law' in 1851, the first measure of state-wide prohibition on the North American continent. (Tyrrell, 1979, pp. 225–89) The leading British prohibitionist organization, the United Kingdom Alliance, was founded under the spell of this American success in 1853. (Harrison, 1971, pp. 196–218) In Germany too, there was an increasing number of demands for state action heard after the mid-1840s.

Once the demand for state action was raised, however, the Drink Question was transformed from a strictly moral and social issue into a political one. But depending on how public power was organized and controlled in each country, temperance reformers faced different obstacles in putting this tactic to work. In Germany claims on the state had only very limited chances of success. To be sure, a bureaucratic state like Prussia could regulate the number of taverns and tax the producers of alcohol, but despite the attraction of social control arguments, traditional ruling elites were by no means disposed to stamp out the drink trade. Weighty interests stood in the way, including the agriculturalists who raised the raw materials from which alcoholic beverages were made, the distillers and brewers who produced them, and the countless number of retailers who purveyed beer, wine and brandy to a growing and thirsty public. But beyond all this, the state itself had a vested interest in the drink trade, for the ruling classes almost invariably saw the vices of the common man as a ready source of tax revenues. (Webb, 1963, p. 46) If this source were to dry up, then the propertied classes themselves would have to bear a greater fiscal burden to meet the growing appetite of the modern state. Hence the movement's need to marshall political power at the grass roots, a tactic that was only viable in a democratic polity with representative political institutions. In Germany, these institutions were almost entirely absent in the first half of the nineteenth century. And partly because they were absent, temperance reformers had no examples of successful popular agitations on which to model their own campaign. In the United States and England, abolitionism and the Anti-Corn Law League provided such examples. (Harrison, 1971; Tyrrell, 1979) Thus, at a time when early prohibitionists in England and the United States were also seeking to harness the power of the state by actively entering the electoral and parliamentary arenas, German temperance reformers had much less room for tactical maneuver and had to content themselves with mere petitions. Their petitions during the acute food shortages of 1845 and 1846 resulted in the prohibition of distilling in some areas, but these were only temporary measures and were not intended primarily to meet temperance objectives.

The revolutionary year 1848 thus marked the end of the first phase of German temperance history. As the movements in Britain and the United States were turning increasingly to prohibitionism, the reform in Germany reached a stopping point, its forces apparently routed by the course of events and the complexities of the German situation, which made large-scale, durable organizations difficult to build and the grass roots political tactics developing in the Anglo-American countries impossible. The reform from above had fallen on fertile but unstable ground. The coalition of forces that had provided both the leadership and the cadres of the temperance army could not endure. The leaders of the reform were frustrated by the signs of flagging vitality in their movement even before 1848, but they had little room for tactical maneuver. Moral suasion and voluntary association were the only means at their disposal. British and American prohibitionists were pioneers in pressure group politics. In Germany the institutional environment in which similar tactics might have developed had not yet taken shape. The movement had thus reached an impasse, and in the following three decades, the temperance impulse lacked organizational expression. By the time public interest again fastened on the Drink Question in the 1880s, only six of the more than 1,200 local associations founded in the *Vormärz* still survived. One of these was in Berlin, the other five scattered through the eastern provinces of Prussia. (Martius, 1886, pp. 35–40)

## Industrialization and Popular Drinking Behavior

It was another thirty-five years before the temperance movement regained any significant public support in Germany. In the meantime, the country had entered the industrial age. The problems of the late 1840s were left behind as a period of sustained economic growth began which was to make Germany one of the world's leading industrial powers. Heavy industry led the way. In 1845 the German railway network had consisted of barely 2,000 kilometers. By 1880, 33,808 kilometers of track were in place. (Henning, 1973, p. 162) Coal production had increased from 3.2 million tons in 1846 to 29.4 million in 1871. German smelters turned out 529,000 tons of pig-iron in 1850; by 1875, output had reached 2 million tons annually. Two thousand steam engines were at work in 1850; by 1875 there were 28,000. (Carr, 1979, p. 69)

As Germany industrialized in the 1850s and 1860s, important shifts in the structure of employment were underway that would be even more pronounced in later decades. In 1850, 600,000 Germans, or 4 per cent of the labor force, had been employed in manufacturing industry. By 1873, the industrial labor force had tripled and included 10 per cent of all German workers. As industry expanded, the number of people in the handicrafts also continued to grow. There were nearly a million more artisans at work in 1873 than in 1850 (up from 1.7 million to 2.5 million), and their share of the labor force increased from 12 to 14 per cent. The only loser within the secondary sector was domestic industry, which experienced both an absolute and a relative decline, from 1.5 million workers and 10 per cent of the labor force in 1850 to 1.1 million workers and 6 per cent of the labor force in 1873. (Henning, 1973, pp. 20, 130)

Germany's economic growth was accompanied by important demographic changes. The population increased by some 5 million between 1850 and 1870. The principal centers of industrial expansion, Greater Berlin, the Rhine and Ruhr, Saxony, and Upper Silesia, became human magnets as thriving enterprises attracted men and women anxious for regular employment and money wages away from the surrounding countryside. The long-term structural imbalance between population growth and economic opportunity that had characterized the *Vormärz* was being redressed, but by now the problems of an emerging urban industrial society were becoming clearly visible. Housing and sanitation problems, long hours and dangerous working conditions, sickness and insecurity plagued German workingmen and their families just as they did the workers of other nations.

As real wages increased in this period of rapid industrial expansion, so too did the consumption of alcohol (see Figure 3.1). Per capita consumption had declined in the 1840s. The temperance movement may have contributed to this trend, but the harvest failures that restricted supply and raised prices were undoubtedly more important. (Baer, 1878, pp. 229–42) Now

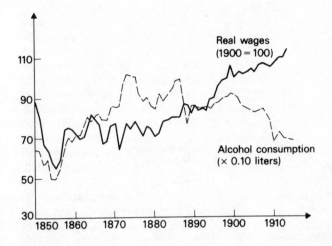

*Source:* Computed from Hoffmann, 1965, pp. 172–4, 650–4; Kuczynski, 1962, Vol. 2 p. 152; Desai, 1968, pp. 112, 117.

**Figure 3.1**   Real Wages and Per Capita Consumption of Absolute Alcohol, 1850–1913

consumption levels reached new heights. Between 1855 and 1873 the per capita consumption of *Branntwein* increased by nearly 50 per cent while the per capita consumption of beer nearly doubled[1] (see Figure 3.2). The consumption of absolute alcohol (an index of the total amount of alcohol contained in both beverages) reached a peak of 10.2 liters per capita in the early 1870s that was not again equaled until the 1960s. (Feuerlein, 1975, p. 59) Beer was beginning to replace *Schnaps* as the principal beverage of the working classes, but in the 1870s these two beverages accounted for roughly equal shares of the German drink bill.

Paradoxically, the sources on popular drinking behavior during this period of rapid industrialization and sharply increasing per capita consumption are poor, largely because there was no broadly based temperance movement to keep the issue in the public eye. Despite the paucity of sources, however, some attempt must be made to account for the dramatic increase of per capita alcohol consumption during these years. In aggregate terms, the upward trend in consumption seems to have been the result of two factors. In the first place, the supply of alcoholic beverages, and especially of commercially produced beer, was expanding rapidly. On the demand side, consumers were enjoying new purchasing power at a time

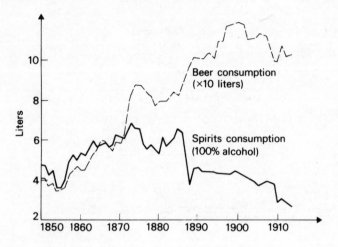

*Source:* Computed from Hoffmann, 1965, pp. 172–4, 650–4.

**Figure 3.2**  Per Capita Consumption of Beer and Spirits, 1850–1913

when there were few alternative consumer goods on the market. Drink – and drunkenness – were traditional objects of expenditure on those relatively rare occasions in the past when cash was on hand. As more and more Germans entered the expanding money economy, they had more money to spend, and in the absence of attractive alternatives, they continued to spend it in accustomed ways. According to Hoffmann's calculations, the percentage of private expenditure devoted to drink increased steadily from the 1850s and reached its nineteenth-century peak of 14.5 per cent in the years 1870–4 (see Figure 3.3). It is no accident that the period of sustained increase in per capita consumption ended when the German economy faced its first severe industrial depression in the mid-1870s. Increasing alcohol consumption was thus by and large a sign of good times rather than bad. This conclusion is borne out by observations of the relationship between alcohol consumption and the business cycle in other societies as well. (Thomas, 1927, pp. 127–32; cf. Mathias, 1960; Dingle, 1978) But the rapidly increasing consumption of the 1850s and 1860s was also a symptom of the general backwardness of the German economy and of the still restricted cultural opportunities available to German workingmen and their families.

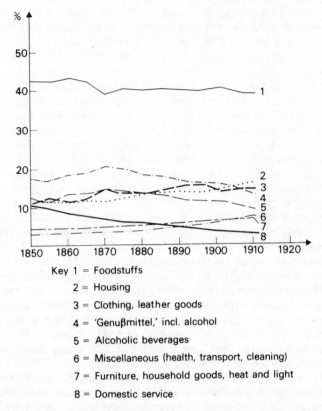

Key 1 = Foodstuffs

2 = Housing

3 = Clothing, leather goods

4 = 'Genußmittel,' incl. alcohol

5 = Alcoholic beverages

6 = Miscellaneous (health, transport, cleaning)

7 = Furniture, household goods, heat and light

8 = Domestic service

*Source:* Hoffmann, pp. 116f, 128. (1850 = 1850/4 etc.).

**Figure 3.3**  The Structure of Private Expenditure, 1850–1913

Alcoholic beverages continued to meet important and legitimate needs in the life of the emerging industrial working class. The dearth of suitable alternatives to drink and the tavern, false beliefs about alcohol's nutritive and medicinal properties, and the deprivations of working-class living and working conditions combined to produce a pattern of alcohol consumption marked not so much by widespread drunkenness as by the use of relatively small quantities of alcohol in a variety of everyday settings. It was this pattern of normal drinking and not the aberrant behavior of those comparatively few men and women who completely lost themselves to drink that constituted the classic nineteenth-century alcohol problem.

The best way to convey what this everyday drinking entailed is to describe a fictive 'drinking day.' (cf. Deutscher Verein gegen den Mißbrauch geistiger

Getränke, 1897a-d; Grotjahn, 1903) It began on the way to work. Men who traveled long distances to and fro, often on foot and exposed to the elements, customarily refreshed themselves at the end of their trek and, eventually, at the hubs of urban transportation. On the job, drinking punctuated the working day at a number of points. Depending on the vigilance of their supervisors and the policies of their employers, workingmen nipped at their brandy flasks at will, whenever they felt the need for refreshment or diversion. The urge to drink was especially great among workers exposed to high or low temperatures, dust, dampness, or noxious fumes. Workers who relied on sheer physical strength also drank heavily, in part to drown out the pain of their exhausting labor. Alcohol was even provided to many workers as a means of increasing their output. Only gradually did employers learn that they could get more out of their workers by prohibiting the use of alcohol at the work-place than by providing it. (Roberts, 1981a) Until the turn of the century, alternative beverages were rarely available. The water supply was unreliable, and workers widely − and often wisely − shunned plain water as an inadequate and even harmful thirst quencher on the job.

Whether or not they actually drank while working, most workingmen consumed alcohol with their meals. German workers typically ate five meals a day rather than the three larger ones familiar to modern-day Americans. Three of these fell within the workday. Workers who consumed their meals in taverns consumed alcohol as a matter of course. Those who remained on the factory premises could buy beer and often *Schnaps* in the canteen. Men whose noonday meals were cold, bulky or greasy found alcoholic beverages an especially welcome addition.

Other kinds of drinking also punctuated the working day. The world of work was also a social world, and drinking was part of working-class sociability. Craft traditions lingered on in the factory setting. Birthdays were celebrated on the job and holidays toasted. The arrival of a new journeyman was celebrated by the customary *Einstand*, the first demonstration of technical skill in an apprentice by a round of drinks. Occasionally, workers simply brought in a barrel of beer or a liter of *Schnaps* and mixed work with conviviality.

At the end of the working day, the road home also brought the opportunity to drink. Workers, like miners and masons, who labored in environments thick with dust or other irritants were especially likely to stop briefly to clear their throats, but married men, at least, were unlikely to linger long in the taverns and bars after work. Exceptions were made only to attend the frequent meetings of the clubs and associations to which so many workingmen belonged. Drinking at such gatherings was mandatory because the meeting rooms were invariably provided by tavern keepers. Single men, depending on their boarding and lodging arrangements, were more likely to take their meals in public accommodations, and many more, for want of alternatives, spent much of their free time in taverns. The solitary drinker drowning his sorrows night after night was a rarity, though many a worker had recourse to the great *Sorgenbrecher* on more than one occasion. In any event, married or single, at home or in the tavern, workingmen were likely to include alcohol in their evening meal.

The drinking day, then, could be long. Drinking punctuated everyday life at a number of points, especially for the working-class male. The variations among individual drinkers were, of course, considerable, and no historical calculus can explain them all. The impression that emerges from the available sources, however, is that most of this daily drinking involved small quantities of alcohol which were consumed in dietary contexts or on the job. Intoxication was not the purpose of this kind of drinking and rarely its result.

Weekend drinking could have a slightly different aspect, especially when wages were paid. The payday was one of the poles around which working-class culture revolved. Preceded by days or even weeks of scarcity, it was followed by a fleeting period of relative prosperity. Drink places were filled on paydays, and drunkenness was frequent. This was not the solitary drunkenness of individual despair but of good times, however short lived, and of well-deserved diversion with friends and workmates. This was especially true for single men. Despite the complaints to which this weekend binge drunkenness gave rise, it was viewed by the people doing the drinking as natural and normal, not in the least incompatible with social respectability. In the long run, however, this kind of recreational drunkenness was on the decline. As workingmen spent more and more of their leisure time in organized clubs and associations, drinking became less an end in itself than an accompaniment of other forms of sociability. Indeed social drinking could also be a family affair, a respite for women as well as for men and an introduction to adult sociability for their children.

All this was normal drinking, widely accepted and widely practiced in working-class communities. The quantities consumed at any one time were generally moderate, but cumulatively they produced the nineteenth-century alcohol problem, which can best be compared to the kind of environmental health risks faced by many twentieth-century workers. (US Department of Health, Education and Welfare, 1973) It was a specifically working-class problem because the factors that sustained it bore especially heavily on the working class. Workers were at risk because of their living and working conditions, because of their shared beliefs about alcohol, and because of the dearth of affordable alternatives to beverage alcohol and the institutions that purveyed it. Though it affected each individual differently, it was a pervasive risk that few workers managed to escape. The net effect was to produce a distinctive pattern of working-class alcohol consumption which, despite the immediate gratifications it offered, must ultimately be seen as part of the larger pattern of deprivation suffered by German workers in the nineteenth century.

## The Rebirth of the German Temperance Movement

In the meantime, efforts to revive the temperance reform in this period of rapidly rising alcohol consumption foundered. After attending the World Temperance Congress in London during the summer of 1862, J. H. Böttcher set out to organize a Continental Temperance Congress to mark the twenty-fifth anniversary of the reform in Germany. In his invitation, Böttcher provided both a lengthy discussion of the movement's history and an assessment of its prospects in the early 1860s. (n.d.; cf. Bode, 1896, pp. 97–100) Germany's economic transformation, he believed, had made the Drink Question even more pressing than in the years before 1848. To be sure, the materialism of the age tended to undermine the spirit of self-sacrifice so necessary to the temperance reform, 'a work of brotherly love,' he noted pointedly, 'which brought neither stocks nor decorations, neither lucrative offices nor posts of honor' (n.d., p. 4). But Böttcher also recognized that Germany's industrial development had made the quality of the labor force a central concern in the nation's economic life. (cf. Jeggle, 1978; Roberts, 1981) Workers who were 'sober, diligent, persevering [and] circumspect' were required by the emerging industrial economy, but precisely these were the qualities that the use of spirits most assuredly undermined. 'As the economy has prospered,' Böttcher reported, 'complaints about lazy, unreliable, disruptive and dissatisfied workers have been heard more and more frequently,' and the desire to meet this threat was increasingly evident 'in the workshops, the factories and on the agricultural domains' (n.d., p. 5).

If Böttcher's observations were an indication that the nature of the Drink Question was changing as Germany entered the industrial age, they were also a recognition that the tactics of the *Vormärz* had been inadequate. Even before 1848, voices had been heard insisting that voluntary association alone could not solve the Drink Question and demanding that the state control – even prohibit – the production and sale of spirits. An attempt at the 1847 General Assembly to direct the movement's energies in this direction had failed, but the idea was never fully abandoned. (Martius, 'Vor fünfzig Jahren,' *Mäßigkeits-Blätter*, vol. 14, no. 11, 1897, pp. 167–9) In 1861 Victor Aimé Huber, a conservative Protestant social reformer who had launched the German co-operative movement, concluded in an analysis of the early temperance reform that its failure to convince the state to adopt energetic measures against the *Schnapspest* was a major source of its weakness. Future efforts to combat the alcohol problem, he argued, would have to involve the state more actively, and future temperance organizations would have to see that government agencies did their duty in this regard. And Johann Hinrich Wichern, the founder of the *Innere Mission*, similarly called in the early 1860s for government action against the spirits producers. (Martius, 1886, pp. 26–7; 1901, pp. 57–8, 77–8) Böttcher continued this line of attack in 1863. He criticized the prevailing licensing system, insisting that 'as long as spirits outlets are privileged by the state, free association alone will never reach its goal' (n.d., p. 8). If the state had the right to grant such a privilege, he argued, it also had the right to take it away. But Böttcher's effort to revive the movement ended in failure.

### The Drink Question and the 'zweite Reichsgründung'

It was another twenty years before organized interest in the Drink Question revived in Germany. In the meantime, the German Empire had been created and the nation had experienced the unprecedented prosperity of the *Gründerjahre*. A severe depression followed that lasted until 1879. The initial crisis brought considerable unemployment to the working class, but subsequent phases of the continuing '*Große Depression*' were marked by a long-term price deflation which buoyed real wages while cutting profits and slowing economic growth. (Borchardt, 1976) Germany's suddenly altered economic prospects were to have profound political consequences. The uncertainty they engendered contributed to the fear and suspicion middle- and upper-class Germans felt for the emerging socialist labor movement and brought the liberal economic doctrines on which the *Reich* had been launched into disrepute. The events of the years 1878–9 have since been called the '*zweite Reichsgründung*,' so drastic was the reversal they witnessed. (Rosenberg, 1967; Wehler, 1975, pp. 41–8; Sheehan, 1978, pp. 181–8) Bismarck abandoned his liberal political allies and their economic principles and embarked upon a policy of economic protectionism, suppression of the socialist labor movement and innovative social insurance schemes. It was within this context of economic uncertainty, political repression and mounting social anxieties that interest in the Drink Question revived in the late 1870s. At the same time, many disillusioned liberals, turning their backs on politics, began to devote their energies to a growing number of formally non-political associations devoted to social betterment. As one leader of the revived German temperance movement later recalled, 'the year 1878 can be understood as the birthdate of the modern German social welfare movement [Gemeinnützigkeitsbewegung]' (Wilhelm Bode, 'August Lammers,' Nordwest, vol. 16, no. 1. Cited in Emminghaus, 1908, pp. 158–9).

Public interest fastened first on the *Reich*'s licensing laws, a product of the economic liberalism written into the Commercial Code [*Gewerbeordnung*] of the North German Confederation and subsequently carried over into the early Empire. The regulations pertinent to the liquor trade, enacted in 1869, did not introduce free trade, but they went a considerable distance in that direction and much further than the Prussian government had hoped. Tavern keepers and retailers [*Kleinhandlungen*] throughout the Empire were required under the 1869 law to obtain licenses from local police authorities. (Reichstag, 1869, Vol. 7, pp. 357–78; Vol. 9, pp. 97, 118; cf. Schmoller, 1883; Meyer and Loenig, 1909) But an application could be denied only if there was evidence that the applicant would misuse his license to receive stolen goods or to promote gambling, immorality or intemperance, or if the premises under consideration did not satisfy the requirements of public health and safety. The question of whether or not local needs were already being adequately met could be considered in the case of establishments that proposed to sell spirits but only in communities of under 10,000 inhabitants and only if the laws of the various *Länder* did not provide otherwise. In contrast to previous Prussian policy, moreover, licenses henceforth did not have to be periodically renewed, and revocation was therefore extremely difficult. The new law was meant to prevent the administrative chicanery the Prussian police had so often used against their political enemies in the years after 1848. (Schmoller, 1883, p. 259; Reichstag, 1869, Vol. 7, pp. 367, 371–2)

A rising tide of complaints about the proliferation of drinking places, especially in industrial areas, led the government to seek tighter licensing regulations in the late 1870s. Under the liberal licensing regime, the number of taverns had risen significantly. (Reichstag, 1879, Vol. 56, pp. 1324–34; Stursberg, 1877) The trend continued into the mid-1870s despite – or perhaps because of – the hard times, for one source of the new recruits to the drink trade was those ruined or left jobless by the depression and forced to find an alternative livelihood. (Stursberg, 1977, p. 16; Thun, 1879, pp. 53–4; Reichstag, 1879, Vol. 56, p. 1300) In the new Prussian provinces, for example, there were 4.5 drinking places per 1,000 inhabitants in 1869; ten years later the figure had reached 5.2. (Baer, 1878, p. 242; Zentrales Staatsarchiv, Reichsamt des Innern, Nr. 16350, Bl. 163–4) The government's proposals were introduced to the *Reichstag* in 1878, just as Bismarck was abandoning his liberal allies and launching his attack on the socialist labor movement. Many contemporaries believed alcohol to be one of the socialist's most important allies, (Stursberg, 1877, pp. 20–1) and there can be little doubt that the revision of the licensing regulations was part of the overall plan for breaking the influence of the social democrats. The anti-Socialist law itself included stiff penalties for tavern keepers who lent their premises to social democratic purposes. (Roberts, 1980b, p. 130)

The government's amendments to the Commercial Code were approved in 1879. (Reichstag, 1879, Vol. 53, pp. 1558–70; Vol. 54, pp. 2135–44) The most important innovation was a more stringent application of the 'Test of Need' [*Bedürfnisfrage*], which allowed local licensing bodies to refuse to grant licenses when in their opinion the community's needs were already being satisfactorily met. Under the new law, this test was to apply automatically to all communities of less than 15,000 inhabitants and include applications to sell beer and wine as well as spirits. Cities over that size could adopt the Test of Need for all three beverages by local ordinance, and state governments could order that it be applied throughout their territories regardless of existing legislation. In effect, the law enlarged the discretionary powers of local government bodies since it provided no objective criteria by which local needs were to be judged. Left Liberals like Eugen Richter rightly saw this legislation as part of the more general trend toward political reaction, and the leader of the Center Party, Windthorst, expressed fears that the new legislation would prove to be only another weapon in the government's *Kulturkampf*. (Reichstag, 1879, Vol. 53, pp. 1560–4)

*A Manifesto for the Temperance Reform*
The year 1878 was important in another respect as well: Dr Abraham Baer, the physician at Plötzensee prison near Berlin, published the classic work of the nineteenth-century German temperance movement, *Der Alkoholismus: Seine Verbreitung und seine Wirkung auf den individuellen und socialen Organismus sowie die Mittel, ihn zu bekämpfen*. Baer's was the first comprehensive treatment of the Drink Question in Germany to draw upon the growing body of international scientific evidence about alcohol consumption and its consequences, and it thus marked a major departure from the predominantly moralistic temperance tracts of the *Vormärz*. Drawing on a wide range of German and foreign evidence, Baer painted an alarming picture of the individual and social consequences of alcohol abuse. He reiterated many of the themes of the *Vormärz* period, but now the moral assumptions of the temperance movement were cloaked all the more impressively in the mantle of science. The underlying motif of the whole panoply of temperance concerns remained self-control and the desire to strengthen it in others. As Baer put it, drink 'is the arch enemy of that mysterious, demanding judge within us – the conscience – because [it] immediately drowns out its quiet warnings and deadens the ear to the counterveiling impulses of the better self.' (Baer, 1878, p. 331) His main concern was the spirits consumption of the lower classes, which he linked to crime, poverty, disease, mental illness, religious indifference and moral depravity. These were the classic themes of nineteenth-century temperance, as common in Germany as they were in Britain or the United States. For Baer, the problem was ultimately an ethical one, the advance of civilization having outstripped the moral foundations of the population. The most essential remedial task was therefore to educate the masses to a higher morality so that they would choose the path of moderation. In Baer's view, this was a foremost duty of the state. Through its schools, the church

and the military as well as through the laws affecting the liquor trade and the conduct of drinkers, he argued, the state could foster the moral elevation of the populace. Baer insisted, however, that the state required assistance in this task. Self-sacrificing men of prominent social standing who were willing to associate for the purpose of this ethical renewal could make their own moderation in the use of alcohol an example for the emulation of others. Looking back to the failure of German temperance in the years before 1848, Baer concluded that the social bases of the movement had been too narrow. Especially in Prussia, it had failed to attract sufficient support from the socially and politically conscious *Bürgertum*.

Baer's book charted the course of future temperance concern in Germany. Reviewing the efforts of the past both in Germany and abroad, Baer laid out a multifaceted approach to the Drink Question with three essential components. In the first place, Baer urged temperance reformers to support responsible efforts to improve the housing and dietary conditions of the working classes. Secondly, temperance reformers had to insist that the state take up the Drink Question. They should demand not prohibition, which Baer rejected as unworkable, but intelligent, enforceable regulation of production, distribution and consumption. For the problem drinker, finally, Baer proposed not punishment but treatment. Baer took the idea of his predecessors in the *Vormärz* that alcoholism was a disease to its logical conclusion. Habitual drunkards should be treated – forcibly if necessary – in specialized asylums whose physical and moral regimen would rebuild the sagging barriers of self-control. Baer had charted the course for the future, but it would be several decades before his last proposal would have any practical impact.

### The Failure of the 'Trunksuchtgesetz' and the Origin of the German Association for the Prevention of Alcohol Abuse

Baer's work was of decisive importance in the re-emergence of an organized German temperance movement. Its most immediate effect, however, was on government policy-makers. With the socialist labor movement banned in 1878, Bismarck turned to winning the industrial labor force to the Empire. Sweeping social insurance measures, unprecedented by contemporary standards, were announced in 1881. Sickness, accident, and old age and disability insurance were approved by the *Reichstag* in 1881, 1883 and 1889 respectively. But with the inauguration of state-supported measures to ease the material plight of the working class also came measures to improve their virtue. The connection between social welfare legislation and concern with the Drink Question was to remain a close one.

In 1881 the government introduced its 'Law for the Punishment of Drunkenness' to the *Reichstag*. Its prologue, drawn extensively from Baer's work, echoed his conclusions about the seriousness of the alcohol problem and its implications. (Reichstag, 1881, Vol. 62, pp. 777–86; Vol. 64, pp. 401–27; Vol. 65, pp. 870–1) Church assemblies, prison officials and legal associations had been clamoring for such legislation for years. The government's proposal struck out in two directions. It sought, first, to make public drunkenness an offense punishable by fines and imprisonment. It included the Draconian provision that repeated offenses would be met with a diet of bread and water and, in some cases, confinement to the workhouse. Secondly, the proposal would have altered existing judicial practice which recognized intoxication as an extenuating circumstance in the judgement of criminal conduct. Under the government's proposal, the commission of a crime under the influence of alcohol would itself be an offense. The bill was opposed on its first reading only by the Left Liberals, who cast doubt on both the seriousness of the drink problem and on the government's proposed remedy. Revised only slightly in committee, the bill never faced a second reading due to the *Reichstag*'s dissolution and was not reintroduced to the new session. The split within the National Liberals and the success of the Progressive party at the polls had apparently drastically reduced the bill's chances of success.

In any case, it was the failure of temperance legislation in 1881 that prompted the measure's supporters – and even some of its opponents – to band together in a new kind of temperance organisation. The most energetic promoter of the new association was the liberal publicist August Lammers. (Emminghaus, 1908) A Hanoverian by birth, Lammers had served as National-Liberal representative for Barmen-Elberfeld in the Prussian Diet, had edited various liberal dailies and, perhaps most important, had developed wide-ranging connections in the voluntary charitable and social service organizations that proliferated in Germany during the social and economic crisis of the mid-1870s. Lammers himself was actually opposed to the government's *Trunksuchtgesetz*, but he was still deeply troubled by the problems alcohol seemed to be creating in German society. Rather than legislative intervention by the state, however, he advocated a revival of voluntary efforts to carry forth the temperance reform. Lammers hoped to unite the 'nobility of birth with the aristocracy of knowledge and ability' in launching a new temperance campaign under royal patronage. (Quoted in Bergman, 1923/5, Vol. 2, p. 418) Though he failed to attract the support of the nobility, Lammers used his connections with other voluntary organizations to bring together doctors, lawyers, clergymen and businessmen who had been disappointed by the failure of the government's legislative proposal. Preliminary meetings were conducted as early as 1881 and 1882. They included Abraham Baer and Dr Werner Nasse, a renowned professor of psychiatry at the University of Bonn, as well as representatives of the conservative Protestant *Innere Mission*. In the course of a meeting devoted to problems of poor relief in Frankfurt a/M in 1882, a public appeal was published announcing the impending formation of a national association to combat alcohol abuse that appealed to all public spirited men for support. ('Aufruf zur Gründung des Vereins,' *Mäßigkeits-Blätter*, vol. 25, no. 9, 1908, pp. 131–4) This call to action was couched in familiar terms. Alcohol was portrayed as a threat to self-control and an obstacle to order and progress in society. The appeal that was to revive the German temperance movement was thus stated in terms of the most essential values of the educated middle classes. It was signed by 143 prominent Germans, including 40 (mostly Protestant) clergymen (28 per cent), 21 university professors (14.7 per cent), 17 high-ranking state and imperial civil servants (11.9 per cent), 16 city government officials and mayors (11.2 per cent), 15 representatives of the free professions (10.5 per cent) and 11 men from commerce and industry (7.7 per cent). Also included were five members of the *Reichstag*, Georg von Bunsen, Wilhelm Loewe, Julius Möller, Karl Schrader and Adolf Stengel, all of them liberals. Only three of the signatories bore titles of nobility and none was identifiably associated with agricultural production.

On 29 March 1883 the *Deutscher Verein gegen den Mißbrauch geistiger Getränke* (DV) [German Association for the Prevention of Alcohol Abuse] was founded at Cassel. (Martius, 1886, pp. 1–16; 1891, pp. 76–93; 1901, pp. 95–112; Stubbe, 1908, pp. 11–15; DV, n.d.) Werner Nasse was elected chairman and August Lammers became the organization's director. The movement's founders saw themselves as part of a larger current of social reform whose task was to improve the condition of the working class in order to ensure the permanence of the existing social and political order. Without the temperance reform, they believed, all other efforts in this direction were bound to fail.

## Note to Chapter 3

1. Wine seldom figured prominently in working-class drinking patterns, even in areas where it was produced, and therefore will not be considered here. (DV, 1897b, p. 2; Hahn, 1967, pp. 27–50, 77–9)

## Chapter 4

# The German Association for the Prevention of Alcohol Abuse, 1883–1914

> Among our artisans, farmers, workers and laborers, family life, domestic peace, the rearing of children, prosperity, decline and progress – in short, everything – depends on the proportion of income that flows into the throat of the family father. Millions and billions vanish through this gorge. The whole way of life of our middling and lower classes, one could say almost without exaggeration, the future of our nation, depends on this question. (Schmoller, 1883, pp. 1347–8)

The second German temperance movement proved to be longer lived than the first, in large part because the movement's leaders adopted tactics much different from their predecessors' in the 1840s. The founders of the DV modeled their organization on French, Dutch and Belgian precedents and consciously broke with the heritage of the *Vormärz*. (cf. Barrows, 1979) They concluded that the broadly based popular agitation of the past had been futile and that the insistence on total abstinence, even if only from spirits, had narrowed the movement's appeal rather than broadened it. They hoped to attract men of power and influence to the new organization, whose main purpose would not be to reach the individual drinker but rather to alter his environment through legislative and administrative reforms in licensing, taxation and the legal treatment of drunkards. They had abandoned the earlier faith in moral suasion, voluntary association and the temperance pledge. Like their British and American counterparts, they looked increasingly to the state for the solution of the social ills that preoccupied them. But unlike their counterparts elsewhere, German temperance reformers after mid-century self-consciously rejected electoral politics and popular agitation. They worked instead as an elitist pressure group, aloof from the masses whose drinking behavior they hoped to reform. In contrast both to its own legacy in the *Vormärz* and the style of its British and American counterparts, the DV promised 'a refined, even-keeled, moderate and not at all agitational approach' to the Drink Question. (Martius, 1891, p. 77) The men who lent their energies to the new movement came from a segment of German society – the *Bildungsbürgertum*

– that traditionally disdained party politics and often put greater faith in Germany's bureaucracy than its national parliament. (Sheehan, 1966, *passim*) This was just as well, for the weakness of parliamentary institutions, the fragmentation of German political culture, and the level of class conflict after the *Reichsgründung* all made electoral politics an unlikely vehicle for a successful temperance reform. German temperance reformers could neither mobilize politically effective popular support nor give what support they had a political expression adequate to overcome the power of vested interests protected by the state and hostile to radical anti-alcohol reform. The entrenched position of the East Elbian *Junkers* who produced the bulk of Germany's raw spirits and the interests of highly profitable breweries now increasingly organized on a joint-stock basis (Struve, 1909; Eckerle, 1933) required that the German approach to temperance reform be moderate and gradual. In this situation, effective initiatives on the Drink Question could come only from above. The best strategy for temperance reform in Germany was thus not electoral pressure but intensive lobbying of government agencies. These exigencies were mirrored in the elitist composition and moderate goals of the German temperance movement before the First World War. Though the DV could claim no striking electoral or legislative successes, it often succeeded in shaping bureaucratic practice to its will, and this could be just as important in influencing the institutional environment in which alcohol was produced, sold and consumed.

## The DV in Wilhelmine Germany

Although the origins of the DV can be traced to the social and political crisis surrounding Bismarck's *'zweite Reichsgründung,'* most of the organization's history belongs to the Wilhelmine age. Indeed, the DV's prospects were uncertain in the first years of its existence. The organization claimed 10,000 members in 1886, but in the next several years membership actually declined. Only in the 1890s did a period of sustained growth begin which would carry the DV to a membership of 41,000 in 240 local organizations by 1913 (see Figure 4.1). These are impressive figures considering the limited constituency to which the DV sought to appeal. The DV was larger than the leading British prohibitionist organization, the United Kingdom Alliance, which never counted more than 30,000 members. (Dingle, 1980, p. 217)

The DV's takeoff coincided with the ascension of William II in 1888 and the beginning of the 'New Course' with Bismarck's dismissal and the lapse of anti-Socialist law two years later. These events raised hopes of a fundamental departure in the nation's social policy. As economic activity revived after a long period of stagnation, interest in the Social Question

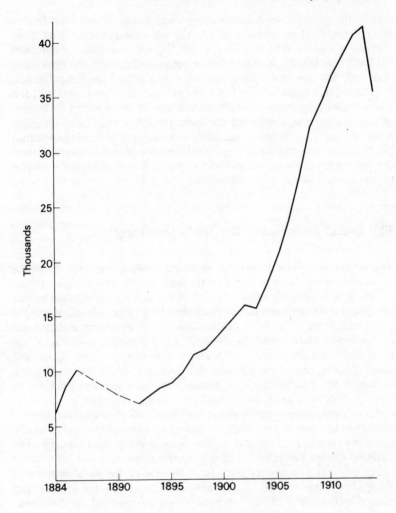

*Source:* Stubbe, 1908, p. 135; DV, *Geschäftsberichte,* 1908–14.

**Figure 4.1**  The Growth of DV Membership, 1884–1914

quickened throughout German society. The German social and economic landscape was transformed in the years after 1890. (Henning, 1973; Hohorst *et al.,* 1975) Trusts and cartels rather than private entrepreneurs and family firms came to dominate the economy. For the first time, more Germans worked in industry than in agriculture; more people lived in cities and towns than in the countryside. A massive migration was underway from East to West, from rural to urban areas. At the same time, the socialist labor movement and the affiliated Free Trade Unions grew apace. After 1890 the SPD was the single most popular party in Germany. By 1904 more than a million men and women were organized in the Free Trade Unions. Bismarck's repressive policies had failed to break the labor movement, and its continued vigor made a solution to the Social Question within the bounds of the existing social order all the more pressing. The Social Question remained the main source of instability in a nation of increasing industrial might whose rulers, generally supported by the liberal *Bürgertum*, were determined to pursue a naval and colonial policy that would give the Empire commensurate power in world politics.

## The Social Activism of the Bildungsbürgertum

The net result of these developments, as one contemporary put it, was the '*sozialisierung* of the conscience of the educated middle classes.' (Willy Hellpach, quoted in Sheehan, 1966, p. 115) The energies released by this new social conscience did not so much flow into party-political activity as into a wide array of voluntary organizations. Both Protestant and Catholic groups were formed in 1890 to advocate social reform and encourage social harmony (Sheehan, 1966, p. 115), and a wide range of more specialized associations were also established. This avenue of social activism, long a domain of the *Bildungsbürgertum*, became even more important as German party politics came to be dominated by economic power blocks and extra-parliamentary pressure groups and as the liberal parties to which university-educated Germans had traditionally adhered continued to decline, unable to tap the reservoirs of popular support open to the Social Democrats, the Catholic Centre party, and even the conservatives.

The DV was first and foremost an expression of this social activism of the *Bildungsbürgertum*. Its leadership was recruited from the academically trained civil service, the universities, the professions and the Protestant church. Business and commercial interests were also represented, but men from these walks of life played a much less prominent role. Although the DV's statutes required strict neutrality in matters of politics and religion, in fact, the new German temperance movement, even more than its predecessor in the *Vormärz*, found its greatest support in politically liberal and Protestant circles. But like many other organizations created by the *Bildungsbürgertum*, the DV considered itself above politics, as the guardians and purveyors of objective truth. They had greater faith in the German bureaucracy than in the *Reichstag* and set their course accordingly.

Table 4.1 permits a comparison of the membership of the DV's leadership

(*Vorstand* and *Verwaltungsausschuß*) in three different years: 1884, at the DV's inception; 1903, just before the period of most rapid growth; and 1913, at the peak of its strength. Civil servants made up the largest contingent of the DV's leaders in all three years, but the contribution of city officials and mayors declined after 1884, while the participation of state and imperial civil servants increased, especially between 1884 and 1903. The importance of the clergy in the DV's leadership also increased during this period and included some Catholic participation by the turn of the century. (Stubbe, 1908, p. 37; Roßnick, 1915, pp. 102–18; Liese, 1922, pp. 167–77) Medical men were also participating more actively in the affairs of the DV by the turn of the century. Men from commerce and industry never accounted for more than 11.1 per cent of the leadership group, but they sometimes played a greater role in local affairs. The most significant change after 1903 was the increased participation of university professors in the DV's leadership. Accounting for only 4.7 per cent in 1903, professors composed 16.5 per cent of the organization's leadership by 1913. The DV's leadership after 1883 was thus recruited increasingly from two sources: the imperial and state civil service, on the one hand, and the universities on the other. This was an indication of the growing prestige and influence of the DV in the decades before the First World War.

Information on the social composition of the local *Bezirksvereine*, though available for only a few cities in the period 1895–1900, sheds further light on the organization's appeal (see Table 4.2). It reveals that the composition of each local organization varied widely and conformed more or less clearly to the social structure of the community in which it operated. Thus in industrial communities like Lüdenscheid, Ruhrort, Gütersloh, Hagen and Dortmund, men from commerce and industry made up a very large proportion of the local membership. (On the social dynamics of towns such as these, cf. Crew, 1979.) On the other hand, the DV in Bonn, a quiet university town, included many professors, and the organization in Koblenz, a regional administrative center, many civil servants. Stuttgart had the most diversified social structure of all the cities for which evidence is available and also the most varied membership in its DV chapter. The local membership lists suggest that industrialists and businessmen had a greater interest in the movement than the analysis of the leadership alone would reveal. But the general social contours of the movement were not markedly different at the local level. The DV was based solidly in the urban *Bürgertum*; it included neither the landed nobility nor the urban working class. Its principal spokesmen came from Germany's university-trained cultural elite.

This information about the DV's leadership points to another important fact about the German temperance movement: in contrast to the situation in the United States, and to a lesser extent England, women played only a modest role in the German temperance movement. There were no women

Table 4.1　*Social Composition of the DV's Leadership*

|  | 1884 | | 1903 | | 1913 | |
|---|---|---|---|---|---|---|
|  | N | % | N | % | N | % |
| PUBLIC SERVICE | 20 | 37.0 | 23 | 35.9 | 40 | 36.7 |
| Imperial/State Bureaucracy | 10 | 18.5 | 19 | 29.7 | 32 | 29.4 |
| City Government | 10 | 18.5 | 4 | 6.3 | 8 | 7.3 |
| MILITARY | — | — | 1 | 1.6 | 5 | 4.6 |
| EDUCATION | 3 | 5.6 | 4 | 6.3 | 21 | 19.3 |
| Professor | 2 | 3.7 | 3 | 4.7 | 18 | 16.5 |
| Teacher | — | — | — | — | 1 | 0.9 |
| Other | 1 | 1.9 | 1 | 1.6 | 2 | 1.8 |
| PROFESSIONS | 6 | 11.1 | 11 | 17.2 | 12 | 11.0 |
| Medical | 5 | 9.3 | 5 | 7.8 | 8 | 7.3 |
| Legal | — | — | 5 | 7.8 | 3 | 2.8 |
| Other | 1 | 1.9 | 1 | 1.6 | 1 | 0.9 |
| INDUSTRY/COMMERCE | 6 | 11.1 | 4 | 6.3 | 11 | 10.1 |
| Industry | 1 | 1.9 | 2 | 3.1 | 6 | 5.5 |
| entrepreneur | 1 | 1.9 | 1 | 1.6 | 3 | 2.8 |
| artisan/overseer | — | — | 1 | 1.6 | 3 | 2.8 |
| Commerce/Banking/Transport | 5 | 9.3 | 2 | 3.2 | 5 | 4.6 |
| CLERGY | 9 | 16.7 | 17 | 26.6 | 16 | 14.7 |
| MISCELLANEOUS | — | — | 3 | 4.7 | — | — |
| INDETERMINATE | 10 | 18.5 | 1 | 1.6 | 4 | 3.7 |
|  | 54 | | 64 | | 109 | |
| NOBILITY | 5 | 9.3 | 3 | 4.7 | 2 | 1.8 |
| ALL MEDICAL MEN | 7 | 13.0 | 13 | 20.3 | 18 | 16.5 |
| ALL PROFESSORS | 6 | 11.1 | 7 | 10.9 | 23 | 21.1 |

*Source:* DV, *Geschäftsberichte*, 1884, 1903, 1913.

*Note:* Since some individuals fit into several categories, the following procedure was followed in compiling this table: public service took precedence over all other categories, and status as a professor took precedence over more specific professional designations. Thus a professor who held a post in the bureaucracy was tabulated as a civil servant; however, a separate tally of all professors was also made. Similarly, professors of medicine were tabulated as professors rather than physicians. In this case too, a separate tally was also made. Women have not been tabulated because only their husbands' social background was provided. In 1884 there were no women in the leadership group; by 1903, there was one. A decade later there were 17 women in the leadership or 13.5 per cent of the total.

in the leadership group in 1884 and only one in 1903. In subsequent years, the DV made positive efforts to enlist women in the fight against alcohol, and virtually all of the important women's groups in Wilhelmine Germany, including the *Bund deutscher Frauenvereine*, the *Allgemeiner deutscher Frauenverein*, and the *Deutsch-evangelischer Frauenbund* took up the issue in their congresses and periodicals. ('Was hat die organisierte deutsche Frauenwelt bisher im Kampfe gegen den Alkoholismus getan,' *Mäßigkeits-Blätter*, vol. 30, no. 11, November 1913, pp. 178–80) As Johanna Steinhausen put it, 'an instinctive opposition to alcohol' was 'rooted in woman's very nature.' ('Die Bekämpfung des Alkoholmißbrauchs eine Kulturaufgabe der Frau,' *Mäßigkeits-Blätter*, vol. 30, no. 11, November 1913, pp. 166–70; cf. Ottilie Hoffmann, 'Über die Mitarbeit der Frauen und des Bundes Deutscher Frauen-Vereine für die Mäßigkeitssache,' *Mäßigkeits-Blätter*, vol. 16, no. 11/12, November and December 1899, pp. 161–3, 177–9) As the educators of German youth, the guardians of family life, and the bearers of a higher morality, women were expected to take up the fight against alcohol.

By the end of 1912, the last year for which figures are available, there were some 5,400 women organized into 22 women's groups or committees within the DV. Altogether, about 80,000 women were active in anti-alcohol organizations of some kind. ('Geschichtliches Rückblick auf die Mitarbeit der Frau in der Antialkoholbewegung,' *Mäßigkeits-Blätter*, vol. 30, no. 11, November 1913, pp. 175–7) Seventeen women sat on the DV's Administrative Committee, making up 13.5 per cent of the total. Most of them were themselves women of the *Bildungsbürgertum* and wives of other prominent members of the DV. Thus, although women were taking an increasingly active role in temperance work after the turn of the century, the anti-alcohol movement never became a major vehicle for advancing feminist goals. Women were never really at the forefront of the German temperance movement, which knew no organizations comparable to Frances Willard's powerful Women's Christian Temperance Union in the United States. (Bordin, 1981; Epstein, 1981) Ottilie Hoffmann's German branch of the International Women's Temperance Union, the *Deutscher Bund Abstinenter Frauen* was but a pale imitation of its American parent. (cf. Planck, 1930, pp. 182–210) The rather limited role women played in the German temperance movement seems to reflect their traditionally subservient role in German society, the complexities of the German suffrage system, and the moderate goals and tactics adopted by the major women's organizations in Wilhelmine Germany. (von Zahn-Harnack, 1928, pp. 137–45; cf. Evans, 1976)

Not surprisingly, the DV's ideals and goals were linked closely to its social composition. However committed to the larger social and political status quo, the DV was neither reactionary nor anti-modern. Its adherents favoured industrial progress, supported Germany's pioneering social legislation and

Table 4.2  *Social Composition of Local Organizations of the DV*

| | Bonn (1897) | | Koblenz (1897) | | Ruhrort (1897) | |
|---|---|---|---|---|---|---|
| | *N* | *%* | *N* | *%* | *N* | *%* |
| PUBLIC SERVICE | 4 | 7.8 | 8 | 36.4 | 4 | 17.4 |
| Imperial/State Bureaucracy | 2 | 3.9 | 8 | 36.4 | 3 | 13.0 |
| City Government | 2 | 3.9 | — | — | 1 | 4.3 |
| MILITARY | — | — | 1 | 4.5 | — | — |
| EDUCATION | 11 | 21.6 | — | — | 3 | 13.0 |
| Professor | 9 | 17.6 | — | — | 2 | 8.7 |
| Teacher | 1 | 2.0 | — | — | — | — |
| Other | 1 | 2.0 | — | — | 1 | 4.3 |
| PROFESSIONS | 6 | 11.8 | 1 | 4.5 | 2 | 8.7 |
| Medical | 4 | 7.8 | 1 | 4.5 | 1 | 4.3 |
| Legal | 1 | 2.0 | — | — | — | — |
| Other | 1 | 2.0 | — | — | 1 | 4.3 |
| INDUSTRY/COMMERCE | 8 | 15.7 | 3 | 13.6 | 8 | 34.8 |
| Industry | 2 | 3.9 | — | — | — | — |
| entrepreneur | 1 | 2.0 | — | — | — | — |
| artisan/overseer | 1 | 2.0 | — | — | — | — |
| laborer | — | — | — | — | — | — |
| Commerce/Banking/Transport | 6 | 11.8 | 3 | 13.6 | 8 | 34.8 |
| CLERGY | 4 | 7.8 | 1 | 4.4 | — | — |
| MISCELLANEOUS | 12 | 23.5 | — | — | 1 | 4.3 |
| INDETERMINATE | 6 | 11.8 | 8 | 36.4 | 5 | 21.7 |
| | 51 | | 22 | | 23 | |

| | Gütersloh (1898) | | Dortmund (1898) | | Lüdenscheid (1898) | |
|---|---|---|---|---|---|---|
| | *N* | *%* | *N* | *%* | *N* | *%* |
| PUBLIC SERVICE | 4 | 7.3 | 13 | 29.5 | — | — |
| Imperial/State Bureaucracy | 3 | 5.5 | 6 | 13.6 | — | — |
| City Government | 1 | 1.8 | 7 | 15.9 | — | — |
| MILITARY | — | — | — | — | — | — |
| EDUCATION | 6 | 10.9 | — | — | — | — |
| Professor | 2 | 3.6 | — | — | — | — |
| Teacher | 1 | 1.8 | — | — | — | — |
| Other | 3 | 5.5 | — | — | — | — |

| | | | | | |
|---|---|---|---|---|---|
| PROFESSIONS | — | — | 12 | 27.3 | — | — |
| Medical | — | — | 8 | 18.2 | — | — |
| Legal | — | — | 4 | 9.1 | — | — |
| Other | — | — | — | — | — | — |
| INDUSTRY/COMMERCE | 32 | 58.2 | 13 | 29.5 | 34 | 82.9 |
| Industry | 20 | 36.4 | 1 | 2.3 | 32 | 78.0 |
| entrepreneur | 12 | 21.8 | 1 | 2.3 | 29 | 70.7 |
| artisan/overseer | 6 | 10.9 | — | — | 3 | 7.3 |
| laborer | 2 | 3.6 | — | — | — | — |
| Commerce/Banking/Transport | 12 | 21.8 | 12 | 27.3 | 2 | 4.9 |
| CLERGY | 8 | 14.5 | 4 | 9.1 | 3 | 7.3 |
| MISCELLANEOUS | 5 | 9.1 | 1 | 2.3 | 4 | 9.8 |
| INDETERMINATE | — | — | 1 | 2.3 | — | — |
| | 55 | | 44 | | 41 | |

| | Hagen (1898) | | Stuttgart (1898) | | All Cities (1898) | |
|---|---|---|---|---|---|---|
| | N | % | N | % | N | % |
| PUBLIC SERVICE | 12 | 12.1 | 10 | 37.0 | 55 | 15.2 |
| Imperial/State Bureaucracy | 9 | 9.1 | 9 | 33.3 | 40 | 11.0 |
| City Government | 3 | 3.0 | 1 | 3.7 | 15 | 4.1 |
| MILITARY | — | — | 1 | 3.7 | 2 | 0.6 |
| EDUCATION | 14 | 14.1 | 1 | 3.7 | 35 | 9.7 |
| Professor | 2 | 2.0 | — | — | 15 | 4.1 |
| Teacher | 9 | 9.1 | — | — | 11 | 3.0 |
| Other | 3 | 3.0 | 1 | 3.7 | 9 | 2.5 |
| PROFESSIONS | 26 | 26.3 | 4 | 14.8 | 51 | 14.1 |
| Medical | 11 | 11.1 | — | — | 25 | 6.9 |
| Legal | 10 | 10.1 | 2 | 7.4 | 17 | 4.7 |
| Other | 5 | 5.1 | 2 | 7.4 | 9 | 2.5 |
| INDUSTRY/COMMERCE | 38 | 38.4 | 7 | 25.9 | 143 | 39.5 |
| Industry | 24 | 24.2 | 3 | 11.1 | 82 | 22.7 |
| entrepreneur | 18 | 18.2 | 2 | 7.4 | 63 | 17.4 |
| artisan/overseer | 6 | 6.1 | 1 | 3.7 | 17 | 4.7 |
| laborer | — | — | — | — | 2 | 0.6 |
| Commerce/Banking/Transport | 14 | 14.1 | 4 | 14.8 | 61 | 16.9 |
| CLERGY | 7 | 7.1 | 2 | 7.4 | 29 | 8.0 |
| MISCELLANEOUS | 1 | 1.0 | — | — | 24 | 6.6 |
| INDETERMINATE | 1 | 1.0 | 2 | 7.4 | 23 | 6.4 |
| | 99 | | 27 | | 362 | |

Source: DV, *Geschäftsberichte*, 1897, 1898.
Note: For the principles of classification employed here, see the note to Table 4.1.

often found themselves at odds with the conservative and socially pre-eminent landed interest, whose domains produced the inexpensive low-grade spirits they found so debilitating (see below, pages 77–81). The men of the DV had more in common with the urban reformers discussed by Andrew Lees (1975, 1979) than with the agrarian romantics described by Klaus Bergmann (1970); more to do with the modernizers in German academic life discussed by Fritz K. Ringer than with the traditionalists (1969); greater affinity to the free traders and defenders of industrial society explored by Kenneth Barkin than to their protectionist and agrarian critics. (1970) Though certainly ambivalent about modern society, these were not the cultural pessimists described by Fritz Stern (1961) or the *völkisch* ideologues discussed by George Mosse (1964). These temperance reformers, like most temperance reformers elsewhere, belonged to the progressive side of the sociopolitical spectrum. Their fundamental purpose was to create a more harmonious and therefore more efficient industrial society, to ensure Germany's success in an increasingly competitive world economy, and to disseminate their own moral and cultural values. A group whose political authority had always been tenuous in Germany, the *Bildungsbürgertum* found itself challenged on two sides, by a growing socialist labor movement whose program and ideology promised conflict rather than cohesion and by the increasing predominance of interest group politics and political demagoguery. (Ringer, 1969, pp. 42–7) If the *Bildungsbürgertum* could not affect Germany's economic and social transformation from within, as participants in these fundamental social processes, they could still try to use their moral authority and technical expertise to shape German society from a position politically outside and morally above the daily fray. The DV's mission was thus to help provide a 'third way' in German politics between the destructive conflict of the class struggle and the stagnation and stalemate of interest group politics. (cf. Frecot, 1976; Zmarzlik, 1976; Linse, 1977) The temperance movement can thus be linked to a kind of liberal subculture – even counterculture – in imperial Germany. Like middle-class feminists, pacifists and other progressives, German temperance reformers shared the limitations as well as the strengths of this parent tradition. (Chickering, 1975; Evans, 1976)

The liberal economist Viktor Böhmert typified the social and political commitments that supported the DV. Böhmert was born in Saxony in 1829 and grew up expecting to follow his father into the Lutheran ministry. But when he left the *Gymnasium* amidst the social and political ferment of 1848, he found his resolution faltering. Filled with zeal for the national cause, he set aside his plan to study theology and instead took his degree in law. His interest in economic affairs was strong even as a student, but it was only after he had begun work as a lawyer in Meißen that his passion for economics turned into a profession. His career was launched when he won an essay contest sponsored by the *Deutsche Schneiderakademie*. Böhmert's subsequent career took him to editorial, administrative and teaching posts in Heidelberg, Bremen, Zürich, and Dresden. In 1875, he was appointed Director of the Royal Statistical Bureau of Saxony and Professor of Economics at the Dresden Polytechnic University. He held these posts for the rest of his working life. He retired from the Statistical Bureau in 1895 and from the university in 1903. Böhmert died in 1918.

Two influences seem to have set the framework of Böhmert's life. He was shaped in the first place by the *Pfarrhaus* in which he was reared. His father, a peasant's son whose hard work had taken him through the University of Leipzig, was a source of continual inspiration. His example of selfless dedication to others was taken over by the younger Böhmert to form an ethic of social service that shaped his whole adult life. The other great influence on Böhmert's life was Germany's national revival. For Böhmert, as for many others of his generation, a passionate commitment to his *Vaterland* was awakened in 1848 when he was a young student. The failure of liberal aspirations at mid-century only intensified the enthusiasm of later years when long-cherished dreams finally found fulfillment. Böhmert was dedicated to Germany's national greatness – economically, politically, culturally, and militarily. But if Böhmert was a nationalist, he remained a liberal nationalist. He continued to defend free trade even after the political tide had turned against that doctrine, and he was a vocal supporter of international law. Part of Germany's mission, he insisted, was to preserve world peace. (Böhmert, 1909, pp. 13–14) Böhmert's life combined these commitments into a seamless web that tied personal and professional aspirations together into a self-consistent whole. His dedication to the public good had both national and individual objectives. He understood – and taught – his professional field of national economy as a kind of social ethics, and he was always more interested in practice – in real social improvement – than in theoretical abstractions. (Böhmert, 1909, p. 13)

What is most remarkable about Böhmert's life is not his professional career but the associations and commitments he developed outside it. The two realms of activity always overlapped, for they derived from a common set of concerns. Böhmert was a tireless organizer and social activist in the mold of the nineteenth-century *Bildungsbürgertum*. In 1856 Böhmert founded the *Kongress deutscher Volkswirte*, an organization crucial in preparing German public opinion for national unification. Four years later in 1860, Böhmert helped organize the German *Handelstag*, a leading advocate of free trade. He also took an active part in the affairs of the *Nationalverein* established by the Hanoverians Rudolf von Bennigsen and Johannes von Miquel in 1859.

But in addition to these sociopolitical activities, Böhmert developed a wide range of other commitments that indicate the dimensions of the liberal subculture of the *Kaiserreich*. From the beginning, Böhmert believed in the necessity of private voluntary action as a means of healing the social wounds of industrial Germany. This view was widely shared by the educated middle class. Social welfare activity was part and parcel of their conception of the social order. Böhmert embodied these ideals perfectly. A list of the associations in which Böhmert played a leading part can only suggest the dimensions of these commitments. In the years after 1872, when he settled permanently in Dresden, Böhmert was the chairman of three important voluntary associations: the *Verein gegen Armennot und Bettelei*, the large and very active Dresden branch of the DV, and the *Verein 'Volkswohl,'* whose purpose was to provide wholesome popular amusements. Böhmert was also deeply involved in the Saxon *Volksbildungsverein*. But Böhmert's activities were by no means only local in scope. He edited the *Arbeiterfreund*, and other publications of the *Centralverein für das Wohl der arbeitenden Klassen* from 1872 until 1914. He was a founder and leading figure in the *Deutscher Verein für Armenpflege und Wohltätigkeit*, for whom he authored an important two-volume study of German poor relief in 1886. The *Deutsche Gesellschaft für Verbreitung von Volksbildung* and the *Verband deutscher Arbeitsnachweise* were among his other commitments. Finally, of course, he took an active interest in the Drink Question. He was present at the founding of the DV and participated in its affairs until his death in 1918.

Looking back on his career in 1899 at the age of 70, Böhmert betrayed that insecurity about the modern world typical of the German *Bildungsbürger*. Proud of Germany's accomplishments, Böhmert nonetheless warned that 'the German people will maintain [their] position of power only if [they] also move forward on the path towards a higher moral and spiritual [geistige] culture' (1900, p. 51). Having acquired economic and military might, it was now imperative, Böhmert wrote, that Germans reconcile their internal differences and chart a course towards social peace. (1900, p. 51) Böhmert put his faith – and invested years of his time and energy – into a brand of social activism which he believed would address this national imperative. Like the liberal temperance reformers of the *Vormärz*, Böhmert believed that there could be no social progress apart from individual virtue. 'Developing character, . . . promoting religious conviction, diligence and temperance appear to me to be the most important public tasks of the day,' he wrote in 1899. (1900, p. 6) Throughout his life, these were the guiding principles of his social activism. Promoting these virtues was a responsibility of men like himself, but they had to look to the state for help. Despite his liberal economic convictions, Böhmert was never a proponent of a *laissez-faire* state. Like most of his educated countrymen, Böhmert conceived the state as a moral entity with a positive historical mission. Böhmert believed this mission included the cultural and moral elevation of the lower classes to a position of social and political equality. (1909, p. 13) In the Drink Question, Böhmert found an issue as central to national as it was to individual well-being, an issue that demanded action both from the state and from private individuals associated in the DV.

## The Drink Question and the Social Question

At the root of temperance concern was thus an ambivalence about industrial society characteristic of German liberalism and a preoccupation, based on social Darwinist premises, with Germany's place in an increasingly competitive world. (Frecot, 1976; Linse, 1977; Sheehan, 1978, pp. 197, 254–6) Germany's rapid material progress seemed a mixed blessing as long as broad sectors of the population lacked the moral maturity to convert it to sensible purposes. That material progress, which in principle should broaden those segments of society with a stake in social stability, might only encourage the proletariat in its worst vices, was a common theme in temperance literature. (cf. Böhmert, 1889, p. 27) The men of the DV were similarly worried about the potential outcome of the various social reforms proposed to ease the plight of the working class and integrate it more fully into the social order. 'Is it not possible,' Wilhelm Bode, the DV's director, asked anxiously in 1898, 'that economic improvement will turn out to be a curse if the temperance reform does not accompany it?' If, for example, the work week is to be shortened, he warned, 'then hundreds of thousands of Germans will have to learn, or be coaxed through appropriate institutional arrangements, or be forced by the law, to use the free time available to them usefully and rationally' (Bode, 1898b, p. 8). The men of the DV, obviously, would have none of that doctrinaire liberalism which would leave up to the individual the choices regarding his moral conduct. The Drink Question was a matter of public concern – and therefore, in their view, a responsibility of the state. (See for example, Schmoller, 1883)

Like their predecessors in the *Vormärz* period, the temperance reformers in the German Empire were concerned above all with altering the drinking behavior of those at the bottom of the social hierarchy, now the industrial proletariat. Despite occasional admonitions to the hard-drinking German officer corps and to the infamous student fraternities, the DV concentrated its attention on the working-class drinker. Although they viewed spirits consumption as the greatest danger to the working classes, they did not demand total abstinence but genuine moderation in the use of hard liquor. But if this stance represented a retreat from the standards of the *Vormärz*, the DV had in another respect expanded the scope of the temperance movement's concerns. The consumption of beer had increased enormously since mid-century, becoming far and away the most popular alcoholic beverage in Germany. In the mid-1870s beer and spirits consumption had claimed about equal shares of the German drink bill, about 45 per cent each. By the First World War, however, that division had changed: 70 per cent of all outlays for alcoholic beverages in Germany went to beer. Only

20 per cent now went to spirits. (Computed from Hoffmann, 1965, pp. 128–9) Though beer was more readily tolerated by German temperance reformers than *Schnaps*, it too threatened working-class sobriety and personal discipline. Beer was no longer quite so unequivocably a temperance beverage.

The DV's concern with the working class was linked to a larger concern for Germany's place in an increasingly competitive world. Despite their ambivalance about industrial society, the men of the DV recognized that. Germany's international prospects depended on its economic vitality. Germany's economic vitality, in turn, depended on the quality of its labor force and the peaceful resolution of the social conflicts that prevented the full mobilization of the nation's productive resources. As we have seen, temperance was advocated as a means to insure that other measures of domestic socioeconomic reform would really succeed. At the same time, true temperance would promote greater productivity and enhance Germany's competitive position in the world. The physician Erich Flade, in a pamphlet revealingly titled *Der Kampf gegen den Alkoholismus – eine Kampf für unser deutsches Volkstum*, stated the position with perfect clarity: 'The more sober the German labor force, the more contented, the more capable they will be – and the more competitive German industry, and the productive segments of society generally, the more resilient Germany will be in the peaceful competition among nations' (1905, p. 20).

After the turn of the century, as a more aggressive nationalism began to pervade the educated middle classes in Germany, the same arguments that were applied to industrial efficiency and international economic competition were also applied to military preparedness and the potential for armed conflict. (Sheehan, 1978, pp. 275–8) The Drink Question could be tied to German nationalist concerns in a variety of ways. In a 1912 article entitled 'Der Alkohol im Wettkampf der Völker,' for example, the physician Arthur Esche raised questions of concern to nationally conscious temperance reformers: 'Will we maintain our prosperity in the economic competition among nations, with England, America and East Asia? Can we emerge victorious from an armed conflict?' (1912, p. 181) For Esche, the answers were uncertain, and he called for renewed efforts to reduce the nation's alcohol consumption and to ensure that military recruits were healthy and sober.

William II himself contributed to the growing sense of the importance of the Drink Question to the national interest. Not only did he endeavor to set a good personal example; in a 1910 speech much celebrated in temperance circles the *Kaiser* told cadets at the new naval academy at Mürick that victory in Europe's next armed conflict would belong to the most temperate people. This, he and other advocates of greater moderation believed, was an important lesson of the recent Russo-Japanese War, in which the abstemious Japanese had convincingly defeated their notoriously hard-drinking opponents. The Emperor recommended total abstinence to his troops and warmly endorsed participation in anti-alcohol organizations. ('1910/1911,' *Mäßigkeits-Blätter*, vol. 28, no. 1, 1911, pp. 1–4; 'Der Kaiser und die Alkoholfrage,' *Mäßigkeits-Blätter*, vol. 30, no. 7, 1913, pp. 101–4)

## 'Better Attitudes, Better Habits, Better Facilities, Better Laws'

The DV's motto – 'Better Attitudes, Better Habits, Better Facilities, Better Laws' – summarized its whole program. (Stubbe, 1908, pp. 27–30; cf. Bode, 1896, pp. 111–32) Unlike their early nineteenth-century predecessors, the men of the DV saw the origins of the drink problem not so much in the moral weakness of the individual drinker as in environmental factors that made drink an accessible and tempting – if not a necessary – accompaniment of working-class life. Emphasizing prevention, the movement's strategy was to alter the environment of the working-class drinker. The organization had abandoned the temperance pledge of the *Vormärz* and made no direct appeal to German workers to curtail their alcohol consumption. Though the DV did favor stringent laws against public drunkenness, it was concerned above all with reducing the temptations to drink through legislative and administrative reform. The DV advocated more stringent licensing laws, closer regulation of taverns and higher taxes that would make alcoholic beverages more costly and presumably less attractive to working-class consumers. But the DV also promoted counter-attractions to beverage alcohol and the tavern. It encouraged the development of non-alcoholic beverages and helped convince many employers to offer coffee, milk and soda water to their workers in order to wean them from beer and spirits on the job. Local associations established coffee halls at busy train depots to encourage commuting workers to abandon their early morning *Schnaps*, and they supported the widespread installation of public drinking fountains. The DV also sought to provide recreational alternatives to the tavern. Its locals supported communal sports facilities and meeting halls, favored the spread of public libraries and other cultural institutions and themselves arranged low-cost entertainment programs. By encouraging employers to provide their workers with adequate dining facilities and shelter from inclement weather, moreover, the DV helped in other ways to reduce the proletariat's dependence on the tavern. These activities were supplemented by efforts in its publications and at its yearly congresses to inform the public, and particularly those with direct influence on the working class, of the latest scientific findings on the individual and social costs of alcohol abuse. By 1907 the DV had distributed over 1.5 million publications – and this figure did not include its own periodicals. The DV, finally, supported efforts to improve working-class living conditions by promoting better housing and encouraging more rational dietary behavior. (cf. Herkner, 1906; Laquer, 1913) Temperance reformers, for example, were among the most enthusiastic early supporters of the German home economics movement. There is no indication, however, that the members of the DV believed that higher wages and shorter hours would be necessary to reduce alcohol consumption. On the contrary, they feared that gains in these areas would be reflected not in higher living standards but in even more destructive drinking practices.

The DV was less concerned with the salvation of individual drunkards than with shaping public policy, and thus a rough division of labor emerged between it and several other anti-alcohol organizations also founded in the 1880s and 1890s. The International Order of Good Templars was the largest of these organizations. The first German chapter of this quasi-masonic brotherhood founded in the United States in 1852 was established in Flensburg in 1889. By 1914 there were some 60,000 Templars in Germany organized into 1,542 lodges. (Martius, 1891, pp. 218–41; Gläß and Biel, 1979, p. 60) Denominational organizations were also established. The first Protestant *Blau-Kreuz* associations were established under Swiss influence in 1884. By 1912 the national organization in Germany claimed 38,000 members in 676 local chapters. (Martius, 1891, pp. 255–320; Krabbe, 1974, p. 41) The Catholic *Kreuz-Bündnis* was founded in 1899 and counted 20,000 members in 315 local associations in 1912. (Liese, 1922, Vol. 2, pp. 174–7; Krabbe, 1974, p. 44) All of these organizations demanded total abstinence from their members. A variety of other organizations were established along occupational lines. (Bergman, 1923/5, Vol. 2, pp. 427–43)

Despite a period of controversy about the comparative advantages of the temperance and abstinence principles which culminated in acrimonious exchanges at the Ninth International Congress against Alcohol in Bremen in 1903, the two wings of the German anti-alcohol movement generally coexisted amicably, both sides accepting the *ad hoc* division of labor. (Martius, 1902, 1903; Hähnel, 1904) Despite its early attempts to aid individual problem drinkers and later systematic support for the creation of alcoholic treatment centers [ *Trinkerheilstätten* ], the DV concerned itself primarily with preventive measures and left the care of individual problem drinkers to the abstinence associations. The DV's role was to provide a prominent public voice for the movement against alcohol and to generate broad-based support for its goals. The abstinence associations went about their work more quietly, concentrating on local organizational activity and efforts to salvage the lives of those already lost to drink.

## Administrative Controls

Concerned about popular drinking behavior and its potential consequences in a rapidly industrializing society, then, the DV's primary objective was to influence public policy on the Drink Question. Though prohibition was never a serious possibility in Germany, the regulation of drinking behavior was nonetheless a serious concern of public authorities. The DV directed its attention to the administrative agencies from which any national temperance legislation would most likely emerge and which, under prevailing German administrative traditions, already had considerable power to regulate drinking behavior locally. Because the DV's approach was moderate and pragmatic, moreover, it was supported from its inception by men influential in precisely these governmental and administrative circles. As local authorities sought to adapt their regulatory practices to the needs of an increasingly urban and industrial society, they turned to the DV for authoritative counsel. Virtually every regulatory or legislative measure produced or even considered after 1883 bore its stamp.

Immediately after its inception, the DV began to convince local administrative bodies to use their discretionary powers to control drinking behavior. (See especially 'Der Kampf der Verwaltung gegen die Trunksucht,' *Mäßigkeits-Blätter*, vol. 16, no. 7, pp. 99–104; Anschütz, 1899) This approach was eclipsed during the late 1880s and early 1890s by the campaign for comprehensive temperance legislation, but as the prospects of such legislation faded toward the end of the century, administrative remedies once again became central to the DV's strategy. Often supported by other influential religious and civic bodies, the DV asked local authorities to suppress public drunkenness, to cease licensing new outlets, to restrict the hours during which alcohol could be sold, and to prohibit sales to minors, notorious drunkards and persons already under the influence of alcohol.

The most important of these discretionary powers lay in licensing new taverns and determining their hours of operation. Under the regulations of 1879, decisions to license or not to license remained arbitrary, officials in each locality determining local needs. Licensing authorities were therefore faced with conflicting pressures as they approached each application. Restriction was favored, however, not only by temperance reformers but also by many local tavern owners, who were happy to see potential competitors kept out of the trade, and by industrialists anxious to keep alcohol away from the factory gates. By 1913 the Test of Need had been introduced almost everywhere, and the ratio of drinking places to inhabitants had decreased. Licensing was strictest in the purely industrial towns of the Rhineland, Westphalia and Upper Silesia, where the highest ratios of inhabitants per drink place were recorded. (W. Böhmert, 1913)

The hours during which alcohol could be sold were also locally controlled. The DV and its allies sought earlier evening closings, the prohibition of sales before 8 a.m. and restrictions on drinking on Sundays and holidays. All of this was clearly intended to reform the drinking behavior of industrial workers, who were to be encouraged to retire early, to abandon their customary *Schnaps* on the way to work and to use their Sundays for the physical recovery necessary to withstand another long, hard work week. Traditional holidays also came under attack, especially in the Catholic Rhineland. Autumnal church festivals, held in each town on a different day, were a frequent source of complaint. They distracted workers from their tasks for weeks on end as they made the rounds from festival to festival, often failing to report at the beginning of the new work week. ('Einschränkung der Lustbarkeiten,' *Mäßigkeits-Blätter*, vol. 15, 1898, p. 173; 'Gesuch der Mäßigkeitskommission der westfälischen Städtetags an den Oberpräsidenten der Provinz Westfalen,' *Mäßigkeits-Blätter*, vol. 19, 1902, pp. 28–9) Some of these proposals, like Sunday closing, were never put into effect, but both morning and evening *Polizeistunde* had become common practice by 1913. (Olhausen, 1905; W. Böhmert, 1913, pp. 231–4) Early morning closings were common in the industrial areas of Prussia, and evening closing times of 11 or 12 o'clock were fairly standard.

The responsiveness of government authority to the DV's efforts is illustrated by the case of Prussia. In 1901 the Free Conservative deputy Wilhelm Graf von Douglas, a member of the DV's executive council and an intimate friend of the Emperor, introduced a resolution in the Prussian Chamber of Deputies that led to extensive discussions of the Drink Question. (Haus der Abgeordneten, 1902, pp. 5068–128, 6143–75, Drucksache nos. 75, 270; cf. Stubbe, 1908, pp. 116–18; Kaiserliches Statistisches Amt, 1910, pp. 93–8) It called on the Prussian government to produce legislation that would unify the regulations controlling the sale of alcoholic beverages. The resolution also encouraged Prussian authorities to take a more active role in educating the public about the potential dangers of alcohol abuse and to provide adequate facilities for the proper care of alcoholics. The resolution was approved the next year by both houses of the Prussian *Landtag*. The resolution was widely supported; only the Left liberals refused to endorse the measure, though they expressed agreement with many of its parts. Socialists were not represented in the Prussian Diet, but *Vorwärts* found many of the proposals reasonable despite the rhetorical excesses of some of the resolution's supporters. ('Trunksuchtsbekämpfung der Schnapsbrenner,' 12 June 1902)

The Prussian government greeted the resolution sympathetically. Although no legislation followed, ministerial decrees instructed provincial authorities to support the temperance movement (and particularly the efforts of the DV), to use their police powers to regulate the retail trade in alcoholic beverages and to promote alternatives to drink and the tavern. (Geheimes

Staatsarchiv, 84A/5235, B1. 76–77a, 95–130; 84A/5236, B1. 14–31) The state railways and the army also joined the campaign to reduce alcohol consumption within their ranks, and the public schools were similarly enlisted in the effort to instruct the public in alcohol's potential dangers. The DV had thus accomplished a great deal in creating and defining a significant public issue and in influencing administrative action on the Drink Question. But the limits of the DV's accomplishments were revealed in its two greatest failures.

## The Failure of Temperance Legislation

What the DV wanted most in its early years, a comprehensive law to combat alcohol abuse, it failed to achieve. Despite the goverment's abandonment of the proposed 'Law for the Punishment of Drunkenness' in 1881, the desire for a bold legislative enactment to combat alcohol abuse and proclaim the state's moral commitment to the cause of temperance remained strong. Such concerns, indeed, had been important in the formation of the DV in 1883. Temperance legislation, as we have seen, was viewed by the DV as an indispensable companion to the social welfare legislation emerging from the German *Reichstag* under Bismarck's guidance beginning in the early 1880s. But whereas the 1881 proposal had had an exclusively punitive character, the DV's proposals after 1883 were more far-reaching. In addition to changes in the criminal code to make public drunkenness a punishable offense, the DV's comprehensive proposal demanded stricter regulation of the licensing and operation of drinksellers, and legislation that would allow civil authorities to commit problem drinkers to special asylums for treatment, entrusting their property to court-appointed guardians. ('Eingabe an Bundesrath und Reichstag des Deustchen Reiches,' *Mäßigkeits-Blätter*, vol. 1, no. 11, 1884, pp. 96–100; 'Vierte Eingabe des Vereins an den Deutschen Reichstag,' *Mäßigkeits-Blätter*, vol. 5, no. 1, 1888, pp. 1–5)

The DV petitioned the *Reichstag* and appropriate government agencies and ministries for legislation along these lines several times during the 1880s. The *Reichstag* endorsed the group's proposals in 1888, voting to send them on to the Chancellor for consideration in future legislation. (Reichstag, 1887/8, Vol. 102, pp. 1110–13) When an active member of the DV's directorate, Johannes von Miquel, the leader of the National Liberals, became Prussia's Minister of Finance in 1890, the organization's voice was carried to the very pinnacle of the Prussian-Imperial government. Von Miquel was a staunch supporter of the DV's comprehensive proposals, which he had helped formulate and publicly endorsed at its annual congress in 1887. (Stubbe, 1908, p. 109) After expressions of government interest in the subject over several years, the Vice-Chancellor, von Boettcher, told the *Reichstag* in January 1891 that the government's proposals were nearing completion and would be presented during the current session. (Reichstag, 1890/1, Vol. 115, pp. 1054–6)

Like its predecessor in 1881, the government's draft of 1891 was developed at a time when social legislation was a major issue on the domestic political scene. (Born, 1957, pp. 7–20) Despite the opposition of Bismarck, William II was determined, after the explosive Ruhr miners' strike that ushered in his reign in the spring of 1889, to broaden the scope of Germany's social legislation. Though the Emperor's proposals were intended only to ensure more favorable working conditions for women and children, his February Decrees, which instructed the Chancellor and the Minister of Commerce and Industry to prepare new legislation, were couched in terms that raised hopes of a fundamental departure from the repressive and fruitless policies of the past. Temperance reformers had high hopes for the new Emperor. 'His courageous bearing,' Wilhelm Martius wrote, 'strengthens the hope that the most difficult task a people has ever undertaken, the peaceful reform of society to prevent the bloody social revolution, really will succeed and that this reform will also include the solution to the Drink Question' (Martius, 1891, p. 391). In the DV's view, new legislation to solve the social question would have to be accompanied by provisions to constrain popular alcohol consumption. The organization's petition to the *Reichstag* in 1890 was based on this premise. Its prologue warned: 'All efforts to bring about an improvement in the conditions of the great mass of the population by means of social legislation must necessarily fail, even be counterproductive . . . unless a way is found to dam that unceasing stream of poverty that flows from the well of drunkenness' (quoted in Stubbe, 1908, p. 110).

The Emperor took a personal interest in the proposed temperance legislation, but for him, restrictions on drinking behavior were apparently to be the prelude rather than the accompaniment to social reform. (Stubbe, 1908, p. 110) Indeed, one reason the Emperor's practical proposal turned out to be so limited was that he personally believed, like many other Germans, that any concessions to the working man in the form of higher wages or shorter hours would only promote more drinking and other untoward consequences. (Born, 1957, p. 12) The sanguine expectations raised by the February Decrees were thus left disappointed. The government did not produce a comprehensive program of social reform but a set of relatively minor restrictions designed to combat the worst abuses of child and female labor. For the workingman, there was another *Trunksuchtgesetz*.

Despite the DV's efforts and government support, however, temperance legislation had little chance of passing the *Reichstag*. Socialists opposed such legislation because it would distract attention from what they believed to be the true causes of the workers' misery. Equally cool to temperance legislation was the Left liberal *Deutsche Freisinnige Partei*. Supported by lower-middle-class elements that included shopkeepers, tavern owners and restaurateurs who could be adversely affected by temperance legislation, the party was also dedicated to defending the interests of the mass of small consumers. On the conservative side, the landed interest might complain about public drunkenness, but since the production of spirits was a rural enterprise closely associated with agricultural production on the estates of East Elbia, the interest of the National-Conservatives (DKP) in energetic measures to reduce alcohol consumption was sharply circumscribed. Not surprisingly, then, the only parties to show any real interest in legislative restrictions in the *Reichstag* were the National Liberals and the Free Conservatives (e.g., Julius Schrader and Stumm-Halberg), the parties with the strongest roots among German industrialists and the nationalist, Protestant *Bildungsbürgertum*. As the fortunes of these two parties faded after 1890, so too did the possibility of comprehensive temperance legislation.

The government's proposals were published in August 1891. Judged by the standard of the most far-reaching British and American temperance legislation, the proposed 'Law to Combat Alcohol Abuse' was quite moderate. Although it did not touch the fiscal aspects of the Drink Question, the government's proposal brought together all other legislation pertinent to the Drink Question, including the licensing and operation of the retail trade, the treatment of habitual drunkards, and the regulation of public drunkenness. The law would have made the Test of Need universal, forced a complete separation of the drink trade from other kinds of retailing, obliged tavern keepers to stock non-alcoholic beverages, prevented sales on credit, provided a legal mechanism for the institutionalization of problem drinkers, prohibited the sale of alcoholic beverages to those already intoxicated, under the age of 17 or known to be habitual drunkards, and, finally, made 'offensive' [*ärgerniserregende*] public drunkenness an offense punishable by fines, imprisonment and/or confinement in an alcoholic treatment center. In addition, the law would have empowered local authorities throughout the Empire to forbid the sale of alcoholic beverages before 8 a.m. The details of the government's proposal reflected the DV's wishes almost perfectly. The only significant discrepancy lay in the government's unwillingness, in view of the great diversity of local customs and needs within Germany, to tie the Test of Need to any fixed standard. The determination of local needs was therefore to be left in the hands of local licensing bodies sometimes inclined, in the DV's view, to excessive leniency.

The proposed *Trunksuchtgesetz* provoked considerable discussion in the political press. (The following discussion is based on the collection 'Bekämpfung der Trunksucht, Äußerungen der Presse, 1881–1931,' Geheimes Staatsarchiv, 84A/5240; and 'Der Gesetzentwurf betr. die Bekämpfung des Mißbrauchs geistiger Getränke,' *Vorwärts*, 28 August 1891.) The National Liberal dailies were consistently behind the government measure, though the influential organ of Rhenish industrialists, the *Kölnische*

*Zeitung,* argued that the proposals were much too moderate. The conservative press was split. The *Kreuzzeitung,* the mouthpiece of government policy, not surprisingly favored the proposals. But the *Hamburgische Nachrichten,* the voice of the agrarian party around the recently departed Bismarck, condemned the legislation and even went so far as to defend occasional drunkenness as a patriotic virtue.

Left liberals and socialists vehemently opposed the government's plan and raised a wide range of objections. They saw in the proposal a clumsy example of class legislation that would not only inconvenience the mass of moderate, responsible consumers but also disadvantage the countless retailers of beverage alcohol. Equally alarming, the new legislation would have increased the arbitrary power of police authorities over tavern keepers whose meeting rooms were vital to opposition political organizations. Other critics questioned the right of a government that spent millions yearly to subsidize the *Schnaps*-producing *Junker* landowners to introduce such legislation and suggested that if the government's object were really to fight drunkenness and improve the condition of the working class, it should shorten the hours of labor and lower the duties on necessary foodstuffs instead of loosing the police on innocent consumers and tradesmen.

The *Berliner Zeitung* summed up the position of the liberal and socialist Left. It saw in the government's draft the 'unmitigated continuation under the 'New Course' of the reactionary police state policies of the *Vormärz.*' But at the same time, there was no real reason for alarm. Accurately, the Left liberal *Vossische Zeitung* concluded: 'No *Reichstag* will be found to introduce the absurdities of the American water apostles into the German legal system.' Without the support of the Progressive party, however, the proposal had no chance of success. The *Kartell* majority, Bismarck's coalition of National Liberals and Conservatives, had been destroyed at the polls in February 1890, and the new Chancellor, Caprivi, was forced to rely heavily on Left Liberal support in the *Reichstag.*

The government's proposals were altered slightly in the *Bundesrat* and then introduced to the *Reichstag* on 15 January 1892. ('Entwurf eines Gesetzes betreffend die Bekämpfung der Trunksucht,' Reichstag, 1890/2, Vol. 125, pp. 3545–89) There they remained untouched until the close of the session at the end of March. The government's draft was not reintroduced during the next session, but the Vice-Chancellor assured the *Reichstag* that this was only because a pressing military bill was expected to absorb the legislators' energies so completely. (Reichstag, 1892/3, Vol. 128, p. 753) Despite this and subsequent assurances that the government had not abandoned the Bill, no such comprehensive solution to the Drink Question was ever again attempted. Important segments of public opinion had opposed the measure, and the political constellation that might have supported it had vanished. The DV continued to petition the *Reichstag* on the matter, but by 1898, even it had begun to set its sights elsewhere. At its 1898 congress, the DV formally recognized that a comprehensive legislative enactment was not forthcoming and resolved to focus its energies instead on making sure that existing means of controlling drinking behavior were being used effectively. ('Der Kampf der Verwaltung gegen die Trunksucht,' *Mäßigkeits-Blätter*, vol. 16, no. 7, 1899, pp. 99–104) Because the DV saw its cause as above politics and eschewed political tactics, it had no recourse when political obstacles stood in its way. This is seen even more clearly in the failure of the DV's effort to extend state control over the spirits industry.

## The DV and the Spirits Monopoly

The comprehensive temperance legislation of 1891 had been aimed at distributors and consumers, but the DV also advocated measures that would affect producers, especially the producers of *Branntwein*. By influencing fiscal policy, they hoped to control the spirits industry. The DV believed that the level of consumption was determined by supply and price. They favored fiscal measures that would raise prices while permanently restricting supply, shutting out normal market mechanisms. But under German conditions, this tactic had to be pursued with great care. The state relied almost exclusively on indirect taxation to meet its ever-growing needs. In 1901, 160.8 million marks, or 11.5 per cent of the Reich's total income came from taxes on beer and spirits. Exclusive of tariffs, 38.5 per cent of all tax revenues derived from these alcoholic beverages. Moreover, almost two-thirds of German spirits were produced on the estates of the East Elbian *Junkers*, the social and political elite of Prussian society whose position was maintained in an increasingly industrial and democratic age by economic subventions, a three-class voting system, privileged access to careers in the army and bureaucracy, and the constitutional position assured to Prussia by Bismarck in 1871. The very complicated tax on spirits was central to the nexus of special fiscal privileges developed by Bismarck during the agricultural depression of the 1870s and 1880s to maintain the financial viability of the *Junker*'s East Elbian estates. (Witt, 1970, pp. 44–54; Wehler, 1975, pp. 142–6; Rosenberg, 1976, pp. 69–91)

Driven out of international markets by Russian and Austrian competition in the early 1880s, German distillers faced a chronic crisis of overproduction. The tax law of 1887, whose goals went beyond filling the treasury, had come to their aid. (Laves, 1887; Heckel, 1909) The law was intended to counter overproduction by discouraging the establishment of new distilleries and by providing tax incentives to limit production. At the same time, the law sought to ensure that at least for the so-called 'agricultural' distilleries, spirits production would again be a profit-making business. The law discriminated in favor of such enterprises, the most productive of which were on the *Junker* estates of East Elbia, on the spurious grounds that distillation was an essential link in the chain of agricultural production in the sandy-soiled East. (Heckel, 1909; Witt, p. 49)

The crucial element in this hybrid of fiscal and social policy was the so-called *Liebesgabe*, the bounty or 'gift of love' that filled the pockets of a relatively small number of privileged producers. Its origins lay in the peculiar system of differential taxation established in 1887. On the basis of the tax law of that year an annual production quota (*Kontigent*) had been established. It was designed to discourage prospective distillers from entering the trade and existing ones from expanding. Only by limiting production in this way could distilling be made profitable for *Junker* landowners. The total volume of production specified by the quota was shared out among the producers then in existence on the basis of their past production, but with preferential treatment for agricultural over commercial distilleries. Each producer's share of the quota was crucial to the profitability of his enterprise because spirits produced in excess of the quota were taxed with an extra 20 marks per hectoliter. The quota for the whole Empire, however, was always set below the total expected demand so that prices revolved around the higher production costs of the surtaxed spirits. As a result, spirits produced as part of each producer's quota earned an extra profit of 20 marks per hectoliter. The sums involved were considerable. In the fiscal year 1907/8 46.18 million marks flowed into the coffers of German spirits producers as a result of the *Liebesgabe*. Between 1887 and 1912, the total amounted to more than a billion marks. (Calculated from Witt, 1970, pp. 46–8) The names of those who benefited from this *Fürsorgepolitik*, as Finance Minister von Sydow openly called it in 1909, remained a closely guarded secret, but there was no doubt that the *Junkers* were its main beneficiaries. (SPD, *Handbuch*, 1911, pp. 261–2)

The men of the DV found it intolerable that the Prussian nobility was lining its pockets with profits from commerce in alcohol. They believed in the power of example, and Germany's leading class was setting a bad one.

> 'We stand before the outrageous fact,' wrote the DV's general secretary Wilhelm Bode in 1898, 'that the richest, most privileged people in Germany will not forego their profits from the *Schnaps* that poisons our people, and that . . . they have even brought matters to such a point that our ministers speak of the interests of the alcohol-producing estate owners in a tone as though the most sacred interests of the nation were at stake.' (1898a, pp. 4, 12)

But if the men of the DV were outraged, they also recognized that they could not hope to achieve their objectives by damaging the interests of the agricultural producers. 'As a neutral association, we cannot take up a principled fight against these landed estates or against agriculture generally,' wrote one DV expert on the production issue. ('Schultz-Lupitz über die

Brennerei-Frage,' *Mäßigkeits-Blätter*, vol. 16, no. 2, February 1899, p. 20.) The fiscal interests of the state were just as important, especially for men who by and large supported Germany's expensive *Weltpolitik*.

The DV's solution to this dilemma was to support a state monopoly, not of production or retail distribution, but of wholesaling and refining. The spirits monopoly established by the Swiss in 1887 was their model. The state monopoly would establish yearly production quotas, apportion them to existing producers, buy all legally produced *Branntwein*, and carry out purification or denaturalization. In contrast to the scheme proposed unsuccessfully by Bismarck in 1886, the monopoly would not itself engage in the retail trade but wholesale the half-finished product for final processing for technical purposes or alcoholic beverages. (Gerloff, 1913, pp. 193–4, 448–52) Despite their criticism of the *Liebesgabe*, the proponents of this plan were willing to see that producers were paid a price well above their costs and thus to continue the subvention of the producers in a new and less visible form. For the state, the monopoly system would ensure a steady source of revenues without the overhead of an enormously complicated system of taxation. Because the state monopoly could set its own prices, it could be expected to yield high returns.

From the point of view of the DV, this plan had several potential advantages. In the first place, the men of the DV expected a sharp rise in the retail cost of spirits and a subsequent drop in consumption. Secondly, the administrators of the monopoly would be required to control the quality of the product that reached the market. As things stood in Germany, there was no effective system of inspection. Finally, the DV hoped that a sizeable proportion of the revenues raised by the monopoly would be put towards combating alcohol abuse, caring for alcoholics, and supporting basic research on the Drink Question. (Möller, 1906; Stubbe, 1908, pp. 122–3; Kubatz, 1909)

The essentials of the DV's plan were embodied in the proposed *Reichsfinanzreform* of 1909, but not out of any suddenly heightened concern with the Drink Question. The rapidly rising costs of Germany's military expansion had plunged the nation's public finances into crisis. The fiscal reform of 1906, which had encroached on the traditional prerogatives of the federal states by introducing the *Reich*'s first direct tax, a moderate levy on some forms of inheritance, had failed to solve the government's financial problems. The naval dreadnought program approved in 1908 made a bad situation worse. Between 1906 and 1908, the national debt increased 20 per cent reaching 4.25 billion marks. (Gerloff, 1913, p. 521) Fiscal reform became the paramount issue on the domestic scene. The Imperial Chancellor Bernard von Bülow introduced a second fiscal reform package in 1908, this time to a new *Reichstag*, elected in 1907 and dominated by a Conservative-Liberal coalition.

The government sought to increase revenues by 500 million marks annually. To this end the Minister of Finance, von Sydow, introduced two Bills. The first proposed a restructuring of the inheritance tax of 1906 and was meant to make the other part of the reform package, substantial increases in indirect taxation, more palatable to the liberal wing of the Bülow block. About three-fifths of the new revenues were to come from taxes on alcohol, tobacco and other items of popular consumption.

The fiscal reform finally enacted in 1909 bore little resemblance to the government's initial proposals, which met stormy opposition in the *Reichstag* and split the ranks of the government's supporters. The major sticking point in the government's proposal was the inheritance tax, adamantly opposed by the Conservatives, who mobilized all the resources at their disposal, both inside and outside the *Reichstag*, to prevent its passage. The Bill was defeated at its second reading on the strength of 194 Conservative, Center and Polish votes. (Witt, 1970, pp. 266–9, 291–4) In its stead, a new conservative-clerical majority voted a new package of property taxes that touched primarily business and trade. (Gerloff, 1913, 461–2, 470–2; Witt, 1970, pp. 312–16) Landed property, including the estates of the East Elbian *Junkers*, thus remained immune from federal taxation.

The government's attempt to raise indirect taxation proved less controversial, but even on this part of the reform package serious disagreements arose about how the new taxes were to be structured. Most important in terms of expected revenues were the proposals regarding beer and spirits. The government's proposal with respect to beer passed with little modification, doubling the effective tax rate while legalizing smaller beer glasses to enable producers and retailers to pass the increase on to consumers. (SPD, *Handbuch*, 1911, p. 272; Wurm, 1912, p. 26; Gerloff, 1913, pp. 453, 469) The government's proposed spirits monopoly fared less well.

The government's proposal, supported by the DV, would have abolished the form of the *Liebesgabe* but not its benefits. Its most enthusiastic supporters were therefore the producers themselves, as anxious to shed the odium of begging for special favors as they were reluctant to relinquish their lucrative advantages. The *Spirituszentral*, the producer's interest organization, had been consulted every step of the way as the government's monopoly proposal was developed in the Ministry of Finance. In the *Reichstag*, however, the proposal met stiff opposition. Though the government's monopoly would have formally abolished the *Liebesgabe* and thus met a long-standing demand of liberals, socialists and deputies of the Catholic Center party, it quite transparently continued the favored treatment of producers by guaranteeing that the monopoly would buy spirits at a price well above that warranted by current market conditions.

Once the monopoly was defeated in committee by the Center, Social Democrats and Left Liberals, the government, desperate for revenues, proved flexible and co-operated with the conservative *Reichstag* delegations in drafting a new bill even more to the producers' liking. The Center party abandoned its opposition to the *Liebesgabe* in order to forge a new parliamentary majority with the conservatives, who had fallen out with the National Liberals on the question of the inheritance tax. Together, they drafted a new tax law even more favorable to *Junker* interests than the monopoly. Under the new law, the differential of 20 marks per hectoliter was retained, but the base was raised from 50 to 105 marks per hectoliter in order to increase government revenue. New technical provisions were introduced to benefit further the agricultural producers. The new law was intentionally structured to give the *Spirituszentral* a private monopoly, and this allowed producers to regulate prices in their own interests even more effectively than if the government monopoly had been created. (Wurm, 1912, p. 36; Gerloff, 1913, p. 465; Witt, 1970, p. 298)

The DV was forced to the sidelines as the proposal it had championed was abandoned and the status quo was maintained. If the men of the DV could express satisfaction that the new taxes were likely to raise prices and reduce consumption, they were nonetheless disappointed at the monopoly's failure, for it had also been expected to ensure that only high quality spirits entered the market, to divert an ever-increasing flow of spirits away from beverage consumption to technical purposes, and to provide a permanent source of public financial support for temperance activities. Once again the DV had proved impotent when confronted with the seemingly intractable political realities with which the Drink Question was ultimately so tightly knotted.

The DV's record was thus a mixed one. It had succeeded in defining a significant social issue and keeping it in the public eye for more than three decades. Its moderate approach to the Drink Question won the support and good will of influential Germans in public service, private industry and the universities. These men in turn used their power and influence to pursue the DV's temperance objectives. But while this approach worked to a point, it was also self-limiting. To the extent that the Drink Question touched the fundamental political realities of the *Kaiserreich*, that is, the privileged position of the East Elbian *Junkers* and the institutions and practices that maintained it, the DV had little room for tactical maneuver.

The men of the DV had no taste for political confrontation, no desire for a radical solution to the Drink Question. We can only speculate about the reasons for this orientation, but certainly it was consistent with the other tendencies of the German *Bildungsbürgertum* and with the wider traditions of German liberalism. Probably they sensed – correctly – that the path of confrontation would be not only incompatible with the National Liberal hats many of them wore but also extremely uncertain of success. On the one hand, given the depth of the class cleavages running through German society and the traditions of hostility that had grown up between liberalism and the labor movement, such a campaign was unlikely to win much popular support. And on the other hand, National Liberals had shown little interest since the *Reichsgründung* in altering the fundamental political realities of the Empire.

The men of the DV thus believed they had little choice but to conform to the political realities in which they operated. The organization's unwillingness to use the Drink Question as a wedge to expand German democracy was illustrated clearly in its reaction to the agitation of German feminists for the Local Option. Like their British and American counterparts, German women's groups linked the proposal for local control over the drink trade to the demand for women's suffrage. In the spring of 1912 a petition bearing 500,000 signatures was presented to the *Reichstag* in support of the Local Option. (Reichstag, 1912/13, Vol. 301, nr. 769) Neither the DV nor the Good Templars, the largest teetotal organization in Germany, would have anything to do with this agitation, both uneasy about its political implications and skeptical of its chances of success. (Gläß and Biel, 1979, pp. 50–1) Christian Stubbe, one of the most prolific writers in the DV cause, was on the mark when he told the organization's executive committee that a society that supported the *Liebesgabe* would never institute the Local Option. ('Die Jahresfeier des Deutschen Vereins g. d. M. g. G. zu Kiel,' *Mäßigkeits-Blätter*, vol. 27, no. 7/8, July/August 1910, p. 101)

*Chapter 5*

# German Social Democracy and the Drink Question

> As with any other problem of the capitalist mode of production, alcoholism can only be checked to a certain point by the class struggle. It can only vanish fully with that which creates and constantly re-creates it. (Kautsky, 1890/1a, p. 130)

The men of the DV opposed socialism, and they ridiculed the materialist argument that drinking was a consequence rather than a cause of the generally deplored conditions of working-class life. But in the 1890s, as isolated voices began to be heard within the labor movement sympathetic to the temperance reform, members of the DV began to see organized labor as a potential ally. They recognized that the SPD and the Free Trade Unions exercised an influence over the working classes far greater than any other institution of national life.

## The DV and the Socialist Labor Movement

The possibility of collaborating with the labor movement was especially attractive because the men of the DV, like the *Bildungsbürgertum* generally, abhorred the idea of class conflict. 'It is high time,' Viktor Böhmert wrote in 1884, 'to bridge the chasm that separates the various classes of the people and to prepare the way for an understanding between labor and capital' (1884, pp. 444–5; 1907). If the social classes could co-operate on 'neutral' ground like the temperance reform, the way would be opened to a more general reconciliation of the social classes. 'The wholly unpolitical concern for the health and domestic happiness of the worker,' Böhmert continued, 'is a means of reconciliation with our social democratically minded fellow citizens.' In practice, this process of social accommodation was to be something of a one way street. If the labor movement abandoned its class hatred and workers learned to appreciate 'the great intellectual, technical, and organizational achievements of our captains of industry; the value of the great landed estates and of the conservative element in the state,' then the way would be cleared for positive social reforms. the wounds in the body politic could then be healed and Germany's position in the competition among nations strengthened. (Weymann, 1915, pp. 13–14).

The men of the DV who cautiously invested their hopes in this strategy were banking on the reformist tendencies increasingly evident in the labor movement during the 1890s. The worst repression of the period of the anti-Socialist law was now a thing of the past, and Germany had entered another period of vigorous industrial expansion, making concrete material gains possible for many German workers. In this situation the labor movement began to alter its practice if not its Marxist theory. To the men of the DV, it seemed inevitable that the labor movement would now take up the Drink Question, for it could only be in its interest to do so. A party which 'no longer pursues distant plans for the future but rather aims to improve the condition of the worker within the present social order,' one DV commentator remarked, was bound to take up the Drink Question. (Möller, 1900, pp. 8–9)

But while almost all members of the DV hoped for a reconciliation with the labor movement and some saw such a rapprochement as inevitable, others remained skeptical that the SPD could really take up an energetic fight against alcohol. Two arguments were advanced by the sKeptics, both of which proved highly perceptive. In the first place, they argued, the labor movement was dependent on the tavern for its meeting places. The ideal of domestic bliss propagated by the temperance movement was thus a threat to the labor movement's foundations in the popular culture of the German workingman. (Möller, 1900, pp. 8–9; cf. Roberts, 1980b) Karl Kautsky, the leading theoretician of prewar German socialism, had admitted as much in a series of 1891 articles critical of the temperance movement. (1890/1a, p. 107) It seemed doubtful that the labor movement could easily dispense with its alliance with the tavern. Skeptics also pointed up the theoretical conundrum the Drink Question posed for the labor movement. ('Die Alkoholfrage im Lichte des Materialismus,' *Mäßigkeits-Blätter*, vol. 16, no. 1, January 1899, pp. 1–5; Möller, 1900.) The temperance movement was rooted in philosophical idealism; the labor movement in materialism. Temperance reformers believed that only self-renewal could create a better world; socialists believed that a transformation of the social world was required to liberate the potential in each individual. Temperance reformers believed the individual could control his drinking and that this was the key to social betterment. Socialists believed that heavy drinking was an inevitable response to a hostile environment and that only socialism could provide an answer to the Drink Question. An energetic temperance campaign, sceptics argued, would snap one link after another in the chain of materialist logic, for a working-class anti-alcohol campaign would have to be predicated on self-help assumptions anathema to the party's Marxist tradition. (Bode, 1898a; von Glümer, 1900).

There was yet another note sounded in the DV's discussion of the labor movement and the Drink Question. Karl Kautsky feared that the temperance movement could corrupt the class struggle (1890/1a); some men in the DV feared that the class struggle could corrupt the temperance movement, making it a matter of partisan political advantage rather than humanitarian social reform.If the labor movement took up the Drink Question not as allies of the DV but as enemies, the temperance army would not only be bitterly divided, the socialists might gain a powerful agitational weapon against the government and the middle-class parties. In a society whose most privileged citizens, the East Elbian *Junkers*, supported by the state, were also the leading producers of raw spirits, there was a radical potential in the Drink Question. The DV was too fragile an organization and its leaders and members were steeped too deeply in the traditions and habits of the *Bildungsbürgertum* to develop an anti-alcohol strategy that would confront head-on the thorny political issues the Drink Question could raise. But what if the socialists, with their organized political might, took up the Drink Question and cast it in these terms, out-trumping the DV? The fight against alcohol, if it were given a radical thrust, could thus be turned against the whole structure of the German Empire. This was a source of anxiety openly expressed in a 1904 article by the DV's chairman Dr Carl C. H. von Strauß und Torney. (1904, pp. 156–7) As we shall see, he had little to fear.

## The Socialist Debate on the Drink Question

Since the DV and its allies defined the drink problem as a problem of the working class, the socialist labor movement had little choice but to confront the Drink Question. From the labor movement's point of view, the issue had two, partially contradictory aspects: on the one hand, socialist concern with improving the conditions of proletarian existence and building effective labor organizations promoted a genuine concern for the problems alcohol could raise in working-class life, but at the same time, most socialists vehemently opposed the often moralistic analysis of the Drink Question offered by middle-class temperance reformers and their suggestion that drink caused the myriad problems of working-class life. The Drink Question therefore required a theoretical as well as a practical response, and the two were not always in harmony.

Except for one brief episode, the labor movement's public response to the Drink Question was essentially defensive. Middle-class temperance reformers and their allies had, in a sense, pre-empted the issue, and their analysis of the link between drink and poverty was a direct provocation to the labor movement. The socialists' response was twofold: to insist on the inevitability of the alcohol problem as a product of industrial capitalism, on the one hand, and to 'externalize' it on the other, to argue that the drink problem afflicted not the organized working class, the class-conscious proletariat of the socialist labor movement, but those outside it. In this way, the middle-class temperance analysis of the Drink Question and the social problem were countered, the integrity of the labor movement defended and the respectable self-image of its members preserved. In its official pronouncements, the party endorsed the temperance ideal, but it refused to make a major public issue of the Drink Question. (cf. Rühle, 1971, pp. 432–43) But while this defensive posture prevailed at the party center, at the periphery, where local party and trade union leaders interacted daily with ordinary workingmen, there was a more practical concern with the Drink Question that spawned productive local efforts to shape working-class drinking behavior.

Karl Kautsky, one of German socialism's most influential thinkers and tacticians, was the architect of the party center's response. Immediately after the expiration of the anti-Socialist law in 1890, a discussion was begun in the socialist press on the nature of the alcohol problem, its consequences for the working-class movement and the appropriate response of the party. The controversy was set in the pages of *Die Neue Zeit*, the prestigious theoretical journal Kautsky edited. Indeed, it was his lengthy response to the advocates of a proletarian anti-alcohol movement that set the tone of party policy on the Drink Question for the next two decades.

Developments within the Swiss labor movement provided Kautsky's point of departure. The physician Ferdinand Simon, August Bebel's son-in-law, argued the position of the abstinent socialists. (1890/1a) Simon argued that a successful socialist anti-alcohol agitation was both desirable and possible: desirable, because a proletariat saturated with alcohol could not prevail in the class struggle; possible, because there was no inevitable causal link between the appalling living and working conditions of German workers and their drinking behavior, as critics of the anti-alcohol movement often implied. Drinking habits could be altered in the present and the material, cultural and political situation of the working class improved. 'Statistics and experience,' Simon wrote, 'tell us nothing more than that alcoholism accompanies social misery; about the relationship between these two factors, however, they say absolutely nothing' (1890/1a, p. 487). But, Simon continued, it was alcoholism, more than any of the other evils accompanying capitalism 'which makes it difficult – and often impossible – for its victim, the proletarian, to work himself out of his misery because it makes him insensitive to his suffering and deprivation and, in advanced stages, breaks forever the will power and endurance necessary to overcome them' (1890/1a, p. 487). If the fight against alcohol was thus necessary, Simon argued that it would have to be carried out on abstinence principles. History had proved the temperance remedy inadequate, and modern scientific research demonstrated that even the smallest amounts of alcohol could be physiologically harmful.

In response to Simon, Kautsky provided a thorough tactical critique of the abstinent socialists' effort to launch a radical anti-alcohol campaign within the working class. (1890/1a; for the sequel see Simon, 1890/1b and Kautsky, 1890/1b) Kautsky admitted that it was important to discourage the abuse of alcohol in the working class, but he rejected the assertion that the consumption of alcohol inevitably bred intemperance. For centuries Germans had enjoyed the use of alcoholic beverages. Only since the beginnings of Germany's industrial transformation had the joys of drink been displaced by the curses of drunkenness and alcoholism. The alcohol problem was thus clearly a product of industrial capitalism. The misery and hopelessness of the masses and the production of cheap, powerful spirits combined to poison one of life's traditional pleasures. 'Like drink,' Kautsky argued, 'so has the drinker, so has the way to drink changed as a result of the revolution in the conditions of production' (1890/1a, p. 40). Because the alcohol problem was inseparable from the conditions of production under industrial capitalism, Kautsky concluded, there could be no meaningful solution until the material bases of the drink problem were transformed. The goal of combating working-class alcohol abuse was thus subsumed by Kautsky in the task of creating socialism. Kautsky was careful to locate the problem in those segments of the proletariat outside the influence of the labor movement, and it was their beverage, *Schnaps*, that was the enemy. Hopeless and demoralized, such men and women lived only for the present and found in spirits − and sex − their principal satisfactions. The forward-looking, class-conscious proletariat, on the other hand, devoted its time and money to nobler causes and had little of either left over to support even moderate beer drinking. (1890/1a, pp. 5, 112–13) Kautsky was delineating a pair of favorite labor movement stereotypes: the respectable, beer-drinking socialist and the demoralized *Lumpenproletariat* awash in *Schnaps*. As we have seen, the cultural evaluation of these two beverages was much the same in middle-class temperance circles. For the spokesmen of the socialist labor movement, this stereotype served to 'externalize' the drink problem and maintain their own sense of respectability in the face of the equally persistent image of the drunken socialist.

Unlike the abstinent socialists, who were also wont to 'externalize' the problem, Kautsky saw no fundamental obstacle to the labor movement in the drinking behavior of the masses of unorganized workers. The tactical implications of Kautsky's position were clear: a proletarian anti-alcohol campaign could only divert energy and attention from far more important tasks. Direct efforts to combat proletarian alcohol abuse, moreover, would play into the hands of those bourgeois social critics who found in working-class drinking a convenient explanation for every social problem. A socialist anti-alcohol campaign could thus only lend credence to the bourgeois analysis of the Social Question. (1890/1a, p. 52).

Even worse, Kautsky argued, the anti-alcohol movement would

undermine important institutions of working-class culture and erode the traditions of social intercourse upon which working-class politics depended. With the experience of party life under the anti-Socialist law still an all too vivid memory, Kautsky called the tavern 'the proletariat's only bulwark of political freedom.' 'Under current conditions in Germany,' he continued, 'the tavern is the only place in which the lower classes can meet unmolested and discuss their common affairs. Without the tavern, not only would there be no social life for the German proletariat, but also no political life' (1890/1a, p. 107). While discounting the possibility that a movement against alcohol on the scale of England's or America's could take hold in Germany, Kautsky nevertheless warned that such a movement might succeed where the anti-Socialist law had failed. If German workers abandoned the tavern for the idealized family life propagated by middle-class social reformers, he wrote, 'the cohesion of the proletariat would be destroyed; it would be reduced to a mass of disconnected and therefore defenseless atoms' (1890/1a, pp. 107–8).

Kautsky's powerful voice temporarily silenced those within the labor movement who wished to see party and trade union organizations pursue a vigorous anti-alcohol policy. His analysis of the origins of the alcohol problem, the primacy of the political struggle and the dangers of the anti-alcohol movement served the party for nearly a decade. But in the long run, his intransigent position was undermined by the increasingly reformist practice of the labor movement and by the theoretical and tactical challenge of a diverse group of younger socialists unwilling to accept Kautsky's fatalistic assessment of the Drink Question or his complacency about its implications for the labor movement.

## The German Abstinent Workers' League

In 1900, the socialist physician Dr Hermann Blocher of Basel undertook an agitational tour through Germany in which he set forth the advantages of abstinence to German workers. (Miethke, 1905) Working-class abstinence associations sprung up in his wake, the most successful, each about 40 members strong, in Berlin and Bremen. By 1902, there were twelve associations of abstinent socialists with a total membership of about 200. In conjunction with the Ninth International Congress against Alcoholism in the spring of 1903, representatives of several of these organizations met in Bremen to form the *Deutscher Arbeiter Abstinenten Bund* (DAAB) [German Abstinent Workers' League].

The DAAB was a thorn in the party's side. Unlike the other organizations of the social democratic subculture, the DAAB sought to win over the whole labor movement to a special cause. (Roth, 1963, pp. 159–63,

212–48; Ritter, 1978; Kocka, 1979) Numerically, the organization enjoyed only moderate success. There were twenty local associations at the DAAB's founding in 1903 and 109, concentrated in the industrial provinces of Rhineland and Westphalia, ten years later. The total membership grew from 196 in 1903 to about 2,600 at the end of 1911, the last year for which figures are available. (DAAB, 1912, p. 12) But despite the organization's unspectacular growth, its influence was sufficient to prod the labor movement to devote more and more attention to the Drink Question.

The DAAB united elements of the labor movement's left and right wings against the party center and brought together cultural and ethical idealists and bread-and-butter pragmatists against the fatalistic intransigence of the party's orthodox leadership. It included men associated with the party's right wing like Simon Katzenstein and Wilhelm Sollmann as well as those associated with the left like Ludwig Frank and Konrad Hänisch. Its membership was recruited from the ranks of organized labor. In 1909, 90.2 per cent of the total membership of 2,019 was affiliated with either the Free Trade Unions or a socialist political organization, and 73.8 per cent of the men belonged to both. Many of the abstinent socialists were activists in other branches of the labor movement. Of the 1,298 DAAB members polled in 1909, 39 per cent held at least one office in other working-class organizations. A total of 18.6 per cent of the membership held two or more positions and 9.7 per cent at least three. Most of the office holders had ties to the trade unions. Of 305 offices held by abstinent socialists in 1905, 47.2 per cent were in the unions, 26.9 per cent in the party, 14.1 per cent in the *Krankenkassen* and 11.8 per cent in the co-operative movement. ('Protokoll der 1. Generalversammlung des Deutschen-Arbeiter-Abstinenten-Bunds," *Der Abstinente Arbeiter*, vol. 3, no. 14, 1905, p. 79) In 1912, 76 members (3.1 per cent) held full-time paid positions in the working-class movement, including 41 trade union officials, 20 *Arbeiter-und Parteisekretäre* and 15 editors of the party and trade union press. (DAAB, 1912, pp. 77–8)

In comparison to the composition of other working-class organizations at this time, three features distinguished the DAAB: the high proportion of women in its membership (19.4 per cent in 1912), the relatively minimal participation of unskilled workers (6 per cent in 1912), and the relatively large contingent of members from non-manual occupations (13.9 per cent in 1912). (DAAB, 1912, pp. 77–8; cf. Fricke, 1976, pp. 249–73) The composition of the DAAB suggests that it was a rather special group, even further removed in its social composition from the mass of unorganized, unskilled workers than other segments of the socialist labor movement. This point should not be overemphasized, however, because the great majority of the abstinent socialists, like the members of other branches of the labor movement, were manual workers, albeit skilled and relatively well-paid ones.

Much less can be learned about the leadership of the DAAB. Though some socialists of prominence were associated with the organization, most of its actual leaders were obscure men whose notoriety rarely reached beyond the local social democratic milieu. The situation in Germany was different than in other Central European countries, where the highest levels of socialist party leadership became publicly involved in the fight against alcohol. (Gordon, 1913, pp. 157–208; Hanauer, 1910/11) Viktor Adler in Austria, Emile Vandervelde in Belgium, Otto Lang in Switzerland and Domela Nieuwenhuis in the Netherlands all lent their influence to the propagation of total abstinence among the working class. In Germany men of similar stature remained uninterested or even hostile to an energetic anti-alcohol campaign. Not a single member of the party's twelve-member executive was actively interested in the problem. The leadership of the DAAB was thus left to relative outsiders.

Of the score or so nationally prominent socialists identifiable as members of the DAAB, only three, Simon Katzenstein, Wilhelm Sollman and Georg Davidsohn, took an active part in the affairs of the national organization.[1] Katzenstein was the group's most prominent spokesman and the most influential figure in the internal affairs of the DAAB. (Osterroth, 1960, Vol. 2, p. 154) Born in Giessen in 1868 the son of a Jewish merchant and a lawyer by training, Katzenstein's socialist inclinations had early forced him to abandon the legal profession. After more than ten years as an author, editor and educator in the service of the labor movement and a stint as *Arbeitersekretär* in Mannheim, Katzenstein took up a post in 1905 at the newly founded party school in Berlin, where he lectured on trade unionism, the co-operative movement and communal politics. Katzenstein was fairly typical of the prominent party members associated with the DAAB. Aged 35 at the DAAB's founding in 1903, he belonged to that second generation of German socialists shaped less by the experience of the repressive anti-Socialist law than by the opportunities for piecemeal social reform and constructive working-class politics that opened up after its repeal. Like the other prominent abstinent socialists, moreover, Katzenstein came from a middle-class background and was exceptionally well-educated; he was committed to making the cultural advantages that derived from that background accessible to those less fortunate than himself. Like many of his abstinent comrades, finally, Katzenstein was deeply involved with the day-to-day work of the labor movement and had a particularly keen interest in working-class education and the socialist youth movement. The most prominent leaders of these two branches of the labor movement, Heinrich Schulz and Ludwig Frank, were also affiliated with the DAAB, and the socialist youth movement had itself adopted an aggressive anti-alcohol stance. (Tramsen, 1973; Phillips, 1977) Such men and women were attracted by the ethical appeal of socialism and committed to making the labor movement a cultural force in the lives of German workers.

The composition and leadership of the DAAB suggests that the organization was supported by two different, sometimes overlapping trends in the labor movement which transcended traditional distinctions between left and right. The first was intensely idealistic, committed to raising the cultural level of the working class and to the spread of knowledge of all kinds. Drink and the tavern were seen as obstacles to these pursuits. The second strain was eminently practical and was represented most clearly by the interest of trade unionists and their officials in the working-class anti-alcohol movement. These were the men who had seen first hand the ill-health, wasted resources and atrophied political faculties that alcohol could leave in its wake and sought by their participation in the DAAB to help rid the working class of these burdens. Both groups were intensely concerned about the plight of the proletariat in the present and cared little about justifying their fight against alcohol in terms of the party's orthodox Marxist theory.

The members of the DAAB were the heirs of the craftsmen who had flocked to the temperance movement in the 1840s, but their emphasis on sobriety was rooted not in the rhetoric of individual self-help but in the language of collective advance. The DAAB's *raison d'être* was to induce the SPD and the socialist Free Trade Unions to take formal and energetic action to inhibit working-class alcohol consumption. Though deeply concerned with the implications of even moderate drinking for the health of the working class, the abstinent socialists were also convinced that the fight against alcohol was indispensable to the ultimate success of the class struggle. In their view, alcohol not only exacerbated the individual and social misery rooted in industrial capitalism; it diverted time and energy from working-class organizations and, more serious still, it allowed workers to forget their troubles, thus promoting a dangerous complacency inimical to the collective struggle of the working class. (Katzenstein, 1907b, p. 765; n.d. (b), p. 5) It was this apathetic proletarian mass outside the organized working-class movement that was the main source of the abstinent socialists' concern. They hoped abstinence could help win these men and women to the labor movement and that the dignity and purpose of socialism would provide a more adequate solution to their problems than the liquor bottle.

Their concern was more than tactical however. Only if the labor movement succeeded in its cultural mission, only if mankind's cultural treasures were made accessible to all workers, they argued, could a socialism worthy of the name be created. (Katzenstein, n.d. (a), pp. 3, 11) Drink and the tavern stood in the way of this mission. The abstinent socialists denigrated the traditional popular culture of the German working class, which they believed to be dominated by drink and ignorance. Their alternative was a cultural vision that derived primarily from classical German *Kultur*. In place of drink and the tavern (and who knows what other working-class pleasures?), the abstinent socialists would have filled working-class leisure with Goethe and Schiller, with botany and astronomy and with party and trade union activities. The fight against alcohol was thus both a tactical and an ethical imperative.

Unlike Kautsky and many other social democrats, the abstinent socialists were convinced that effective action on the drink problem was possible in the immediate present. Again and again, the abstinent socialists took issue with the fatalism of the Kautskyian approach. 'The whole workers' movement,' argued Katzenstein, 'is a thousand-sided proof that we are not only creatures of our environment, but creators as well; it is a constantly renewed appeal to the power of individual revolt and redemption' (1907b, p. 766). Whereas Kautsky had argued that alcoholism, as a manifestation of industrial capitalism, could only vanish with that which created it, the abstinent socialists insisted that the enlightened worker could renounce alcohol in the present. Their own example was meant to prove it. The abstinent socialists by no means denied the close connection, emphasized by Kautsky (and Friedrich Engels before him [1962b]), between drinking behavior and the material conditions of working-class life; they argued, however, that the connection was neither necessary nor automatic. If alcoholism was a sympton of the plight of the working class, it was not *only* a symptom, for it so compounded the conditions that gave it rise that it could stand as an autonomous obstacle to any real improvement in the material and cultural conditions of working-class life and thus hinder the development of the standards and expectations essential to the further progress of the labor movement. (1907a, p. 465) The alteration of drinking behavior was therefore the reasonable starting point of efforts to break the vicious circle of material and spiritual degradation, heavy alcohol consumption and political apathy. What stood in the way was not necessity but individual habits reinforced by powerful social traditions and systematically encouraged by the capitalist drink interest.

The abstinent socialists looked to the party and the trade unions to lead the fight against alcohol. If drink limited the cultural horizons and material expectations of the working class and thus directly obstructed the development of class consciousness, effective working-class organization and a new and worthy proletarian culture, then it was the obvious duty of the labor movement to provide forceful leadership on the Drink Question. Like Emile Vandervelde, the leader of Belgian socialism who had brought an energetic anti-alcohol campaign to his party, the abstinent socialists believed that the party of the working class 'must have the courage to tell the world-conquering proletariat what it needs to be worthy to rule the world' (Vandervelde, 1901/2, p. 750; cf. Katzenstein's speech in: SPD, Protokoll, 1903, p. 191). In addition to its efforts to improve the material conditions of working-class life, the labor movement could help dispel false beliefs about alcohol's worth, foster alternative patterns of leisure and recreation and open new cultural horizons to the working class. (cf. Vandervelde, 1907)

Ultimately, the abstinent socialists hoped to see a society without alcohol and were willing to countenance local or even national prohibition if it reflected the democratic choice of an enlightened proletariat. (DAAB, 1911, p. 6; SPD, Protokoll, 1907, pp. 375–6) For the present, however, they imposed abstinence upon themselves and advocated it to others. They adopted the principle of total abstinence for two reasons: first, because they were convinced on the basis of their reading of the available scientific and medical evidence that even the smallest amounts of alcohol were both physiologically and socially harmful. And second, because they saw abstinence as a necessary tactic in a proletariat already saturated with alcohol. As Brian Harrison has suggested in his study of the temperance question in nineteenth-century England, abstinence is a means to reclaim the intemperate while temperance tends only 'to confirm the sober in their sobriety' (1971, p. 115). The flexible standard of moderation was devoid of agitational value. What was required was a radical, absolute standard to reform the working-class drinker and to prevent coming generations from succumbing to alcohol's temptations. (Katzenstein, 1907a, p. 465; n.d.(b), pp. 9–10)

Through its meetings and traveling speakers, the DAAB brought a consciousness of the Drink Question even to small town Germany. Its agitation produced an ambivalent response. Few accepted the plea for total abstinence, but appreciation of the potential dangers of alcohol for German workers and their organizations was growing. The organizations of the labor movement sponsored periodic lectures on the Drink Question, and the issue was discussed with increasing frequency in the working-class press. (Störmer, n.d.) In addition, trade unions supported and sometimes even initiated efforts to curtail alcohol consumption on the job. These gains made at the local level were reflected in increasing pressure on higher party institutions to put the Drink Question on the agenda of a socialist party congress for the kind of full-scale consideration reserved for the most pressing issues of the working-class movement.

## The Party Congress at Essen (1907)

Even before the formation of the DAAB in 1903, the Drink Question had been raised at congresses of the SPD. In 1899 August Bebel spoke against three motions urging the party to agitate more vigorously against working-class alcohol abuse. (Schröder, 1910, p. 27) Though sympathetic to the goals of the motion, Bebel insisted that such '*Kleinkram*' was not fit for a full party discussion. Despite this and similar rebuffs in the years following, pressure to have the Drink Question placed on the agenda of a party congress mounted. After 1904, members of the DAAB pushed the issue at every opportunity, and by 1906 Bebel was forced to admit that due to the intense concern of so many delegates, the problem would have to be considered in the near future. By this time, even opponents of the anti-alcohol agitation within the labor movement were willing to accede in order to settle the question once and for all. (SPD, Protokoll, 1900, pp. 181–3; 1901, pp. 306–7; 1904, pp. 190–8; 1905, pp. 359–60; 1906, pp. 223–7) At the 1907 party congress in Essen, the Drink Question was finally discussed at the most important forum of the German labor movement. The abstinent socialists had apparently convinced the party to give serious attention to the Drink Question.

Those who expected the party to inaugurate a new, more dynamic policy on the Drink Question were disappointed by the outcome of the congress at Essen. The party executive charged Emanuel Wurm, a member of the SPD's *Reichstag* delegation especially interested in factory hygiene, with preparing a lengthy report and accompanying resolution on the Drink Question. Wurm had previously demonstrated an acute awareness of the problems alcohol could raise in working-class life, but the abstinent socialists were nevertheless disgruntled by the party executive's choice since Wurm had always rejected the doctrine of total abstinence and had hitherto steadfastly resisted efforts to bring the Drink Question before a party congress.

Wurm's address was a polemic against critics of popular drinking behavior who continued to see in alcohol consumption a major source of the contemporary social problem. Wurm countered these arguments in the course of his two-and-a-half-hour address. He began from the premise that alcoholic beverages were not intrinsically harmful if consumed in moderation. But under the conditions of modern industrial capitalism, excesses were inevitable, especially among those workers most vulnerable to economic exploitation, poverty and hopelessness. Responsibility for the alcohol problem therefore lay not with its individual victims but rather with the system of industrial capitalism and the social groups which supported it. The best way to combat the alcohol problem, therefore, was to attack the social and economic conditions that underlay it. The labor movement could help workers learn about the potential ill effects of alcohol consumption, but ultimately, the decision of whether, what and how much to drink had to be left up to each individual.

The party congress at Essen unanimously adopted a resolution based on these principles and thus established a formal position on the Drink Question. (SPD, 1907, Protokoll, pp. 345–66, 375–6) Both tolerant of popular drinking behavior and fatalistic about its sometimes untoward consequences, it attacked the evils of industrial capitalism while asserting the essential respectability of the labor movement. The resolution adopted at Essen was not a call to action but rather a reaffirmation of the *de facto* position long since established. The Drink Question remained a matter of individual choice and conscience. The labor movement's task was not to reform drinking behavior but to root out the underlying social and economic causes of alcohol abuse. Its prescription for the future was to continue the practices of the past, to fight for the emancipation of the working class, and the improvement of its living and working conditions.

The abstinent socialists did not accept the either/or dichotomy presented by Wurm. Katzenstein made it clear in his brief rejoinder that the choice was not between combating long hours, abysmal housing conditions and low wages, on the one hand, and empty preaching and invidious moral condemnations on the other. (SPD, 1907, Protokoll, pp. 366–9) A vigorous propaganda campaign on the Drink Question could go hand in hand with agitation for more far-reaching social reforms, as was the case in other European countries. The abstinent socialists were more flexible in their conception of cause and effect in the Drink Question and sought to use the only realistic means at their disposal – the prestige, the agitational resources and the self-sacrificing idealism of the socialist labor movement – to cut through the nexus of causality where it seemed most vulnerable, in the beliefs and habits of individual drinkers. A worker could not by himself declare the eight-hour day, solve the housing problem or raise wage levels, but he could alter his drinking behavior and thus make his lot a little less bleak and at the same time increase his contribution to the labor movement.

If Essen brought no major innovation on the Drink Question, it nevertheless served as an important public notice of socialist concern with the problems alcohol could raise in working-class life. Socialists disagreed about how best to go about alleviating these problems, but the very fact that the Drink Question was even debated in the labor movement's most important forum must have provoked discussion in every working-class organization and at many a work-place. The resolution adopted by the congress at Essen called on the organs of the labor movement to educate the working class about the potential dangers of excessive drinking. Whether this precept was put into practice depended largely on the personalities and commitments of local leaders and editors, but it was not without effect. Though the SPD remained unwilling to launch an unequivocal anti-alcohol campaign, the reports of German factory inspectors suggest that the labor movement's local educational activities were in fact helping to reduce working-class alcohol consumption (see below, pages 110–12, 118–19).

## The Schnapsboykott of 1909

Just two years after the congress at Essen, the SPD called resoundingly on all German workers to renounce the use of *Schnaps*. The SPD thus abandoned, at least temporarily, the cautious approach to the Drink Question established in the years since Kautsky first wrote on the subject in 1891. For the first and only time, the SPD publicly seized the initiative on the Drink Question, linking it creatively to the labor movement's larger concerns and goals as political opposition movement, defender of popular living standards, and cultural vanguard of the working class. Such an approach, much feared by some middle-class temperance reformers, had always been a possibility. The new indirect taxes enacted as part of the Imperial fiscal reform were the catalysts of this sudden change of direction.

## Responses to the Imperial Fiscal Reform

The socialist *Reichstag* delegation had fought hard in 1909 to give the Imperial fiscal reform a more progressive shape. (Schorske, 1955, pp. 147–62; Witt, 1970, ch. 4) Once they were defeated, however, the socialists could only welcome and encourage the widespread popular indignation which the new taxes evoked. Having suffered a serious electoral setback in 1907, they now hoped to give political voice to the discontents of German consumers. The SPD's agitational leaflets sought to display in graphic terms what the new tax increases would mean. In one leaflet preserved in Amsterdam, working-class consumers were confronted with drawings that compared the cigars, beer mugs and *Schnaps* glasses they had enjoyed before the tax increases with the shrunken delights of the coming age. It left no doubt about who was to blame for the new taxes and to what dangerous military purposes they would be put. (International Institute for Social History, Iconographic Department, Deutscher Arbeiter Abstinenten Bund, 1909; cf. Friedrich Ebert Stiftung, Archiv der sozialen Demokratie, Flugblätter Sammlung, 1908–10)

Popular disenchantment with the fiscal reform focused first on the new tax on beer and the efforts of the brewers who actually paid the tax to introduce a general increase in prices. In many areas, tavern keepers and other retailers also announced price increases that would have more than compensated for the new taxes.

The price of beer had long been a sensitive issue in Germany. One of the bloodiest civil disturbances in the history of the Empire erupted in Frankfurt a/M in 1873 when local brewers attempted to raise their prices. (Tilly, 1975, p. 311) Fearing the political consequences of pushing up the cost of this increasingly popular beverage, successive sessions of the *Reichstag* had refused the government's not infrequent requests to increase the tax on beer. (Struve, 1909) Even in 1906, when taxes affecting beer were increased for the first time since 1871, the *Reichstag* tried to ensure that the tax increase would not be passed on to consumers in the form of higher prices. (Gerloff, 1913, pp. 431–2) But in 1909 this caution was abandoned. In fact, a contrary approach was taken. In order to win the support of the German brewing industry for this second tax hike in three years, the government's draft, which passed the *Reichstag* with only minor modifications, envisioned a tax on beer structured both to favor existing breweries against new competitors and to make it easy to pass the new tax on to consumers. To the same end, the *Reichstag* also legalized the use of smaller beer glasses in the retail trade, a strategem not likely to fool many beer-drinking workingmen. (SPD, 1911, Handbuch, pp. 270–1, 273; Gerloff, 1913, p. 469)

In the summer of 1909 workingmen throughout North Germany demonstrated vigorously against the impending increases in the cost of beer. (The progress of the *Bierkrieg* can be followed in the pages of *Der Abstinente Arbeiter* and *Vorwärts*.) Similar protests occurred in Baden and Bavaria in the following summer, when the tax increases were due to take effect there. Popular indignation often resulted in boycotts, dubbed 'beer strikes' in the working-class press, designed to prevent brewers and tavern keepers from raising their prices more than was warranted by the new tax law. In Brunswick, for example, a 'gigantic popular demonstration . . . of a kind never before seen' in the city gathered to protest the efforts of brewers and middlemen to up their prices. The crowd was estimated at 6,000 to 7,000 strong and resolved to drink no beer at increased prices. ('Vom Bierkrieg,' *Vorwärts*, 27 August 1909) Similar actions were reported in Frankfurt, Leipzig, Breslau, Essen, Dortmund and at least a score of other North German cities and towns. The boycotts were often successful, at least in the short run. Tavern keepers and their associations rolled back their prices. Brewers also felt the consequences of the 'Beer War' and were forced to come to terms with popular pressures. In some places, as in Duisburg and Gera, the local labor movement negotiated settlements with producers and distributors to hold down the price of beer. ('Vom Bierkrieg,' *Vorwärts*, 8 September 1909)

The 'Beer War' demonstrated vividly the working class's determination to defend its standard of living – including customary levels of alcohol consumption – against the new indirect taxes. The labor movement supported and sometimes guided this popular movement. Its response to the new tax on spirits, however, was markedly different. There was nothing like the 'Beer War' to protest the impending increase in the cost of spirits, partly because beer rather than *Schnaps* was by now the real staple beverage of most German workingmen, especially in urban areas. But the labor movement's response to the new tax on spirits was shaped less by consumer protests than by the political and cultural issues that surrounded the production and consumption of *Schnaps*. Its *Junker* producers, supported by the infamous *Liebesgabe*, were among the labor movement's most bitter enemies. Its consumers, at least in popular stereotypes, were the demoralized and apolitical masses traditionally beyond the labor movement's reach. (cf. Bromme, 1971, pp. 360–1)

The idea of turning popular revulsion against the new taxes into a boycott against distilled liquor was discussed first in the *Volkswacht* of Breslau, an SPD newspaper in one of the most important industrial areas of eastern Germany. (On the genesis of the *Schnapsboykott* see 'Vorpostengefechte,' *Der Abstinente Arbeiter*, vol. 7, no. 16, 1909, pp. 133–5; 'Zum Schnaps-Boykott,' *Der Abstinente Arbeiter*, vol. 7, no. 17, 1909, pp. 143–4; 'Vom Bier und Schnapskrieg,' *Der Abstinente Arbeiter*, vol. 7, no. 18, 1909, pp. 150–1) By the eve of the socialists' party congress, scheduled for Leipzig in mid-September, just before the new taxes were to take effect, the party and trade union press was full of similar sounding appeals urging workers to smash their brandy flasks and renounce the use of *Schnaps*. Boycotts had already begun on local initiative in some places, and Breslau, Bielefeld-Wiedenbruck, Hamburg and Bunzlau all addressed motions to the party congress calling on the SPD to endorse a nationwide *Schnaps* boycott.

*The Leipzig Resolution*

The party congress convened in Leipzig on 13 September. Paul Löbe of Breslau introduced the *Schnaps* boycott resolution, which won the assembly's unanimous endorsement amidst stormy applause from the rostrum, the floor and the galleries. Despite the unanimity and enthusiasm of the congress's endorsement, however, there remained an ambiguity about the boycott's real purpose that would provide the seeds of later disagreements. (SPD, 1909, Protokoll, pp. 283–6)

Löbe made clear that he was motivated by political concerns and that he intended the boycott to achieve political ends. In his view, the boycott's primary purpose would be to keep the inequity of the government's fiscal reform in the eye of a working-class public prone to forget too quickly. By actively engaging the working population in some form of continuing protest, the boycott would keep the issue alive until the next *Reichstag* election and thus help the socialists recoup their losses of 1907. But at the same time, even for Löbe, the *Schnaps* boycott was inextricably bound up with the fight against alcohol consumption per se. For Löbe, as for many others, this was no doubt a secondary motivation, but he nonetheless made clear that the 'favorable economic and hygienic by-products that a boycott of spirits would call forth are naturally very welcome' (SPD, 1909, Protokoll, p. 283).

Other voices only added to the ultimate confusion about the real purposes of the boycott. Luise Zietz spoke for the Party Executive Committee and urged that the resolution be unanimously endorsed. The party's leadership, she announced, supported the boycott not only as a tax protest but also because its members expected from it an 'extraordinary moral victory' (SPD, 1909, Protokoll, p. 286). She expressed confidence that the labor movement's adherents would make the boycott effective, and she suggested that agitation for the boycott could be used to reach the men and women not yet actively involved in the collective struggle of the working class.

The exuberance that greeted Zietz's announcement of the party executive's support for the *Schnaps* boycott was echoed in the party and trade union press. The Leipzig Resolution evoked a sense of pride, enthusiasm and confidence. The moral dimensions of the action, moreover, were as much in the foreground as were the political. 'The boycott strikes two enemies,' wrote *Vorwärts*, the party's leading daily newspaper, 'the external and the internal, the exploitation and repression of the *Junkers* and the apathy and ignorance in our own ranks.' The boycott would not only undermine the social and material foundations of *Junker* rule by striking directly at the vulnerable *Liebesgabe*, it also promised the 'proletariat's liberation from chains of its own making' ('Zwei Kulturaufgaben,' *Vorwärts*, 15 September 1909). The party's confidence that this great moral and political mission would succeed, the newspaper suggested, was founded on the close relationship between the proletariat and the labor movement established over the course of many years. As the paper's editorial put it:

> The party can count on the fact that its moral influence in the proletariat is stronger than the evil customs of the past and the tremendous force of habit. Social democracy can count on this fact because its educational work in the working class has gone on for decades and because it has succeeded in bringing the masses of its followers to the realization that the individual has to make sacrifices in the interests of the whole. This resolution is therefore a living testament to the inner strength of the party, to the fact that it is one with the forward striving proletariat' ('Die Leipziger Tagung,' *Vorwärts*, 19 September 1909).

*Vorwärts* was joined by the *Correspondenzblatt* of the General Commission of German Trade Unions and a host of lesser lights in the working-class press in calling for energetic agitation in all branches of the labor movement to insure the boycott's success.

The party, followed spontaneously by the free trade unions, had thus embarked upon a path it had long eschewed in its previous confrontations with the Drink Question. It had, in Ludwig Frank's terms, committed its moral capital with the working class in the hopes of reaping both moral and political rewards. (SPD, 1909, Protokoll, p. 285) The older view that the individual drinker was powerless in the face of overwhelming environmental pressures was decisively abandoned. An action made possible by political events and intended, to be sure, to produce political consequences was thus also conceived as an end in itself. This was true in two senses, for the boycott was meant both to reduce alcohol consumption and to broaden political education by involving workers directly in a concrete form of class struggle. The risks in this course of action were considerable. Kautsky had long before warned that the Drink Question could seriously fragment the labor movement. And, as Franz Mehring now observed, from one point of view the *Schnaps* boycott placed the party in a double bind (see below, page 101). If the boycott brought about a dramatic reduction in *Schnaps* consumption, the old caricature of the red-nosed socialist that the party had long sought to dispel would be embarrassingly confirmed. On the other hand, if the boycott failed to produce a substantial decline in consumption, the enemies of the labor movement could ridicule its tenuous hold on the masses and continue to propagate the image of the drunken and irresponsible worker.

### The Aftermath: Conflict and Retreat

Despite the enthusiasm that accompanied the adoption of the Leipzig Resolution, dissension over the interpretation and implementation of the boycott was soon rampant in the German labor movement. It is difficult to determine what went on in the local meetings at which the *Schnaps* boycott was discussed and debated, but inevitably differences of opinion arose about how it should be carried out and by what means it should be enforced. Conflicting interests within the labor movement produced local tensions. A headline appearing in *Vorwärts* in early November – 'Is Cognac Schnaps?' – was indicative of the confusion. (*Vorwärts*, 7 November 1909)

In response to this chaos, the party executive issued a clarification of the Leipzig Resolution that was published in the working-class press on 20 November. ('Der Branntweinboykott,' *Vorwärts*, 20 November 1909) Its purpose was both to quell dissent about the boycott and to provide guidelines for its further implementation. The party's leadership interpreted the *Schnaps* boycott in extremely narrow terms, focusing exclusively on its political origins and purposes. The economic and social motives behind the Leipzig Resolution were ignored, and there was no mention of the 'extraordinary moral victory' Luise Zietz, the executive's spokeswoman at Leipzig, had foreseen. The party's leaders called for the boycott's continuation, but they warned that it could be conducted only by means of 'moral influence' and that there could be no question of intra-party disciplinary measures for those who failed to comply with the Leipzig Resolution. The party executive insisted, moreover, that the *Schnaps* boycott had not altered the position on the Drink Question adopted at the 1907 Essen congress, which emphasized the socioeconomic roots of the alcohol problem and condoned the moderate use of alcohol.

If the party executive's declaration sought to recast the boycott in a narrower mold, the comments of the influential socialist publicist Franz Mehring, appearing a week later in *Die Neue Zeit*, the party's most prestigious theoretical journal, cast doubt on the wisdom of the whole enterprise. (1909/10a, pp. 289–91; cf. 1909/10b) Mehring's article was a lucid restatement of the arguments that in the past had prevented the SPD from seizing the initiative on the Drink Question. According to Mehring, the Leipzig Resolution was based on faulty assumptions and was thus unlikely to achieve its political goals; in the end, therefore, it could only embarrass the party. In the first place, Mehring argued, the resolution's appeal to organized workers seemed to suggest to the German public that the labor movement was 'more or less saturated with alcohol' (1909/10a, p. 289). Yet the assumption that party and trade union members could bring about a drastic reduction in spirits consumption, Mehring contended, was not only unflattering; it was false. It was the hopeless masses not yet touched by the working-class movement who accounted for the level of spirits consumption in Germany, and these segments of the working population were unlikely to heed the party's call. But since the resolution could have little real effect on consumption, the boycott was bound to fail in its political objective, and – what was apparently equally troubling to Mehring – the party would be open to the derision of its enemies as a result. Mehring's remarks betray a certain insecurity about whether the boycott would be supported even within the organized working class. Nevertheless he concluded with bitter irony: 'It is a tricky business to pass resolutions that can only be carried out on the condition that the party is more underdeveloped than it actually is' (1909/10a, p. 291).

Taken together, Mehring's article and the party executive's clarification raised important questions not only about the wisdom of the Leipzig Resolution and the way it was being executed but also about the cultural differences between the organized and unorganized segments of the working class, the extent of the labor movement's influence beyond – indeed, even within – its own membership, and the possibility that that influence could be extended by an action like the *Schnaps* boycott. About these issues there were now serious disagreements.

In the working-class press, there was an immediate and for the most part negative reaction to the cautionary note sounded by Mehring and the party executive. ('Der boykottierte Schnapsboykott und die Arbeiterpresse,' *Der Abstinente Arbeiter*, vol. 7, no. 24, 1909, p. 203) Resentment against the '*Flaumacherei*,' the defeatism, of both Mehring and the party leadership was the dominant theme. Editorial writers naturally agreed that there could be no question of disciplinary action against those who continued to drink *Schnaps*, but this sentiment appeared so obvious as to go without saying. To advocate caution so soon after the boycott was launched seemed to provide a ready excuse for local leaders and rank-and-file socialists to evade the demands the party had made on itself at Leipzig. Such evasions were intolerable to many socialists whose views now appeared in the party press. For the boycott's most enthusiastic supporters, the decision of the party congress, in this as in other matters, established the guidelines socialists should be expected to follow. To be sure, the deeply ingrained character of drinking habits required some flexibility, but fundamentally, the principles of the party and the discipline of its members were at stake. The socialist *Volksblatt für Anhalt*, for example, conceded that 'external measures of coercion' were out of the question but insisted that the 'full force of moral criticism' should be levelled against those who continued to drink *Schnaps.* ('Der boykottierte Schnapsboykott und die Arbeiterpresse,' *Der Abstinente Arbeiter*, vol. 7, no. 24 1909, p. 203) Attitudes such as these, however justifiable in principle, were bound to produce conflict and resentment in the labor movement's local organizations.

Mehring was taken to task for other reasons as well. Most significant was the criticism, repeatedly voiced, that Mehring simply had no conception of the realities of working-class life. 'Such naiveté and pedantry,' wrote the Breslau *Volkswacht*, 'we had not thought possible.' Mehring's ' "class conscious" worker' was 'about as far removed from the real German worker as the idealized goddess of liberty is from the real proletarian housewife' (cited in 'Zum Schnapsboykott,' *Metallarbeiter-Zeitung*, vol. 27, no. 50, 1909, pp. 399–400). Mehring had asserted that the boycott was bound to fail because organized workers did not consume *Schnaps* and because the labor movement had no influence on those who did. These propositions were roundly disputed in both theoretical and empirical terms. In the first place, it was argued, the level of *Schnaps* consumption in Germany was determined neither by the drunken *Lumpenproletariat* nor by the numerically declining agricultural labor force but by the mass of moderate drinkers, among them many socialists and trade unionists. It was a delusion, Mehring was repeatedly told, to believe that organized workers had abandoned the taste for hard liquor. 'The author can never have been even once in one of the thousands of proletarian taverns in Berlin, not to mention East Elbia, in which organized workers gather, if he does not know how it is with the *Schnaps* consumption of our workers' (cited in 'Zum Schnapsboykott,' *Metallarbeiter-Zeitung*, vol. 27, no. 50, 1909, pp. 399–400).

This line of attack was not to suggest that socialist workingmen were a lot of hopeless drunkards, but it was the linchpin of the boycott's more realistic supporters' argument that the *Schnaps* boycott, culturally necessary, could be politically effective. If, as one supporter argued, the greater part of the millions of marks expended each year on *Schnaps* 'is composed of the individual pennies, which respectable and sober working men spend one after the other,' then it would be possible to make the boycott a success. (Darf, 1909/10, pp. 380–1) It was not a question of reforming drunkards or curing alcoholics but of appealing to class-conscious workers to make a small personal sacrifice. Surely, the class-conscious proletariat would respond to an appeal endorsed by the highest party authority and designed not only to move the labor movement closer to its political goal but also to enhance the cultural and material quality of working-class life. The key was to give the boycott energetic and consistent leadership. The boycott's supporters were under no illusions that they could eliminate the use of spirits from working-class life altogether. But any decline was an improvement in cultural terms, and even a moderate reduction could affect the *Reich*'s treasury and the financial resources of the *Junkers*.

The boycott's proponents took issue just as strongly with the second part of Mehring's pessimistic argument. In those segments of the proletariat in which drinking really was excessive, Mehring had suggested, *Schnaps* consumption was an inevitable response of workers to the hopelessness of their objective situation. The boycott, as a moral appeal, could have no impact where such hopelessness and apathy were so deeply rooted in basic material conditions. Numerous editorials, particularly in the trade union press, took exception to this line of reasoning and offered an interpretation of the *Schnaps* boycott at once more optimistic and more ambitious. Mehring's premise was often accepted, but not his fatalistic conclusion. Economic exploitation, cultural degradation and the psychology of hopelessness were surely conducive to excessive alcohol consumption, but Mehring, his critics argued, left the autonomous force of the alcohol problem out of his historical equation. As one rebuttal insisted,

> the consumption of *Schnaps* is not only rooted in the hopeless condition of the modern proletariat; it also helps to prevent the worker from freeing himself from this hopelessness. For thousands of workers, a determined decision to renounce the use of *Schnaps* would make it possible for the first time to begin the fight for better conditions. (Darf, 1909/10, p. 380)

If this were so, then it was necessary to take the fight against alcohol well beyond the confines of the organized working class and to use the agitation for the *Schnaps* boycott as a way to reach and win over those workers previously outside the influence of the labor movement. Luise Zietz had made this argument at the Leipzig congress, and it was repeated now in much of the working-class press. The socialist *Volkswacht* in Bielefeld took up this line of thought:

> If there were a clear-cut boundary line between the class conscious proletariat, between the workers who have joined the modern labor movement and those under the influence of the bourgeois world-view, then the effectiveness of the *Schnapsboykott* would be very much in doubt. But such is not the case; everywhere there are points of contact, and precisely the *Schnapsboykott* offers a way to gain influence over those workers who do not yet count themselves among the members of our party and to draw them over to our side. (Cited in 'Der Passionsweg einer Resolution,' *Der Abstinente Arbeiter*, vol. 7, no. 23, 1909, p. 193)

The proponents of this broader strategy were to be disappointed.

*The DAAB to the Defense*

Thus far, the abstinent socialists have been treated only in passing. In fact, the genesis of the SPD's *Schnaps* boycott owed very little to their efforts. At Leipzig the abstinent socialists sought to make themselves inconspicuous, recognizing that the boycott would have a better chance of gaining the party's endorsement if, in Simon Katzenstein's words, it was not allowed to seem the product of the still unpopular 'water apostles' (*Wasserfanatiker*) within the party. (1909, pp. 157–9)

The adoption of the Leipzig Resolution thus presented the abstinent socialists with a new situation, but it by no means constituted a victory for their principles. Although the years of growing concern with the Drink Question, fueled by the agitation of the abstinent socialists, no doubt paved the way for the *Schnaps* boycott, its immediate source was the peculiar constellation of political and economic forces brought to public consciousness by the Imperial fiscal reform. The abstinent socialists harbored no illusions on this point, but they believed the boycott could be cast in terms that would reduce working-class alcohol consumption generally. Katzenstein announced a wait-and-see policy, hoping that the party would take its self-imposed task seriously but warning that the abstinent socialists were ready 'to defend the party energetically against its leaders' if the execution of the boycott proved unsatisfactory. (1909, p. 158) In the months following, they found much to criticize.

By the beginning of 1910, the *Schnaps* boycott had ceased to attract much attention in the party press. Interest rose only slightly with the approach of each year's party congress, where the boycott was renewed in Magdeburg (1910), Jena (1911) and Chemnitz (1912). (SPD, Protokoll, 1910, pp. 393–5, 475–6; 1911, p. 401; 1912, pp. 274–81) Otherwise, the periodic exhortations that continued to appear from time to time in random issues of the working-class press provided the only outward sign that the boycott was still in force. Despite the demand, heard fairly frequently early on, that the party *organize* and *lead* the boycott, its execution was ultimately left up to local editors and labor movement functionaries. The *Schnaps* boycott thus meant different things in different places, but it appears that nowhere was it followed – or enforced – very strictly.

Although there is no way of knowing how typical their examples were, the abstinent socialists made it their mission to point up the laxity of the boycott's execution. This not only stiffened the opposition of the action's detractors but also delighted the labor movement's critics. Opposition to the Leipzig Resolution showed itself in a number of small gestures. To order a 'Leipzig Resolution Shot' became a standard joke in the labor movement. Placards supporting the boycott were ripped from walls. The party's agitational pamphlet was left undistributed. Excuses for evasion were readily at hand. Not rum or arak, the recalcitrant told themselves, but the

*Junker*'s rotgut brandy was banned by the Leipzig Resolution. The boycott was meant not for upstanding and moderate drinkers like us, they said in Berlin or Hamburg or Munich, but for the wretches of East Elbia or the Ruhr. More serious was the fact that union halls continued to offer the boycotted *Schnaps* for sale, while the working-class press continued to advertise it.

Individual inertia, conflicts of interest and temperament, and the caution of the central institutions of the labor movement all contributed to the movement's stagnation. By the beginning of 1910, the DAAB was convinced, despite subsequent efforts to revivify it, that the *Schnaps* boycott was dead. In a lead article in its April number, the DAAB's official organ, *Der Abstinente Arbeiter*, suggested that the party had failed to provide the energetic leadership necessary to counteract the public's natural tendency to lose sight of the purposes and importance of the boycott and become absorbed in other issues. ('Die "Wirkung" des Schnapsboykottbeschlußes,' *Der Abstinente Arbeiter*, vol. 8, no. 7, 1910, p. 57) An action born of momentary discontents, the memory of which was constantly eroded by the succession of equally aggravating events, was bound to lose its impetus unless given a larger meaning and goal that would focus the public's discontents and keep the issue in the public eye. Such a strategy, explicit in Löbe's Leipzig speech, would have made the boycott a political success and provided a useful agitational vehicle in the struggle against the ruling class and the militarist state. But the early disagreements within the party, rooted, the DAAB believed, in the economic interests of influential party circles in the drink trade, had led to both active and passive resistance to the boycott. Instead of serving to expand the party's influence, the boycott threatened to undermine it; the moral conquests made by the resolution would be more than undone by the party's inability to execute it.

The denouement of the SPD's *Schnaps* boycott was played out in 1912. Agitation on behalf of the Leipzig Resolution was stepped up, at least temporarily, after the government was forced to modify the spirits tax once again. This time the bounty for privileged producers was formally abolished, but the massive subvention of the East Elbian distillers was to continue under the new law. *Junker* producers were rid of the odium but not of the benefits of the *Liebesgabe*, and the power of the *Spiritusring*, the cartel of major East Elbian producers, to limit production and control prices remained unbroken. (SPD Protokoll, 1912, pp. 120–1; Gerloff, 1913, pp. 502–3)

The abstinent socialists saw the events of 1912 as a final opportunity to win the party over to a more energetic and meaningful execution of the Leipzig Resolution. At that year's party congress at Chemnitz, Georg Davidsohn, the DAAB's spokesman, put a direct challenge to the assembled delegates: either carry out the boycott in a way befitting the reputation of German social democracy or rescind the Leipzig Resolution. (SPD, 1912,

Protokoll, pp. 274–6) Asking the party congress to support a more radical and energetic approach to the boycott, Davidsohn introduced a resolution calling for more active leadership from local party functionaries, an end to liquor advertisements in the party press, and a ban on the sale of the boycotted beverages in union halls and social democratic meeting houses.

Davidsohn's plea was rejected. He was answered, among others, by Paul Löbe, the 'father' of the Leipzig Resolution. Löbe's argument, apparently accepted by the overwhelming majority of the delegates present, showed that the party had come full circle from the position of aggressive moral and cultural leadership implicit in the Leipzig Resolution. Löbe had proposed the boycott principally as a political weapon. Now that the weapon was backfiring, Löbe's tactical sense changed accordingly. In response to Davidsohn, Löbe warned that by prohibiting the sale of *Schnaps* in the labor movement's establishments, the party would only drive away the people it most hoped to influence, not only on the question of the *Schnaps* boycott but also on the whole range of other social democratic concerns. (SPD, 1912, Protokoll, p. 280) Löbe's caution suggests that little remained at Chemnitz of that glowing faith in the proletariat's willingness for self-sacrifice that had resounded through the Leipzig meeting hall three years before.

### Success or Failure?

By now the boycott was little more than a face-saving operation. Unable to admit defeat, the party's spokesmen resorted to familiar images of proletarian virtue and heroism, insisting that the *Schnaps* boycott was a great success. Löbe, who only moments before had warned that the boycott could cut into the labor movement's support, now provided its eulogy. Löbe attributed the decline in consumption since 1909 to the efficacy of the boycott and the self-sacrificing idealism of the proletariat. Behind this reduction, Löbe suggested, were 'hundreds of thousands of our functionaries who used to drink *Schnaps* as they went off in the early morning cold to distribute leaflets [but who] now say: enough of that, my party discipline forbids it.' Thanks to the Leipzig Resolution, he went on, there were now 'hundreds of thousands of families in which the children no longer see their fathers drinking *Schnaps*, [and] in which the money that previously went to rot gut liquor is now devoted to more refined and useful amusements' (SPD, 1912, Protokoll, pp. 279–80).

Löbe had thus proclaimed a great victory where Davidsohn saw only defeat. Disagreement was built into the logic of the situation. The abstinent socialists, stressing the moral and cultural side of the boycott, undoubtedly set higher standards than most of their party comrades; no matter what was achieved, it could always be bettered. The party leadership, on the other hand, was in a position to be too complacent. Consumption was bound to decline simply because the new taxes would raise prices. The party was quick to claim this reduction as evidence for the boycott's effectiveness. The boycott undoubtedly did have some effect on consumption, but judged in relationship to the expectations raised in Leipzig and echoed in the party and trade union press, the SPD's *Schnapsboykott* must be counted a failure.

## German Social Democracy and the Drink Question

The SPD proved no more capable of exploiting the political potential of the Drink Question than the DV. This failure is attributable in part to the inability and unwillingness of the labor movement's central institutions to organize and lead the boycott. But the boycott's failure and the continuing isolation of the DAAB within the labor movement also bespeaks the breadth of consensus within the labor movement supporting moderate social drinking. For most workers, drinking was something to be defended rather than curtailed. From their point of view, the labor movement's efforts to defend the consumption of beer while condemning the use of *Schnaps* was ultimately an inconsistent policy. It was not possible to capitalize on the workers' sense of deprivation and encourage the spirit of self-sacrifice simultaneously.

Yet it would be a mistake to think that the DAAB had labored in vain. The DAAB's failure was only relative. Few workers adopted its teetotal stance, but it was largely due to the abstinent socialists' efforts that the Drink Question was so widely discussed in working-class circles. By provoking these discussions – and serving as a kind of negative reference group – the DAAB helped shape the labor movement's response to the Drink Question. In retrospect, perhaps the most striking thing about this response was the extent to which it converged with that of middle-class temperance reformers. To be sure, there were disagreements between the DV and the SPD about the causes and consequences of problem drinking and also about what should be done about it. These differences were rooted in their most fundamental assumptions about the social order. But despite these disagreements, both the SPD and the DV promoted an ideal of moderate social and mealtime drinking, and both worked actively, not only to educate the working class to this temperance ideal, but also to provide the material and cultural infrastructure that would make its attainment feasible. This positive temperance work sprang from different and often conflicting motives. For this reason it would be a mistake to interpret the labor movement's temperance work as evidence of its *Verbürgerlichung*. As Eric Hobsbawm has written, the 'line between personal and collective improvement, between imitating the middle class and, as it were, defeating it with its own weapons' was an extremely thin one in the nineteenth-century working class. (1975, pp. 226–7) In an emerging industrial society, there was nothing middle class about sobriety.

## Note to Chapter 5

1 Among the prominent members of the labor movement identified as members of the DAAB but not otherwise discussed here were Otto Braun, Oskar Cohn, August Erdmann, Alfred Grotjahn, Hildegard Wegscheider-Ziegler and Rudolf Wissel. Identification was made on the basis of participation in DAAB general assemblies, mention in DAAB publications, and statements made at the congresses of the SPD.

*Chapter 6*

# The Changing Shape of the German Drink Question

Temperance must be rooted in self-discipline, morality and good manners, in the sense of shame and in self-respect, and in those individuals in which these virtues are not fully developed, the popular conscience must make itself decisively felt as an authoritative force and establish the limits of what is proper and acceptable. (Brinkmann, n.d., p. 11)

After nearly a century of concern with the Drink Question, there were clear indications by the turn of the century that popular drinking behavior had begun to change. Few Germans abandoned drink altogether, but this had never been the objective of the German temperance movement. The beliefs and customs that had once made alcohol seem obligatory and necessary had begun to change; alternative beverages were now more widely available; and rising living standards gave consumers new choices and expectations.

The evidence of changing behavior is abundant. In the first place, there was a clear shift in the trend of per capita consumption statistics. Throughout the nineteenth century, increasing alcohol consumption had accompanied economic growth and rising real income. Now that trend was abruptly reversed. Beginning in 1899, the per capita consumption of absolute alcohol in the form of beer and spirits began a sustained decline amounting to some 25 per cent by 1913. (See Figures 3.1 and 3.2.) The consumption of both beverages was in decline. Tax increases in 1906 and 1909 reinforced but did not initiate this trend. By 1913 aggregate absolute alcohol consumption had returned to roughly its 1850 level of 6.4 liters per capita. The figure had peaked in 1873 at 10.2 liters per capita, then levelled off for most of the rest of the century as rapidly rising beer consumption offset declines in spirits. Between 1900 and 1913 aggregate consumption fell from 9.1 to 6.9 liters per capita. (Calculated from Hoffmann, 1965, pp. 172–4, 650–4) Spirits consumption had actually fallen to below its mid-century level, while beer consumption in 1913 was about 2.5 times as great as it had been in 1850. Alcohol was also claiming a shrinking share of Germany's aggregate purchasing power. According to Hoffmann's calculations, the share of private expenditure devoted to alcohol peaked in 1870/4 at 14.5 per cent. By 1895/9 the figure had reached 11.6 per cent and declined rapidly thereafter to 8.7 per cent in 1910/13. (See Figure 3.3.) The First World War and the economic dislocations of the early Weimar Republic continued this tendency. The levels of 1900 were not again reached in the Federal Republic until the 1960s. ( Feuerlein, 1975, p. 59; Vogt, 1982)

## Alcohol and the Work Place

Per capita consumption statistics are of course no guide to the behavior of the workingmen who were the main source of the temperance movement's concern. But there is other contemporary testimony which fits remarkably well with this aggregate picture, suggesting that if workers did not set the aggregate trend they at least followed it. This evidence allows us to discern changes not only in the volume of alcohol consumed but also in the way alcohol was integrated into the daily lives of German workers, for underlying per capita consumption trends were changes in how, when and where workers used alcohol. Some of the most eloquent testimony in this regard was provided by the German factory inspectorate.

The factory inspectorate was established throughout the German Empire in the 1870s. From the beginning, its officials, many of them physicians by training, had shown considerable interest in the Drink Question. The factory inspectors were not, however, mere mouthpieces for employers' complaints; they actively encouraged factory owners and managers to provide warm meals, decent dining facilities and, above all, low-cost non-alcoholic beverages in order to offer positive alternatives to drink and the tavern. After the turn of the century, factory inspectors reported substantial changes in drinking behavior at the workplace. It was not the threat of fines and firings to which many employers resorted that proved effective in bringing about this transformation but the growing availability of low-cost alternative beverages. Over and over again, the factory inspectors reported the success of measures to provide coffee, tea, milk and mineral water to German workers. Presented with a viable alternative, most workers were willing to abandon or at least curtail their alcohol consumption on the job. One railway-carriage factory in Dortmund, for example, reported in 1904 that it had begun to offer flavored and unflavored mineral water to its employees at a price per bottle of 4 Pf. and 2 Pf. respectively. During the course of the first summer the beverages were available, the plant's 800 workers consumed 80,800 bottles. In addition, 102,500 liters of coffee were sold during the course of the year for just 1 Pf. per liter. The result, according to the local factory inspector, was impressive: 'The use of *Schnaps within the plant has ceased, and drunkenness on the job, which was earlier* the source of frequent complaints, has not been observed since these beverages were introduced.' (Reichsamt des Innern, 1904, Vol. 1, pp. 373–4)

The success of these alternative beverages depended on new attitudes on the part of working-class consumers. Above all, the close connection between virility and heavy drinking that had once made alcohol consumption socially obligatory had to be broken. As late as the 1890s, one observer reported, workers who preferred non-alcoholic beverages were forced to disguise them in brandy flasks in order to avoid the derision of their fellow workers. (von Glümer, 1897, p. 3) But a decade later the factory inspector for Hildesheim could report that 'workers are no longer afraid to drink milk, coffee or tea during their breaks instead of beer or *Schnaps.*' (Reichsamt des Innern, Vol. 1, pp. 86–8). This would have been nearly unthinkable a few decades before.

A special survey conducted by the Prussian factory inspectors in 1907 revealed that with few exceptions, alcohol consumption had ceased to be a major problem for Germany industry. (Reichsamt des Innern, 1907) Only in a few of Germany's technologically most primitive industries and economically most backward areas was the heavy drinking of the past still prevalent, perhaps because living standards there were especially low, the labor movement weak, and the work-force particularly close to its largely rural and preindustrial origins. Both the survey of 1907 and a study by A. H. Stehr in 1903 revealed that it was in the East – particularly in East and West Prussia and Silesia – that workers defended traditional drinking habits most tenaciously and that employers were most cautious in attempting to alter them. (Stehr, 1903, p. 40; Reichsamt des Innern, 1907, Vol. 1, pp. 11–12, 34–5, 45–6, 126, 148–50, 201–3; cf. Levenstein, 1912, pp. 247–82) Occupations little affected by mechanization and the factory system of production also continued to be plagued by heavy alcohol consumption. From all over Germany came reports of the continued heavy drinking of stone-cutters, brick-makers, construction and cement-workers. Workers in these categories, employed out of doors and in isolated locations in the countryside, were probably the last to have access to low cost alternative beverages.

But elsewhere, alcohol's role at the work-place had changed considerably in the decades before 1914. To this day, drinking remains a part of the life of labor in Germany to an extent unimaginable in the United States, where alcohol is rarely tolerated at the work-place. In Germany workers continued to drink beer on the job, but they did so more moderately and more responsibly than in the past. The conclusion of the factory inspector in Baden, where there was a long tradition of concern with the Drink Question, was typical: 'The powerful temperance movement of the last decade,' he wrote, 'has brought such enlightenment to working class circles that it is no longer possible to speak of alcohol abuse in Baden's working class; exceptions only prove the rule' (Reichsamt des Innern, 1913, Vol. 2, pt 5, p. 52).

## Drink and the Diet

If the most striking changes in working-class drinking behavior occurred at the work-place, there were also changes in the relationship between drink and working-class dietary patterns. (cf. Dingle, 1972) Alcohol's role in meeting the energy needs of German workers receded in importance as other aspects of their diets improved. (The contours of this process of dietary improvement – and the persisting inadequacies in many workers' diets – are outlined in Teuteberg and Wiegelmann, 1972; Teuteberg, 1976.) Alcohol gradually became less a nutritional 'necessity' in the lives of German workers than a dietary supplement or refinement, much as it was for other Germans. What was perhaps the nub of the nineteenth-century alcohol problem – that workers were forced to resort to alcohol to meet their basic physiological needs – was thus for the most part overcome, albeit gradually and unevenly, in the decades before the First World War.

One way to make clear this line of development is to examine Friedrich Wörishoffer's pioneering study of the dietary standards of factory workers in the Mannheim area in 1890. (Wörishoffer, 1891) Wörishoffer, a physician by training, was the widely respected chief of the factory inspectorate in Baden. His was the first detailed investigation of working-class living standards that recorded not only expenditures but also the actual quantities of foodstuffs consumed. On the basis of this information he was able to estimate fairly precisely the protein, fat and carbohydrate content of the diets of the workers he studied.

By modern standards, none of the workers in Wörishoffer's study was adequately nourished. The average intake of calories (2,490) was only 59 per cent of the modern norm of 4,200 for males engaged in heavy physical labor and even fell short of the norm of 2,740 calories necessary to perform light to moderate industrial work. (Teuteberg and Wiegelmann, 1972, p. 142; National Academy of Sciences, 1974, p. 27) Their diets were especially deficient in fats and carbohydrates. In order to meet modern standards for heavy labor, the average worker would have required an additional 21 grams of protein, 64 grams of fat and 242 grams of carbohydrate per day.

Wörishoffer himself considered most of these men to be undernourished, and he held their drinking behavior partly responsible. About 10 per cent of the family budget went to alcohol in these men's households, mostly to support the male's beer drinking during the so-called 'Zwischenmahlzeiten' on the job. Wörishoffer saw these short repasts, and the beer drinking that went with them, as extremely inefficient from a nutritional point of view, and he urged that the working day be shortened and the pauses curtailed in order to eliminate them. (Wörishoffer, 1891, p. 287) Certainly some of the money devoted to drink in these pauses could have been better spent, but only if the amount allocated to beer each day had been devoted to other foodstuffs like bread and potatoes could a substantial gain in calories have been made without increasing total expenditure. But these Mannheim workers, like workers generally, *already* ate large quantities of these bland, bulky foods – an average of 1.5 pounds of bread and 1.2 pounds of potatoes per day. Under these circumstances, and in the absence of widely available alternative beverages, it is understandable that drink constituted an integral part of these men's diets. Despite the overall improvement in dietary standards over the previous two or three decades, the situation of these Mannheim workers suggests that alcohol remained an essential part of the working-class diet. It provided necessary calories in palatable form. The sharp flavor of alcoholic beverages could add spice to otherwise monotonous fare, providing a sense of warmth and fullness even when meals were cold and unsatisfying. Perhaps most important, alcohol provided energy in concentrated form. Alcohol, whether in the form of beer or spirits, enabled workers to reduce the sheer quantity of food that had to be gotten down each day. The distinguished physiologist Max Gruber calculated that a worker who consumed even a tenth of a liter of *Schnaps* with a meal could, with no energy loss, reduce his potato and rye bread consumption by some 288 and 122 grams respectively. 'Try eating . . . a kilo of black bread or two or more kilos of potatoes day after day,' Gruber told his well-fed middle-class readers in 1888, 'and you will discover what a relief it can be to substitute a pungent and stimulating beverage for more than a tenth of this mass' (1888, p. 305).

After the turn of the century, as we have seen, the per capita consumption of both beer and spirits declined, and the percentage of private expenditure devoted to alcohol fell to its lowest point since the middle of the nineteenth century. (Hoffmann, 1965, pp. 116–17, 128) The per capita consumption of traditional working-class staples like bread and potatoes also declined, while the consumption of fish, meats, eggs and dairy products all increased (see Table 6.1). In addition, Germans were consuming more vegetables and legumes and substantially more sugar, fruits, fats and oils. Hoffmann has calculated that Germans enjoyed an average calorie surplus of between 18 and 24 per cent in this period, up from the 8 per cent aggregate surplus in 1890–4. (1965, p. 659) These aggregate figures suggest an important change in the dietary context of drinking. As the working class's nutritional status improved, its energy needs could more readily be met without alcohol.

Many workers, it appears, partook of the dietary improvement suggested by these trends. The 1908 survey of 320 households of German metal workers, can be usefully compared to Wörishoffer's 1890 findings. (For another indication of substantial dietary improvement, see

Table 6.1   *Changes in the Per Capita Consumption of Selected Food Items, 1896–1910 (Five Year Averages)*

|  | Percentage Change |
|---|---|
| GAINERS | |
| Tropical Fruits | 91.7 |
| Fruit | 67.3 |
| Sugar | 52.3 |
| Rice | 29.2 |
| Fish | 28.1 |
| Eggs | 23.5 |
| Dairy Products | 12.6 |
| Pork | 14.3 |
| Poultry | 12.2 |
| Beef | 8.0 |
| Legumes | 5.1 |
| Vegetables | 4.6 |
| Wheat Bread & Flour | 0.8 |
| LOSERS | |
| Potatoes | −25.2 |
| Spirits | −24.0 |
| Rye Bread & Flour | −13.1 |
| Beer | −7.6 |

*Source:* Calculated from Hoffmann, 1965, pp. 172–4, 622–5, 630–3.

the follow-up study of workers in the Mannheim area by the factory inspector Eduard Föhlisch (1910); cf. Bocks, 1978, pp. 458–79.) The 1908 survey did not include precise information on the quantities of foodstuffs consumed by individual households, but its compilers did provide estimates of the per capita consumption of basic food items based on information about local retail prices and per capita expenditure. (Deutscher Metallarbeiter Verband, 1909, pp. 75–82) For present purposes, these estimates have been weighted to give a more reliable indication of the nutritional status of the male head of household. The values thus obtained have been converted to calories. On the basis of these calculations, the daily caloric intake of adult males has been estimated and compared to the figures obtained by Wörishoffer in 1890. The results are reported in Table 6.2.

Even taking into consideration the inevitable imprecision of these estimates, the net gain in calories consumed between 1890 and 1908 appears to have been substantial. The figures suggest that metal-workers in 1908

Table 6.2  *Estimated Daily Caloric Intake of 299 Metal-Workers*

| FOOD SOURCE | Average Annual Household Expenditure (in marks) | | |
| --- | --- | --- | --- |
| | Under 1600 N=92 | 1600–2000 N=116 | 2000–2500 N=91 |
| | CALORIES | | |
| Meat | 270.4 | 318.7 | 386.2 |
| Butter | 154.1 | 173.5 | 169.1 |
| Flour | 153.0 | 166.0 | 165.3 |
| Bread | 1317.7 | 1416.1 | 1492.5 |
| Sugar | 148.8 | 176.1 | 185.3 |
| Potatoes | 518.3 | 513.4 | 525.4 |
| Milk | 234.8 | 284.1 | 340.7 |
| Eggs | 22.8 | 28.1 | 37.6 |
| Subtotal | 2819.9 | 3076.0 Mean=3066.0 | 3302.1 |
| Beer | 263.9 | 332.2 | 441.6 |
| Total | 3083.8 | 3408.2 Mean=3410.5 | 3743.7 |

*Source:* Calculated from Deutscher Metallarbeiter Verband, 1909, p. 79; Arlin, 1977, pp. 405–37.

*Note:* To further comparability, the weighting scheme employed here is identical to that adopted by Wörishoffer. Adult men and women are each weighted 1.0, while children are assigned a value of 0.5. The 21 families in the uppermost bracket of total expenditure (over 2,500 marks annually) have been eliminated from consideration here because inspection of the data revealed that their greater spending power frequently resulted from the presence of extra adult wage-earners in the household.

had a caloric intake roughly 25 per cent greater than that of the Mannheim workers studied by Wörishoffer in 1890. Though the average worker still fell short of the caloric norm of 4,200 required for heavy physical labor, the norm for light to moderate work (2,740) had been surpassed in all income categories. In this new nutritional context, alcohol's place in working-class diet was beginning to change. Alcohol served less as a substitute for foodstuffs beyond the financial reach of many workingmen than as a dietary supplement, a 'Genußmittel' rather than a 'Nahrungsmittel.' As alcohol began to play a less essential role in working-class diets, popular drinking patterns became more and more like those of better-placed social groups who enjoyed alcoholic beverages – especially beer – as a social amenity and a welcome mealtime refreshment.

## Social Drinking

As alcohol's importance on the job and in the diet declined, it lost none of its importance in working-class social life. But the social uses of alcohol were also changing. Social drinking continued to be an important part of working-class life, and in contrast to the situation in England and the United States, such drinking was almost universally approved by the larger culture. Yet there is evidence to suggest that social drinking itself was undergoing a disciplining process that was a result partly of changing attitudes towards drunkenness and partly of larger changes in the use of leisure. Drunkenness, especially on paydays and weekends, had been a fairly typical feature of early industrial life. This was not so much the drunkenness of individual despair and psychological escape as of socially shared good times, a 'time out' from everyday cares in an environment starved of recreational and cultural alternatives. (Roberts, 1980a; MacAndrew and Edgerton, 1969; for an interpretation that stresses escape and despair, see Schivelbusch, 1980, pp. 159–78) Though middle-class moral reformers condemned them, workers, even respectable workers, saw nothing wrong with occasional drunkenness.

We see this clash of values, for example, in Paul Göhre's account of his experience with Chemnitz factory workers in 1891. A young theologian passionately interested in the Social Question, Göhre disguised himself as an ordinary factory hand and went to work as an unskilled laborer. Göhre noted approvingly that habitual drunkards were shunned by their workmates, but he was dismayed that even solid and respectable workers defended periodic drunkenness. (1891, p. 201) During the next two decades, the climate of opinion within the respectable working class seems to have changed. As one trade union official reported in 1907, the antics of drunken workers were no longer amusing to their peers but sharply condemned. As a result, he reported, 'even those who are inclined to drink heavily exercise more self-control and are therefore more cautious' in their behavior than in the past. ('Arbeiter und Alkoholkonsum,' *Der Abstinente Arbeiter*, vol. 5, no. 19, 1907, pp. 165) Changes in popular attitudes towards drunkenness were also noted in surveys conducted by the temperance movement, which reported that while tavern life continued to flourish drunkenness was actually declining. 'People used to drink to get drunk,' the DV in Baden reported in 1895, 'now they just drink' (Badischer Landesverein gegen den Mißbrauch geistiger Getränke, 1896, pp. 20, 37; cf. Stubbe, 1905, pp. 6, 14). The impression that drunkenness declined is also supported by the available statistics on arrests for public drunkenness. Though such statistics may reflect changes in police practices as well as changes in behavior, their overall tendency is the same as that in the more impressionistic accounts just discussed. In Berlin, for example, the average number of arrests each year declined from 8,158 in the period 1883/7 to 3,153 in 1909/13. (*Statistisches Jahrbuch der Stadt Berlin*, Vols 12–33, 1886–1916) Berlin's population had nearly doubled in this period.

The decline of public drunkenness apparently had less to do with the declining volume of alcohol consumption than with changes in the way it was consumed. Here the interdependence of the tavern and working-class associational life was especially important. The competition that had been created by liberal licensing policies led to a progressive improvement in the attractions tavern keepers, often backed by brewery capital, were able to offer their customers. (von Leixner, 1891, pp. 57, 62–3; Reichsamt des Innern, 1899, Vol. 4, pp. 931–2; 1913, vol. 3, pt 26, p. 112; Stubbe, 1905, pp. 19–20; Eckerle, 1933, p. 13) More comfortable furnishings, better food, and various kinds of cheap entertainment made the tavern an increasingly attractive place to spend leisure time, especially in view of the miserable housing conditions most workers and their families endured. (cf. Niethammer, 1976) The tavern was thus the locus of working-class social life. It was there that workers gathered to pass the time and discuss their common concerns. But the tavern's attractions did not necessarily promote increased drunkenness or even greater alcohol consumption. More likely, similar quantities of alcohol were consumed over longer periods of time. The replacement of *Schnaps* by beer as the principal working-class beverage both reflected and encouraged this development. *Schnaps* was often tossed down in a single gulp. But beer was a more social beverage, consumed slowly over the course of a whole evening.

The working class's extremely varied associational life also influenced drinking behavior. Whatever the express purpose of the numerous voluntary associations that spread within the working class after 1890, they all served to alter working-class leisure patterns. (Gonser, 1903; Lidtke, 1973; Ritter, 1978, pp. 172–3) Organization infused the ever-increasing time off the job with greater content, tied leisure activity to particular times and places and just as important, bound working-class leisure in large measure to the tavern. Taverns offered the only public facilities generally open to workers and their associations. In exchange for their meeting rooms, tavern keepers insisted on a lively trade in alcoholic beverages. Alcohol thus continued to play an important role in working-class social life, but organization disciplined drinking behavior by subordinating it to other goals and purposes. Social drinking was thus beginning to provide less the content of working-class leisure pursuits than an accompaniment to them.

Thus a number of changes could be observed in popular drinking behavior after the turn of the century. Some of them, like the displacement of *Branntwein* by beer in popular consumption patterns, continued long-term trends. But the sustained decline in aggregate per capita consumption was new. Behind the quantitative changes lay more fundamental changes in attitudes and behavior. Drunkenness declined as alcohol was integrated into and disciplined by new forms of leisure activity. There was a relative decline in drinking on the job and a relative increase in the importance of social drinking. Drinking habits thus mirrored the more general separation of work and leisure characteristic of industrial societies. Finally, though mealtime drinking continued, alcohol ceased to function as a dietary substitute – taking the place of more nutritious foodstuffs – and served instead as a dietary supplement.

## Drink, Temperance and the New Consumer Mentality

Why did these changes occur when they did, and what role did the temperance movement have in bringing them about? A number of factors were certainly at work, most of them gradual and cumulative in their effects. Better diets, shorter hours and new recreations helped make the use of alcohol less pressing, while a wide array of increasingly attractive consumer goods began to compete successfully for working-class purchasing power. But these factors, important as they were, do not explain why alcohol consumption declined when it did. This timing can best be understood as the result of rising living costs (including the costs of alcoholic beverages) and the slowed advance of real wages after the turn of the century.[1] In the face of this budgetary pressure many workers apparently curtailed their drinking in order to advance or defend their living standards in other areas.

Three additional facts support this hypothesis. In the first place, Germany was not the only Western European country to experience a decline in per capita alcohol consumption after the turn of the century. The budgetary squeeze that affected German workers also affected consumers elsewhere. Per capita alcohol consumption declined in every other country where beer and spirits were the principal alcoholic beverages. (Wlassak, 1923, pp. 183–4) Secondly, as the percentage of German private expenditure devoted to alcohol declined after the turn of the century, the proportion devoted to clothing, housing, furniture, and household goods all increased. (See Figure 3.3; cf. Minchinton, 1976, pp. 153–5) Finally, there is a striking correlation between changes in per capita alcohol consumption and changes in working-class fertility rates, which also declined in this period. (Linse, 1972) This congruence suggests a fundamental shift in working-class mentality, a more long-term orientation and a finer reckoning of costs and benefits. It bespeaks above all the working class's integration into the fundamental values of a consumer society. (cf. Stearns, 1970)

Changes in popular drinking behavior after the turn of the century depended as much on the spread of new attitudes to alcoholic beverages as they did on the availability of suitable alternatives. The view that alcohol was an essential element of the workingman's diet, a quasi-medicinal prophylactic against insalubrious working conditions and an indispensable ingredient of genuine manliness, was giving way to an ideal of moderate social drinking tolerant even of the abstainer. Under the temperance movement's influence, this new view was propagated by the public schools, the army and navy, the churches, the medical profession, industrial employers and a variety of other middle-class reform movements. Together they contributed to a long-term learning process.

But perhaps even more important in this process was the contribution of the socialist labor movement. Recognizing the hygienic and financial advantages of reduced alcohol consumption as well as the importance of sobriety to occupational safety, trade unions and other organizations of the labor movement worked actively from the turn of the century to alter working-class drinking behavior. They used their meetings and the columns of their press to educate workers about the true properties of alcohol and to encourage them to curtail their alcohol consumption, especially on the job. Though Christian trade unions more fully echoed the point of view of employers in blaming industrial accidents and inadequate living standards on immoderate drinking, the socialist Free Trade Unions also used their influence to combat working-class alcohol consumption. By justifying moderation to workers in terms that spoke directly to their needs and experiences and by using the prestige of the working-class press to dispel prevailing myths about alcohol's medicinal and nutritive properties, trade unions contributed significantly to the reduction of working-class alcohol consumption.

The success of these efforts was noted in a variety of factory inspectorate reports. In the Minden district of Westphalia, for example, the 1911 report concluded that it was due to the influence of the local wood-workers' union in Bielefeld 'that its members, among whom *Schnaps* consumption already has no place, are now limiting their beer drinking during breaks and, especially in the morning, increasingly prefer milk as a beverage.' (Reichsamt des Innern, 1907, Vol. 1, p. 407) Labor leaders agreed with this assessment of their unions' influence in reducing popular alcohol consumption. ('Arbeiter und Alkoholkonsum,' *Der Abstinente Arbeiter*, vol. 5, nos 18–20, 1907, pp. 157–9, 165–6, 170–2) The propaganda of the labor movement and the example of its adherents, moreover, had an impact beyond the rather narrow confines of its formal membership. As a factory inspector in Württemberg reported, where the labor movement set the tone, drunkenness was rare and there were few complaints about working-class drinking behavior. (Reichsamt des Innern, 1903, Vol. 2, pt 4, p. 113)

## Consensus and Continuity

None of this is to suggest that any more than a tiny minority of workers abandoned the use of alcohol altogether. Total abstinence was never a highly prized ideal in Germany, where, as we have seen, the anti-alcohol movement emphasized genuine moderation. Even in the middle classes, abstinence never became the symbol of respectability that it was in the United States and, to a lesser extent, in England. Workers were no different. It was not abstinence that symbolized respectability but how and in what forms alcohol was consumed. It is thus not surprising that the major household budget surveys of the early twentieth century reveal that workers attached considerable importance to alcohol even as they modified their drinking behavior.

The three most extensive compilations of family budgets were those published by the Statistical Bureau of the City of Berlin in 1904, the German Metal Workers' Union in 1909 and, in the same year, the Division of Labor Statistics of the Imperial Statistical Bureau. (Statistisches Amt der Stadt Berlin, 1904; Deutscher Metallarbeiter Verband, 1909; Kaiserliches Statistisches Amt, 1909) The Berlin survey included 908 budgets from the city and its suburbs and was based on workers from all sectors of the local economy – industry, handicrafts, trade, transport and commerce. The metal-workers' budgets were gathered in 42 different cities and towns throughout Germany. Altogether 14 different metal-working trades were represented as well as a sprinkling of the union's officials. The Imperial study, finally, included household budgets from 852 families of workers, civil servants, school teachers and management employees [Privatangestellte] from throughout the Empire. Altogether 522 workers' households from all sectors of the economy were represented, and the study included a special survey of the drinking behavior of 155 working-class families and 60 families of civil servants. Skilled workers predominated over the unskilled in all three surveys, and many of the participants were won to the project through the assistance of local trade union organizations.

The results of these studies can be taken as widely representative of popular expenditure patterns, but several cautions are in order. The poorest and socially most disorganized proletarian families were probably underrepresented in their findings since they were unlikely to have been successful participants in projects requiring careful and persistent record-keeping. Moreover, few single men were included in these surveys; yet their propensity to drink may have been greater than married men's. They had fewer family ties, were more dependent on the tavern for meals, and often had more pocket money to spend. Finally, of course, it is possible that expenditure on alcohol may have been underreported because of the stigma sometimes attached to it by the people conducting the investigations. The figures that follow are thus intended to convey orders of magnitude rather than precise quantitative realities. (For a useful survey of the development of family budget studies in Germany and some of their weaknesses, see Teuteberg, 1976, pp. 205–23.)

The information available in these family budget studies suggests that the percentage of working-class expenditure devoted to alcoholic beverages was, on the average, quite modest. Table 6.3 summarizes the relevant findings, which indicate that the proportion of all expenditure devoted to alcohol by these three groups of workers ranged from 4.8 to

6.7 per cent. Since all three surveys were made at a time of declining per capita alcohol consumption, it is probably safe to assume that the proportion of working-class purchasing power devoted to alcohol would have been a few percentage points higher in previous decades.

Table 6.3  *Alcohol Expenditure in Working-Class Households*

| Total Expenditure | Expenditure in Marks and as a Percentage of Total Expenditure | | | | | | | | |
|---|---|---|---|---|---|---|---|---|---|
| | Imperial Study | | | Berlin Study | | | Metal-Workers Study | | |
| | N | M | % | N | M | % | N | M | % |
| Less than 1200 M | 6 | 63.31 | 5.6 | 51 | 54.66 | 5.6 | 12 | 57.72 | 5.0 |
| 1200–1600 M | 52 | 82.20 | 5.7 | 295 | 91.29 | 6.2 | 80 | 74.36 | 5.2 |
| 1600–2000 M | 56 | 83.87 | 4.6 | 353 | 121.31 | 7.0 | 116 | 86.32 | 4.9 |
| More than 2000 M | 41 | 98.19 | 4.3 | 209 | 166.29 | 7.0 | 112 | 123.89 | 5.5 |
| All Households | 155 | 86.30 | 4.8 | 908 | 118.16 | 6.7 | 320 | 98.25 | 5.3 |

*Source:* Calculated from Statistisches Amt der Stadt Berlin, 1904, pp. 64–75; Deutscher Metallarbeiter Verband, 1909, p. 56; Kaiserliches Statistisches Amt, 1909, pt 2, pp. 202–3.
*Note:* The budget post in the survey of metal-workers also included some non-alcoholic beverages and is therefore probably slightly inflated.

Despite the relatively low levels of average alcohol expenditure, however, it is important to note that families with greater resources spent more on alcohol than those at the bottom of the financial scale. (cf. Blocher and Landsmann, 1903) This was true in all three studies. The more detailed information in the Imperial study's special section on alcohol consumption reveals that expenditure on all three beverages – beer, wine and spirits – rose as the household's total outlays increased. But the differences in absolute terms were not great. Linear regression suggests that in the Imperial study, each additional mark of income was accompanied by an increased alcohol expenditure of only 3 Pf. Among the metal-workers and Berliners, the corresponding figures were 6 and 8 Pf. respectively.[2] Greater expenditure did not, of course, necessarily mean increased consumption, but the Imperial study suggests that in the case of beer, the only beverage for which such information was provided, the quantity consumed did increase as total expenditures rose.

If working-class expenditures on alcohol do not appear to have been patently excessive, there is still some evidence that workers spent more on alcohol than did other social groups. The special section devoted to alcohol expenditure and consumption in the Imperial study of 1909 makes possible a direct comparison between the households of workers and middle-level civil servants and teachers. (Kaiserliches Statistisches Amt, 1909, pt 1, p. 7; pt 2, pp. 202–5) Although their total yearly expenditure was 52 per cent less than the civil servants', workers spent more of their money on alcohol – in both absolute and relative terms. Whereas working-class households in this study devoted an average of 4.8 per cent or 86.30 marks of their annual expenditure to alcohol, civil servants spent 2.5 per cent of their resources on drink or 71.43 marks annually. The working-class households consumed an average of 272.1 liters of beer per year, while the civil servants consumed only 171.2. This contrast was indicative of other differences in drinking styles. Beer was the most widely consumed beverage among both groups, but wine was consumed more heavily by the civil servants than by workers. Spirits, on the other hand, took second place in the workers' drink budget and last in the civil servants'. Moreover, the main study suggests that workers probably did more of their drinking in taverns than did the civil servants, who spent most of their budget for alcohol on beverages consumed at home. Workers spent 56.2 per cent of their alcohol budget in taverns and 43.8 per cent for beverages consumed at home. The figures for school teachers and civil servants were 44.2 and 55.8 per cent respectively. (Calculated from Kaiserliches Statistisches Amt, 1909, pt 2, p. 185)

What priority was assigned to alcohol consumption within the larger package of family expenditure in these two groups? The main Imperial study indicates how narrow were the financial margins of working-class existence even among these relatively secure families. As Table 6.4 suggests, 80.6 per cent of the average working-class budget was taken up by life's basic necessities: food, clothing, and shelter. Little was left for other expenses. Of the purchasing power remaining, however, alcohol absorbed the largest share, 3.9 per cent. A greater proportion of working-class expenditure went to alcohol than to such budgetary items as health care, reading and instructional materials, insurance or savings. In contrast, the families of middle-level civil servants and teachers devoted only 71.5 per cent of their greater resources to necessities. They were consequently able to spend more of their incomes, both proportionately and absolutely, on important items slighted in working-class budgets. In the context of these other expenditures, the 66.89 marks (2.1 per cent of all expenditures) devoted to alcoholic beverages appears insignificant.

The picture of popular drinking behavior that emerges from these early-twentieth-century family budget studies suggests, then, that working-class expenditure on alcohol was on the whole quite modest. Nevertheless, workers spent more on alcohol, both absolutely and relatively, than other social groups for which information is available. This difference between social groups cannot, however, be adequately explained with reference to the relative poverty of the working class, for in fact the households with the greatest resources spent the most on alcohol. But what is most striking

Table 6.4 *Allocation of Resources in Households of Workers and Civil Servants*

| | 522 Working-Class Families | | 218 Families of Middle-Level Civil Servants and Teachers | |
| | Marks | % | Marks | % |
|---|---|---|---|---|
| Total yearly expenditure | 1835.06 | 100.1 | 3187.83 | 100.0 |
| Necessities | 1478.27 | 80.6 | 2295.32 | 72.0 |
| Food | 883.09 | 48.1 | 1101.50 | 34.6 |
| Clothing | 204.67 | 11.2 | 460.41 | 14.4 |
| Housing/Utilities | 390.51 | 21.3 | 733.41 | 23.0 |
| Other Expenditures | 356.79 | 19.5 | 892.51 | 28.0 |
| Alcohol | 71.97 | 3.9 | 66.89 | 2.1 |
| Insurance | 55.52 | 3.0 | 129.05 | 4.0 |
| Newspapers, books, associations | 51.47 | 2.8 | 66.88 | 2.1 |
| Transportation | 25.74 | 1.4 | 36.56 | 1.1 |
| Amusement | 21.23 | 1.2 | 76.12 | 2.4 |
| State, municipality, church | 19.21 | 1.1 | 63.06 | 2.0 |
| Savings | 17.57 | 1.0 | 40.58 | 1.3 |
| Health care | 15.26 | 0.8 | 106.27 | 3.3 |
| Education | 11.63 | 0.6 | 75.23 | 2.4 |
| Miscellaneous | 67.19 | 3.7 | 231.87 | 7.3 |

*Source:* Kaiserliches Statistisches Amt, 1909, pt 1, pp. 58–65.
*Note:* The total in column 2 is greater than 100% because of rounding.

about these surveys is the high priority assigned to alcoholic beverages in the hierarchy of working-class consumer choices. This was possible only in a society that continued to value the social uses of alcohol. In this rather indulgent atmosphere, social drinking was viewed as one of the good things in life, something to be enjoyed rather than deprecated, something to be refined as living standards improved rather than curtailed. Not surprisingly, then, just as consumers might improve their diets, their housing or their wardrobes as their purchasing power increased, they also invested a portion of their incremental income in the enjoyment of alcoholic beverages and the activities of which they were conventionally a part.

This was not simply a question of more of the same. New purchasing power opened new choices and opportunities to working-class drinkers. Apart from mere quantity, a number of other important decisions were also involved. First, there was the question of *what* to drink, whether brandy, beer or wine. Each of these beverage types, moreover, subsumed a broad range of products differentiated by quality and price. It is impossible to be very precise about what choices people actually made. The point is that the array of alcoholic beverages available in the market place offered considerable possibilities for consumer choice and that these choices were structured in a hierarchical way. With rising income it was possible therefore to increase not only the quantity of alcohol consumed but also the quality, understood both in a hygienic and in a social or symbolic sense. As it does today, the choice of beverage, particularly in the public arena, offered workingmen an opportunity to demonstrate their relative social standing. It is no accident therefore that the poorest Germans drank the cheapest alcoholic beverages, low quality brandy or *Schnaps*. As greater purchasing power became available, however, both at the aggregate level over the whole course of the nineteenth century and in the life cycle of each individual, *Schnaps* was typically displaced as the principal working-class beverage by beer, a beverage that was not only more expensive and more prestigious but also of higher quality from a dietetic and hygienic point of view. (cf. Grotjahn, 1898, pp. 271–3; 1903)

Just as one might alter the kind and quantity of the beverages consumed as income increased, so too the settings in which people did their drinking could change. The range of drinking places was wide, at least in urban areas, and their clienteles were largely self-selecting. Most of the places workers frequented were no doubt neighborhood-based, but even in this sub-local context they faced choices that offered a significant means of cultural self-expression. The options ranged from nefarious *Schnapshöllen* to spacious *Bierpaläste*. Where one drank could be as important as what one drank. It could be a way of demonstrating social status and (relative) economic power, of reinforcing occupational or neighborhood identification, even of expressing political preferences. (cf. Roberts, 1980b)

But if workers were far from abandoning drink, it is still possible to argue that the distinctively working-class alcohol problem that had characterized the nineteenth century had by and large vanished by the eve of the First World War. There was now very little that distinguished the way workers used alcohol from the way it was used by middle- and upper-class Germans. Alcohol was valued as a social amenity, a dietary supplement, and as an occasional thirst quencher. In contrast to the situation in the United States and England, there was a single cultural system governing alcohol consumption which encompassed virtually the whole German people. (cf. Bacon, 1967)

## The Changing Shape of the German Drink Question

The creation of this national consensus did not mark the end of the Drink Question in Germany; it simply gave it a new form. The era of mass movements was over. The DV never regained its prewar following, and other temperance organizations suffered similar declines. (Bergman 1923/5;

Gläß and Biel, 1979) The goal that dominated temperance activity after the war was not to reshape the drinking habits of the working class as a whole but to attend to the deviant drinker, the man or woman unwilling or unable to conform to widely shared social norms. This shift in emphasis was signalled in the new name the DV adopted after the war – the German Association against Alcoholism (*Deutscher Verein gegen den Alkoholismus*). (Stubbe, 1933, pp. 6–8)

The temperance movement had always spoken of drunkenness as a disease, but in the past this language had been largely metaphorical, meant to indicate that drunkenness was both unnatural and ungodly. Now a more literal conception of alcoholism as a disease, elaborated and validated by the latest scientific and medical research, was applied to the problem drinker. The alcoholic was the man whose 'pathological disposition' [*'krankhafter Hang'*] had deprived him of 'the power to withstand the temptation to drink excessively' (quoted in Elster, 1923, p. 233). A medical model of alcoholism was thus being created and with it, a new strategy in a long chain of efforts to cope with alcohol's destructive potential. If alcoholism was a disease beyond the individual's control, then it was no longer appropriate to confine the drunkard in prisons or insane asylums. But by the same token, the alcoholic had to be cured, and this required a social policy of active intervention in the lives of problem drinkers.

Although the first efforts to provide specialized institutional care for problem drinkers dated back to the 1850s, it was only after the turn of the century that an alcoholism treatment movement emerged in Germany – its first congress was in 1909. ('Die erste Konferenz für Trinkerfürsorgestellen,' *Mäßigkeits-Blätter*, vol. 26, no. 11, 1909, pp. 173–9) By the spring of 1912, there were 48 alcoholic treatment asylums (*Trinkerheilstätten*) and 158 alcoholic counselling centers (*Trinkerfürsorgestellen*) operating in the German Empire. (Elster, 1923, p. 235) Despite the medical and scientific rhetoric of the men who founded these institutions, their cure was essentially moralistic. Their prescription for the problem drinker was total abstinence, moral rigor and hard work – all under a doctor's care. (Stubbe, 1908, p. 100; Wlassak, 1923, pp. 204–8) The inebriates' home was similar to the poor house. After 1900 it was possible under German civil law to commit drinkers to treatment centers against their will. (Stubbe, 1908, pp. 98–103) As coercive institutions, alcoholism treatment centers were bound to touch only the lower classes. But even as voluntary institutions, their class character was equally pronounced. Middle- and upper-class drinkers, if they could not hide or camouflage their problems, could seek their cures at fashionable spas or expensive *Heilstätte* reserved for the well-to-do.

The new treatment movement located the source of the problem not in social relations and cultural values or even in drink itself, as the classic temperance movement had done, but in individual predispositions that rendered some men and women unable to control their drinking. This analysis of the source of the problem was significant, for it allowed the broader consensus supporting moderate social and mealtime drinking to go unchallenged. At the same time, this focus on the individual problem drinker shifted attention away from the social, economic and political components of the Drink Question. (cf. Müller and Tecklenburg, 1978) In one sense then, the medicalization of the Drink Question also marked its individualization and thus its end as a classic nineteenth-century social problem. It was no longer the province of a social reform movement but a narrow concern of professional medical men.

From that time to this, medical researchers have sought to determine the origins of the disease they call alcoholism. Although there has been no shortage of theories, no lasting consensus has ever emerged within the professional alcohol studies community about the etiology of alcoholism. (Room, 1983) In the early twentieth century, it was widely assumed that alcoholism was a hereditary disease. German medical men (and temperance reformers) were by no means the only ones to adopt this explanation and to link it to eugenic concerns. But only in Germany, during the Third Reich, did racialism become the official ideology of the state, and only in Germany did this conception of the alcohol problem help justify the sterilization, incarceration and murder of human beings in the name of racial hygiene. (Gruchmann, 1972; Dawidowicz, 1975, pp. 175–80; J. Stern, pp. 213–14; Gläß and Biel, 1979, pp. 161–2) Like so many other aspects of Nazi social policy, this measure had its origins in attitudes and ideas born in the *Kaiserreich*. (cf. Zmarzlik, 1963) To their credit, many men and women active in temperance work during the Third Reich abhorred these policies. They retained their faith that alcoholics could be helped and cured. (Gläß and Biel, 1979, pp. 161–2) But there were others in the temperance tradition who welcomed these decisive actions and who willingly placed themselves at the head of this branch of Nazi social policy.

## Notes to Chapter 6

1  The development of real wages after the mid-1890s remains a subject of controversy. There seems to be general agreement, however, that real wages continued to rise in the early part of the twentieth century but at a much slower rate than in the period 1873/96. Despite the continued – if considerably slowed – advance in real wages, however, there was a widely articulated sense among the working class's spokesmen that wages were not keeping pace with rising living costs. This subjective sense of narrowing financial straits is more important to the argument being advanced here than the actual movement of real wages. It is this subjective sense that would have impelled workers to alter their choices as consumers. For a summary of recent findings on this issue, see Lee, 1978, pp. 471–3.

2 Linear regression provides a convenient way to summarize the relationship between total expenditure, a measure of overall wealth, and expenditure on alcohol. It is used here with aggregate data strictly for descriptive purposes. The regression of alcohol expenditure (Y) on total expenditure (X) (as expressed in Table 6.3 and using the mean of each total expenditure interval) yields the following equations:

155 Working-Class Families (Imperial Study)

$Y = 35.84 + 0.03X$     $(r = 0.95)$

908 Berlin Families

$Y = -23.46 + 0.08X$     $(r = 0.99)$

320 Metal-workers' Families

$Y = -12.14 + 0.06X$     $(r = 0.99)$.

## Chapter 7

# Conclusion: Drink, Temperance and the Working Class in Nineteenth-Century Germany

In Germany, as in other countries, the temperance movement looked far beyond the individuals who suffered the immediate consequences of heavy drinking, for in drink they saw a key to all the great social evils of their day. Poverty, crime, class conflict, and the breakdown of family life – all were linked in one way or another to the pernicious effects of alcohol. As Harry G. Levine has argued in the American context, alcohol was the favorite scapegoat of nineteenth-century society. Alcohol acquired this role because it seemed to threaten the virtues of individual self-control upon which rational self-government and the delicate economic interdependence of modern industrial capitalism depended. (1978, pp. 233–4, 242–3) Yet this was a classic act of reification, for in attributing the whole panoply of contemporary social problems to drink, temperance reformers ascribed to alcohol a power to shape the social order that really resides in man himself and the institutions and ideals he creates. Middle-class temperance reformers thus loaded the Drink Question with a significance that far outweighed its real potential to shape industrial society. Their hopes were too high for the remedies they proposed.

But even without subscribing to all the claims of over-zealous temperance reformers, it is still possible to argue that there was a significant alcohol problem in the nineteenth-century working class. The problems that workers were likely to experience as a result of their drinking were not necessarily the ones that most preoccupied middle-class temperance reformers. I have argued that the classic nineteenth-century alcohol problem was the consequence of 'normal' drinking practices widely accepted within the working-class community. It was not the result of socially deviant drinking, the drinking of the habitual drunkard or the genuine alcoholic. I have argued further that the problem was a physiological rather than a psychological or social one. Workers drank not so much to drown their sorrows, though this undoubtedly occurred, as they did to meet their legitimate physiological and social needs. Their problems with alcohol were consequently less those of demoralization, marginalization and the destruction of significant social ties, though these things sometimes happened, than the less visible, long-term consequences of dietary insufficiency and physical disability. This distinctive pattern of working-class alcohol consumption was the product of the countless daily choices of ordinary workingmen. In seeking to meet their everyday social and physiological needs, they almost inevitably consumed small quantities of alcohol in a variety of settings throughout the day.

The classic nineteenth-century alcohol problem persisted because a number of factors combined to reinforce patterns of consumption that had taken shape in the early nineteenth century. Workers saw in alcohol an essential ingredient of masculine sociability, a valuable thirst quencher and stimulant on the job, a welcome mealtime beverage, and an occasional means of escape from everyday cares. Alcohol was readily available and alternative beverages unpalatable and scarce. The workingman's need for refreshment, dietary stimulation, and diversion outside the home was especially great because of his basic living and working conditions. These factors receded in importance in the decades before the First World War, and eventually, confronted by new budgetary choices after the turn of the century, workers began to alter their drinking behavior. As they did so, the Drink Question was given a new form. The issue in the twentieth century has been how to treat the deviant drinker, and this has generally been left up to medical specialists. In the meantime, however, the classic nineteenth-century alcohol problem had by and large been overcome.

The DV's efforts were only tangentially related to the real problems alcohol could raise in working-class life. The proposed *Trunksuchtgesetz* of 1891, for example, would have done little to address these problems. Nevertheless, the DV did make some positive contributions to ameliorating the problems alcohol could raise in working-class life, and these positive contributions seem to have influenced the choices workers made about their drinking behavior after the turn of the century. First and foremost, the temperance movement was instrumental in encouraging employers to provide non-alcoholic beverages at the work-place, thus loosening considerably the ties that bound workers to drink. Secondly, the temperance movement initiated a long-term learning process in which the popular beliefs which had made drinking an inescapable part of everyday life were replaced by values that were still fundamentally positive but which put greater emphasis on alcohol's role as an occasional *Genußmittel* rather than an essential *Narhungsmittel*.

But if the DV helped shape popular attitudes towards drink, preserving a social consensus around the uses of alcohol that was destroyed in England and the United States, it probably did very little to alter middle- and upper-class stereotypes of the working-class drinker. There is an interesting parallel here to Gertrud Himmelfarb's observation about the reception of Henry Mayhew's work in the Victorian middle class. (1973) The more Mayhew attempted to distinguish the reputable from the disreputable poor in his pioneering and widely read social investigations, the more his descriptions of the latter came to dominate the middle-class image of the laboring classes. Similarly, the German temperance movement's effort to provide a sober, scientific approach to the Drink Question only reinforced popular stereotypes by calling attention again and again to the drinking behavior of the working classes. As social democrats were well aware, the temperance campaign not only reinforced the social stereotypes that people in power created to justify their own wealth, power and prestige, it also diverted attention from more thoroughgoing social analyses and more far-reaching proposals for reform. It is worth remembering that the Emperor himself based his social policy on such stereotypes, refusing to shorten the hours of labor in 1890 on the grounds that doing so would only allow workers more time to fill the taverns. (Born, 1957, p. 12) If this was the attitude of the Emperor, it is easy to imagine that many employers and politicians held equally primitive views. (cf. the speech by the conservative Rhenish industrialist Julius Vorster, Reichstag, 1902, Vol. 4, pp. 501–8)

Despite this complex, uneven relationship between the temperance movement and the alcohol problem, I have argued throughout this study that the temperance movement belongs to the progressive tradition in German society and politics. The temperance reform is part and parcel of the ambiguous heritage of German liberalism. In making this argument, I am also suggesting that the concept of 'social control,' frequently applied to temperance and similar nineteenth-century reform movements, is too thin to do justice to the complex attitudes and aspirations of the men who made the Drink Question a significant public issue. (cf. Thompson, 1981) Certainly temperance reformers were trying to order the social world according to their own values and interests. But these men were not guided only by personal motives and narrow self-interest, as the concept of 'social control' would seem to imply. Steeped in an ethic of social responsibility and believing in their own world-historical mission as the bearers of a higher *Kultur*, they sought to open the path of social advance and cultural attainment to the new working class. The liberal rhetoric of the *Vormärz* reveals this strain of temperance thought most clearly. Temperance promised to fit men for economic and political independence at a time when these ideals were just beginning to be realized on German soil. Although this rhetoric gave way to a form of discourse more in tune with the *Realpolitik* of an age concerned with industrial efficiency and world economic supremacy, this thread was never completely lost. For a man like Viktor Böhmert, the promise of this liberation through self-discipline remained the key to the temperance movement's appeal. To summarize the aspirations of Böhmert and others like him as an effort at social control obscures more than it illuminates. As Hans-Günther Zmarzlik has argued, it is partly the legacy of men such as these, failures in their own time, that has provided the foundation of liberal values in the *Bundesrepublik*. (1976, pp. 120–1)

The themes of control and liberation also run through the labor movement's treatment of the Drink Question. To be sure, the motives of these two poles of what might be called the larger German temperance movement often differed, but both brought liberation and self-control into a positive dialectical relationship. In keeping with its general orientation, however, the labor movement advanced the argument from the individual to the social plane. The working class had a stake in creating an orderly industrial society at least as great as that of the middle class, for if anyone suffered the consequences of disorder, workers did. Nothing shows this more clearly than drinking, for the problem drinker of the middle and upper classes could generally conceal his condition. The workingman was more vulnerable. (Badischer Landesverein gegen den Mißbrauch geistiger Getränke, 1897, p. 14; cf. Hoggart, 1970, pp. 80–1) Along with his family, neighbors and workmates, he faced the consequences of his drinking without the resources that financial security could provide. It was perhaps for this reason, because of his own vulnerability and the threat he posed to others, that the habitual drunkard was condemned in working-class circles with a vehemence at least as great as that of the most outspoken middle-class critic. Working-class culture did not demand self-denial, but it did demand self-control. Drinkers were expected to hold the line against the debilitation of habitual drunkenness. It was a narrow line, the line between respectability and disgrace, but once it was crossed the abyss into which the working-class alcoholic fell was deep, dark, and usually inescapable. There was thus nothing intrinsically 'middle class' about punctuality, frugality or sobriety. Workers had reasons of their own to develop these character traits, and this suggests the power of industrial society itself to shape the social and cultural agenda. Indeed, it is in this context that the concept of 'social control' makes the most sense, for what we see in the labor movement and the temperance movement are convergent efforts to create order out of the potential chaos of industrial society. Despite their disagreements about the control of the new industrial society and the distribution of its products, the middle and working classes were not antagonists but allies in this long-term social process.

But if the temperance movement shared many of the strengths of German liberalism, it also shared its weaknesses. This is seen most clearly by comparing the relationship between temperance and liberalism in England and Germany. In England, the temperance movement was but one piece in a larger mosaic of progressive, humanitarian social reform. As Brian Harrison has argued, the values and aspirations of the temperance movement were part of an ethos with appeal beyond the middle classes. In fact, Harrison argues, this ethos helped hold English society together in the years after mid-century by uniting labor aristocrats with key elements of the ruling classes. This alliance provided the social bases of labor's co-operation with the Liberal party, a relationship that broke down only in the first years of the twentieth century.

German liberals, on the other hand, never developed the grass roots organizations and points of contact with respectable workingmen upon which late Victorian liberalism depended. In England the temperance movement helped build this support, providing an important component of the liberal infrastructure in the era of mass politics that took shape after the passage of the Second Reform Bill. In Germany this infrastructure was almost entirely lacking. The history of the temperance movement helps us to understand why. The collapse of the German temperance movement in 1848 was symptomatic of that much more fundamental parting of the ways which was to mark the relationship between the politically conscious *Bürgertum* and the emergent labor movement for decades to come. (Mommsen, 1964, pp. 149–66) The temperance movement that re-emerged in the 1880s was elitist and aloof, never departing from the tradition of reform from above, never trusting the good will or intelligence of the men and women whose behavior they hoped to reform. This organizational style, the style pre-eminently of the German *Bildungsbürger*, and the inability of liberals at all levels to transcend it, contributed, as scholars like James J. Sheehan, Dan White and Geoff Eley have shown in other ways, to the basic weakness of German liberalism and its failure to shape the course of events in an era of increasingly turbulent mass politics. (White, 1976; Sheehan, 1978; Eley, 1980) The German temperance movement moved in encrusted political forms. Lacking the strength and confidence to challenge them, the temperance movement could only conform to the larger political world in which it operated.

# References

## A Note on Sources

Research for this project took me to some fifteen state and private archives in the Federal Republic of Germany as well as to the *Zentrales Staatsarchiv* of the German Democratic Republic. I used the resources of an almost equal number of libraries and research institutes. In my search for materials I was not able to locate the archives of either of the two major temperance organizations central to this study. The archive of the *Deutscher Verein gegen den Mißbrauch geistiger Getränke* was destroyed by fire late in 1944 or early in 1945. (I am grateful to Dr Curt Meyer, Berlin, for this information.) The archives of the *Deutscher Arbeiter Abstinenten Bund* were not to be found in either of the two principal repositories of materials on the prewar German labor movement, the *Archiv der sozialen Demokratie* at the *Friedrich Ebert Stiftung*, Bonn-Bad Godesberg, or the International Institute of Social History, Amsterdam. They were presumably destroyed, like so many other documents of the German labor movement, after Hitler came to power in 1933.

My work in archives and specialized research institutes yielded occasional gems of information (especially for the period before 1848), but for the most part, the extensive files under such enticing rubrics as '*Bekämpfung des Alkoholmißbrauchs*' served only to document the tireless lobbying efforts of the DV, whose petitions, proposals, reports and requests for financial assistance filled the files of government agencies at all levels. In the absence of a single set of rich archival sources, this study has relied heavily on the extensive publications of the DV and the DAAB – periodicals, pamphlets, yearly reports, and the published proceedings of periodic conferences.

These documents produced by different branches of the German temperance tradition have been supplemented by a wide array of other printed sources. The Drink Question was a subject for economists and sociologists, natural scientists and medical men, theologians and politicians, and – not least – the agencies of national, state and local government. The list of references that follows is not intended as a comprehensive guide to the vast German literature on the Drink Question. It does include, in addition to temperance sources, the major general works on the Drink Question as well as the principal articles and pamphlets dealing specifically with drink and the working class.

Anyone wishing further bibliographical assistance should consult the following comprehensive bibliographies:

Emil Aberhalden, *Bibliographie der gesamten wissenschaftlichen Literatur über den Alkohol und den Alkoholismus* (Berlin: Urban & Schwarzenberg, 1904).

Mark Keller, *International Bibliography of Studies on Alcohol, 1901–1960*, 3 Vols (Rutgers, NJ: Publications Division, Rutgers Center of Alcohol Studies, 1966).

Peter Schmidt, *Bibliographie des Alkoholismus der letzten zwanzig Jahren* (Dresden: Böhmert, 1901).

The period before 1848 is not extensively covered in these works, and to my knowledge no comprehensive bibliography exists for this period. A useful, if unfortunately very early starting-point is the 'Literarischer Anhang' in J. H. Böttcher's *Geschichte* (1841, pp. 672–9). The most useful guide to temperance periodicals in this period is Joachim Kirchner's *Die Zeitschriften des deutschen Sprachgebietes von 1831 bis 1870* (Stuttgart: Hiersemann, 1977). Otherwise I have relied on the catalogue of the *Staatsbibliothek Preußischer Kulturbesitz*, Berlin, for references to the early literature.

## Archival Sources

*Badisches Generallandesarchiv*, Karlsruhe

| | |
|---|---|
| Abt. 236/16260 | Bekämpfung des Mißbrauchs geistiger Getränke, 1853–1923 |
| Abt. 237/34017 | Die wegen Überhandnahme des Branntweintrinkens getroffenen Maßregeln und die Bekämpfung des Mißbrauchs geistiger Getränke, 1853–1923 |

*Bayerisches Hauptstaatsarchiv*, Munich

| | |
|---|---|
| Abt. 1/ MInn 62572 | Das Überhandnehmen des Branntweintrinkens, Schädlichkeit des Kartoffelbranntwein, Bd. I: 1833–1836, Bd. II: 1837–1884 |

*Deutscher Caritasverband, Archiv*, Freiburg i. Br.

| | |
|---|---|
| CA XIV, 6A | Trinkerfürsorge |

*Friedrich Ebert Stiftung/Archiv der sozialen Demokratie*, Bonn-Bad Godesberg
Flugblätter Sammlung,   1908–1910

*Geheimes Staatsarchiv Preußischer Kulturbesitz*, Berlin

| | |
|---|---|
| 84A/5235, 5236 | Bekämpfung der Trunksucht, 1899–1902, 1903–1906 |
| 84A/5240 | Bekämpfung der Trunksucht: Äußerungen der Presse, 1881–1931 |

*Hauptstaatsarchiv Düsseldorf*

| | |
|---|---|
| Reg. Aachen 4793 | Mäßigkeitsvereine, 1833–1887 |

*International Institute of Social History*, Amsterdam

| | |
|---|---|
| Iconographic Department | Deutscher Arbeiter Abstinenten Bund, 1909 |

*Niedersächsisches Hauptstaatsarchiv*, Hanover

| | |
|---|---|
| Hann Des 74 Hann VIII H5, Nr. 5 | Allgemeine Maßregeln und Voschriften gegen den übermäßigen Genuß von Branntwein, auch Föderung von Entnhaltsamkeits- und Mäßigkeitsvereinen, 1834–1904 |

| Hann Des 80, | Die Bildung und Föderung von Mäßigkeitsvereine, |
|---|---|
| Hildesheim I, E18 | 1839–1863 |

*Staatsarchiv Münster*
Oberpräsidium      Die deutschen Enthaltsamkeits vereine, 1847
703

*Staatsarchiv Osnabrück*
Erw A16, no. 152      Familie Stüve, Drucksachen, 1848/50

*Zentrales Staatsarchiv*, Potsdam
Reichsamt des      Die gesetzlichen Maßregeln zur Bekämpfung des
Innern, 16350      Mißbrauchs geistiger Getränke, Bd. I: 1885–1889

Reichslandbund      Pressearchiv, Bd. I: 1905–1910, Bd. II: 1910–1914
2613, 2614

## Temperance Periodicals

*Die Alkoholfrage* (1.1904–9.1913)
*Der Alkoholismus* (1.1900–3.1902)
*Der Abstinente Arbeiter. Organ des deutschen Arbeiter-Abstinenten-Bundes* (1.1903–12. 1914)
*Blätter des Hamburgischen Vereins gegen das Branntweintrinken* (1.1841–3.1844)
*Blätter des Osnabrücker Mäßigkeits-Vereins. Zu Rath und That.* (8. 1848)
*Central-Blatt der Vereine gegen das Branntweintrinken für die Provinzen Brandenburg, Sachsen, Pommern und die Insel Rügen* (3.1848)
*Central-Blatt für die Enthaltsamkeits-Angelegenheit im Großherzogthum Posen* (1.1841–3.1843)
*Central-Blatt für die Rheinisch-Westphälischen Enthaltsamkeitsvereine* (1.1846–2.1847)
*Centralblatt sämmtlicher Enthaltsamkeits-und Mäßigkeitsvereine in Ost-und West-Preußen* (9.1848–25.1864)
*Generalblatt für die Mäßigkeits-Reform in Deutschland* (1.1846)
*Mäßigkeits-Blätter. Mitteilungen des Deutschen Vereins gegen den Mißbrauch geistiger Getränke* (1.1884–31.1914)
*Mäßigkeitsherold für die Preußischen Staaten* (4.1844–5.1845)
*Mäßigkeits-Zeitung* (Stade) (1.1840–10.1849)
*Monatsblatt für die Enthaltsamkeitssache* (1.1844–3.1847)
*Der Volksfreund. Monatsblatt des Breslauer Vereins gegen das Branntweintrinken* (1.1847–39.1885)

## Other Printed Sources

Abel, Wilhelm (1972), *Massenarmut und Hungerkrisen im vorindustriellen Deutschland* (Göttingen: Vandenhoek & Ruprecht).

Anschütz, Gerhard (1899), *Die Bekämpfung der Trunksucht im Verwaltungsweg* (Hildesheim: Mäßigkeitsverlag).

Anton, Günter (1891), *Geschichte des preußischen Fabrikgesetzgebung*. Staats- und Sozialwissenschaftliche Forschungen, no. 12, pt 2 (Leipzig: Duncker & Humblot).

Arlin, Marian (1977), *The Science of Nutrition*, 2nd edn (New York: Macmillan).

Bacon, Selden D. (1967), 'The Classic Temperance Movement of the U.S.A: Impact Today on Attitudes, Action and Research,' *British Journal of Addiction*, vol. 62, no. 1/2, pp. 5–18.

Badischer Landesverein gegen den Mißbrauch geistiger Getränke (1896), *Der Mißbrauch geistiger Getränke in Großherzogtum Baden* (Karlsruhe: Selbstverlag).

Badischer Landesverein gegen den Mißbrauch geistiger Getränke (1897), *Die Aufgaben des Vereins gegen den Mißbrauch geistiger Getränke in Großherzogtum Baden* (Karlsruhe: Selbstverlag).

Baer, Abraham (1878), *Der Alkoholismus, seine Verbreitung und seine Wirkung auf den individuellen und socialen Organismus* (Berlin: Hirschwald).

Baird, Henry M. (1886), *The Life of the Rev. Robert Baird, D.D.* (New York: Randolf).

Baird, Robert (1836), *Histoire des sociétés de tempérance des États-Unis d'Amérique* (Paris: Hachette).

Baird, Robert (1837), *Geschichte der Mäßigkeits-Gesellschaft in den Vereinigten Staaten Nord Amerikas* (Berlin: Eichler).

Balser, Frohlinde (1959), *Die Anfänge der Erwachsenbildung in Deutschland in der ersten Hälfte des 19. Jahrhunderts* (Stuttgart: Klett).

Barkin, Kenneth (1970), *The Controversy over German Industrialization, 1890–1902* (Chicago, Ill: University of Chicago Press).

Barrows, Susanna (1979), 'After the Commune: Alcoholism, Temperance, and Literature in the Early Third Republic,' in *Consciousness and Class Experience in Nineteenth-Century Europe*, (ed.) John M. Merriman (New York: Holmes & Meier), pp. 205–18

Bergman, Johan (1907), *Geschichte der Antialkoholbestrebungen*, trans. from the Swedish by Reinhard Kraut (Hamburg: Verlag von Deutschlands Großloge II, International Order of Good Templars).

Bergman, Johan (1923/5), *Geschichte der Nüchternheitsbestrebungen*, 2 vols trans. and edited by Reinhard Kraut (Hamburg: Neuland-Verlag).

Bergmann, Klaus (1970), *Agrarromantik und Großstadtfeindschaft* (Meisenheim am Glan: Anton Hain).

Beyreuther, Erich (1963), *Die Erweckungsbewegung*, in: *Die Kirche in ihrer Geschichte*, (eds) Kurt Dietrich Schmidt and Ernst Wolf, Vol. 4, pt 1 (Göttingen: Vandenhoek & Ruprecht).

Bigler, Robert M. (1972), *The Politics of German Protestantism: The Rise of the Protestant Church Elite in Prussia, 1815–1848* (Berkeley, Calif: University of California Press).

Billington, Ray Allen (1964), *The Protestant Crusade, 1800–1860* (New York: Macmillan, 1938; repr. Chicago, Ill: Quadrangle).

Blasius, Dirk (1976), *Bürgerliche Gesellschaft und Kriminalität: zur Sozialgeschichte Preußens im Vormärz* (Göttingen: Vandenhoek & Ruprecht).

Blocher, Hermann and Landsmann, J. (1903), *Die Belastung des Arbeiterbudgets durch den Alkoholgenuß* (Basel: Reinhardt).

Blocker, Jack S. (1976), *Retreat from Reform: The Prohibition Movement in the United States, 1890–1913* (Westport, Conn: Greenwood).

Bocks, Wolfgang (1978), *Die Badische Fabrikinspektion. Arbeitershutz, Arbeiterverhältnisse und Arbeiterbewegung in Baden 1879–1914* (Freiburg i. Br.: Alber).

Bode, Wilhelm (1896), *Kurze Geschichte der Trinksitten und Mäßigkeitsbestrebungen in Deutschland* (Munich: Lehmann).

Bode, Wilhelm (1898a), *An die Politiker* (Hildesheim: Selbstverlag des Verfassers).

Bode, Wilhelm (1898b), *Arbeiterschutz gegen den Alkohol* (Berlin: Sittenfeld).

Bodnaer, John (1977), *Immigration and Industrialization: Ethnicity in an American Mill Town, 1870–1940* (Pittsburgh, Pa: University of Pittsburgh Press).

Böhmert, Viktor (1884), 'Das Arbeiterwohl und der Kampf gegen den Mißbrauch geistiger Getränke,' *Der Arbeiterfreund*, vol. 22, pp. 435–45.

Böhmert, Viktor (1886), *Das Armenwesen in 77 deutschen Städten und einige Landarmenverbände* (Dresden: Selbstverlag des armenstatistischen Bureaus des Deutschen Vereins für Armenpflege und Wohltätigkeit).

Böhmert, Viktor (1889), *Der Branntwein in Fabriken*, neue Bearbeitung. (Leipzig: Duncker & Humblot).

Böhmert, Viktor (1900), *Rückblicke und Ausblicke eines Siebzigers* (Dresden: Böhmert).

Böhmert, Viktor (1907), 'Die Alkoholfrage auf dem sozialdemokratischen Parteitage in Essen,' *Die Alkoholfrage*, vol. 4, pp. 277–90.

Böhmert, Viktor (1909), *Erinnerungen und Lebensauffassungen eines Achtzigers* (Dresden: Böhmert).

Böhmert, W. (1913), 'Die Gast- und Schankwirtschaften, nebst Angaben über die polizeiliche Regelung des Wirtschaftsbetriebes und über die alkoholgegnerischen Vereine,' *Statistisches Jahrbuch Deutscher Städte*, vol. 29, pp. 213–42.

Borchardt, Knut (1972), *Die industrielle Revolution in Deutschland* (Munich: Piper).

Borchardt, Knut (1976), 'Wirtschaftliches Wachstum und Wechsellagen, 1800–1914,' in *Handbuch der deutschen Wirtschafts- und Sozialgeschichte*, (eds) Hermann Aubin and Wolfgang Zorn, Vol. 2 (Stuttgart: Klett), pp. 198–275.

Bordin, Ruth (1981), *Women and Temperance: The Quest for Power and Liberty, 1873–1900* (Philadelphia: Temple University Press).

Born, Karl Erich (1957), *Staat und Sozialpolitik seit Bismarcks Sturz* (Wiesbaden: Steiner).

Bosl, Karl and Weis, Eberhard (1976), *Die Gesellschaft in Deutschland: Von der fränkischen Zeit bis 1848* (Munich: Lurz).

Böttcher, J. H. (1839a), *Der Branntwein, ein sicherer Zerstörer des Wohlstandes, der Gesundheit, des häuslichen Glücks und der Zufriedenheit* (Hildesheim: Gerstenbergschen Buchhandlung).

Böttcher, J. H. (1839b), *Das Hauskreuz, oder was vom Branntweintrinken zu halten sei* (Hanover: Hahn'schen Hofbuchhandlung).

Böttcher, J. H. (1839c), *Über den Branntwein-Genuß, dessen Größe, Ursachen, Folgen und Heilung* (Hanover: Hahn'schen Hofbuchhandlung).

Böttcher, J. H. (1840), *Der Patriot: Eine vorurteilsfreie und grundliche Untersuchung über die Mäßigkeits-Angelegenheit*, 2nd edn (Hanover: Hahn'schen Hofbuchhandlung).

Böttcher, J. H. (1841), *Geschichte der Mäßigkeitsgesellschaften in den norddeutschen Bundes-Staaten, oder General-Bericht über den Zustand der Mäßigkeitsreform bis zum Jahr 1840* (Hanover: Hahn'schen Hofbuchhandlung).

138  *Drink, Temperance and the Working Class*

[Böttcher, J. H.] (1896), 'Böttchers Leben: Von ihm selbst beschrieben,' *Mäßigkeits-Blätter*, vol. 13, no. 1, pp. 6–9, 31–4.

Böttcher, J. H. (n.d.), *Continentaler Mäßigkeits-Congress in Hannover (n.p.).*

Brinkmann, Wilhelm (n.d.), *Der deutsche Verein gegen den Mißbrauch geistiger Getränke und die Mäßigkeitsbewegung in Deutschland* (Wiesbaden: Wiesbaden Bezirksverein).

Bromme, Mortiz Theodor Wilhelm (1971), *Lebensgeschichte eines modernen Fabrikarbeiters,* edited with an Afterword by Bern Neumann (Jena: Diederichs, 1905; repr. edn, Frankfurt a/M: Athenäeum).

Burnham, John C. (1968), 'New Perspectives on the Prohibition 'Experiment' of the 1920s,' *Journal of Social History,* vol. 2, no. 1, pp. 51–68.

Bynum, William F. (1968), 'Chronic Alcoholism in the First Half of the 19th Century,' *Bulletin of the History of Medicine,* vol. 42, no. 2, pp. 160–85.

Carr, William (1979), *A History of Germany, 1815–1945,* 2nd edn (New York: St Martin's).

Chickering, Roger B. (1975), *Imperial Germany and a World Without War: The Peace Movement and German Society, 1892–1914* (Princeton, NJ: Princeton University Press).

Clark, Norman H. (1976), *Deliver Us from Evil: An Interpretation of American Prohibition* (New York: Norton).

Conze, Werner (1954), 'Vom 'Pöbel' zum 'Proletariat': sozialgeschichtliche Voraussetzungen für den Sozialismus in Deutschland,' *Vierteljahrsschrift für Sozial- und Wirtschaftsgeschichte,* vol. 41, no. 4, pp. 333–64.

Conzen, Kathleen Neils (1976), *Immigrant Milwaukee, 1836–1860: Accommodation and Community in a Frontier City* (Cambridge, Mass: Harvard University Press).

Crew, David F. (1979), *Town in the Ruhr: A Social History of Bochum, 1860–1914* (New York: Columbia University Press).

Cumbler, John T. (1979), *Working Class Community in Industrial America: Work Leisure and Struggle in Two Industrial Cities, 1880–1930* (Westport, Conn: Greenwood).

Dannenbaum, Jed (1981), 'Anti-Alcohol Mass Movements: The Cross Cultural Perspective,' paper presented to the 96th Annual Meeting of the American Historical Association, Los Angeles, December 28–30.

Darf, R. (1909/10), 'Wirkt der Schnapsboykott,' *Die Neue Zeit,* vol. 28 pt 1, no. 11, pp. 380–1.

Dawidowicz, Lucy S. (1975), *The War against the Jews, 1933–1945* (New York: Holt, Rinehart & Winston).

Dawly, Alan (1976), *Class and Community: The Industrial Revolution in Lynn* (Cambridge, Mass: Harvard University Press).

Desai, A. V. (1968), *Real Wages in Germany, 1871–1913* (Oxford: Oxford University Press).

Deutscher Arbeiter Abstinenten Bund (1909), *Protokoll der III. ordentlichen General-Versammlung des Deutschen-Arbeiter-Abstinenten-Bundes zu Hannover, Pfingsten 1909* (Berlin: Michaelis).

Deutscher Arbeiter Abstinenten Bund (1911), *Was Wollen die Arbeiter-Abstinenten?* (Berlin: Verlag DAAB).

Deutscher Arbeiter Abstinenten Bund (1912), *Protokoll der IV. ordemtlichen Generalversammlung des Deutschen-Arbeiter-Abstinenten-Bundez zu Berlin 5. bis 8. April 1912* (Berlin: DAAB7.

Deutscher Metallarbeiter-Verband (1909), *320 Haushaltsrechnungen von Metallarbeitern* (Stuttgart: Schlicke).

Deutscher Verein gegen den Mißbrauch geistiger Getränke (1897a), *Der Alkohol auf Arbeitsplätzen: Dritte Sammlung von Gutachten an den Deutschen Verein gegen den Mißbrauch geistiger Getränke* (Hildesheim: Geschäftsstelle des Deutschen Vereins gegen den Mißbrauch geistiger Getränke).

Deutscher Verein gegen den Mißbrauch geistiger Getränke (1897b), *Arbeiterschutz gegen den Alkohol: Mitteilungen von Fabrik-Inspektoren, Arbeitgebern, Arbeitern und Andern für den Deutschen Verein gegen den Mißbrauch geistiger Getränke* (Hildesheim: Geschäftsstelle des Deutschen Vereins gegen den Mißbrauch geistiger Getränke).

Deutscher Verein gegen den Mißbrauch geistiger Getränke (1897c), *Erste Gutachtensammlung des Deutschen Vereins gegen den Mißbrauch geistiger Getränke* (Hildesheim: Geschäftsstelle des Deutschen Vereins gegen den Mißbrauch geistiger Getränke).

Deutscher Verein gegen den Mißbrauch geistiger Getränke (1897d), *Weitere Mitteilungen zum Kapitel 'Arbeiterschutz gegen den Alkohol'* (Hildesheim: Geschäftsstelle des Deutschen Vereins gegen den Mißbrauch geistiger Getränke).

Deutscher Verein gegen den Mißbrauch geistiger Getränke (n.d.), *Verhandlungen der constituierenden Versammlung in Kassel, am 29. März 1883* (Bremen: Roussel).

Deutscher Verein gegen den Mißbrauch geistiger Getränke, *Bericht des Geschäftführers* (Hildesheim and Berlin: Mäßigkeitsverlag, 1893–1914).

Dieterici, C. F. W. (1838/57), *Statistische Uebersicht der wichtigsten Gegenstände des Verkehrs und Verbrauchs im Preußischen Staate und im deutschen Zollverbande*, 5 vols (Berlin: Mittler).

Dingle, A. E. (1972), 'Drink and Working Class Living Standards in Britain, 1870–1914,' *Economic History Review*, 2nd series, vol. 25, no. 4, pp. 608–22.

Dingle, A. E. (1980), *The Campaign for Prohibition in Victorian England: The United Kingdom Alliance, 1872–1895* (New Brunswick, NJ: Rutgers University Press).

Dodd, Jill Siegel (1978), 'The Working Classes and the Temperance Movement in Ante-Bellum Boston,' *Labor History*, vol. 19, no. 4, pp. 510–31.

Eckerle, Karl Günter (1933), *Die deutsche Brauindustrie und die moderne Konzentrations-und-Expansions-Bewegung* (Freiburg i. Br.: Poppen & Ortmann).

Eley, Geoff (1980), *Reshaping the German Right: Radical Nationalism and Political Change after Bismarck* (New Haven, Conn: Yale University Press).

Elster, Alexander (1923), 'Alkoholismus,' *Handwörterbuch der Staatswissenschaften*, 4th edn (Jena: Fischer), Vol. 1, pp. 207–41.

Emminghaus, A. (1908), *August Lammers: Lebensbild eines deutschen Publizisten und Pioniers der Gemeinnützigkeit aus der zweiten Hälfte des vorigen Jahrhunderts* (Dresden: Böhmert).

Engel, Ernst (1853), *Die Branntweinbrennerei in ihren Beziehungen zur Landwirtschaft, zur Steuer und zum öffentlichen Leben* (Dresden: Kuntze).

Engel, Ernst (1864), 'Zur statistischen Ermittelung der Consumption pro Kopf der Bevölkerung im preußischen Staate,' *Zeitschrift des Königlichen Preußischen Statistischen Bureaus*, vol. 4, pp. 128–35.

Engels, Friedrich (1962a), 'Briefe aus dem Wuppertal,' in *Marx-Engels-Werke* (East Berlin: Dietz), Vol. 1, pp. 413–32.

140    Drink, Temperance and the Working Class

Engels, Friedrich (1962b), 'Die Lage der arbeitenden Klassen in England,' in *Marx-Engels-Werke* (East Berlin: Dietz), Vol. 2, pp. 225–506

Engels, Friedrich (1962c), 'Preußischer Schnaps,' in *Marx-Engels-Werke*, (East Berlin: Dietz), Vol. 19, pp. 37–51.

Engelsing, Rolf (1973), *Sozial- und Wirtschaftsgeschichte Deutschlands* (Göttingen: Vandenhoek & Ruprecht).

Epstein, Barbara Leslie (1981), *The Politics of Domesticity: Women, Evangelicalism, and Temperance in Nineteenth-Century America* (Middletown, Conn: Wesleyan University Press).

Esche, Arthur (1912), 'Der Alkohol im Wettkampf der Völker,' *Mäßigkeits-Blätter*, vol. 29, no. 12, pp. 181–7.

Evans, Richard J. (1976), *The Feminist Movement in Germany, 1894–1933* (London: Sage).

Faler, Paul (1974), 'Cultural Aspects of the Industrial Revolution: Lynn, Massachusetts, Shoemakers and Industrial Morality, 1826–1860,' *Labor History*, vol. 15, no. 3, pp. 367–94.

Fallati, Johannes (1844), 'Das Vereinswesen als Mittel zur Sittigung der Fabrikarbeiter,' *Zeitschrift für die gesammte Staatwissenschaften*, vol. 1, no. 4, pp. 737–91.

Ferber, C. W. (1829), *Beiträge zur Kenntnis des gewerblichen und commerciellen Zustandes der preussischen Monarchie* (Berlin: Trautwein).

Feuerlein, Wilhelm (1975), *Alkoholismus: Mißbrauch und Abhängigkeit* (Stuttgart: Thieme).

Fischer, Wolfram (1963), 'Soziale Unterschichten im Zeitalter der Frühindustrialisierung,' *International Review of Social History*, vol. 8, no. 3, pp. 415–35.

Flade, Erich (1905), *Der Kampf gegen den Alkoholismus – ein Kampf für unser deutsches Volkstum* (Berlin: Mäßigkeitsverlag).

Föhlisch, Eduard (1910), 'Die wirtschaftliche Lage der Arbeiter in 35 Mannheimer Fabriken,' in *Jahresbericht der Badischen Fabrikinspektion*, pp. 79–131.

Forsander, Olaf F. (1963), 'The Influence of Alcohol on the General Metabolism of the Body,' in *Alcohol and Civilization*, (ed.) Salvatore Pablo Lucia (New York: McGraw-Hill), pp. 43–60.

Franz, Günther (1976), 'Landwirtschaft 1800–1850,' *Handbuch der deutschen Wirtschafts- und Sozialgeschichte*, vol. 2, (eds) Hermann Aubin and Wolfgang Zorn (Stuttgart: Klett), pp. 276–320.

Frecot, Janos (1976), 'Die Lebensreformbewegungen,' in *Das wilhelminische Bildungsbürgertum: Zur Sozialgeschichte seiner Ideen*, (ed.) Klaus Vondung (Göttingen: Vandenhoek & Ruprecht), pp. 138–52.

Fricke, Dieter (1976), *Die Deutsche Arbeiterbewegung 1869–1914* (Berlin: Verlag das europäische Buch).

Gerloff, Wilhelm (1913), *Die Finanz-und Zollpolitik des Deutschen Reiches* (Jena: Fischer).

Gläß, Theo and Biel, Wilhelm (1979), *Der Guttempler-Orden in Deutschland*, Vol. 1 (Hamburg: Neuland).

Glümer, H. von (1897), *Schutz der Arbeiter gegen den Alkoholmißbrauch* (Hildesheim: n.p.).

Glümer, H. von (1900), 'Zu "Mäßigkeitsbewegung und Arbeiterpartei",' *Mäßigkeits-Blätter*, vol. 17, no. 2, pp. 18–20.

Göhre, Paul (1891), *Drei Monate Fabrikarbeiter und Handwerksbursche* (Leipzig: Grunow).

Goldberg, Leonard (1963), 'The Metabolism of Alcohol,' in *Alcohol and Civilization*, (ed.) Savatore Pablo Lucia (New York: McGraw-Hill), pp. 23–42.

Gonser, J. (1903), *Verein und Wirtshaus* (Berlin: Mäßigkeitsverlag).

Gordon, Ernst (1913), *The Anti-Alcohol Movement in Europe* (New York: Revell).

Graf, Christa Volk (1970), *The Hanoverian Reformer Johann Carl Bertram Stüve, 1798–1872* (Ph.D. dissertation, Cornell University).

Grotjahn, Alfred (1898), *Der Alkoholismus, nach Wesen, Wirkung und Verbreitung* (Leipzig: Wigand).

Grotjahn, Alfred (1902), *Über Wandlungen in der Volksernährung*, Staats- und Sozialwissenschaftliche Forschungen, no. 20, pt 2 (Leipzig: Duncker & Humblot).

Grotjahn, Alfred (1903), *Alkohol und Arbeitsstätte* (Berlin: Mäßigkeitsverlag).

Gruber, Max (1888), 'Der Osterreichische Gesetzentwurf zur Bekämpfung der Trunkenheit,' *Archiv für soziale Gesetzgebung und Statistik*, vol. 1, pp. 293–320.

Gruchmann, L. (1972), 'Euthanasie und Justiz im Dritten Reich,' *Vierteljahrshefte für Zeitgeschichte*, vol. 20, no. 3, pp. 235–79.

Gusfield, Joseph R. (1962), 'Status Ideologies of the American Temperance Movement,' in *Society, Culture and Drinking Patterns*, (eds) David J. Pittman and Charles R. Snyder (New York: Wiley), pp. 101–20.

Gusfield, Joseph R. (1963), *Symbolic Crusade: Status Politics and the American Temperance Movement* (Urbana, Ill: University of Illinois Press).

Hahn, Helmut (1956), *Die deutsche Weinbaugebiete, ihre historisch-geographische Entwicklung und wirtschaftliches- und soziologisches Struktur* (Bonn: Geographisches Institut der Universität).

Hähnel, Franziskus, (ed.) (1904), *Bericht über den IX. Internationalen Kongress gegen den Alkoholismus* (Jena: Fischer).

Hamer, D. A. (1977), *The Politics of Electoral Pressure: A Study in the History of Victorian Reform Agitations* (Sussex: Harvester Press).

Hamerow, Theodore S. (1958), *Restoration, Revolution, Reaction: Economics and Politics in Germany, 1815–1871* (Princeton, NJ: Princeton University Press).

Hanauer, F. (1910/11), 'Die sozialistischen Parteien und die Alkoholfrage,' *Die Neue Zeit*, vol. 29, pt 2, no. 49, pp. 828–33.

Harrison, Brian (1965/6), 'Philanthropy and the Victorians,' *Victorian Studies*, vol. 9, no. 4, pp. 353–74.

Harrison, Brian (1971), *Drink and the Victorians: The Temperance Question in England, 1815–1872* (Pittsburgh, Pa: University of Pittsburgh Press).

Harrison, Brian (1973), 'Teetotal Chartism,' *History*, vol. 58, no. 193, pp. 193–217.

Haus der Abgeordneten, *Stenographische Berichte über die Verhandlungen des Preußischen Hauses der Abgeordneten*.

Heath, Dwight B. (1975), 'A Critical Review of Ethnographic Studies of Alcohol Use,' in *Research Advances in Alcohol and Drug Problems*, (eds) Robert J. Gibbins et al. (New York: Wiley), Vol. 2, pp. 1–92.

Heath, Dwight B. (1976), 'Anthropological Perspectives on Alcohol: An Historical Review,' in *Cross-Cultural Approaches to the Study of Alcohol: An Interdisciplinary Perspective*, (eds) Michael W. Everett et al. (The Hague: Mouton), pp. 41–101.

142   *Drink, Temperance and the Working Class*

Heckel, Max von (1909), 'Branntweinsteuer,' in *Handwörterbuch der Staatswissenschaften*, 3rd edn (Jena: Fischer), Vol. 3, pp. 207–36.

Henderson, W. O. (1975), *The Rise of German Industrial Power, 1834–1914* (Berkeley, Calif: University of California Press).

Henning, Friedrich-Wilhelm (1973), *Die Industrialisierung in Deutschland 1800 bis 1914* (Paderborn: Schöningh).

Henning, Hansjoachim (1977), *Sozialgeschichtliche Entwicklungen in Deutschland von 1815 bis 1860* (Paderborn: Schönigh).

Herkner, Heinrich (1906), *Alkoholismus und Arbeiterfrage* (Berlin: Mäßigkeitsverlag).

Herlemann, Hans-Heinrich (1952), *Branntweinpolitik und Landwirtschaft* (Kiel: n.p.).

Himmelfarb, Gertrude (1973), 'The Culture of Poverty,' in *The Victorian City: Images and Realities*, (eds) J. H. Dyos and Michael Wolff, 2 vols (London: Routledge & Kegan Paul), Vol. 2, pp. 707–36.

Hirsch, Susan E. (1978), *Roots of the American Working Class: The Industrialization of Crafts in Newark, 1800–1860* (Philadelphia: University of Pennsylvania Press).

Hirsch, Joseph (1949), 'Enlightened 18th Century Views on the Alcohol Problem,' *Journal of the History of Medicine and Allied Sciences*, vol. 4, no. 2, pp. 230–6.

Hitzig, Julius Eduard (1837), *Votum über die Bildung eines sogenannten Mäßigkeits-Vereins in Berlin* (Berlin: Vereins-Buchhandlung).

Hobsbawm, Eric J. (1962), *The Age of Revolution, 1789–1848* (London: Weidenfeld & Nicolson).

Hobsbawm, Eric (1975), *The Age of Capital, 1848–1875* (London: Weidenfeld & Nicolson).

Hoffmann, Ottilie (1899), 'Über die Mitarbeit der Frauen und des Bundes Deutscher Frauen-Vereine für die Mäßigkeitssache,' *Mäßigkeits-Blätter*, vol. 16, no. 11/12, pp. 161–3, 177–9.

Hoffmann, Walter G. *et al.* (1965), *Das Wachstum der deutschen Wirtschaft seit der Mitte des 19. Jahrhunderts* (Berlin: Springer).

Hofstadter, Richard (1955), *The Age of Reform: From Bryan to F.D.R.* (New York: Vintage).

Hoggart, Richard (1970), *The Uses of Literacy* (London: Chatto & Windus, 1957; reprint edn, New York: Oxford University Press).

Hohorst, Gerd, Kocka, Jürgen and Ritter, Gerhard A. (1975), *Sozialgeschichtliches Arbeitsbuch. Materialien zur Statistik des Kaiserreichs 1870–1914* (Munich: Beck).

Holborn, Hajo (1964), *A History of Modern Germany,1648–1840* (New York: Knopf).

Honnigmann, John J. (1979), 'Alcohol in its Cultural Context,' in *Beliefs, Behaviors and Alcoholic Beverages*, (ed.) Mac Marshall (Ann Arbor, Mich: University of Michigan Press), pp. 30–6.

Hufeland, Christoph Wilhelm (1796), *Makrobiotik, oder die Kunst das menschliche Leben zu verlängern* (Leipzig: Reklam).

Jantke, Carl and Hilger, Dietrich (1965), *Die Eigentumslosen: Der deutsche Pauperismus und die Emanzipationskrise in Darstellungen und Deutungen der zeitgenössische Literatur* (Freiburg i. Br.: Alber).

Jeggle, Utz (1978), 'Alkohol und Industrialisierung,' in *Rausch-Ekstase-Mystik. Grenzformen religiöser Erfahrung*, (ed.) Hubert Cancik (Düsseldorf: Patmos), pp. 78–94.

Johnson, Paul E. (1978), *A Shopkeepers' Millenium: Society and Revivals in Rochester, New York, 1815–1837* (New York: Hill & Wang).

Kaiserliches Statistisches Amt (1910), *Quellen-Material zur Alkoholfrage* (Berlin: Mäßigkeitsverlag).

Kaiserliches Statistisches Amt, Abteilung für Arbeiterstatistik (1909), *Erhebungen von Wirtschaftsrechnungen minderbemittelter Familien im Deutschen Reiche*, Sonderhefte zum *Reichs-Arbeitsblatte*, no. 2 (Berlin: Heymanns).

Kantzenbach, Friedrich Wilhelm (1969), *Geschichte des Protestantismus von 1789–1848*, Evangelische Enzyklopädie, Vol. 21, (eds) Helmut Thielicke and Hans Thimme (Gütersloh: G. Mohn).

Katzenstein, Simon (1907a), 'Die sozialen Beziehungen des Alkoholismus,' *Sozialistische Monatshefte*, vol. 11, no. 6, pp. 463–71.

Katzenstein, Simon (1907b), 'Die deutsche Sozialdemokratie und die Alkoholfrage,' *Sozialistische Monatshefte*, vol. 11, no. 9, pp. 760–7.

Katzenstein, Simon (1909), 'Der Parteitag,' *Der Abstinente Arbeiter*, vol. 7, no. 19, pp. 157–9.

Katzenstein, Simon (n.d. [a]), *Moderne Jugendbewegung und Alkoholfrage* (Berlin: Michaelis).

Katzenstein, Simon (n.d. [b]), *Wofür Kämpfen Wir?* (Berlin: Michaelis).

Kaufhold, Karl Heinrich (1976), 'Handwerk und Industrie 1800–1850,' in *Handbuch der deutschen Wirtschafts- und Sozialgeschichte*, Vol. 2, (eds) Hermann Aubin and Wolfgang Zorn (Stuttgart: Klett), pp. 321–68.

Kautsky, Karl (1890/1a), 'Der Alkoholismus und seine Bekämpfung,' *Die Neue Zeit*, vol. 9, pt 1, nos 27–30, pp. 1–8, 46–55, 77–89, 105–16.

Kautsky, Karl (1890/1b), 'Noch einmal die Alkoholfrage,' *Die Neue Zeit* vol. 9, pt 2, no. 37, pp. 344–54.

Kendis, Joseph B. (1967), 'The Human Body and Alcohol,' in *Alcoholism*, (ed.) David J. Pittman (New York: Harper & Row), pp. 23–30.

Kocka, Jürgen (1979), 'Arbeiterkultur als Forschungsthema: Einleitende Bemerkungen,' *Geschichte und Gesellschaft*, vol. 5, no. 1, pp. 5–11.

Köllmann, Wolfgang, (1974a) 'Bevölkerung und Arbeitskräftepotential in Deutschland 1815–1865,' in id., *Bevölkerung in der industriellen Revolution* (Göttingen: Vandenhoek & Ruprecht), pp. 61–98.

Köllmann, Wolfgang, (1974b) 'Die deutsche Bevölkerung im Industriezeitalter,' in id., *Bevölkerung in der industriellen Revolution* (Göttingen: Vandenhoek & Ruprecht), pp. 35–46.

Köllmann, Wolfgang (1976), 'Bevölkerungsgeschichte 1800–1970,' in *Handbuch der deutschen Wirtschafts- und Sozialgeschichte*, Vol. 2, (eds) Hermann Aubin and Wolfgang Zorn (Stuttgart: Klett), pp. 27–50.

Koselleck, Reinhart (1962), 'Staat und Gesellschaft in Preußen, 1815–1848,' in *Staat und Gesellschaft im deutschen Vormärz, 1815–1848*, (ed.) Werner Conze (Stuttgart: Klett), pp. 79–112.

Krabbe, Wolfgang (1974), *Gesellschaftsveränderung durch Lebensreform* (Göttingen: Vandehoek & Ruprecht).

Krout, John A. (1925), *The Origins of Prohibition* (New York: Knopf).

Kubatz, Alfred (1909), 'Staat und Alkoholsteuern,' *Mäßigkeits-Blätter*, vol. 26, no. 12, pp. 189–91.

Kuczynski, Jürgen (1962), *Die Geschichte der Lage der Arbeiter unter dem Kapitalismus*, 38 vols (East Berlin: Akademie Verlag).

Lambert, W. R. (1975), 'Drink and Work-Discipline in Industrial South Wales, c. 1800–1914,' *Welsh History Review*, vol. 7, no. 3, pp. 289–306.

Laquer, B. (1913), 'Einfluß der sozialen Lage auf den Alkoholismus,' in *Krankheit und soziale Lage*, (eds) M. Mosse and G. Tugendreich (Munich: Lehmann), pp. 473–95.

LaRoche, L. A. (ed.) (1845), *Die Branntweinschrecknisse des neunzehnten Jahrhunderts* (Posen: Busse).

Laurie, Bruce (1980), *Working People of Philadelphia, 1800–1850* (Philadelphia: Temple University Press).

Laves, Theodor (1887), 'Die Entwicklung der Branntweinproduktion und die Branntweinbesteuerung in Deutschland,' *Jahrbuch für Gesetzgebung, Verwaltung und Volkswirtschaft im Deutschen Reich*, vol. 11, no. 3/4, pp. 1193–306.

Lee, J. J. (1978), 'Labour in German Industrialization,' in *The Cambridge Economic History of Europe*, (eds) Peter Mathias and M. M. Postan (Cambridge: Cambridge University Press), Vol. 7, pt 1, pp. 442–91.

Lees, Andrew (1975), 'Debates about the Big City in Germany, 1890–1914,' *Societas*, vol. 5, no. 1, pp. 31–47.

Lees, Andrew (1979), 'Critics of Urban Society in Germany, 1854–1914,' *Journal of the History of Ideas*, vol. 40, no. 1, pp. 61–83.

Levenstein, Adolf (1912), *Die Arbeiterfrage* (Munich: Reinhardt).

Levine, Harry Gene (1978), *Demon of the Middle Class: Self-Control, Liquor and the Ideology of Temperance in 19th Century America* (Ph.D. dissertation, University of California, Berkeley).

Lidtke, Vernon L. (1973), 'Die Kulturelle Bedeutung der Arbeitervereine,' in *Kultureller Wandel im 19. Jahrhundert*, (ed.) Günter Wiegelmann (Göttingen: Vandenhoek & Ruprecht), pp. 146–59.

Liebetrut, Friedrich (1844), *Zur Revision der Nüchternheitsreform* (Berlin: Oehmigke).

Liebig, Justus von (1851), *Chemische Briefe*, 3rd edn (Heidelberg: Winter).

Liese, Wilhelm (1922), *Geschichte der Caritas* (Freiburg i. Br.: Caritas Verlag).

Linse, Ulrich (1972), 'Arbeiterschaft und Geburtenentwicklung im Deutschen Kaiserreich von 1871,' *Archiv für Sozialgeschichte*, vol. 12, pp. 205–71.

Linse, Ulrich (1977), 'Die Lebensreformbewegungen,' *Archiv für Sozialgeschichte*, vol. 17, pp. 538–43.

MacAndrew, Craig and Edgerton, Robert B. (1969), *Drunken Comportment: A Social Explanation* (Chicago, Ill: Aldine).

Mandlebaum, David (1979), 'Alcohol and Culture,' in *Beliefs, Behaviors and Alcoholic Beverages*, (ed.) Mac Marshall (Ann Arbor, Mich: University of Michigan Press), pp. 14–29.

Marquandt, Frederick D. (1975), 'Sozialer Aufstieg, sozialer Abstieg und die Entstehung der Berliner Arbeiterklasse,1806–1848,' *Geschichte und Gesellschaft*, vol. 1, no. 1, pp. 43–77.

Marshall, Mac, (ed.)(1979a), *Beliefs, Behaviors and Alcoholic Beverages: A Cross-Cultural Survey* (Ann Arbor, Mich: University of Michigan Press).

Marshall, Mac (1979b), 'Conclusions,' in *Beliefs, Behaviors and Alcoholic Beverages*, (ed.) Mac Marshall (Ann Arbor, Mich: University of Michigan Press), pp. 451–7.

Martius, Wilhelm (1886), *Die zweite deutsche Mäßigkeitsbewegung, oder der Deutsche Verein gegen den Mißbrauch geistiger Getränke und die Enthaltsamkeitsvereine* (Heilbronn: Henninger).

Martius, Wilhelm (1891), *Handbuch der deutschen Trinker-und Trunksuchtsfrage* (Gotha: Perthes).

Martius, Wilhelm (1901), *Die ältere deutsche Mäßigkeits-und Enthaltsamkeitsbewegung* (Dresden: Böhmert).

Martius, Wilhelm (1902), 'Der Deutsche Verein gegen den Mißbrauch geistiger Getränke und die Abstinenz,' *Mäßigkeits-Blätter*, vol. 19, no. 4, pp. 49–72.

Martius, Wilhelm (1903), 'Randbemerkungen zum Kongress in Bremen,' *Mäßigkeits-Blätter*, vol. 20, no. 5/6, pp. 74–94.

Marx, Karl and Engels, Friedrich (1978), *Manifesto of the Communist Party* [1848], in *The Marx-Engels Reader*, 2nd edn (ed.) Robert C. Tucker (New York: Norton).

Mathias, Peter (1958), 'The Brewing Industry, Temperance and Politics,' *Historical Journal*, vol. 1, no. 2, pp. 97–114.

Mayhew, Henry (1865), *German Life and Manners as Seen in Saxony at the Present Day* (London: W. H. Allen).

Mehring, Franz (1909/10a), 'Der Schnapsboykott,' *Die Neue Zeit*, vol. 28, pt 1, no. 9, pp. 289–91.

Mehring, Franz (1909/10b), 'Gegen den Sektenfanatismus,' *Die Neue Zeit* vol. 28, pt 1, no. 12, pp. 385–8.

Meyer, G. and Loenig, E. (1909), 'Schankgewerbe,' in *Handwörterbuch der Staatswissenschaften*, 3rd edn (Jena: Fischer), Vol. 7, pp. 197–207.

Miethke, Wilhelm (1905), 'Die Abstinenz in der deutschen Arbeiterbewegung,' *Die Alkoholfrage*, vol. 2, pp. 320–6.

Minchinton, Walter (1976), 'Patterns of Demand, 1750–1914,' in *The Industrial Revolution, 1700–1914*, (ed.) Carlo M. Cipolla (Sussex: Harvester Press).

Moleschott, Jacob (1853), *Lehre der Nahrungsmittel für das Volk*, 2nd edn (Erlangen: Enke).

Möller, Karl (1900), 'Der Eintritt der sozialdemokratische Partei in die Mäßigkeitsbewegung,' *Mäßigkeits-Blätter*, vol. 17, no. 1, pp. 8–9.

Möller, Karl (1906), 'Die Branntweinsteuer im Reichstag,' *Mäßigkeits-Blätter*, vol. 23, no. 12, pp. 197–9.

Mombert, Paul (1921), 'Aus der Literatur über die soziale Frage und die Arbeiterbewegung in Deutschland in der ersten Hälfte des 19. Jahrhunderts,' *Archiv für die Geschichte des Sozialismus und der Arbeiterbewegung*, vol. 9, no. 2, pp. 169–236.

Mommsen, Wilhelm (1964), *Größe und Versagen des deutschen Bürgertums*, 2nd edn (Munich: Oldenbourg).

Mosse, George L. (1964), *The Crisis of German Ideology: Intellectual Origins of the Third Reich* (New York: Grosset & Dunlap).

Müller, Richard and Tecklenburg, Ueli (1978), 'Die Medikalisierung des Alkoholismus,' *Drogalkohol*, vol. 2, no. 1, pp. 15–27.

National Academy of Sciences (1974), *Recommended Dietary Allowances*, 8th edn (Washington, DC: National Academy of Sciences).

Niethammer, Lutz, with the assistance of Franz Brüggemeier (1976), 'Wie wohnten Arbeiter im Kaiserreich?' *Archiv für Sozialgeschichte*, vol. 16, pp. 61–134.

Nipperdey, Thomas (1976), 'Verein als soziale Struktur im späten 18. und frühen 19. Jahrhundert,' in id., *Gesellschaft, Kultur, Theorie: gesammelte Aufsätze zur Geschichtswissenschaft* (Göttingen: Vandenhoek & Ruprecht), pp. 174–205.

Noyes, P. H. (1966), *Organization and Revolution: Working Class Associations and the German Revolutions of 1848–1849* (Princeton, NJ: Princeton University Press).

Odegard, Peter H. (1928), *Pressure Politics: The Story of the Anti-Saloon League* (New York: Columbia University Press).

Olhausen (1905), 'Die Frühpolizeistunde im Deutschen Reich,' *Jahrbuch für Gesetzgebung, Verwaltung und Volkswirtschaft im Deutschen Reich*, vol. 29, no. 3, pp. 845–82.

Osterroth, Franz (1960), *Biographisches Lexikon des Sozialismus*, 2 vols (Hanover: Dietz).

Ott, Stephan (1933), *Die politische Anschauungen Johann Carl Bertram Stüves und ihre Beeinflussung durch Justus Möser* (dissertation, Tübingen).

Phillips, Dieter (1977), 'Die Arbeiterjugendbewegung zwischen Arbeiter-und Jugendbewegung' (Zulassungsarbeit, History, University of Freiburg).

Pittman, David J., and Snyder, Charles R. (eds) (1962), *Society, Culture and Drinking Patterns* (New York: Wiley).

Planck, Mathilde (1930), *Ottilie Hoffmann. Ein Beitrag zur Geschichte der deutschen Frauenbewegung* (Bremen: Leuther).

Recum, von (1827), *Ueber freien Gewerbs-Betrieb, besonders in Bezug auf die kleinere landwirtschaftliche Branntwein-Brennerei im Rheinland* (Mannheim: Löffler).

Reichsamt des Innern, *Jahresberichte der Gewerbeaufsichtsbeamten und Bergbehörden.*

Reichstag, *Stenographische Berichte über die Verhandlungen des Reichstags.*

Ringer, Fritz K. (1969), *The Decline of the German Mandarins: The German Academic Community, 1890–1933* (Cambridge, Mass: Harvard University Press).

Ritter, Gerhard A. (1959), *Die Arbeiterbewegung im Wilhelminischen Reich* (Berlin-Dahlem: Colloquium Verlag).

Ritter, Gerhard A. (1978), 'Workers' Culture in Imperial Germany: Problems and Points of Departure of Research,' *Journal of Contemporary History*, vol.13, no. 2, pp. 165–90.

Ritter, Kurt (1955), *Agrarwirtschaft und Agrarpolitik in Kapitalismus* (East Berlin: Deutscher Bauern Verlag).

Roberts, James S. (1980a), 'Der Alkoholkonsum deutscher Arbeiter im 19. Jahrhundert,' *Geschichte und Gesellschaft*, vol. 6, no. 2, pp. 220–42.

Roberts, James S. (1980b), 'Wirtshaus und Politik in der deutschen Arbeiterbewegung,' in *Socialgeschichte der Freizeit*, (ed.) Gerhard Huck (Wuppertal: Hammar), pp. 123–40.

Roberts, James S. (1981), 'Drink and Industrial Work Discipline in 19th Century Germany,' *Journal of Social History*, vol. 15, no. 1, pp. 25–38.

Room, Robin (1983), 'Sociology and the Disease Concept of Alcoholism,' in *Research Advances in Alcohol and Drug Problems*, vol. 7, (New York: Plenum Press) pp. 47–91.

Rorabaugh, W. J. (1979), *The Alcoholic Republic* (Oxford: Oxford University Press).

Rosenberg, Hans (1967), *Große Depression und Bismarckzeit: Wirtschaftsablauf, Gesellschaft und Politik in Mitteleuropa* (Berlin: de Gruyter).

Rosenberg, Hans (1972), 'Theologischer Rationalismus und vormärzlicher Vulgärliberalismus,' in id., *Politische Denkströmungen im deutschen Vormärz* (Göttingen: Vandenhoek & Ruprecht), pp. 18–50.

Roßnick, F. (1915), *Deutsche Nüchternheitsbewegung* (Hamm/Westf.: Beer & Thiemann).

Roth, Guenther (1963), *The Social Democrats in Imperial Germany* (Totowa, NJ: Bedminster Press).

Rühle, Otto (1971), *Illustrierte Kultur- und Sittensgeschichte des Proletariats* (Berlin: Neuer Deutscher Verlag, 1930; reprint edn, Frankfurt a/M: Verlag Neue Kritik).

Rumbarger, John J. (1968), *The Social Origins and Function of the Political Temperance*

*Movement in the Reconstruction of American Society, 1825–1917* (Ph.D. dissertation, University of Pennsylvania).

Sagarra, Eda (1977), *A Social History of Germany, 1648–1914* (New York: Holmes & Meier).

Scharfe, Martin (1980), *Die Religion des Volkes. Kleine Kultur- und Sozialgeschichte des Pietismus* (Gütersloh: Gütersloher Verlagshaus Mohn).

Schivelbusch, Wolfgang (1980), *Das Paradies, der Geschmack und die Vernunft. Eine Geschichte der Genußmittel* (Munich: Hanser).

Schmoller, Gustav (1883), 'Der deutsche Verein gegen den Mißbrauch geistiger Getränke und die Frage der Schankkonzessionen,' *Zeitschrift für Wirtschafts-und Sozialwissenschaft*, vol. 7, no. 4, pp. 1347–66.

Schnabel, Franz (1951), *Deutsche Geschichte im Neunzehnten Jahrhundert*, 2nd edn, vol. 4: *Die Religiösen Kräfte* (Freiburg i. Br.: Herder).

Schorske, Carl E. (1955), *German Social Democracy, 1905–1917* (Cambridge, Mass: Harvard University Press).

Schröder, Wilhelm (1910), *Handbuch der Sozialdemokratischen Parteitage* (Munich: Birk).

Schüler, Fridolin (1884), *Über die Ernährungsweise der arbeitenden Klassen in der Schweiz und die dadurch bedingte Ausbreitung des Alkoholismus* (Bern: Schmidt).

Seld, Albert von (1865), *Sechzig Jahre, oder ein Leben an Bauern- und Fürstenhöfen, unter Säufern, Kindern und Verbrechern* (Leipzig: Bredt).

Shanahan, William O. (1954), *German Protestants Meet the Social Question* (Notre Dame: University of Notre Dame Press).

Sheehan, James J. (1966), *The Career of Lujo Brentano: A Study of Liberalism and Social Reform in Imperial Germany* (Chicago, Ill: University of Chicago Press).

Sheehan, James J. (1978), *German Liberalism in the Nineteenth Century* (Chicago, Ill; University of Chicago Press).

Simon, Ferdinand (1890/1a), 'Zur Alkoholfrage,' *Die Neue Zeit*, vol. 9, pt 1, no. 15, pp. 483–90.

Simon, Ferdinand (1890/1b), 'Herrn Kautsky zur Entgegen,' *Die Neue Zeit*, vol. 9, pt 2, no. 36, pp. 309–15.

Smith, Timothy (1955), *Revivalism and Social Reform in Mid-Nineteenth Century America* (New York: Abingdon Press).

Sozialdemokratische Partei Deutschlands, *Protokoll über die Verhandlungen des Parteitages der Sozialdemokratischen Partei Deutschlands* (Berlin: Vorwärts, [annually]).

Sozialdemokratische Partei Deutschlands (1907), *Handbuch für sozialdemokratische Wähler anläßlich der Reichstag Auflösung 1906* (Berlin: Vorwärts).

Sozialdemokratische Partei Deutschlands (1911), *Handbuch für sozialdemokratische Wähler. Der Reichstag 1907–1911* (Berlin: Vorwärts).

Statistisches Amt der Stadt Berlin, *Statistisches Jahrbuch der Stadt Berlin*.

Statistisches Amt der Stadt Berlin (1904), *Lohnermittelungen und Haushaltsrechnungen der minderbemittelten Bevölkerung im Jahre 1903*, Berliner Statistik, no. 3 (Berlin: Stankiewicz).

Stearns, Peter N. (1970), 'Adaptation to Industrialization: German Workers as a Test Case,' *Central European History*, vol. 3, no. 4 pp. 303–31.

Stehr, A. H. (1903), *Alkoholgenuß und wirtschaftliche Arbeit* (Jena: Fischer).

Stein, Hans (1936), 'Pauperismus und Assoziation: soziale Tatsachen und Ideen auf dem westeuropäische Kontinent von Ende des 18. bis zur Mitte des 19. Jahrhunderts, unter besondere Berüchsichtigung des Rheingebiets,' *International Review of Social History*, vol. 1, no. 1, pp. 1–20.

Stern, Fritz (1961), *The Politics of Cultural Despair: A Study in the Rise of the Germanic Ideology* (Berkeley, Calif: University of California Press).

Stern, J. P. (1975), *Hitler: The Führer and the People* (Berkeley, Calif: University of California Press).

Stolleis, Michael (1981), ' "Von dem grewlichen Laster der Trunckenheit:" Trinkverbote im 16. und 17. Jahrhundert,' in *Rausch und Realität: Drogen im Kulturvergleich,* (ed.) Gisela Völger, *Ethnologica*, Neue Folge, Vol. 9 (Cologne: Gesellschaft für Völkerkunde), pp. 98–105.

Strauss und Torney, Carl C. H. von (1904), 'Die Alkoholfrage und die Sozialdemokratie,' *Mäßigkeits-Blätter*, vol. 21, no. 10, pp. 156–7.

Struve, Emil (1893), *Die Entwicklung des Bayerischen Braugewerbes im neunzehnten Jahrhundert*, Staats- und Sozialwissenschaftliche Forschungen, no. 12 (Leipzig: Duncker & Humblot).

Struve, Emil (1909), 'Bier, Bierbrauerei und Bierbesteuerung,' in *Handwörterbuch der Staatwissenschaften*, 3rd edn (Jena: Fischer), Vol. 2, pp. 1038–82.

Stubbe, Christian (1905), *Das Trinken in Schleswig-Holstein* (Berlin: Mäßigkeitsverlag).

Stubbe, Christian (1906), *Die ältere Mäßigkeits- und Enthaltsamkeitsbewegung in Schleswig-Holstein* (Berlin: Mäßigkeitsverlag).

Stubbe, Christian (1908), *Der Deutsche Verein gegen den Mißbrauch geistiger Getränke, 1883–1908* (Berlin: Mäßigkeitsverlag).

Stubbe, Christian (1911), *Hamburg und der Branntwein: Die ältere Mäßigkeits- und Enthaltsamkeitsbewegung in Hamburg* (Berlin: Mäßigkeitsverlag).

Stubbe, Christian (1933), *Der deutsche Verein gegen den Alkoholismus* (Berlin: Verlag 'Auf der Wacht').

Stubbe, Christian (n.d.), *Das alte Bremen gegen den Brantwein (n.p.).*

Stürmer, A. (n.d.), *Die Stellung der Arbeiterpress zur Alkoholfrage* (Berlin: Michaelis).

Stursberg, H. (1877), *Die Bekämpfung der Völlerei* (Düsseldorf: n.p.).

Stüve, Gustav (1900), *Johann Carl Bertram Stüve nach Briefen und persönlicher Erinnerungen* 2 vols (Hanover: Hahn'schen Buchhandlung).

*Tagesblatt der dritten Generalversammlung der deutschen Vereine gegen das Branntweintrinken*, 1847 (Brunswick: Waisenhaus-Buchdruckerei).

Teuteberg, Hans J. (1976), 'Die Nahrung sozialen Unterschichten im späten 19. Jahrhundert,' in *Ernährung und Ernährungslehre im 19. Jahrhundert*, (ed.) Edith Heischkel-Artelt (Göttingen: Vandenhoek & Ruprecht), pp. 205–87.

Teuteberg, Hans J. and Wiegelmann, Günter (1972), *Der Wandel der Nahrungsgewohnheiten unter dem Einfluß der Industrialisierung* (Göttingen: Vandenhoek & Ruprecht).

Thomas, Dorothy Swaine (1927), *Social Aspects of the Business Cycle* (New York: Knopf).

Thompson, F. M. L. (1981), 'Social Control in Victorian Britain,' *Economic History Review*, vol. 34, no. 2, pp. 189–208.

Thun, Alphons (1879), *Die Industrie am Niederrhein und ihrer Arbeiter*, pt 1, Staats- und Sozialwissenschaftliche Forschungen, no. 3, pt 2 (Leipzig: Duncker & Humblot).

Tiesmeyer, [Ludwig] (1902/12), *Die Erweckungsbewegung in Deutschland während des 19. Jahrhunderts*, 4 vols (Cassel: Röttger).

Tilly, Charles, Tilly, Louise and Tilly, Richard (1975), *The Rebellious Century, 1830–1930* (Cambridge, Mass: Harvard University Press).

Timberlake, James H. (1966), *Prohibition and the Progressive Movement, 1900–1920* (Cambridge, Mass: Harvard University Press).

de Tocqueville, Alexis (1945), *Democracy in America*, 2 vols (New York: Vintage).

Tramsen, Eckhard (1973), *Bibliographie zur geschichtlichen Entwicklung der Arbeiterjugendbewegung bis 1945* (Frankfurt a/M: Verlag Roter Stern).

Tyrrell, Robert Ian (1979), *Sobering Up: From Temperance to Prohibition in Antebellum America, 1800–1860* (Westport, Conn: Greenwood).

United States Department of Health, Education and Welfare (1973), *Alcohol and Health: Report from the Secretary of Health, Education and Welfare* (New York: Scribner's).

Valentin, Veit (1930/1), *Geschichte der deutschen Revolution von 1848–49*, 2 vols (Berlin: Ullstein).

Vandervelde, Emile (1901/2), 'Die oekonomische Faktoren des Alkoholismus,' *Die Neue Zeit*, vol. 20, pt 1, no. 22, pp. 740–51.

Vandervelde, Emile (1970), *Alkohol, Religion, Kunst: Drei Sozialistische Untersuchungen*, trans, Engelbert Pernerstorfer (Jena: Fischer).

Virchow, Rudolf (1879), *Gesammelte Abhandlungen zur öffentliche Medizin und der Seuchenlehre*, 2 vols (Berlin: Hirschwald).

Vogel, Walter (ed.) (1959/60), *Johann Carl Bertram Stüve, Briefe*, 2 vols (Göttingen: Vandenhoek & Ruprecht).

Vogt, Irmgard (1981), 'Cultural Beliefs and Government Propensities to Control or Ignore Drinking Problems: An Historical Comparison between Germany and the United States,' *The Drinking and Drug Practices Surveyor*, no. 17, pp. 4–8.

Völger, Gisela (ed.), *Rausche und Realität: Drogen im Kulturvergleich, Ethnologica*, Neue Folge, Vol. 9 (Cologne: Gesellschaft für Völkerkunde).

Walkowitz, Daniel (1978), *Worker City, Company Town: Iron and Cotton-Worker Protest in Troy and Cohoes, New York, 1855–84* (Urbana; Ill: University of Illinois Press).

Walters, Ronald G. (1978), *American Reformers, 1815–1860* (New York: Hill & Wang).

Webb, Sidney and Webb, Beatrice (1963), *History of Liquor Licensing in England* (1903; repr. London: Frank Cass).

Weber, Max (1892) *Die Lage der Arbeiter im ost-elbischen Deutschland* Schriften des Vereins für Sozialpolitik, no. 55 (Leipzig: Duncker & Humblot).

Weber, Max (1958), *The Protestant Ethic and the Spirit of Capitalism*, trans. Talcott Parsons (New York: Schribner's).

Wehler, Hans-Ulrich (1975), *Das Deutsche Kaiserreich, 1871–1918*, 2nd edn (Göttingen: Vandenhoek & Ruprecht).

Weymann, Konrat (1915), *Der Kampf gegen die Alkoholschäden – eine Kulturaufgabe* (Berlin: Mäßigkeits-Verlag).

White, Dan (1976), *The Splintered Party: National Liberalism in Hessen and the Reich, 1867–1918* (Cambridge, Mass: Harvard University Press).

Witt, Peter-Christian (1970), *Die Finanzpolitik des Deutschen Reichs von 1903 bis 1913* (Lübeck: Matthiesen).

Wlassak, Rudolf (1923), 'Der Alkoholismus,' *Handbuch der Hygiene*, (eds)

M. Rubner, M. von Gruber and M. Ficker (Leipzig: Hirzel), vol. 4, pt 3, pp. 117–221.

Wörishoffer, Wilhelm (1891), *Die soziale Lage der Fabrikarbeiter in Mannheim und dessen nächster Umgebung* (Karlsruhe: Thiergarten).

Wurm, Emanuel (1912), *Die Alkoholgefahr, ihre Ursachen und ihre Bekämpfung* (Hamburg: Dubber).

Zahn-Harnack, Agnes von (1928), *Die Frauenbewegung. Geschichte, Probleme, Ziele* (Berlin: Deutsche Buch-Gemeinschaft).

Zmarzlik, Hans-Günther (1963), 'Der Sozialdarwinismus in Deutschland als geschichtliches Problem,' *Vierteljahrshefte für Zeitgeschichte*, vol. 11, no. 3, pp. 246–73.

Zmarzlik, Hans-Günther (1976), 'Das Kaiserreich in neuer Sicht?' *Historische Zeitschrift*, vol. 222, no. 1, pp. 105–26.

# Index

# SHAKESPEARE & SON

## CHAPTER TWENTY-THREE

THE citizens of Stratford had begun to stop talking about that Willy and poor Anne when the two of them turned up brightly on the morning of the twenty-sixth of May, riding with a company of young fellows who called themselves Shakespeare's Boys.

"Damn me if it isna that Willy!"

"And poor Anne!"

"What's that she carries in the pannier?"

"Damn me if it's not a wee baby!"

"And who are these fellows with 'em? More rogues to knock our constables about?"

"Say they're Shakespeare's Boys."

"Shakespeare's Boys! Players?"

"Bah, look like stable-boys to me. Who is he to have a company?"

"Ill-beseeming, ill-gotten, and illegal."

But the happy children just coming out to school believed it, and went shouting with the parents, the boys, and two or three other parents to the house of Dr. Haycroft, where they knocked and cried for him to come out.

"A christening! A sprinkling!" cried the boys.

"A new citizen of England, Sir Henry," explained the new father.

Dr. Haycroft was not able to speak very well for a few moments. But when he did speak he spoke a good deal. While he was speaking the new father had time to go round to the house of his parents and roust them both out, with his sister and brothers, and with these allies and many neighbours all clacking their tongues at the father of this new female child Susanna with the red hair, the good preacher could do nothing but agree to the proper baptizing of the small traveller so newly arrived in England.

213

"Susanna, h'm," said Dr. Haycroft. "Her godmother's name? Where is the godmother?"

"O la, me!" piped Judy Sadler, tripping forward to take the baby, a complicated performance because she had first to get rid of the two of her own she was carrying. The dreamy Hamlet, however, took them, looking confused. Mine? H'm . . .

"But you are not Susanna, you are Judith," said Dr. Haycroft, who was getting to be quite an old man.

"The name of her patron saint, Sir Henry," the new father gently explained.

"Zounds, the day she was begotten!" said Mr. Shakespeare. "And be sure you spell our surname with a whoreson *e*."

Then he burst out laughing, put his arm round the father, and they went ho-hoing from the preacher's house to the church, followed by a goodly company.

After the girl was given her name they all went to the Angel and had a large nourishing dinner, which consisted of a peacock, a pheasant, some prawns, a gooseberry pie, a few slices of buck in beef, some kid with a pudding, some hartichokes, and sufficient quantities of May wine to make them all as merry as crickets. And Mrs. Shakespeare gave the best imitation of a happy grandmother that had ever been seen in that part of the country.

End of *Shakespeare & Son*,
first in a Trilogy to be called
*The Silver Falcon*

# Shakespeare

# & Son

*A Novel by*

EDWARD FISHER

ABELARD-SCHUMAN
London   New York   Toronto

| LONDON | NEW YORK | TORONTO |
| --- | --- | --- |
| Abelard-Schuman | Abelard-Schuman | Abelard-Schuman |
| Limited | Limited | Canada Limited |
| 8 King Street | 6 West 57th Street | 896 Queen St., W. |

To Betty, who had faith in this book even

before I knew it was going to be written.

# PREFACE

*Sir, it is a mystery.*
*Measure for Measure*

This is not a biography, but a novel. I hope that when you have finished it the son of the Stratford alderman will seem more mysterious than ever.

All the details it is possible to know about his outward life will be found in the works of scholars who have devoted their lives to the study of Shakespeare. But a novelist "is obliged to enter into the inward life . . . an obligation from which the biographer is mercifully free," as Marchette Chute said.[1]

This little book is an attempt to imagine what it was like in Stratford-on-Avon when the eldest son of John Shakespeare was beginning the long war he had to win before he could even hope to conquer his greatest antagonist — himself.

The necessity for the first war will be appreciated when his natural antagonists are revealed. These inevitably were his father, his mother, his teachers, his preachers, his friends, and anyone else who tried to control him or direct him beyond the limits of his own conscience, which was just as great a genius as he was. His chief antagonist, however, was that passionate witch who haunted his boyhood — Anne Hathaway by name. She could only be conquered, temporarily, by marriage. The mystery of that marriage has fascinated many generations of biographers, who have not been as kind to Anne as Shakespeare was at the time. My Anne Hathaway is not so much the daughter of a Shottery farmer, who married suddenly, at an out-of-town church, in a forbidden season, with no time for the banns, a boy with no money or prospects who was eight years younger than herself. My Anne is rather the bright vision he carried in his mind which made it so difficult to appreciate the wise, kind, incredibly patient woman he inadvertently married. One thing about Shakespeare's Anne that has been neglected is to pay

[1] *Shakespeare Quarterly* V, i, p.90.

her her honest due as the woman who set him free to win his greatest victory of all. There is a tradition that Anne was a shrew, but it is too logical for me to believe. And so the only original thing I can claim about my portrait of Shakespeare the husband is that he loved his wife.

But far greater battles are still ahead, to be published as soon as may be. Next to follow will be TWO LOVES I HAVE, an attempt to imagine what it was like for a "lame, poor, despised" young man to find the door to success in a despised profession, against all the attempts of the righteous to destroy it even before he could enter it. In my account of two fascinating people who may (or may not) have entered his life in the difficult years between 1583 and 1593, I shall attempt my own imaginative solution to a mystery which has baffled the biographers of Shakespeare, and perhaps always will. Who was the Dark Lady of the Sonnets? Who was Mr. W. H.?

I think he invented the lady, but there was nothing to prevent him from going out afterwards and finding her.

As for Mr. W. H., there was at least one man of power he certainly would have tried to please. This was Mr. William Honing, Clerk Controller in Her Majesty's Office of the Revels. Many biographers, and less scrupulous people, have diligently sought "A man in hew all *Hews* in his controwling," but here is one man who really had them.

Until that story of "a trial of friendship" which may (or may not) have been alluded to in Ben Jonson's *Bartholomew Fair*, we must get the first war over with.

Date when it begins: St. Susanna's Day, August 11th, 1579.

Time: Three o'clock in the morning.

Light: The moon.

## ACKNOWLEDGEMENT

My thanks are due to Dr. Louis B. Wright, Director of the Folger Shakespeare Library, for welcoming a novelist to that paradise for scholars, and to Miss Dorothy E. Mason, administering angel there.

For inspiration I must thank Harold Cantor, the ideal editor, who encouraged me to write this book, and Ernest Brennecke, the ideal critic, who said (*Shakespeare Quarterly*, I, 4) that if you must write a novel on this mysterious subject "it is better to throw caution to the dogs and improvise freely . . . Just have fun!"

Whether it has been any fun for the fascinating lady who asked me if I was interested in Shakespeare, she has certainly listened patiently to my answer, which has been going on now for about fifteen years. So this book belongs to Betty King Fisher, who has been the constant and hopeful inspiration for *Shakespeare & Son* from the day we met.

BOOK ONE
# THE OBSTINATE
# ALDERMAN


## CHAPTER ONE

T HE little town of Stratford-on-Avon lay sleeping under the moon. The noble river gleamed, the dark trees rustled, a pleasant breeze blew over the roofs.

It was the eleventh of August in 1579, the Feast of St. Susanna the Virgin.

How innocent the little houses looked beneath the rustling trees! How good and peaceful while everybody was asleep!

But everybody was not asleep.

Out of an upstairs window in the house of John Shakspere the alderman peeked the face of a youth with a high brow, large dreaming eyes, and auburn hair which shone like a pot in the spangled light of the lopsided moon.

Anybody in Stratford would have recognized that face at once. It was Willy, the alderman's eldest son, weighing his heavy thoughts between earth and heaven while sensible people were asleep. Already well into his sixteenth year, he still had accomplished nothing. He was a disappointment to his father, a torture to his teachers, a puzzle to his preachers, and a scandal to his friends, who all thought they had a right to expect better things of him.

He sighed deeply, his chin upon his hand. An owl hooted in the garden.

It was dark down there. He could hardly see the dovecote roof below. Water was dripping from the thatch and from the orchard trees.

The owl hooted again.

Willy hooted in answer, then climbed up on the window-sill and jumped, reaching for the apple-tree branch on the way down. It broke right off in his hands, and he fell all the way to the dovecote roof, rolled down it and crashed to the ground, hearing the imprisoned mournful lovers wake up and begin to bustle and hoo-hoo, and feeling the wet leaves, broken twigs, and a few apples falling on him from the tree.

1

Creeping toward him from beneath a mulberry bush came a stocky youth whose fair hair gleamed in the moonlight.

"Get up, Willy, for God's sake!" he whispered. It was Dick Field, the eldest son of Henry Field the tanner.

"Are you an angel? When did I die?" murmured the fallen son of the alderman, spitting out leaves.

"What's the matter with you *now?*"

"Meditating upon the attributes of angels. I think they smell to heaven."

"Pox on thy nose. Get up."

"Alas!" groaned Willy. "Alive again?" And he began systematically testing his joints.

"Nick Bott's in the stocks."

"Oh, oh, tell him I'm dead, and pile the dust on me."

"I said you'd help get him out," said Dick, hauling him to his feet.

"But how? How?"

"You'll think of something," said Dick, dragging him out by the back gate and around into Swine Lane, where a stinking trickle of slops and slime shimmered between the privy and the pigpen.

"Ah, poetry!" said the son of the alderman, preparing to make a speech.

"Pox on thy poetry. Poor Nick will be hanged for sure this time."

"I have often predicted it."

"Come on, come on," said Dick, urging his schoolmate along past Dick Hornby's blacksmith shop. "What the devil makes thee halt so hard?"

"Alas, the silver sockets of my golden bones are all unseated from their hinges," Willy groaned, trying a few experimental limps to see which was most horrible.

"You'll never make a Queen's soldier now."

They turned into Henley Street, first passing the house of William Smith the haberdasher, for whom John Shakspere had named his first-born son, in the way of good business, though no profit yet. Next came Dick Hornby's house, then Wedgwood the tailor's, who slept lightly, for he had a young wife, and then the long staring house of wattle and daub in which the large and swelling Shakspere family lived. A low passageway led be-

tween living quarters and glove-shop to the stables back in
Swine Lane, where the alderman kept three horses. Over the
shop, above the penthouse roof, hung a creaking sign:

JOHN SHAKSPERE

GLOVER

An old horn lantern hung by the door, casting its feeble rays
over the sagging walls and into the winking windows behind
which slept the parents of the young heir to all the thumbs and
fingers of the glove business, who was now limping by, assisted
by his friend Troublesome Richard.

"Woe, woe," said William the Worthless as he and his friend
dragged their wavering shadows along Henley Street in the
mellow moonlight. "Alas, poor people, for virtue passes by
them, and they do not regard it."

"They caught him stealing a roe deer."

"Who?"

"Nick Bott."

"God save me from my fat-witted friends."

"Thy father's a justice."

"And Nick Bott's is a thief."

"Wake him, Willy, he's a good fellow. Oh, he roars at times."

"No, no, let justice sleep, or we'll all hang," said the son of
the alderman as they crossed the market square, with their long
shadows going before them to join the deeper shadows of the
lock-up, which was called the Cage, with the stocks and whip-
ping-post before it.

"Whose deer was it?" Willy asked.

"Sir Thomas Lucy's."

"Oh, he did wrong."

"Can young men not live? Must we be hemmed about with
grim and horrible laws? Is there no freedom?"

"None, Bloody Richard. Where's the deer?"

"Ah, the damned keeper has it, and there is no justice under
heaven."

"You shall find it, my son, with a little asking." The voice of
the alderman's son grew rich with unction and sorrow. "With
thy too much blood and too little brain, though an honest fellow enough, and one that loves quails, I fear me that thou, in
thy youth, art little better than one of the wicked."

"Pox on all catbirds, all apes, and all mockers! What art thou but another counterfeited lump of —"

"Of sinfully miscarried flesh, I know it. Well, I shall repent, and say my prayers."

"I dropped a bottle in the path of the constable, Willy."

"What, of old Hugh Pyggin?"

"And he's drunk himself asleep."

A wild yelp of laughter, quickly muffled, came from the son of the alderman. An answering grunt came from the stinking darkness of the bear pit.

"Where's the constable now?"

"Come," whispered Dick. They tiptoed past the bear pit, in which Alfred, the town bear, was kept.

"Hey, Catbird!" came a piercing whisper from the darkness by the Cage.

Two disembodied hands in a moon ray wagged a greeting.

"I'm sorry to see thee pinned, Bottom," Willy said, tiptoeing to the stocks.

"What's the time, Catbird?" asked Nick Bott. Now his head was visible, with its wild locks, scraggly beard, and glittering eyes.

"Three o'clock."

"By the moon? I steal by the moon," said the prisoner.

"By the Market House clock, under which you will hang."

"Fine friends I have. The mouldy rogues ran away. I'll starve ere I rob a foot farther."

"Why not join me and we'll be players, Nick?" said Willy.

"A plague on all players, I say," mumbled young Bott. "Show me where the money is."

"In London, where the playhouses are. I might run off and join 'em if you would."

"Get me out first, Catbird, and I will consider it."

"Good, I will consider trying," said Willy, wandering among the deep, dark shadows beneath the Market House roof.

He stumbled against a large, well-padded form.

"Hey, who's this dead man?"

Young Bott yawned. "He's not dead yet, he's drunk. And gave me not a drop. Is that justice?"

"Look not for justice in nature, Nick, or you'll run mad. Who's the sleeper?"

Dick Field bent down and felt the fat face of the sleeping man. "Hugh Pyggin, as drunk as life."

"A piece of him," said Bott. "Catbird, get me out. Wake the justice, call the court, plead my case, put me to bed."

"This is a sad lesson to youth," said the son of the justice meditatively, examining the sleeping constable with practiced hands. "I am afraid if my father sits on you, there'll be a drawing and quartering of old Billy Bott's boy. You know he has been patient with all the lads who follow you, save one."

"Who? What one?"

"Me, Nick, me," Willy said, cautiously unhooking a large key from the belt of the sleeping constable.

"Hey, is it his knife?" muttered the prisoner.

"A better engine, to knick thee hence, I hope."

"Thou art the very genius of simplicity," said the prisoner with a windy sigh. And he chuckled with joy as the son of the justice tiptoed to the stocks and began clanking the key in the lock. Young Nick Bott, too young to be good, for he had three better brothers, all older, was going to escape the consequences again. If he had only had a father as respected as Willy's he might not have caught it so many times; but old Billy Bott had been kicked out of Council many years ago, for swearing, cheating, and stealing everybody's property he could get into his lawmanly hands. And everybody suspected his youngest son of villainy even when he tried, sometimes, to be good.

"I am sorry they have treated thee so badly, Nick."

"Quick, Cat, scratch me out of here."

"The lock is rusty. Old Fossicar ought to oil it."

"Hey, I hear the Watch," said Dick.

And indeed the feeble thumping of their staves upon the stones gave ample warning to all naughty people that the old men of the Watch were coming. No able-bodied men ever volunteered for this heavy duty; it was the enforced and feeble elders of the town who yelped the hours at night, and trailed their long bills over the paving stones.

"Oh!" groaned Nick, as his wrists and ankles came free. "I'll be lame for life."

"Take thy freedom, go, run," said Willy, lifting the lank and limping Bott.

"Where'll we meet?"

"In Snitterfield Wold. Now fade, empty thyself on the air," said Willy as the feeble lantern of the leading watchman came bobbing round the Market House.

"Come *on*, Willy!" said Dick.

"In a minute," said his friend, now dragging the heavy body of the constable to the stocks and propping him up in the ancient and dishonourable position.

"They'll catch thee!"

"Then run, run, save thy sinful carcass," said Willy, clamping the ponderous jaws of the instrument of justice upon the ankles and wrists of the constable.

"Why do you always have to do better than good, and worse than worst?" moaned Dick, unable to go and leave him.

The watchmen were stopping beneath the roof of the Market House to have a little drink together.

"Now which is the constable, which is the thief?" asked the son of the alderman, admiring the constable sleeping peacefully in the stocks. "Is it not written that the humble shall be exalted? And that a haughty spirit goeth before a fall?"

"This is no time for speeches," Dick said, pulling at him.

"It is always time for speeches," Willy answered.

"Hey! They're coming!"

And off they went down the High Street, into the merciful mist that was beginning to roll over the roofs from the river.

Two little old watchmen came plodding into the market square.

"A quiet night, neighbour," said old Tom Gybbs, setting down his lantern.

"A peaceful night, blessed be God," said Ned Bassett, the other watchman.

They sat down by the bear pit to rest awhile, and to visit with Alfred.

Skimming along like swallows, Willy and Dick had now passed the corn market and the swine market and were heading for Dead Lane, a street of barns that were splendid to hide in, of old gardens now overgrown with weeds, very good to crawl under, and a haunted house that had been closed up for years. A narrow stream, little better than a ditch, ran along this lane all the way to the river. The two escaping friends could smell it even before they came to it, for the tenants of the big houses on Chapel Street threw their refuse into it, and it was foul.

"Hey! Not in there," Dick muttered, as his companion suddenly disappeared through a narrow opening in a crumbling wall.

The mewing of a cat was Willy's answer.

So into the mouldy garden the son of the tanner went.

He peered all round the ghostly garden for his friend. "Willy, Willy!" he called.

A fearful groan answered him, from beneath a hedge. Dick sprang back and bumped into a tree.

"Come in here, ye cuckoo," said his friend, reaching up and grabbing him.

"Damn thee, Willy, don't be a ghost here," said Dick, his teeth clacking together.

"Repent thy sins, marry the wench, patch up thy body for heaven," said Willy like a hedge-priest, lying back against a mossy stump with a happy sigh. "Oh, Dick, what a lovely seat! Could we buy it, some time?"

"Who wants this filthy old ruin? It's haunted."

"All these barns too, this garden, the old horse mill. Marry her, Bloody Richard, and live here."

"Marry who-who?"

"Lizzie Fisher loves thee."

Dick groaned.

"She'll have all old John's property, and his manure piles."

"Oh, curse thee, Willy, why did we ever get Nick out again? And lock Hugh Pyggin in the stocks?"

"Think of the future, Dickie-bird. Shall we be poulterers, full of fleas and feathers? Shall we be cogging lawyers, and own these great warehouses, and be rich? What are we to be?"

"I fear me only what my father will say when he finds out from Hugh Pyggin that we —"

"What if we were haberdashers, little Richard? Think of the knotheads, hogsheads, loggerheads —" His voice suddenly went away downstairs into the cellar, and he was gloomy with the hopelessness of ever escaping from such narrow destinies as were open to them in this trading town.

"Willy."

"Alas, yes."

"Willy, what's that moving there?"

"Where?"

"By the haunted house."

The son of the alderman looked up at the shadowy wall of the old timber structure that had once belonged to the famous Clopton family, but was now owned by an absentee landlord named Underhill. Did forbidden priests meet behind those shuttered windows, as they did in so many country manors, to say Masses in dead of night? Mr. Underhill was a secret Catholic. The old house had a ghost too — poor Charlotte Clopton had been buried alive in the plague year of 1564 and they had found her skeleton pressed against the door of the tomb. The year Willy was born, too — he often woke up sweating and gasping from some dream of the poor ghost.

His powerful right hand suddenly clutched Dick by the arm. "Hark!"

"Whu-what is it?"

"Creeping forms there, by the prior's cottage!"

"It is thy wormy imagination."

"Hist!"

"Now what does thy diseased imagination see?"

"A light in the gable window!"

"It is thy haunted brain. Let us go home, sweet Willy."

"Come on!"

"Hark!" said old Tom Gybbs, setting down his lantern.

"O Lord, what is it now?" moaned little Ned Bassett.

"Is it not a light in old New Place?"

"Precious Master, where?"

"There, neighbour, there."

"I see it not," said Ned Bassett as the moon went behind a cloud. Pale rays streamed out from it through the mist, a breeze sprang up and wagged the trees, a shutter clattered, a voice cried out at the Market Cross.

"See, see, see, see!"

"O Jesu, what does thy diseased eye see now?"

"Art thou blind, neighbour? O Lord, look there!"

"Let us be about our lawful business and not seeing behind every garden wall!"

"Under the quince tree! Oh!"

"How am I to keep from tripping over thy staff and falling into holes in this street if I must be looking under every quince tree and thorn bush?"

"I think I heard a voice cry, 'Burglary!'"

"Then let him duly report it to the justice of the peace in good time and order," said old Mr. Bassett.

The two aged watchmen picked up their lanterns and turned the corner into Dead Lane.

"I do not think I like this duty, neighbour," said Mr. Gybbs.

"Thou must learn not to hear and see what does not become a dutiful man," said Mr. Bassett.

The moon died in the mist. A wind came over the foggy fields, bringing rain from the Cotswolds.

"What's that?" quavered Mr. Gybbs.

An owl hooted somewhere in the garden of New Place. A cat came creeping out of the bushes and crossed their path.

"Murder! Help! Flat buggery as ever was committed!" cried a voice from the direction of the Market Cross.

Quickly the two little watchmen turned and ran in the opposite direction.

"Hark!" said Mrs. Shakspere, sitting up in the second-best bed.

Sighs and mutters came from her sleeping husband.

"Wake up, John!" she said, shaking the large powerful body of the solid, darkly sleeping man she had married twenty-two years ago against her better judgement.

"Is a man never to get his sleep?" groaned the alderman.

"Is a man never to wake to the truth?" cried his wife, eager to begin the old complaint again. Alas, she was a lady, daughter of one of the finest families in England, or so it had become in her bitter dreams. Had not the Ardens once owned all this green country roundabout? And who were the Shaksperes? Everybody knew they were nobody. "Oh, if I had married a gentleman, and not the son of my father's shepherd! Alas, we will all die in this mouldy old smoky house."

"Then let us all lie down and be about it," grumbled Mr. Shakspere, putting a pillow over his head.

But she snatched it away. Then she shook the second-best

bed until the huge old structure of uneasy sleep and troubled dreams began to creak and groan.

"Go to bed!" growled her husband.

"I heard a cry," said Mrs. Shakspere. "It is thy duty as justice of the peace to wake up and listen."

"I resign my last office in this ungrateful town tomorrow."

"A cry! I heard a dreadful cry!"

"Who cried, woman?"

"Someone cried, 'Murder!' "

"Where?"

"In the High Street," said Mrs. Shakspere, the music of grief singing in her beautiful voice as she stood gracefully in the doorway, wringing her hands.

"Then we will hang him in the High Street tomorrow," said Mr. Shakspere, turning over with a groan.

Mrs. Shakspere ran sobbing into her eldest son's room and threw herself upon the bed. "Wake up, Willy, and help thy mother," she moaned. "I married a fool, a fool. My father advised me against it."

Suddenly her writhing hands touched the bare pillow.

"My boy is gone! He has run away! It is all the fault of his father!" she cried, running back into the room where her husband was now climbing out of bed in desperation.

"Now plague take a town that cannot keep Christian order in the streets or a quiet tongue in the house of a tired businessman!" he groaned, as his wife shook him again. Her long black hair streamed over her shoulders in the faint light from the lantern above his door. She was still slender, and had the ruins of her beauty; but he was not slender, he was not beautiful, and he could not find his breeches.

"You've driven him from me at last! Are you happy now?" whispered his wife.

"No!" bawled John.

"Think of the neighbours, if you don't think of me."

"O God, why did I not run off with the Coventry players and be a rogue of the highways and a stallion of the stews?"

"Much you could do there," said his wife. "Are you going after my lovely son and bring him back to me?"

"Let me but get my hands on him and I'll lame him with blows from one end to the other," said her husband, suddenly finding his breeches and nearly tearing them apart in his mad haste to get them on and be out of this house of talk, talk, talk.

"You hear your father!" sobbed Mrs. Shakspere, swooping toward the children who stood in the doorway in their smocks: first Gilly, a loving fat boy of twelve, then good Joan, who would be ten in two weeks, and after her little Dickie, who was five.

Now half-clothed and wrestling with his doublet, Mr. Shakspere stumbled over his sword-belt and kicked his nightgown across the room. It flapped like a ghost hurrying home to churchyard after a night of good haunting. He stamped on his boots, buckled on his sword, and clapped his hat on his head.

"My poor boys are cold, see how they shake!" moaned Mrs. Shakspere. "Alas, three daughters dead in this mouldy old smoky house, and my heartless son off running the wild roads with wasters and wantons and worse, and does his father care?"

"Bah!" said Mr. Shakspere, wrapping his black cloak about his powerful body and plunging out into the darkness. He gasped, he panted, he drew in great draughts of air. Sniffing the wind and pawing the muddy cobblestones like a bull let loose, he barged off solidly toward a dim figure carrying a lantern.

Ten feet away he knew the man: it was his old friend Henry Field the tanner, for he could tell him by his smell.

"What's amiss, Henry?" he barked.

"Ah, some mad doings at the Market House. Tom Whittington has broke the town pump and the constable has locked himself in the stocks and can't find the key."

"We're going to have to depose Hugh Pyggin, I'd say it in Council if there was any use going these mad days, this drinking will be the ruin of him. It was not so in my day, when I was High Bailiff," said Mr. Shakspere.

"My boy Dick is out, John."

"Ah, now I begin to comprehend," said Mr. Shakspere.

"And is thy boy Will in his bed, old friend?"

"Well, Henry, it has to be admitted that he is not."

"The time has come for us to be stern with the boys."

"Alas, I hate to beat him, Henry, and besides, he is stronger than I now. What he will be in another year the merciful Father in heaven knows. I've tried, Henry, you know I've tried with the boy, being my eldest and all, and what have I got for a son?"

"Well, I don't know, John, but I think many a lad in town would not have been in trouble if he had not first thought of the trouble for them to be in. My Dick is a good boy."

"If he's aught like thee, Henry, no woman is safe in one more year."

"What of they housemaid? What of Anne Hathaway?"

"And what d'ye mean by that?" suddenly roared Mr. Shakspere, shaking his fist under the tanner's nose.

"Why did she leave, then?"

"Because my wife sent her back to Shottery," said the alderman, the passion all gone out of him. He sighed deeply. "Her old father's going, Henry. Then what's to become of the girl? No man will marry her."

"I would," Henry said. "And you too, John," he added, digging his friend in the ribs.

"She could have had any man in the parish, if she'd not lost her heart to the priest," said Mr. Shakspere sadly.

"John, I have decided. There's too much troth-plighting and bedding amongst our younkers nowadays anyhow. It will do our boys good to pack 'em off as apprentices to a solid trade for their next seven years. If you'll send Willy, I'll send Dick."

"I'd have sent him off long ago, if he weren't my eldest," Mr. Shakspere said. "No, Henry, the boy will grow out of his mad ways."

"There's a printer in London, John. Firm with his prentices, and his wife's a godly woman. How if we send the two of 'em off bound to him?"

"What? There's no money in books, Henry. Who reads 'em?"

"Our boys do, John."

"Aye, and much good it's done 'em."

"But John, look all the leather we'd sell to their masters," said Mr. Field. "My mind's made up, John. I'll pack Dick off tomorrow."

"Tomorrow, Henry?"

"With a cloak-bag of calfskins, John, for the whoreson book trade. He can be bound from the Feast of Saint Michael Tharkangel next. We're just in time."

"Well, Henry, I do not like to bind my boys to hard masters. God grant this man has not a heavy hand."

"What harm has a little beating done a boy, now and again?
I beat Dick every Sabbath day, he expects it."

"I think Willy will beat me next time I try," said the mighty
alderman with a sigh.

"No hard feelings about Anne Hathaway, John? I meant it
not."

"Thou art not the first, nor the last, who has demeaned her,"
answered the alderman. They walked on in silence toward the
Market Cross.

Now other lawful citizens had come out and were plodding
through the streets, up which the smoky mist was rolling from
the river. Where had the moon gone? It had gone behind the
English clouds, it had drowned in the English mist.

"There's the light again, Willy," whispered Dick.

"I never saw a ghost carry a candle."

"I'm fraid, Willy."

"Why, what is there to fear?"

"I know not, but I'm fraid anyway."

"Come on, Bloody Richard! Poor Nick has given me an idea.
Is not his father the agent for this house?"

"Sweet Willy, let us make no more trouble tonight," whimpered Dick as his friend tugged him toward the back door of
New Place.

"How, and not inspect my house? I have decided to buy it."

"And I to run all the way to London."

A reedy whisper, full of joy, came from the alderman's son.
"It's open, Dick. The door is not locked."

"For God's sake, let us go!"

But Willy was already creeping into the back entryway of
the house. Black dark in here, but a darkness full of rustles and
a strange murmuring sound. A thrill of fear ran along his spine.
He knew the sound. Something brushed his face, and he started
back.

"Willy, where are you?" moaned his friend in the dark.

"Shhh!"

Mustering all his courage, he groped forward, felt the heavy
folds of an arras, and cautiously drew it a little to one side.

A long panelled room stretched before him, tremulous with

shadow and a little winking light in a red bowl. At the head of the room stood a tall, bearded priest holding a golden chalice and murmuring in Latin, while before him knelt half a dozen people.

"Spies!" cried out somebody, starting up. Staring faces were turned toward him. Then the little winking light went out and he heard people scuttling away like rats.

He heard Dick Field falling into the arras and yelling with fear.

"Run, Bloody Richard!" he cried at the top of his voice, and then felt someone reaching for his throat in the dark. He kicked out and heard a grunt, sprang sideways and got his back against a wall. If they only knew it, I'm their friend, he thought.

But it was too late to explain to these secret Catholics who had met here for Mass at peril of their lives.

Why, my own mother used to go in Lady Jocosa's manor until they caught Father Gerard, he was thinking as a shower of meteors went up in his head, and a rain of rockets like the ones they had shot off at Warwick Castle where he saw the Queen. Alas, I'll never see her again, he thought, and made an act of contrition as he fell. A powerful arm went round him. He got his left hand free and grasped the face of this man. "I love the old religion too, neighbour," he explained, feeling a long nose, fat cheeks, and a little beard. A chill of fear went through him. He knew this face from a tavern brawl last Michaelmas. It was the face of the mad squire of Edstone, John Somerville the Oxford scholar, who went all round the country swearing to shoot the Queen.

"I know thee, Johnny," he whispered. "Remember me?"

"I'll remember thee better dead, thou sneaking spy," snarled the mad squire.

Feeling his spine ready to snap as Somerville bent him farther and farther back, Willy squeezed the face as hard as he could. Suddenly the terrible pressure was gone. He fell to the floor and immediately started crawling away.

Another voice whispered in the dark. "Where are you, Johnny? Give the fool to me and I'll slit him like a pig."

And he felt the other man creeping toward him. He could not get to his feet yet, but he could roll. So he rolled right into this other man and brought him down with a crash.

"I'm a friend," he explained.

But the fallen man grappled with him and they rolled over and over, hitting out blindly. I really do not want to be any trouble to either one of these gentlemen, thought Willy as he knocked the unknown grappler's noggin on the stones of a hearth until he stopping thrashing about.

Suddenly he heard a voice raised in high ringing whoops out in the street: "Help! Murder! Ring the alarm bell!"

Now I will have to explain all this to mother, thought Willy, and I do not understand it myself. He felt the hands of Somerville reaching for him again, and knew that this time he would be done for. Down the hands came, clawing for his throat. I must warn Cousin Maggie and Anne against this fellow, he thought, remembering how Somerville had courted every comely girl in the county. He got one of Somerville's hands in his mouth, and bit it hard.

Then while the mad squire was still screaming he rolled away from the two of them in the direction he thought the arras would be. Something rang on his head like a gong, and that was all he knew until torches shone in his eyes and he was lying in the ashes of a great hearth, staring up into his father's face.

"Alas, unhappy boy, what hast thou done?"

"Nothing, father," he answered, as usual.

"Then who is this here beside thee?"

He became aware of a large man groaning on the floor. It was all too evident who the large groaning man was. Somehow the murderous squire had got away, but his friend remained, and he was Tom Barber the skinner, who had married the widow of Francis Harbage and skinned her out of her business, and was now High Bailiff too, and had been skinning everybody in Stratford for years, including the Shaksperes.

CHAPTER TWO

IF Tom Barber had not been stunned Willy would have gone right to jail. As it was, Mr. Shakspere at least got him home in the morning for a short visit before justice should fall upon him.

"Oh, alas, it is my doing, I drove thee from me," sobbed Mrs. Shakspere, embracing her bruised and confused son. "Oh, my darling, my dear one, my love, what shall thy poor mother do now without thee?"

"Pox, he is not hanged yet," said Mr. Shakspere with a snort. "I have a plan."

"Ah, what good are thy plans now? What shall we do to save him?"

"He need only tell who was there saying Mass, and who was hearing it," Mr. Shakspere said.

At this his wife moaned and made the sign of the cross. "Never! Better to die than betray the true religion. Oh, my boy, my boy," she sobbed, embracing her son most passionately until she was in a very ecstasy of grief.

"Well, mother, I'm not dead yet," Willy said cheerfully. She always loved him when he suffered.

"Let us see, my boy," said the alderman kindly, "if by thy investigation of this ghost we may not make a ghost of Tom Barber, or at least do a little skinning of him. I have stayed away from Council in honest protest for two years come Michaelmas. Shall my patience bear fruit now? Let us see, let us see." And he rubbed his large hands thoughtfully. "There's Lewis ap Williams' vote. There's John Wheller's vote. George Whateley would vote for me. Now then, my son, attend to me with great care. Who was in the house conspiring against the Queen, and who was the forbidden priest saying Mass?"

"I would rather he died on the scaffold than tell," said Mrs. Shakspere, lifting her chin high as though standing at the scaffold herself, a doomed and beautiful queen.

"Pay thy mother no heed but attend carefully and in good conscience to me," said Mr. Shakspere.

Their son heaved a mournful and hopeless sigh and rested on the other foot for a change.

"What if Tom Barber skins us again and prosecutes him for assault?" cried his mother. "Where is the money to buy his bail and pay his fines, as thou hadst to do for thy mad brother Henry the last time he got drunk and was put in the Clink?"

"The woman does not know that the only point at issue is whether or not the people in New Place were gathered unlawfully to assist at the saying of Mass in clear disobedience of the Act of 1571 which declares it high treason and subject to fine, forfeiture of property, ah! and under the Statute of *Praemunire* to capital punishment and to torture."

"Tom Barber is High Bailiff till Michaelmas! No one dares prosecute him for anything!"

"Ah, but I dare," said Mr. Shakspere, drawing himself up and folding his arms.

"They do not know and they shall not know that any Mass was said in the house," Mrs. Shakspere declared.

"Then for what other purpose was such a company of Catholics banded together, eh?"

"They may have been looking at the house to buy it," said Mrs. Shakspere.

"Who would buy that great ark of a house? Who could afford it?"

William raised his hand. "I would like to buy it, sir."

"Silence in the courtroom!" bawled John, banging on a table with a silver-gilt bowl.

"My best silver bowl! A wedding gift from Cousin Edward Arden of Park Hall! I have been saving it all these years till you marry his daughter Maggie, and live with her at Asbies, and be a gentleman, and an esquire, and get children who will be a joy to me in my old age —"

"Order in the court!" cried Mr. Shakspere. "The constable will clear the court."

"Sir, the constable is asleep again, and has locked himself in the stocks," said William respectfully.

"Hem! Now, sir," said Mr. Shakspere. "Attend to me, boy. Art attending, eh?"

"It does no good to shout at him. After all, he is my son and has the rudiments of a gentleman."

"Are you attending, boy?"

"I am, sir, yes."

"I recite you once more the Act of 1571 of our Majesty the Queen which makes it high treason to assist in any way at the papistical rites or practices declared hereandunder to be heretical and subject to fine, forfeiture, prison, or, for exercising the priestly ministry, namely, the saying of Mass, or to cooperate in any way with such treasonable act, subject under the Statute of *Praemunire* to capital punishment and in the discretion of her Majesty's ministers, to torture for bringing to the light of justice any and all confederates who may have assisted in such heinous and traitorous acts. Did you or did you not see, apprehend, or by any of your five senses detect, the observance of any of the acts aforesaid on the night of the tenth of August or the morning of the eleventh of the same, in the empty house of the said Underhill, now know as New Place, it being the Feast of good St. Susanna the Virgin, and did you or did you not see, hear, observe, mark or apprehend what crucifixes, candles, missals, rosaries, Agnus Deis, medals or the like vain and superstitious trumperies, or what robes, copes, or other papistical accoutrements were upon or about the persons of the suspected practicers of damnable and abhominable forbidden acts, answer yes or no."

"Would you repeat the question, your honour?"

John Shakspere arose from his armchair. He took off his hat and flapped it against the table. Then he grabbed some thirty pairs of gloves from the sample case at his side and sent them flapping and smacking against the walls. After that he put his foot in a bucket and crashed the thing against the chimney.

His son regarded this demonstration of energy with his head on one side. It was that looking look, that bleak and mindless stare of somebody who had no human tripes and heart, that drove the old man wild. He might have been a clown in a scurvy old filthy play. When he had kicked the bucket awhile he sat down again and mopped his steaming neck and cheeks.

He talked for some time. The upshot of it was that people didn't love him, people didn't care about all he had done, but by blood and oons even if he was the son of a shepherd he had risen above his origines, and he could hold up his head in any company. People respected him. Did not people respect him?

"Answer, woman!" he shouted.

"An end of this babble before I reach the end of my wits!" screamed Mrs. Shakspere, with such superior passion that the ordinary grumbling and growling of the alderman was reduced to nothing.

Their regretful son began pensively eating a peach while waiting for them to resume the examination of his wandering and dreamy memory.

What a furnace of passion goes roaring forth from my parents, and all vanity, he thought. Alas! Where got I such a father? In what bolting-hutch of eternity did the seed of this windy fool encounter my doomed and naked spirit, shivering for human form? And my mother — will her woe ever be assuaged by dusty time, or will she go wailing through eternity, hunting for a sorrow that will stick?

"What art mooning about, eh? Art asleep again, eh?" cried his father, whacking him on the back.

This caused William the Worthless to swallow the peach stone and to go strangling and gasping and clawing about the whole house like a cat gone mad, with his startled sister Joan following him with a teaspoonful of sugar, thinking he had the hiccups again, and his two young brothers skulking out of his way.

When the discussion was resumed he was lying hopelessly on his bed, his loving little sister holding his limp hand, his two brothers crouching and peering at him to see if he might be dying, and his mother distractedly rubbing his stomach with the grease of geese, a very good remedy for something, though in her grief she could not remember what.

"It is not his stomach, it is his windy brain," said Mr. Shakspere. "The boy can swallow anything, he has the guts of a pelican. Now then, everybody out of this room. Let us go over the whole scene again, my boy, and see if thou canst remember this time if thou didst see aught that would lead thee to assume, or, in thy good judgement believe, that any member or members of this company were engaged in the act, or about to be engaged in it, of seeing or hearing Mass. Eh?"

A groan came from the prostrated form upon the bed.

"Hear how he groans! Has the man no heart?" cried Mrs. Shakspere.

"Then let him groan aye, or let him groan no," said her husband. "Eh?"

"Oh!"

"What dost mean, Oh? Thou wert in the house, eh? There were candles lighted, eh?"

"Candles, father? Oh! What candles did anybody find?"

"Now pox take me if thou art answering the questions in this court or I am! Didst thou see any light or didst thou not see any light?"

"What light, father? Was there any light? Oh!"

"Oh, my poor boy. Oh, my unhappy suffering boy," said Mrs. Shakspere. "With an ass for a father who thinks he is in the magistrate's court when he is in this old mouldy bedroom!"

"Attend to me, boy! Art attending?"

"I think I could attend better, sir, if I had a little good foamy ale to heal my bruised oesophagus. Oh!"

"Then come with me out of this windmill and to the Swan where we can talk of this matter with no further idle interruptions," said Mr. Shakspere.

"Very well, father," said his son, mournfully kissing his sister goodbye and shaking hands with his brothers. As for his mother, she threw her arms around his neck, while tears stood in her beautiful eyes.

"Oh, my son, my son, I fear thy nature, remember thy mother will be with thee always, and change that dabbled doublet for the russet one," she whispered, attempting to comb his wild hair, sprinkled with hay, burdocks and thistles from his wanderings.

"Peace, woman! The boy is not going to court today!" grumbled his father, clapping on his black hat and draping his black cloak over his shoulders with no help from any of the family.

"Remember my teachings, do not betray our holy religion," whispered Mrs. Shakspere, embracing her eldest son with such passionate sorrow that he began feeling a little worried himself.

"Mother, I'm just going to have a swig of ale, or so," he said. "It is not poison, I will live."

But she looked at him with so many more years of sorrow and wisdom than he had suffered himself that he began to doubt it before he got out of the mouldy old dark house in which the smell of leather always won out over all other smells, and where duty always waited at the bottom of the stairs.

Out in Henley Street he looked uneasily up at the window of his parents' bedroom. It was open. In it was framed the tragic and beautiful figure of Mrs. Shakspere, her chin lifted bravely, her long aristocratic fingers trailing a message of melancholy warning on the air.

Alas! thought the escaping boy, hurrying along beside his growling father, what a pity my mother was not born a boy! She would have been the greatest player in England.

How right she was! Sadly afterwards, father and son agreed that something always seemed to happen when they went to the Swan, and that this was one of the worst times in their bruised and brawling history.

Willy's fight with the two Cawdreys in the street was not an unusual whacking and thumping, and might never have happened if he could have told them quickly enough that he was a friend. But the Cawdreys were Catholics and didn't care who knew it. Moreover, this biter of Squire Somerville and beater of Tom Barber aroused all their muscular animosity as soon as they saw him come amiably along past Lizzie Fisher's house, bowing most politely to her mother and winking at the button-nosed girl who would inherit old John Fisher's money almost any day now. As Mr. Shakspere stopped to salute the lady and beam paternally upon the girl, George Cawdrey brushed by Willy and hissed, "Shaky Spear, the sneaking spy," while his brother Rafe tripped him and called him the Knight of the Fallen Staff. Down he went, in a mud puddle.

"Cannot the boy walk a good English rod without tumbling on his moon face?" gasped Mr. Shakspere, ashamed before these people who had so much money.

Meanwhile the two big-shouldered Cawdrey boys were rapidly disappearing down Back Bridge Street.

"It is this windmill of a name, it dizzies me," explained the fiery-faced boy, scrambling to his feet. "Sweet father, a little minute of muddy time, I pray thee, and I will join thee at the Swan."

"Very well, unlucky boy, but try to keep on thy pins," said

his father amiably, turning to confer gravely with Mr. Wheller, one of the burgesses whose vote he wanted on the town council.

Off went Willy like the skipping wind which was then blowing from the butcher shops along Bridge Street. He caught up with the Cawdreys just in front of their family barrow, piled high with the parts of slaughtered animals. Old Rafe Cawdrey was chopping up some more animals in the Shambles, while doomed calves bleated and a squealing pig bled out his last singing minutes. This bloody man was the worst enemy of old John Shakspere and had been stewing up a bitter pot of revenge ever since John had arrested him twenty years ago for making a fray upon Alex Webb, who had married Mrs. Shakspere's sister Maggie. Clearly a family matter, this, thought Willy with keen legal, or illegal, insight as he accidentally stumbled against the smaller Cawdrey, hit him in the guts with his elbow, knocked over the barrow of bloody meat with one flying foot and kicked the larger Cawdrey in the shins with the other. "Oh!" he cried loudly, rolling over and over.

"It's Willy Wagstaff, the upside-down jack from the jakes!" roared George Cawdrey, dancing among the tripes and sweetbreads.

"Sadbird is down again! Kill him!" yelled Rafe Cawdrey, falling upon the prostrate Shagstaff, Wagstaff, Fagstaff, or Fallstaff, as his best friends often called him, depending upon his condition. It was a misery and a weariness to wear this old rag of a name and suffer the idiot fancies of village clowns wherever it was known.

He had been willing to be friends until he heard them mocking him again.

He gave the lesser Cawdrey a sudden snap of the neck, which he had learned from Tom Tiddler, who was king of the vagabonds in Warwickshire and had taught him gypsy fighting last year, when he ran off with the Coventry players.

"War! War! Blood! Murther!" cried William the Conqueror in a voice like a trumpet. Wandering and dreamy friends, hearing that well-known cry, lifted their noses and snuffed the good air like war horses, crying Ha ha. Dick Quiney came galloping first, and after him, with holy joy, Abe Sturley, Hal Walker, and Roger Sadler. Also the long pale baker named Hamnet Sadler, carrying two full armfuls of loaves fresh from his ovens, calling after his brother to be mindful of the tarts.

These tarts, however, soon splattered across the faces of the battling Cawdreys and their friends Jack Russell, Tom Logginge, and Ned Young, all vigorous Catholics and eager for a religious argument.

Unfortunately Willy was friendly with all these people and sympathetic with their cause, while he thought that most Puritans were solemn asses, righteous, colicky, pompous, and sang too many windy hymns.

So he was caught in the middle of the discussion, and might have been squeezed badly if some few moderate young men, belonging to the Queen's official religion, had not bustled in between the followers of Rome and the followers of their own noses, urging them, with a whack here, a thump there, to moderate their choler, beshrew their bile, and subdue their spleen, until the whole argument was settled with an agreement to go into the Swan and drink to the health of her redheaded Majesty while she had a little hair left.

As for the fallen tripes, sweetbreads, hearts, brains, and other fragments of slaughtered animals, the young men threw them all back in the barrow and they looked as tempting as ever.

Their arms around Willy the Shaky, Frank Halliday and Bob Bratt led the way down the High Street, singing.

It was true that they muted their voices when coming into the Swan, where so many grave businessmen were taking their ale and beer. Their entrance was modest. Their demeanour was subdued and seemly. Nevertheless these old baldheaded and greybearded inhabitants regarded them with popping eyes.

"Now what a plague hast thou done this time?" cried Mr. Shakspere, regarding the blood, the bruises, the mud, the rips and gashes of his eldest son and principal heir.

"Nothing, father," murmured Willy modestly, attempting to seat himself this time without some enemy tripping him up. The Cawdreys were looming dangerously near.

"Say, who tore thy doublet? Who ruined thy trunk-hose? Cannot a man turn his back but thou art in a brawl again?"

The bemused innocence in young William's eyes would have made his mother weep for pity.

"It was not his doing, sir, it was the Cawdreys' fault," said Dick Quiney respectfully, spitting out a tooth.

"That is true, John," said Hamnet Sadler with a groan, lying upon a padded bench to mourn his tarts, his loaves. Then too, he had a nosebleed, so that Judy Stanton, the pitiful orphan who had been done out of her country manor by three greedy brothers and now worked as a barmaid, had to stoop over him and stanch his crimson flow with her handkerchief.

Ah, ah, it might move, thought young Shakspere, wondering for the first time since early this morning where Dick Field was. Could he be, by any chance, still running?

But a still older, bigger Cawdrey shoved forward and inserted his nose into the discussion. "You lie, hymn-singers!" he brayed. He was Peter, whom they called Bullcalf.

The dreamy Hamnet, or Hamlet, as his loving friends called him, was staring in astonishment and admiration at the young girl's rosy breasts, which came tumbling out of her bodice two inches above his nose, for it was the fashion among barmaids, French ladies, and some well-bosomed married women of easy persuasion to wear no covering in this region at all, if they were not among Puritans or other sour-stomached people.

But if Bloody Richard is running, thought Worthless William as the sound of a new discussion began rising around him, is it not I who am guilty? His powerful conscience awoke and began to scream in his ear, even as Peter Cawdrey and Dick Quiney snatched up pint-pots, joint-stools, and other handy instruments of persuasion, and began attempting to convince each other.

The discussion rapidly became general, for indeed it was a dull life in this market town, what with weather and wives, not to mention work, and the citizens of Stratford were well known to be as contentious as any in Warwickshire.

All would probably have dwindled away into some sociable drinking in a little while, if the Earl of Warwick, Lord of the Manor of Stratford, had not come amiably riding into town that afternoon on his way back to his castle nine miles up the road. He had been paying a visit to the Queen at Giddy Hall in Romford, where she had gone to dally with the young French Duke of Alençon, the brother of the most worthless king that France had ever had, and that was a great worthlessness. How to keep her amorous Majesty from marrying the useless duke, that was the question. All England waited to see how the game would come out. If she married him, the bloody gentry would try to make all England Catholic again. If she did not, the bloody Puritans would keep England divided as it was among the Protestants.

That is to say, if some angry country gentleman whose property had been taken by the Crown did not murder the Queen first. Many of them threatened, more of them plotted, and all of them wished to shoot her or stab her as much as mad Squire Somerville, to whose mutterings nobody paid any attention.

Willy looked up from his position on Peter Cawdrey's head and saw the great and dangerous Earl himself staring down at him. Earl Ambrose of Warwick was a large, limping, fat old man in ermine and velvet, with an ostrich plume, who often sat beside his father in court and called him Mr. Shagsbye. Looming behind him were some startled gentlemen of the county, including Sir Richard Moryson and Sir Fulke Greville, a dozen or more men-at-arms, and two other people Willy did not want to see right now: Tom Barber the High Bailiff, and Squire Somerville, both looked bruised and unfriendly, and in a mood to make trouble.

Alas, there is already trouble enough here, thought the son of the alderman, arising hastily from the fallen Cawdrey and bowing before the mighty Earl.

The other members of the Startford debating society also made a leg before the sad old man who was reproachfully staring at them from beneath his velvet hat with the ostrich plume, as if all their blows had been struck at him, though he loved them.

The Fat Knight of the Ragged Staff, as his grateful retainers called him, liked nothing better in these bad old days than to loll upon a padded bench in a tavern and drink sack all day long, remembering his deeds of war and forgetting his wounds, which hurt all the time, and perhaps dallying with a tavern wench, or so. "What! I must be a father to my people," the good old gentleman would say.

There was also some recruiting to be done this year, for not only was the Privy Council in fear of an uprising among the Protestants, a conspiracy among the Catholics, an invasion by the Spaniards, and a revolt among the swarming poor, but there was some good profitable pacifying to be done among the Irish, and some peace to preserved among the Dutch.

Rolling his eye around among these young men now bowing before him, as if already he saw them as soldiers, the Earl cried out in his muffled old voice, like a frog of muddy antiquity in a pool of juvenile frogs: "Peace! Ye swaggerers, peace! Fetch forward the instigator of this broil!" He then seated himself at the hearth and put his bad leg up on a padded bench. But his eye kept on rolling, as if in search of something, until it encountered the bobbing breasts of Judy Stanton, and there rested.

In his lonely and painful old age, the Earl had forgotten about the classes of people, and sought only for quality. This he appeared to observe in the generously breasted girl now bobbing to her knees with a cup of sack for him. His weary old hand reached. "God bless thee, child, what is thy name?" he murmured, and lifted the cup to his lips.

"Still Judy Stanton, your worship, but I have hopes," said the rosy girl.

"What, of Longbridge Manor? Is it possible? Is it come to this?"

"Oh, my Lord," said Judy, sobbing. "Not a friend in the world, and no dowry either."

"Alas, poor girl, I knew thy father, and we must find thee a dowry," said the good old Earl, handing her the cup to refill. "Ah, why do my silly people require me to be stern, when all I desire is to love them? For in the days of darkness, my dear, there is no time for anything but love."

"Hear that, Hamlet?" whispered Willy to the dreamy baker. "She will have a good dowry. And has been staring at thy leg with admiration all this while."

"Is it possible?" mumbled the bashful baker.

But the two large Cawdrey brothers got hold of Willy and began dragging him forward. This aroused his dormant friends, and an obscure and agonized struggle began, to reveal him or to conceal him. Sir Fulke Greville and Mr. Shakspere both attempted to shield the culprit from the old Earl's eyes, and this aroused his interest.

"What is the trouble back there, Greville?" he called. "And is that Mr. Shagsbye with you? Let him come forward."

And then suddenly he saw the center of the confusion, a

tall youth with shining auburn hair, with mud and scratches, blood and bruises, and the most extraordinary eyes.

"That boy again," muttered the Earl.

Once he had seen Willy act out killing a calf, with a long speech, at a fair, and had always been puzzled about him since, whenever he had seen him, especially that time he had been caught playing a ghost in the churchyard, and had been brought to justice, and that awful time the old mare had run away, on the hill below Warwick Castle, when the Queen herself was about to address the welcoming committee.

"A word in your ear, my Lord, and all will be understood," said Mr. Shakspere, bowing before Earl Ambrose with dignity and a very good conscience, which was one of his weaknesses.

At this significant utterance the mud-coloured countenance of Tom Barber faded to the tint of clay.

"My Lord, his father would tell a tall tale. Do not give ear."

And boosting forward the well-breasted girl, he propelled her into the lap of the lame old lord, so that in order to save herself from undue bruising, she needed to embrace the good Earl round the neck.

"Why, how thy pulse beats, child! It is a pretty pigeon," stammered the old man.

"Oh, it's a lonely, cruel, hard world it is, sweet honey Lord," sobbed Judy, hanging on tight.

"Alas, what bitter truth is in thy words," said the old man, sighing deeply. "Well, fetch me a cup of sack and I will remember thee. Let me see, let me see, let me see. Now, where is the culprit? Is it thee again, unlucky boy? Come hither, fear not, my justice will not harm thee, if thou art half as innocent as they face avers. Now, thou art the boy that did fright the Queen and gravely endanger her with thy runaway mare, on that St. Susanna's Day when she did visit me at my castle, in '72. I believe thou art the boy, alas."

"He is, it is the same cullionly rascal," declared Mr. Barber.

"My Lord, it was a burr under the mare's tail, slipped there by some idle fellow, and no friend to majesty," said Mr. Shakspere. For this was the version of the unlucky story which his son had allowed him to believe these seven years.

"My Uncle Henry's mare, named for her Majesty in respect of resemblance, being long in the body and short in the legs, just like our noble soverign, God bless her," explained the eager young son of the alderman, lifting his shining head and raising high a glass full of wine, which he had just sinfully sneaked from the sideboard on his way forward to the Earl. "To her glorious Majesty, gentlemen! The heart of a lion, the stomach of an oxe, the brow of an eagle, the eye of a basilisk which turns to stone all creeping and shameful enemies of our mighty England, which never did, nor never shall lie at the foot of a conqueror! England and Elizabeth, all hail!"

Quite a few hearty cries of "To the Queen! To her Majesty! England!" burst forth from the large company now squeezed into the Swan, and the old Earl had to get groaning up and drink a cup of sack to the powerful lady too.

"Alas, my boy, thou art better than a play, and hast a tongue like a clapper," said Earl Ambrose, sinking down once more with a weary yawn. "I remember thee, no more than a pint-pot boy, on the greensward below my castle among the people, careering and caracoling after the ramping mare, while our horses all did dance, and the grooms had old coil keeping the coach of her Majesty secure, and how she did laugh at it afterwards, and say it was a boy with such tulip-coloured hair as she had herself, formerly, and did inquire if he had a Welsh father as she did, and quothe that he did cling well to the rein if not to the saddle, and saved her from the poor addled beast bravely. It was a happy visit, gentlemen, a happy day. Would it were come again in these sad times!"

He was growing so mellow it looked as if Tom Barber would fail to provide a culprit for anything today. "Now as to the riot, my Lord," he whispered. "He has broke open and entered property in dead of night, and created disturbances in the church, and has been in and out of the bone-house, stealing skulls which he talks to most horrible, and has been always tetchy and wayward, your worship, and his school days were frightful."

"There stands Tom Barber who met in secret to hear forbidden Mass and here is the witness!" suddenly roared out Mr. Shakspere, freezing the whole company into fear and amazement. "And conspirators with him too, as my boy shall name! As my boy shall name!"

He turned to draw his son closer, his hand clutching at air.

A jostling and stumbling swept through the crowd as Willy dove among them, wildly fighting to gain the doorway.

A howl of rage and pain went up from Peter Cawdrey and a whimper from old Hugh Pyggin the constable, who had inadvertently become one of the company.

Then Willy was out sailing through the air, skimming the cobblestones, leaping a hedge, springing into the saddle of the first horse he could reach, and whacking his heels into the startled creature's sides. Two stupefied grooms leaped for their lives as the stallion kicked, whinnied, squealed, and sprang over their heads. Then, plunging and rearing, he crashed into a market barrow piled high with cabbages, knocked over that, and made for the butcher stalls along Bridge Street.

Oh, my poor mother, thought Willy, crouching low in the saddle. I wonder whose crazy horse this is. He looked down at the saddle skirt and saw the arms of the Earl of Warwick, a bear and ragged staff, tooled in gold, surmounted by a coronet.

I'll be hanged for sure now, he thought, just as the Earl's powerful stallion plunged through a flock of sheep, knocking the shepherd to the ground, and came clattering to the bridge.

Shouts and screams rose on the summer air. Looking over his shoulder as the stallion went galloping across the bridge, Willy saw many people pouring out of the Swan, their mouths open, their arms waving.

I wonder why I always seem to excite people, he thought sadly. I am only trying to do good.

How if I turn round and go riding back? No, for the Earl's horse does not wish to turn, and secondarily, I do not desire to hang. Sixth and lastly, my father must have no witness to gallop with him in the way of his own folly, and I am doing him a great deed of kindness, if he but knew it. Well, I will write to him from the country, so that he will love me in absence. And, to conclude, here comes Squire Somerville with four men-at-arms to speed me in my decision.

Indeed at that very moment the murderous squire and a body of the Earl's men came trotting on their horses out of the innyard of the Swan and looking all around and whichways to see where the missing witness had gone.

Then they caught sight of him on the far bank of the bridge, hanging onto the runaway stallion as hard as he could. He saw them pointing, and other men leaping on horses, and then a screen of alders hid them from view.

He dug his heels in hard, crouched low in the saddle, and gave the stallion a good loose rein.

Where the road forked beyond the tithebarns he signalled the galloping stallion to take the road to Alveston. The animal chose to leap a hedge instead and go plunging into the marshes beside the Avon.

In a few moments they were deep in a clump of reeds among bullfrogs and dragon-flies.

Is it possible? Willy thought. This horse is wiser than I am. I think we are going to escape.

The tall reeds hid them from the road. He heard the Earl's men go galloping by toward Alveston.

Why, this is wonderful luck, he thought. This is a shrewd horse.

Now if the mad squire has but gone with them, I will meet my father and mother alive in a few days, after this little storm has blown over, and be good forever after. Ah, how they will love me then!

"As for Earl Ambrose, I'll send you back to him from my Uncle Henry's stable," he told the horse.

His spirits rose and he began to feel happy. Old John's younger brother Henry was just the reverse of the alderman: no dignity, no sense of business, content to be a poor tenant farmer like his father; no children either; whatever was, he was against it; whatever was not, he believed in it.

I wonder how much of my nature comes from dead Shaggy-spurs like Uncle Henry, thought the fugitive.

The only times he seemed to meet Uncle Henry were when the indignant farmer was arrested again for refusing to wear his statute cap on Sundays, or obey old John Fisher, the tyrant of the Warwick Corporation, or for just being loud and happy in a tavern.

I'll visit all my aunts and uncles and decide once and for all what I am, where I came from, and where I am going.

Who are we anyhow? And why?

His gloomy philosophical speculations were suddenly interrupted by a new manoeuvre of the stallion.

Instead of tucking in his hindquarters, sliding down the river-bank, and swimming across the sky, trees, and golden fields having an upside-down dream of themselves in the river, the giddy charger began dancing among the dragon-flies in the reed mace by the stream.

"A fine cavalry horse you are," said the fugitive. Again he signalled the dancing charger to take to the water.

But the stallion tossed up his mad head, sniffed the tender air, and whinnied.

Then he danced up the bank, clattered across the Alcester road, plunged down into the marshes along the other side, and began trotting south-southwest along the muddy bank till he came to Ad Quiney's mill-dam.

"No, horsie, no, Uncle Henry is in the other direction," said the reproachful rider.

"Hay, Sir Jakes!" called out Tom Quiney from over the shining water-wheel. "Where's the war?"

"Where is it not?" replied the baffled rider.

Young George Badger looked peacefully up from the bank where he sat fishing and waved a lazy hand. He had got caught with Alice Court last November and had to marry the girl in a hurry, but nobody in town thought anything about it. George had claimed he had a troth-plight with Alice, but some of the drinkers and wenchers at the Swan had heard him tell a different story.

I suppose if it happened to me, and I got Lizzie Fisher with child, the whole town would be screaming, thought the gloomy equestrian, who had now given up trying to persuade the dancing stallion to do anything at all.

He is too full of high breeding for me. "Thou art a seat too wanton for my head, O horsie," he remarked as the stallion lifted up his ear-crowned head again, snuffed the air as if it was delicious, and then darted off sideways up the bank until he came to a little party of young naked boys, jumping in and out of the pool the Quineys had made here under the willows.

With a magnificent splash, in leaped the stallion among the yelling boys.

Their cries piping all around him and after him, young William the Shaken, with wet legs, sat his seat and rode across the river on his swimming bearer, trying to look half as dignified as the most dignified man he knew, namely, his father.

O Lord, what would my mother say to this sight? he thought, and felt as damp in his spirits as in his body.

A few narrow punts were drawn up along the bank, and the stallion pointed his nose toward these.

"Hey!" said a ruddy-faced boy, sitting up suddenly. The girl beside him hid her face.

The whole creation goes to't, except me, thought the frustrated rider. Gnats and botflies, they wanton in my sight, the winged, the horned, the furred, and yon mincing dame too, if her looks are any beacon of that fire which f —

Always when he worried about what his mother would be thinking of him he became very bitter about the great universal lechery of everybody else in the world.

She's bound me on a wheel of fire, and I'll never get off, he thought. Whispered little sermons about sin, from the pillow beside him, while her cool arms embraced him and her beautiful dark eyes stared into his, had strangled any hope of enjoying a healthy romp in the bushes with a willing girl. The sad dark eyes would loom above them, the whispers of sin would drown any joy.

Some day my mother and I must drown in her holiness together, or I must become a thief like Nick, he decided.

Lust and corruption seemed to be creeping, crawling, squirming, and writhing all round him in the teeming air. Always when he tried to be holy, like Robin the priest who had once been his teacher, he became more and more diabolical.

By the time the stubborn stallion reached the tree-lined bank and clambered up, snorting with pleasure at the new coolness of his crupper and belly, his rider had given up all hope of ever finding any love, any understanding, any sweet comfort and kindness in the world of hypocrites and fools that would be all over in a few years anyhow, according to the forbidden books of prophecy he had been surreptitiously reading lately.

Everything that is good is against some law, he decided, as the stallion began cheerfully trotting off among tall mossy trees smothered with ivy, as if he knew where he was going.

A cat fled across their path, a beagle loped out from a thicket of alders and rang a chime of bells at them, and a few peaceful farmers, raking and tossing the hay, looked up lazily and went on with their work as the horse and rider trotted right on, east by southeast, toward Shottery.

CHAPTER THREE

𝕻EACEFULLY nibbling the tender
grass by a little brook, a chestnut mare lifted up her head and
whinnied.

Her mistress was a country girl in a faded blue gown, with
a modest hood. She was not beautiful, but wonderfully tall and
strong, and in spite of her humble costume there was a pride
and dignity about her. Slim and agile as a boy, she had climbed
out on a willow branch growing aslant the brook and with a
hooked knife was cutting the young green shoots. These she
carefully laid in a basket.

A loud splashing and snorting came from around the bend
in the stream. Then the voice of an angry youth reasoning with
a horse.

A stallion rather, rearing and squealing, flinging his proud
head above the nettles and reeds, then suddenly springing up
the bank and dancing toward the mare.

The young breeder whinnied again, swivelling her ears and
snuffing the air, tossing her head, dancing among the butter-
flies, glancing shyly down at a bee, pretending to be startled
and scudding away in the greenwood.

In after her romped the stallion, neatly shedding his rider
beneath a low-hanging branch.

The young woman burst out laughing. "Oh, Willy, must I
jump in and save thee again?"

The dignified ex-cavalryman picked himself up, waded out
of the little stream, and stood before her, dripping water. "Any
time you're so minded, Anne."

Once when he was small he had fallen into Quiney's Pool
and she had leaped in and saved him. He had pretended to be
drowned for a long blissful time while she kissed him, and
spoke kind words to him, but then his father had come, and
thumped him both therapeutically and paternally.

He did not speak yet, only looked deep into her grey eyes,

34

so candid and clear, beneath the modest shade of her virginal hood. A little ripe to be a virgin, old gabbling goodwives in Stratford and Shottery said: twenty-three this year, and still yearning after Bob Debdale, her neighbour, who had gone away to Reims to be a seminary priest.

Meanwhile the stallion and mare were dancing among the willows and elms, whinnying, snorting, and neighing to each other as if they were the first stallion and the first mare ever born.

Anne Hathaway slid down the sturdy branch, her basket of osiers held with care. Arranging her voluminous petticoat and skirt with still greater care, she smiled peacefully at him and said, "I'm brewing the willow-bark for poor dad. Will you sit beside me?"

He fixed her with his skeptical eye, green as a goat's. "I haven't the time."

"I am happy to see thee in service to Earl Ambrose," Anne said. "Does John know it?"

A little twinge of jealously always ran through him when she called his father *John*. How many people in the county dared do that? And this daughter of a shepherd had been their housemaid — his nursemaid too, when he was small and innocent, and could not appreciate it.

He often tried to remember, when he was lying in bed at night, her tender words and her kisses then.

"John?" he said. "John a Who?" **U. S. 1192993**

The wide-set grey eyes smiled at him as sweetly and tenderly as the lips. They looked delicious, and all going to waste.

"The only one worth half a minute of our time, unless you sit, honey-lamb."

He twitched suddenly. She had a maddening way of using endearments she did not mean. Or could she, if she used the same one to a mongrel cur, a gib-cat, or a lugged bear? Her heart went out to all life, any old life.

"Even to mine, I suppose," he said with a windy sigh, but not sitting down beside her. He began to pace up and down the bank, as if he were a harlotry player in the yard of some inn. "Ah, women! Why will they not be soft, mild, pitiful, and stamp our signets in their waxen hearts? But what are their weapons? What are they?"

"Take mine," said Anne, handing him the hooked knife as he went striding by.

"Thank you. Their weapons are coifs, caps, and love-locks. Their weapons are rings, bows, ribbons, garlands and girdles. Their weapons are words, words, words, while men's hearts bleed."

"I am glad he has given his permission for you to serve the good Earl, honey-lamb."

He glared at her. "He'll never give it. I am doomed to fingers and thumbs forever."

"Then what service are you in, dear?"

"It is not I who am in service, it is this wasp-stung, giddy, and impatient horse. Well, I have done my best."

He glowed with wrath, woe, misery, and frustration; but he was usually glowing with something anyhow, when he was not plunged into the dark pool of gloom he seemed to live in lately, wondering what he was going to Be.

"Then let him do his best, angel, and praise the Lord for all gifts, expected and unexpected."

"You should have been a nun," he said and saw her bite her lip.

"Perhaps."

She took off her hood and the white wimple that usually lay along her glowing cheek. When, how, and where had she ever become so brown? As far as he could see down the sweet throat and the noble bosom, she was as toasted by the sun as the naked boys who romped by the river these warm August afternoons.

"Is it true Spooner the painter caught thee at thy bath?"

"Did he say so? I thought Spooner was a gentleman," Anne said.

"He? Hang him, mouldy rogue! Nick Bott caught him t'other night stealing timber from old New Place. There ought to be more law in this town."

"You sound like John."

He twitched.

"Is Nick back from the wars already?" asked Anne, with a look so innocent he could not help laughing.

"He wants me to be a player, and join him and Davy Jones at next Coventry Fair."

"What does J — ?"

"My father has not liked players for three years, and you know why."

"I always thought it was a pity, going after you like that when you were so happy playing shepherdesses. Such a pretty lass you made too!"

"Indeed," he said, lowering himself to the bank beside her and beginning to nibble at one of the green willow-shoots. "Is this what you brewed for my father, sweet witch, when he had the black melancholy?"

"When he brought thee back from the players?"

"When little Anne died last April."

She lowered her eyes before he could see the quick tears in them. Mrs. Shakspere had named her last daughter after Anne Hathaway, in gratitude for her patience with the children. But the child had coughed her life out — the third daughter to die in that old smoky house.

"Why did you leave us?" he whispered. "We miss you."

"My father is dying," said Anne.

He could have told her what everybody in the county knew: old Dick Hathaway had been dying before he married his new wife, and now he was dying because he had married her.

"He's the hardiest man in Shottery," he said.

"So my stepmother says."

Except for the lustful snorting of the stallion, and the amorous squealing of the mare, the green woods were quiet. Beyond the feathery trees he could see Anne's brother Bart up on the roof of the Hathaway cottage, ripping off mouldy thatch. A cloud of dirt puffed up around him, and the brooding son of the businessman heard his sneeze. In these old cottages, when you tore off the rotted thatch before laying on the new, you might uncover anything from rats' nests to swallows' lairs; once while patching the mouldy thatch over the counting-room, Willy himself had found some crucifixes, rosaries, and a chalice wrapped in a cope. No doubt these had been stuffed up there by the frugal alderman after some raid on church or chapel, in case the country went Catholic again. Another time Willy had found an old hacked statue of Our Lady among some rotted hides in the chopping-shed, where John Shakspere trimmed the skins torn off the carcasses of baby lambs (for the softest

cheveril gloves), or poor dogbodies (for hunting gauntlets) or
the ordinary cadavers of sheep and calves.

One thing neither we nor the Hathaways have is any petticoats or kirtles made from the chasubles of the priests, he
thought, stealing a look at the noble line of thigh revealed by
the faded blue skirt of the gloriously living woman beside him.

I will die of this lusting, he thought. A wholesome aroma of
woman's flesh, cowbarns, clover, and bleeding grass prickled
his sensitive nostrils. A vision of Anne naked swam through his
teeming brain and swam away. He decided to snatch some
willing wench from a dance around some St. Susanna fire and
stop her giggling with kisses until these hellish visions of lust
were killed and dead.

"Who'll inherit the cottage?" he suddenly asked.

Her candid eyes looked him through. The hot blood rose
over his remose and made him angry.

"You sound like a law-clerk," she said.

"No fear I'll be one," he said.

"Why not? You could be anything," said Anne with such
intensity he was startled. It was true that she had sat through
many desperate sermons preached by his father about the woes
of the glove business and his plans for his eldest son to inherit
them all.

"Does a bee have to worry over what it's to be? Does a
flea?" he asked her passionately. "Why is it only man, proud
man, must wait so long for his wings, and then beat himself
to flaming death against some h'm . . ." Images and metaphors
crowded so thickly upon him when he was with a listening
friend that he sometimes felt choked with hopelessness ever
to get them all out in time.

"I love your voice so it makes me sleepy," said Anne, yawning luxuriously, stretching her magnificent arms. "Ah, honey-
sweet boy, how you used to read about Cain and Abel to the
children, and the Flood, and the coming Fire, till the heart in
me was like to burst with the beauty of it. And Sir Henry told
me last Sunday he misses thy glory out of the choir, that voice,
Willy, that voice singing like what's that thing you played in
the pageant, St. George's Day?"

"*Viola da gamba.*"

"Oh, if I had a son," Anne said, reaching up to undo her

long chestnut hair, "I'd want him just like you, all sorrow and joy, scaring me one minute and making me laugh the next, only to weep for pity. And when you played that other thing, darling, at the barber's, when I went by and the boys were all laughing and whistled after me —"

"The lute, the lute."

"And sang, angel, those bawdy songs, I could not tell whether to hurry up out of hearing, or creep under the penthouse roof and listen. What *are* you going to be, anyhow?"

His bitterness all melted now, he only looked over at her and smiled, though he wanted to fling himself upon her and weep against that lovely bosom. He still had a faint and deliciously guilty memory of doing it, the night his mother had gone storming out of the house to stay with Goody Thatcher, screaming that her husband was a murderer and she would never lie with him again. That was the year John Shakspere had led the burgesses into the gild chapel to smash the stained-glass windows and hack the pretty saints and angels.

"Could you love me if I were a harlotry player?" he asked. "Davy Jones and Nick Bott might make up a troupe with me, if we could find a nobleman to lend us his badge."

"I couldn't stop loving you if you were a harlotry anything."

He was so grateful to her he could not speak. How wonderful she was to dream with, laugh with, eat with, work with, rest with, or simply to breath the same air with, and be grateful, and peaceful, and quiet!

He looked over at her, and she looked over at him, sideways. Then she looked away, at anything, at the gnats dancing on the water perhaps. Yes, he knew why she had left the Shakspere house.

And did the neighbours? Did his mother know?

"I was going to say," he told her, having almost forgotten now that he was probably a fugitive, like Nick Bott from time to time, "I was going to declare that from the moment I first looked up at grey-eyed Venus from the muddy bank of Quiney's Pool and saw that tender smile as if Our Lady herself were bending down to me, with a crown of stars —"

"Rest now, darling, and speak not of Scripture."

"It is not in Scripture, it is out of me, me, me."

"It is wrong anyhow."

"It is soon righted, with a word from thy lips. I swear to thee, goddess of the shade, daughter of the stream, the Nymph Salmacis of the Stolen Joys —"

"Mmm, that's not me at all."

"Joined forever to the drowning boy —"

"Willy, who is that riding by Mr. Richardson's manure pile?"

He looked, and flattened himself to the ground.

"I'm dead. It's Squire Somerville."

"Well, he's only collecting his dream rent, darling."

For one of the mad fancies the poor young squire had been having lately was that he still owned the lands and manors taken away from his family by the Earls of Warwick and Leicester, under good Presbyterian law and lordly custom. So every month or so, the good farmers of Shottery, Edstone, Lower Hampton, even as far as Tiddington, would see the dreaming squire plodding round, asking for his rents.

"No, no, he's not dreaming of money, he's dreaming of murder."

The vengeful squire, muttering to himself, had got down off his horse, tethered him to a barnyard post, and was now going toward the Hathaway cottage.

"Quick!" Willy said, seizing Anne's arm.

"Oh, Willy, what is it anyhow?"

"He's after me, he's after me. They all are, they all are."

"I know that, but what for this time?"

"Nothing at all," he gasped, crawling under a hedge and beginning to creep toward the Hathaway barn.

But she was as lithe and sinewy as he was, did not give a whoop for her skirts or anything else when her heart was in anything intense, hasty, exciting, and honest, so that she was after him now through the bushes, among the little apple trees, pausing only to snatch up two ripe apples and bite into one, toss him the other.

Her brother Bart had come down off the roof now and was talking with the squire. Neither one noticed the two figures stealing past a haycock and dodging into the barn through the corncrib.

In here with the crunching animals, so good and friendly, they immediately quieted down.

Breathing gently and sweetly, right beside him, so that with his forearm against her side he could feel the current of life, the very rhythm of her blood, Anne stood and listened to the voices of her brother and the squire.

"Treason. Danger. Stole a horse."

"Willy never did that afore."

"He might be in your barn."

"Only the cows in the barn."

Then Anne and the fugitive heard more horsemen come trotting into the stable-yard.

She sighed, like a fond mother. "Oh, lamb, what is it in the world? And how did you do it this time?"

"People are after me. They always are."

"Which people now? Constables again?"

"Earl Ambrose's men. I stole the horse, and I'm leaving for the wars. Where are we fighting now? Ireland? Holland?"

She looked at him, her eyes peering in alarm through the long chestnut locks, which she had forgotten to twine around and pin up, or whatever she did.

"Oh, darling, I'd die to see thee hanged."

He folded his arms and looked so noble she began to cry. "I'll but kick the air awhile, let not thy heart be troubled, I'll be soon quit, and cast on a dung pile for ravens."

"I'll not let 'em take thee," she said, her fair grey eyes shining with honest tears, her bosom heaving with sighs, as she pulled him earnestly toward the rude ladder which led to the hayloft.

"It is useless," he said, so affected by his coming end that he was staging the scene already, as he had staged the Whitsun pageant last spring for Mr. Jenkins the schoolmaster. Old Ananias Nason, in black, would be the hangman, standing on the scaffold with a pole-ax. Dr. Haycroft the vicar would be upstage, holding a Bible. All the pretty girls in Stratford would be weeping and kissing the prisoner. Mrs. Shakspere would just have fainted, after her great speech of despair, and would be disposed gracefully downstage, where all the men could admire her profile. Uncle Henry and Aunt Maggie would be brawling with the Earl's men-at-arms and would have to be thrown into the Cage. As for sweet Anne Hathaway, she would run mad and drown herself in this very stream, or perhaps it would be better to go floating along a little while, singing snatches of old tunes, or some new tunes if he had time to write them.

He was enjoying his execution and everybody's sorrow so much that he was slow on the ladder and she had to boost him upwards.

"Too late! Lost, lost!" he groaned as she shoved him over the top and into the hay.

They rolled over and over together into the dark womb of the hay-mow, until they were snug and hidden.

"Let's solve the mystery of eternity," he said, holding on for dear life, for the dearness of life, for any old excuse he could think of.

"We haven't time," said Anne.

"Oh, to die, to die, roll onward to that shore together, thy heart against my heart —"

"Stop that, Willy, I'll slap you."

"Sweet death, dark mother, fair bride —"

"Here, put on my petticoat and kirtle. You've done it in the harlotry plays enough, now do it for some good."

"My wild bird tangled in a net, kiss me to death —"

"Stop raving about death now and put on my smock."

"Fair queen, generous goddess, unspotted Venus —"

"Stop it, I say, and give me thy breeches."

He was stricken with the sudden glory of her plan. Old Roman comedies fled mockingly through his mind, and those new Italian farces the Earl of Worcester's men had done at Kenilworth last summer — girls being boys, boys being girls, everybody in everybody else's clothes, and nobody suspecting who was which till the last act, when there was a wholesale marriage.

"But will it work? I doubt it," he said.

"Oh, I'll strap myself in here and stuff myself there, and you do just the opposite. Who'll know the difference?"

"Who cares anyhow?"

"None of those blue moods. Think what a pretty wench you'll be, with that lovely auburn hair. We'll stuff thee out here with a bunch of hay."

"It tickles! Ah!"

"Pox on thee, boy! Be a man! I mean, a woman."

"What if they harm thee? I'll come back and kill 'em."

"Do that, Willy darling, that's an angel," Anne said, and kissed him a hearty smack.

"Hell and death! You're a better man than I am."

"Wait a few years, pretty one."

"I hate being a girl."

"So do I," said Anne, kicking her legs gaily in the close-fitting nether-stocks and slapping her thigh like a young buck in a tavern.

"It may move, it may proceed, it might amble," said Willy thoughtfully, looking down to see if he was bulging properly, or improperly.

"Farewell, sweet maid," said Anne, and kissed him like a sister. "Now go, steal away, melt, melt!"

"Another kiss, another kiss, I may be dead next week."

"Go, ye ape, go, vanish, go off by the sheepfold calling the lambs," she said, pushing him to the ladder. Down he went, almost on his head. But he made it, in spite of the flapping skirts. Wouldn't even kiss me, he thought. Ah, nobody loves me.

Gloomily he crawled into the twilight and then, remembering to be a girl now, and one with a clear conscience, he stood up and began mincing away through the barnyard among the haycocks until he came to some bushes. Here he began to move faster, and when he reached the woods he was running.

The Earl's men rode into the barnyard a few minutes later, making a great noise. It took them quite a good while to find Anne in the hay.

And when they did, they did not hold her long. Squire Somerville wanted to keep her, but the Earl's men laughed at him, and his angry going was hastened by her laughter also.

CHAPTER FOUR

IN the yard of the Crown Inn at Warwick it was a busy morning. The players of the Earl of Leicester had come to town, six bold-looking handsome men leaning upon the padded benches in the taproom and yawning out curses and complaints about muddy roads and flea-bitten country inns.

"Why, they will allow us never a jordan, and there's no more good company in bed since Doll Trapp died."

"All save the fleas are gone."

"And so will we be gone too, ere many more meals."

"Or the country justices will hang us."

Townspeople gathered in the High Street, waiting for the players to ride to St. Mary's Hall to petition the sour old Puritan, John Fisher, for license to perform before the burgesses, in case there was sedition or prophecy in their plays. Boys crowded into the yard of the Crown to watch the unloading of the treasure cart, with its apes' heads, kings' crowns, hell gates, purple robes, devils' pitchforks, and swords and daggers to clash and kill with.

In the doorway to the inn kitchen the girls giggled and gabbled. Among them was a tall, strapping figure in hood and blue gown.

"Who art thou, wench?" asked John Greene, the host of the Crown.

An idiotic cackle came from the facial regions within the hood. The wench flung out an awkward hand and slapped him on the paunch.

"Lor', Cousin John, not know little Joan?"

"Little Joan? *Little* Joan?"

"Here for the fair with my father's ewes from Stratford."

"What, Cousin John Shagspear's wench? Great God, upon what meat hast thou fed since last Michaelmas?"

"We grow, cousin. May I sleep with Mildred tonight?"

44

"Well, make thyself useful in the scullery," said Mr. Greene, hurrying away.

Off went Joan, with one powerful arm around Mildred, the fairest and best-smelling of the chambermaids. They were busy around the inn all morning, running with pots and basins, climbing the stairs to the gallery that ran all round the interior court, helping the players get out their robes, wigs, swords, and copper finery.

A slim boy, alarmingly handsome, kept staring at Joan.

"An Amazon!"

"Should I have been a boy, and played queans?" Joan asked him, nearly kocking him to the ground with a whack between the shoulder blades.

"Fry thy gizzard in hell, thou cow!" said the lovely boy, who spoke as boldly as any of the swearing players, for he was Dick Burbage, the manager's son.

After a morning of insults, blows, and knocks, they had become friends, having the fatal attraction of opposites.

"A peevish wench thou art, Joan, but what a tongue for talking, all the same!"

"And thou too, Dickie, speakest fair as a calf at throat-cutting time."

"Well, all my life, these thirteen long bitter years, have I not been trained for it by my father? I had rather be a painter of fools' faces."

"What wouldst say to this fellow?" asked Joan, taking up a murdered head.

"That's Catiline," said Dick Burbage. "Bob Wilson kills him."

"How if I clap on a queen's wig and crown, and a robe, and pattens, and fool the company?"

"Thou!"

"Just for a little minute, anyhow? I'll steal thee a fat capon."

Dick finally decided to let the ignorant wench do it, for the sake of something horrible. They went behind the treasure cart.

When they came out Joan was taller than ever, because of pattens three inches high, and a copper crown clapped on over a fierce black wig. What with purple robes, and the strutting, and young Dick's blowing of a bugle, the apparition got some attention.

Then the purple-robed figure advanced to the center of the innyard, and began to speak.

Two of the lounging players stood up and stared. Some gabbling wenches and commercial travellers stopped their clatter.

The voice of the visitor from Stratford rose among the galleries. More people came out. Mr. Burbage himself appeared.

After it was over, after the strange dark music was still, and the country queen was bowing before the cheering players and the shouting travellers, Mr. James Burbage came running.

When he could speak, this strong blunt man, who had been a carpenter before he built the first playhouse in London, called upon the Lord for pity. "For 'tis pity, that in the name of morality, we must have only boys in companies to play our queens and shepherdesses! O Lord, girl, why were you not born a boy? And what was that speech you spoke? And who taught you to play a queen?"

The glowing eyes, so merry and yet so sad, looked at him straight. "Why, her Majesty herself, for I saw her once, here in Warwick, when she came to visit Earl Ambrose years ago. What better teacher could there be?"

Burbage stared hard. "Who art thou, girl?"

"Your servant, sir, if you will," said the visitor from Stratford, opening the bosom of the blue gown and baring a powerful masculine chest. Off came the crown, robe, and wig too, and Will Shakspere stood there laughing, his auburn locks bright as a bonfire.

"A boy! A whoreson boy! Who's your father?"

"Alas, sir, is it necessary to know my father? Will not Mr. Greene do? He's my cousin."

And the fugitive from Stratford looked apprehensively toward the arched gateway.

"I'll go to thy father and get thee bound into my company this very day."

"Can we not do it without him, sir?"

"The law says, father. Do you know your father?"

"Too well, sir," said Willy Shakspere. All the light had gone out of his face.

"And have you asked him?"

"Five hundred times," the boy said, turning away so that the tough and angry man could not see the tears in his eyes.

He saw the archway into the High Street all wavy and bright, with strange shapes swimming in it. Strangers were riding in, calling for the ostler, and for fresh horses.

Well-dressed travellers, fine people from the great world, the world he never would see. No, it was hopeless, he was doomed to the glove-shop, the shambles, and the grave.

"Hold that runaway! Hold that horse-thief! The Earl of Warwick himself has said it!"

A gouty old burgess, followed by two ugly constables, rode into the courtyard. It was the scribbling chamberlain of the Warwick Council, crotchety John Fisher, who was not a Fisher at all, but a Hawkins.

In two shakes, Willy Shakspere had snatched up his hood and leaped to the roof of the treasure cart. One more shake, and he had vaulted over the rail and onto the gallery.

"Hey!" cried a commercial traveller.

"Halt!" said another.

Down they both went as Willy dived between them, and through an open window, straight into bed.

"Help!" screamed an old lady, in the middle of it.

"Not from me," he said, leaping to the door.

Old John Greene was just backing out of another room, bowing to somebody in there. "Oh!" he cried, sitting down.

"Goodbye, cousin!" hastily called out a figure in flapping skirts at the head of the back stairs.

"Where the pox art thou going, unlucky boy?"

"To see some other cousin, cousin," answered the escaping visitor, and was gone down the back stairs.

Mr. Greene sat sullenly on the floor, cursing the ins and outs of the inn business while screams and barks came from the kitchen, and in the scullery there was a sudden banging and clanging of falling pots and pans.

"Where is the host? Oh!" cried a hasty traveller, appearing at the top of the front stairs and tripping over Mr. Greene's outstretched left leg, in which he had sciatica.

Down came the hasty traveller, sword, spurs and all, with such a clanging of metal he was like a falling war, all by himself. But he was not by himself, he was by Mr. Greene, who was speaking unto him in curses and little old English words.

"Where is that bloody boy?" cried another jingling traveller, appearing suddenly above them and joining them on the floor.

"Pox on the inn business!" shouted Mr. Greene.

"And on thee, lard-belly!" snarled the most recent arrival, who was Mr. Somerville, the murderous squire.

They then began fumbling, stumbling, and scrambling to get away from one another and back onto those unreliable members, their feet.

"Where art thou going, thou goose-faced knave?" Mr. Greene demanded of Mr. Somerville.

"To a wedding, you fat fool!" said the squire.

"May all the issue of this marriage have horse-tails, pig-snouts, and goat-feet!" called Mr. Greene after him.

And whimpering pitifully as he unlimbered his sciatic leg, he began lamely staggering toward the scullery.

Peeking out from beneath a mulberry bush, young Willy the Hasty took stock of his situation. A dawdling dog came by to sniff at him, and he retreated under the bush. There was a haycock nearby, and beyond that a barn. Beyond the barn was the river, and beyond the river was the Forest of Arden, which had belonged to his ancestors for a thousand years until it had been stolen by the godly Puritans.

Alas, I was born at the wrong time, he thought as he crawled through briars and brambles until he got to the river.

Here he sat down to think.

Should I drown myself?

This made him remember how Anne Hathaway had kissed him in the hay. I wish it had been less like a sister, he thought.

I'll drown myself later. No time now.

For the thing to do next is visit some other cousins. Which should it be? The Webbs, no. The Morysons? No. Uncle Henry and Aunt Maggie? Too far in the other direction.

My mother's lordly cousins, the Ardens of Park Hall?

The very people, he decided. For young Maggie is very beautiful, and has a merry eye.

Ah, but how visit them in this hood and gown?

I have been a slight zany too long already. The game wearies me.

A morbid blue gloom was beginning to sit heavily on him.

Is it possible that I am too stupid to be a success in this life? I could have hooked an Italian slashed doublet, it was right there before me, and I could have snaffled some French hose too, and such a pretty dagger.

Oh, oh, the crimes I have not committed do hang heavy on me.

*Milkmaid!*

CHAPTER FIVE

**N**OW all peace was gone from the smoky old house of the Shaksperes. The wife of the alderman wept from parlour to kitchen, from bedroom to counting-room, and followed her swearing husband into the orchard with her lamentations.

"My son! My son! I will never see him again!"

"Peace, woman! Think of the neighbours."

"It was thy doing, glove-maker! It was they doing, butcher!"

"Let us have peace."

"Thou hast driven my son from me, constable!"

The baffled eye of the alderman, rolling round for someone to blame for all this, caught sight of young Gilly, his second son, eating an oaten cake, some cheese, an apple, and some manchets, a bite of this, a bite of that. He was far too fat already, and only twelve years old.

"Eat, eat!" cried his baffled father. He stamped to the stable and glared at his horses' backsides. Old Dick Hornby the blacksmith peeked out at him from his forge.

"Do ye gape? Do ye stare?"

"No, John. No, John, no."

"Have I horns on my head? Have I wheels on my feet?"

"God forbid, old friend. Rest thee now. Have a beer."

"Shall we guzzle while England falls? What ails this town?"

"Naught that I know of, John. Same as always."

"Same as always!"

John grabbed up a saddle and flung it on the back of Crispin, his black stallion.

"Take us with you!" cried little Dickie and young Joan, running into the stable.

"Go to your mother!" barked their father. In another moment he had Crispin saddled and bridled and was riding out of the orchard.

Half an hour later he was sitting by the bedside of his old

friend Dick Hathaway. A hornet's nest of trouble had stung the old man half to death. His wife, greasy Joan, was raving at Anne in the kitchen. "Shamed on account of thee! Disgraced on account of thee! I'll have to sit in the back of the church."

The two men sighed and looked at each other.

"I'll not last much longer, John. My daughter disgraced."

"You'll not die yet, Dick. What! We're young men still."

"Hear her, John. I should never have married again."

Dame Hathaway came to the bedroom door and shook her finger at John. "It is your son has done this! My stepdaughter disgraced. The whole town laughing."

John looked at her with patient dignity. "Calm, woman, calm."

"I've been calm too long! I've been calm too long! She is leaving this house today!"

And back to the kitchen she ran to scream at Anne again.

"We must rise and tame our women, Dick. We have endured too long."

But old Hathaway groaned and folded his hands. "The race is run, and I am for the dark."

"I'll take her into my house. She shall help my wife with the children. Is it thy wish, Dick?"

"Ah, what is my wish, before a woman's will?" groaned old Hathaway, turning his face to the wall.

John strode to the kitchen and spoke with quiet authority. "Silence, woman! Know your place. Anne, I have decided. Come to my house."

Dame Hathaway's voice rose higher than ever. "She could have married Debdale! She could have married Mosely! John Pace wanted her! The best land in the parish! 'I'll not wed,' she says. 'I cannot love,' she says, as if she were too young. Too young, forsooth! I tell thee this, girl, go where thou wilt, I'll not have thee here any longer!"

"Silence!" roared John.

"Out of my house! Both of ye! Do I not know what the whole parish knows?"

"And what mean ye by that? What mean ye by that?" cried John, beginning to choke.

"Shame!" said greasy Joan, darting her head at him like a snake. "Oh, shame, and you an old fat man!"

"I'll hear no more in this house," muttered the alderman, taking Anne by the arm. "Come with me, girl. My wife shall make thee welcome."

But Anne gave him a long sad look and turned away. John dropped his hands and went trembling out of the house. He heard the woman screaming at the girl after he had mounted Crispin and ridden out of the stable-yard.

For a long time he rode aimlessly. He went into a tavern, called for a cup of sack, tossed it down, had another, and knew instantly what he would do. He went out, mounted Crispin again, and rode back to Shottery. Behind a clump of willows he watched the thatched cottage until he saw Anne come out, carrying a sack over her shoulder. She was dressed in the old mourning for her mother, with a hood which made her look like a nun. She went quickly up the path and through the hedgerows to the deep banked lane.

He waited awhile, then went riding after her.

"Give it to me," he said.

Without a word from her, he took up the heavy sack and laid it across the saddlebow.

"Where will anyone love thee more than I?" he asked, his voice thick.

"Are you mad?" Her grey eyes would not look at him.

"Not yet, I think."

"I will go to Aunt Kate Whittington, in Temple Grafton," Anne said. "She loved my mother."

"She's the worst shrew in the county," John said as he dismounted and took her by the arm.

"No, no, never, never."

"Is it because you still love the priest that you will not have any man?"

She whirled round, her eyes wild. "You dare speak of him!"

"Oh, I dare anything, these mad days. Is it because you still love Robin Debdale?"

"I forbid you to speak of him!"

"Why do you love him?" he cried, his powerful fingers digging into her arm.

"Because he is holy," Anne said, her voice trembling. Tears came to her eyes.

"A mad reason, to love a man!"

She tore herself out of his desperate hands and cried, sobbing, "You are not fit to touch the hem of his garment!"

"And are you?" whispered John, staring into her eyes.

She put her hands to her face and wept.

Then she started walking up the lane, and he followed her in weary silence, leading Crispin with the sack full of her belongings.

When he rode back up the High Street in Stratford it was early afternoon. Anger and sadness rode with him, and a desire for violence. Round eyes of neighbours were staring at him now, and no mistake. Let 'em stare.

As he came near to his little dark house on Henley Street he heard the voice of his wife raised in steady lamentation to the children.

Four Catholics muttering together under a penthouse roof grinned as he rode darkly by.

"Sir John of the Fallen Staff," said Rafe Cawdrey the butcher.

"Squire Poorjohn of the Jakes," Bill Russell muttered.

"The master of the mill, who cries 'Hold!' to the breeze," said Tom Logginge.

"The Knight of the Shaky Spear," Rafe Cawdrey added.

John gave them a long slow stare as he rode by. All Catholics, and all carrying arms in clear disobedience of the Queen's orders.

Now the voice of his unhappy wife was louder and sang in his head like an imprisoned bee.

"Cannot keep order in his own house, and would impose it on the whole town," Tom Barber called after him. They all burst out laughing.

The alderman rode by his house and into Back Bridge Street, where his loyal friends would be at their barrows and stands. At first it was a great comfort to talk to old Starky and Kindall about the high price of crossbeams and scantlings, and he made a good bargain on some timber from his wife's estate of Asbies, in Wilmecote. But he was uneasy. Why did people look at him?

"The Earl of Leicester's faction is loud in the Privy Council, they say," Bassell Burditt was saying to Bob Bratt. "If the Catholics rise there'll be many a broken head before Michaelmas."

"England is sore troubled, and needs peace," said John, riding on to confer with Ad Quiney. But he could not find his old friend the mercer in his shop, and so he rode on to the Bear Inn, where there might be some commercial travelers interested in bargains in gloves, malt, corn, wool, or timber.

But the Bear was crowded with Catholics. The Debdales were there, and Mr. Cottam. In the center of a whispering group stood Sir William Catesby with Mr. Underhill, owner of New Place. His two sinister sons, Fulke and Hercules, stood somberly glaring at anyone who came near.

John glared back at them and sat down on a padded bench alone. He had three, four, five, or six beers, and in the ensuing clarity and relief, not to say marvelous acuity of vision and mind, perceived that all these Catholics were armed and equipped for travel.

Young Somerville, the vengeful squire, came jingling in, all spurs, plumes, slashed doublet, and velvet.

Immediately his dark brooding eye caught John. They stared at each other with hatred.

Then the squire smiled and held out his hand. "I'll tell you a secret, cousin," he said.

Cousin? Old John's neck began to swell.

"Shall I tell you a secret?"

John dropped the hot hand of the squire and picked up his glass. "If you like, sir."

Somerville leaned down and whispered in his ear. "The day has come," he said. Then he straightened up, still smiling, and went jingling over to join the group of Catholics.

"Ah, Johnny! Well met for the wedding!" said Sir William Catesby, shaking hands with the squire.

Wedding! John's eyes bulged.

Now he knew why all these Catholics had gathered for a journey. He finished his beer, got quietly up, paid the shot, and left the inn. Two ostlers helped him climb onto Crispin, who had grown taller.

Time to warn his loyal friends. Whatley the sheriff would make one. Williams the fishmonger, Symonds the scrivener, Sadler the baker, Smith the haberdasher, Dickson the keeper of the Swan, Biddle the cutler, Whateley the vintner, Quiney the mercer — all were godly Puritans and loyal to England and the Earls of Leicester and Warwick.

To hell with the frog-faced Frenchman! Marry the Queen, would he? All England was ready to arise at the word.

John was smiling grimly as he headed Crispin toward Hamlet Sadler's shop.

Henry Field the tanner called out to him on the way by. "Where to now, John? Back to Temple Grafton?"

John glared at him and rode by in silence. He dismounted at Hamlet Sadler's shop and went striding in. The dreamy young man was there among his pies and crumpets.

"Well, neighbour," said John, "the time is at hand. The Queen is to marry the Frenchman, unless all loyal Englishmen arise."

Hamlet Sadler yawned and said, "I'm tired, John. Up all night I was."

"Awake, ye blind owl! Would ye be murthered in your bed?"

"Oh, John, England will muddle through. Always done it afore, and —"

"Can ye not see? Can ye not hear? The Catholics are all armed and ready."

"Now, John, do na be like thy old father Diccon Shagshaft the shepherd, bawling out to the sheep and cows to awake. We'll handle the Catholics in our own way."

"Sheep and cows! Sheep and cows!"

"Calm, friend, calm. The dough must rise, the yeast must work."

And the dreamy young man yawned peacefully among his tarts and pies.

"Fall in your dough tub and never get out!" cried John. "Let 'em rape your women and burn down your scurvy bakery, I'll not come to help thee!"

A rosy young girl peeked out from among the ovens: Judy Stanton, in a modest blue gown.

"O Lord, Master Shagsbird, those be very bitter words!" said the rosy girl.

"Ah, ah, so that's where the yeast rises, eh?" grumbled John, backing out of the shop.

Bah! Bah! Bah!

He was standing under the penthouse roof of the pie place

when the man he hated most in all the world came haughtily riding up the High Street — Edward Arden, the Squire of Park Hall, as proud and arrogant as any lord in Warwickshire, with his ancient family arms in rusty gold on his saddle skirt, and on the badges of his four servants riding behind him. He was High Sheriff of Warwickshire, as his ancient ancestor Robert of Arden had been, and he looked just like the jealous alderman's wife: same haughty nose, same high-riding chin, same dark and scornful eye.

The leading Catholic conspirator in the country!

Could none of these people see?

The Fossicar brothers were whispering together and goggling at John, who had no family arms, either ancient and honourable or dubious and new.

"Ah, Muster Sadspur, off riding to Temple Grafton again?" inquired old Henry the clock-maker.

Sadspur! Shakebag! Could the clowns never get his name right?

John glared at them as he climbed heavily up into the saddle. As for Squire Arden, he was riding grandly toward the Bear, where all the Catholics waited.

Hark! Was that the sound of a trumpet? Crispin pricked up his ears, and whinnied.

"Alas for England, when the beasts have more wit than the men," said John.

Just then Lewis ap Williams, the fishmonger, came trundling by, bawling "Eels! Fishes and eels!"

John spoke urgently to him, saying, "The time is at hand, neighbour. Have ye your sword?"

Williams shook his head and replied, "No, John, fishes and eels, fishes and eels." And he went trundling along the High Street, calling his wares.

John kicked his spurs into Crispin's flanks. The stallion groaned, shuddered, and began to kick. The alderman pulled hard on the reins. Crispin turned round and round, then began dancing sideways into Back Bridge Street, overturning a few barrows of vegetables.

"So, boy, so, boy," said John patiently while tradesmen cursed and shouted. A flock of geese came waddling over the bridge, the old gander sticking out his neck and hissing at the dancing stallion.

Tom Barber, Norman Fitts, Ted Tinsley, and Bill Russell came briskly trotting by on obedient horses, all armed and ready for something.

"Where goest thou sideways so fast, Master Crabspear?" called out Barber as the alderman passed them broadside on, speaking earnestly to Crispin.

"Ask rather, where goes the horse with the ass?" Ted Tinsley inquired.

And they all went ho-hoing up the road to Warwick.

John Shagspear went sideways to the house of Whatley the sheriff.

The lazy man was asleep again.

"Awake! England is waiting!"

"Well, England has waited afore, John," mumbled Whatley.

"The papists are gathering! The time is at hand!"

"I'll see about it in the morning," said Whatley, and went back to sleep.

When John Sagspear came out his face was dark with anger, but his eyes saw a great light. The scurvy knave was a sleeping Catholic. They were all in the plot together.

"Are ye stocks? Are ye stones?" he wheezed to Smith the haberdasher and Quiney the mercer. "The Queen is marrying the Frenchman! The fatal day has come! Rise now, ye English, or die forever!"

Smith and Quiney looked solemnly at him. "Calm, John, calm. Remember the choking sickness thou hadst last winter. We get old, John, we get old. We must hang onto our five wits."

"Fools' wits! Ninnies' wits! Can ye not see? Can ye not hear?"

"Thou'lt have to send for Anne Hathaway to nurse thee again, John. How does Anne Hathaway, John? How does she without her petticoat?"

He strode away from them, climbed delicately and gently into the saddle, spoke reasonably to Crispin, and took the road to Bidford, which would lead to Chipping Norton, which would lead to Oxford, which would lead to London. He was out of the town now, passing farms and sheepfolds, passing common fields where mowers and gleaners were working, where cows were eating and windmills were turning. "Arise!" he shouted, waving his rusty sword. "Defend England! Save the Queen! A rescue! A rescue from the Frenchman! Awake! Awake!"

The cows went on chewing, the windmills went on turning, the peaceful farmers went on mowing and gleaning.

"The time has come! The day is at hand!"

Round eyes in fat faces were turned toward him, and a few boobies stopped to watch him gallop by in a cloud of dust.

The eager whinny of a mare came clearly over the fertile fields. Crispin pricked up his ears and began dancing sideways toward a small meandering stream.

"So, boy, so, boy," said Mr. Shakspere soothingly. They danced to the bank of the stream. Crispin snorted, craned his neck, whinnied, and began mincing toward the bulrushes. In another moment he had tucked in his hindquarters and was skating down the bank.

Mr. Shakspere was beginning to shout again. The farmers in the fields heard his voice roaring from the water, and leaving their work and strolling down to good positions along the stream they peacefully watched and listened to the show.

"Help! Help!" cried the alderman, thrashing among the **waterlilies.**

# CHAPTER SIX

$\mathcal{G}$ATHERING roses in her pleached garden, a fine lady in a silken gown and a hat of plaited straw looked up suddenly and said "Hark!"

"O Lord, mother, have they come?" cried a young girl in a brocaded gown, dropping a pair of garden shears.

"Calm thyself, it is not thy husband yet, it is a cat in the hedge, I think."

They both listened and heard a creeping and a rustling coming toward them.

"Mother, I wish he would not come."

"Peace! Thy father has chosen."

"I like not his eye, mother."

"It is but maidenly. Hark!"

There was a louder rustling, and then a tall figure in a blue gown and hood crawled out from the hedge and came toward them, waving.

"Who art thou, wench?" cried the fine lady, starting back.

"Cousin Mary! Do you not know me?" called the wench, pulling off the hood. The auburn locks of Willy Shakspere glowed at her.

"I know thee not, thou dirty doxie," said Mrs. Arden, stepping quickly back. "Margaret, run to the house and tell Middens to come at once!"

The young girl obediently started away toward the house. But the visitor from Stratford ran after her through the flower beds, explaining: "It is I, Maggie! Cousin Willy from Stratford! Wait for me!"

Maggie burst out laughing and flung her arms around him. "Oh, Willy, you've joined the players!"

"Not yet, sweet cousin," he said, kissing her several times.

"Alas, Willy, if I were but marrying you," she whispered. "Take me with you and we'll be milkmaids?"

"Why, who art thou marrying then?"

Tears came into her fine eyes. "Johnny Somerville from Edstone. My father has gone as mad as he."

"Oh no, do not do it," he groaned. But Mrs. Arden had now reached them and sternly took her daughter by the arm.

"Art thou mad, girl, to be kissing and hugging clowns? In with thee at once!"

"He's no clown, he's my sweet cousin Willy, and I love him."

"Shame! So soon before the wedding! In, I say!"

"I can explain everything," sweet Cousin Willy declared eagerly, but Mrs. Arden gave him a haughty stare, pulled the girl with her into the house and slammed the door in his face.

He stood there muttering in the garden until two rude grooms, one carrying a broom, the other a pitchfork, suddenly came at him from out of the scullery and drove him off the property of the Ardens of Park Hall.

"Wait till I tell my mother about this!" he called back from behind a tree.

"Aroint thee, wench!" cried the groom with the pitchfork, leaping after him.

The visitor from Stratford took to his heels.

It is harder being a girl than I had expected, he thought as he crawled out of the woods into a stable just as dusk was falling. He was up in the hayloft before the cows knew anything about it.

The warm scratchy darkness made him think of Anne Hathaway again. He was dreaming of her when somebody climbed in beside him and whispered, "Who are you?"

"Joan," he answered, half asleep.

It was a farm girl, ready to crawl in and go to bed.

"Have you run away from your master, Joan?"

"My mistress."

"Did she beat thee?"

"Every day."

"I am sorry for thee, Joan. My lady beats me too."

"A hard world for poor wenches. What's thy name?"

"Mildred."

"I'm sorry for thee, Mildred."

"I'm sorry for thee, Joan," said the farm girl, lying down beside him.

"Naught for us poor souls but work and starvation."

"Why, did she starve thee too?" asked the farm girl, snuggling up to him. "How big and strong thou art, Joan!"

"Alas, but a shadow of my former self."

"Poor Joan," said the farm girl. "I'll creep in the kitchen and steal thee a honey-cake."

"Now, Mildred dear?"

"When mistress has gone to bed."

"Steal me some ale too?"

"Thirsty, poor Joan? Cruel mistress!"

"Cruel world, sweet Mildred."

"There's no joy in it for such as us," said the farm girl, beginning to weep.

"Oh, there's some," said the bogus Joan, putting his strong arms round the weeping Mildred.

"Where? Tell me where."

"Here, Mildred dear."

A scream, quickly muffled, in the hayloft. Then the sound of thrashing and kicking. Then low laughter. Then soft rustles and sighs, and then silence.

Willy slept very little that night. But long before daylight he left the dreaming Mildred and went down the ladder.

Out in the farmyard all the chickens were having their breakfast. So was a family of thrushes, tossing dry leaves over their heads and crying "Early bird! Tee hee hee!"

The air smelt fresh and clean, and the larks were up hunting for the sunrise. He was into the woods and down on the river bank before the sky was light. He went to sleep here, and awoke in full morning, with birds chirping all around him. Down in the river a country girl was bathing.

"Hallo!" he called, waving.

"Hallo! Come on in!" cried the county girl, standing up in the water and waving back.

"I'd rather just watch!" he explained, and sat there awhile watching. But he was too hungry and thirsty now for anything but a good loaf and a bird, a bottle too, and crept back among the trees to see if he could steal some breakfast.

I must shed these garments, though there are compensations, he decided.

Just then he heard horses jingling toward him through the

forest. He crept into some bushes and went to sleep again.

He awoke suddenly, feeling a rough hand travelling up his thigh. From deep in the bushes he saw the looming form of a large bearded man. The eyes of this man were very bright.

In another moment it would be too late. Willy Shakspere raised his right knee, reached up and grasped the large bearded man by the ears. He then gave a good gypsy twist and stood the fellow on his head. Then he spun him over on his back, and leaped upon him.

A choked cry came from the bearded man.

Then silence.

Willy came crawling out of the bushes, dressed in a ragged old doublet and slops.

Groans and curses came from inside the bushes. "What will I wear? Have pity on me, a moral man."

"I have left thee my petticoats, O moral one. Wear them in humble Christian repentance for thy evil desires."

"May all the devils of hell cut all thy two stones till thou shalt not have a stone to throw at a dog."

"A sad curse from one in thy position," said Willy, taking a tuck in the doublet he now wore, for it was very great. "I leave thee now to think upon thy sins committed and uncommitted. Amen."

And he melted away among the shapes and shadows of the trees.

CHAPTER SEVEN

ONE foggy morning a ragged old man with a sack over his shoulder appeared at Alderman Shakspere's back door. A torn old hat of plaited straw came down to his eyes. He was dressed in old muddy slops and a ragged doublet tied around him with rope. Out of his marvellously dirty face two strangely glittering eyes peered at Mrs. Shakspere.

"Lord have mercy on us!" she cried.

"Amen," said the ragged old man in a rusty voice, coughing. "Well, kiss thy cousin, lass. Dost not know thy Cousin Poorjohn?"

"Oh!" screamed the proud lady, starting back.

Meanwhile Mr. Shakspere had come into the kitchen for a couple of cold squabs and was now staring at the ragged visitor with his mouth open.

"A fine world, master, when Peascod Arden's favourite son is sneezed at by his little cousin he's kissed a thousand times, aye, and bounced on his knee too," said the ragged old countryman, plodding into the kitchen and setting his filthy sack down on the table. "That's gratitude, master! Eh?"

"I cry you mercy, good sir, we did not expect to see you," stammered the alderman.

"Bah! A mad world," grumbled the old ragged man, snatching up the wine bottle from the table and seizing one of the squabs. He sat down by the hearth and began gobbling the squab and gulping the wine. "And how's the glove business, eh?"

Mrs. Shakspere had been looking suspiciously at her unknown and awful cousin for some moments. Now she suddenly crept up on him and snatched off his hat. The fiery locks of her missing son glowed at her. "I knew it!" she cried.

Out of the wonderful dirtiness and from among the painted

wrinkles of the visiting cousin's face a pair of merry eyes sparkled at her.

"Oh, my boy! my boy!" she cried, embracing him. "Oh, I could murder thee with these hands!"

The alderman's neck swelled, his eyes bulged, he panted like Dick Hornby's bellows. Then he began to laugh.

"A bastard cousin of the Ardens!" he wheezed, and then was seized with a fit of coughing. The ragged countryman arose and beat the alderman upon the back. Groans, grunts, sighs, sneezes and ha ha's came from the master of that household. "I knew it all the time," he said weakly. "Old Peascod Arden's favourite son Poorjohn. How does the glove trade? Oh, oh, I've always wanted to meet these fine Arden cousins and now I've had my wish. Pray sit at my table, sir. Make yourself welcome. Hast any news of Cousin Surecard and Cousin Flap-ear?"

"They sent thee their blessings from Dogpond Common," said his son, reaching for his little sister Joan who was staring at him with big eyes. "Give me a kiss, little cousin."

"Thou art no kissing cousin of mine," said the child, and ran away.

"Then I must kiss thy wife, master," the auburn-haired visitor said. "And what's for dinner?"

"Not until thou hast washed that face and taken off those filthy rags," said Mrs. Shakspere. "Oh, thou naughty varlet, where hast been these long aching nights and weary days?"

"Not so far away, sweet mother," said her son, beginning to haul out various kid-skins, deer-skins, and leathern aprons from among the articles in his sack. "There's for the glove business. Let me see, let me see."

"Oh, thy good suit, Willy, what has become of thy good suit?"

"We shall find it in the hayloft," he answered. "And how does Anne Hathaway, mother?"

A sudden silence greeted this question.

"No news? When I have so much to tell?"

He looked inquiringly at his mother, then at his father. Both looked dark.

"Well, I will go and claim my suit of her," he said, bringing out some baubles, pins, poking-sticks, ribands, and a dried snakeskin. "Good for the choking sickness, father. I had it of

Tom Tiddler, who is King of the Vagabonds and taught me the secret of adding fifty years to my age. He is better at it than the players."

Old John Shakspere looked darker still. "With the players again? Did I not forbid it?"

"Oh, alas, my son consorting with vagabonds and strolling players," said Mrs. Shakspere with a few tragic gestures. "Oh, to think that he should come to this!"

"I'll tell thee where he inherits it from," said the alderman. "For the last twenty years —"

"Twenty-two years," said Mrs. Shakspere with a suffering sigh. "And before I ever married the son of our shepherd was *he* not always running off with the players?"

"I — you — he —" began the alderman again, gasping and blowing.

"Mad Jack of Snitterfield!" said his wife, her fine eyes flashing. "The woe of all modest maids, the blight of my life too, when all's done. What about that time you ran off with the Coventry morris-men and your poor witless father had to send the constables to fetch you? The less you have to say about harlotry players the better."

"Let us hear all about it, Cousin Shagback," said the prodigal son eagerly.

"Thou shalt hear more than that, Cousin Ragbag," said his father.

Mrs. Shakspere gave a tragic cry. "Alas! My son is a thief!" Out of the sack she drew a handsome silk gown of sea-water green.

Willy jumped up, waving his arms wildly. "That's for Anne Hathaway! That's for Anne Hathaway!"

Now both parents became marvellously united in disapprobation. "Oh, I have feared this day!" moaned his mother.

"It is as I have always predicted," growled his father.

Willy indignantly shouted that he had won the gown fairly at Coventry Fair with two throws of the dice, and he might better be dead than with parents who did not believe him, and had never loved him. Nor his fine cousins neither, the Ardens of Pox Hall, who had thrown him upon a dunghill to be eaten by ravens. A plague on all cousins! To the devil with 'em, and let 'em marry what mad rascals they willed, he would not go to

the wedding, no, if they begged him, High Sheriff of Warwickshire or Low Sheriff of Hell, it was all one to him who these
Ardens were, yea, and the Shagstaffs too, and the Wagstaffs
also, may they be afflicted with the cramp.

So in one neatly twisted minute he had them both humbly
begging for details, and all wrath, bogus or otherwise, was
forgotten.

"Oh, alas, poor Maggie married to that gloomy squire, who'll
weigh her down with brats and sorrow! And I had planned for
her to marry thee, Willy!"

"The fellow's mad," growled Mr. Shakspere.

"Tell me what Maggie wore," said his wife eagerly.

"Well, mother dear, I was not invited to stay very long."

"Shame, shame, not to invite thee to the wedding! Thou,
named for our common ancestor William, a great lord of many
manors, whose estates extended farther than the eye could see,
and rightly so, for our ancestors were kings, my dear, kings of
Britain and lords of this whole country roundabout before
Unholy Harry stole their lands from them. But our day will
come, my son. And thou shalt be a gentleman, and an esquire,
and live at Asbies, our estate we inherited from my father, and
thou shalt get many children, and be a joy to me in my old
age —"

"But mother, sweet mother, how can I get children when I
have not even shaken hands with my wife yet, and besides,
women are a dish I love not, for they are all made of tongue."

Old John's eye gleamed at this hit, and he gave his eldest
son and heir a good nudge with his elbow.

"Was Maggie's dress very fine? Of what fashion was it?"

"I was in a hurry, mother."

"Alas, where were your eyes? Had it a kirtle? A French
bosom? Italian laces? How many flounces?"

"I looked only at her dark eyes."

"Surely you can remember what she wore!"

"It was my chief study to remember my own petticoats,
mother."

"And that is the worst thing of all! That is the worst thing
you ever did! If it had been anyone else in this world but sweet
Anne Hathaway, by the blessed saints and martyrs in heaven
I would think my son was lewdly given!"

Another nudge from the elbow of the alderman.

"Would ever woman in this world do so much for thee as poor Anne? I remember the day she fished thee out of the pool, and thou dank as a dog. 'It seems this one will always be my special care,' she said. And when thou wert but a tender infant, did she not bathe thee in the basin and play with thee like a very mother with her darling child, and she but seven years old?"

"Mother, can we please control ourselves? Is there no shame in this house?"

"Thou owest her thy very life, aye, three times it is now, for did she not save thee from choking too, and thy face as black as a Moor's with the fishbone in thy throat? And now the poor creature disgraced and sent from home to be no better than a beggar."

Now it was Mr. Shakspere who was choking. He rose from the table and staggered out of the kitchen into the orchard.

"What did you say, mother?"

Willy's voice had gone weak.

"Ah, the work of evil tongues! The only home she has ever known, though but a poor cottage at best. May God forgive that wicked woman, and thee, Willy, for bringing this upon her!"

"Mother, for God's sake tell me."

"The purest virgin in all Stratford, Shottery I mean to say, and might have been won to our holy religion and even become a nun if Unholy Harry had not closed all the convents and stolen their lands! But a day will come —"

"Mother! Tell me where Anne is."

"Our religion will not always be flouted. Saints have shed their blood, martyrs have lost their heads, and will again."

"Will you tell me, mother?" shouted her son.

"Hear the boy shouting like his father! And in this house!"

"Then I will shout out of the house! I will shout out of the house!"

His arms waving in the air, her son went rapidly out of the theatre, that is to say house. But that beautiful and inexhaustible voice of tragedy followed him. He clapped his hands to his ears, he ground his teeth, he took hold of his head with both hands and tried to unscrew it and throw it away. It would not unscrew. He ground his teeth, moaned, groaned, and began cursing the several devils' names that were his ancestors. He cursed the Shakebags, he cursed the Sacksbeers, he cursed the Wagstaffs, the Sagstaffs, and then began on the Ardens, whom he cursed all the way into history and back again.

He had the whole story by the time he came slinking into the house late that night, like a harmless necessary cat. Sleep lay over the old sagging house like a veil, and he reached his room under the dripping eaves without even a mouse hearing him, as far as he knew.

Into his lumpy bed he crept, and immediately a whole calumnious web of gossip began spinning itself all over him, so that he almost strangled with it.

I must think, he thought.

But his mind bustled all over like sixty-five families of crabs in a basket. How am I ever going to stop it? he wondered. It rides off with me like a scattering team of wild horses and I am even more mixed than my metaphors.

What is to become of her now? And of me, of me?

And my poor mother, fighting the whole lost battle of the old religion every day?

Which one of us will run mad the first?

Sleep, sleep, come knit me up, mend me, mend us all, sweet sleep.

But he was afraid of sleep, for as soon as he slept he would dream of gore, he would dream of murder. The madcap, the catbird, the jester, was only his mocking envelope in daytime hours, when anybody was listening and looking. In his dreams he wandered through a dark kingdom of evil and despair.

What is to become of me anyhow? I cannot forever hold all this madness in my head.

Poor Cousin Maggie marrying the mad squire, and my parents becoming mad with the bloody question that will tear England to pieces before it is answered.

O sweet religion of love, how have you become this addle-headed battle of hate?

At last he slept, but he fought his way with monsters and devils, no, they were the angels in the windows his father had broken, angels with broken wings of glass. A bleeding martyr with stumps of arms, his tongue cut out because he had sung a hymn in Latin, was drawn and quartered high on a gory scaffold before a screaming crowd. Mothers held up their children to see, and the darling babes were spattered with blood. The saint arose from the red and slippery planks and snatched back his head from the executioner.

"Follow me, Willy," the head said.

"I'll do it, Robin," said Willy in his sleep. Then he was awake, sweating and shaking.

A snore came from the bed beside his own. Gilbert was strenuously sleeping, his large mouth open, while beside him lay the peaceful Dickie, not old enough or bright enough to be a problem.

Ah, why am I the one that makes the trouble? Willy thought. What is it about me that is wrong?

The old apple tree was rubbing its scarred boughs against the timber-and-plaster sagging wall of the glove-seller's house. The whole night was awake, the whole breathing and stirring creation of small creatures living in darkness.

Slowly gleaming through the feathery trees, the fair moon rose into the sky of night. His heart contracted with a pain he had never felt before, his throat ached, the tears sprang to his eyes.

Why was I born too late? Why am I doomed to live in this old, tired, divided, frightened world? The great times are gone, the Queen of Heaven no longer reigns in the Kingdom of Innocence, men are greedy, thinking only of gain, and my mother and father are disappointed in me.

But higher rose the moon, shining on the bosom of the river where it lay in the embrace of the sleeping town, shining on the housetops and the orchard trees. Brightly and more brightly shone the moon, and the unattainable beauty sweetly disclosed herself to him. Now he knew that all his dreams were not in vain, that he would go out into the great world beyond these little shops and houses, he would see Rome, Venice, Athens, all the great cities of antiquity and glory, and he would come home to her, rich, famous, noble, and lay his gifts at her feet.

"Welcome home, my son," she would say.

And he would lead her to the door of the best house in town, or second-best anyhow, called New Place, on the corner of Dead Lane.

But now miraculously she became transmuted into a loving woman with grey eyes and chestnut hair.

"Is it you, Anne?"

"Oh, don't you know, lamb?" said Anne.

In another moment she was in his arms. Unknown ages passed. He opened his eyes and looked out of the window. A breeze was blowing from the river, a cloud was blowing over the moon.

He heard a weary sigh from the room where his parents slept, and knew it was his father hunting through darkness for some solution to the puzzle of his scorning wife, his worthless son, the ever-mounting heap of worry and debt. In all his years of trade and loss, had the baffled businessman ever had time to think of a thing so alien as his own happiness?

Alas, my father, thought Willy, slipping out of bed and softly picking up the handy bundle he had made of his clothes. He began putting on his shirt, his breeches, moving to the window, slipping on his stockings, ungartered, and his shoes, unlaced. Then he climbed up on the window-sill.

No owl hooting in the orchard this time.

"Alas, Bloody Richard, shall I ever see thee again?" he whispered.

Then he reached into the spangled darkness for a branch that was not broken.

He made it without disaster, and only a little scraping and scratching. Picking himself up in the wet grass, he picked up also a few juicy apples.

Beginning to eat these, he crept out of the orchard, hiding from the moon, now peeping out again, stole out the back gate, tiptoed over the shining trickle in Swine Lane, and started off among the shadows of trees, haycocks, manure piles, and miscellaneous messuages between here and the river.

And then, when he reached the mossy bank, he had to find his narrow boat among the others tied up here, and be sure of his oars. Soon all was right, he had the good little boat headed out of the reeds and into the broad shining stream.

As streaky-fingered dawn was combing back the English clouds over the pale sky he hid his boat in the reeds two miles above Bidford, where the Avon made a broad curve, and struck out through the fields and across the highway over the hills and into the vale of Temple Grafton. The ruins of another plundered church and priory rose black against the white sky twittering with birds. He shivered, thinking of the voices that had sung matins there for centuries of English mornings.

I'll never understand religion, he thought.

My godly father murdered fair hope and charity in his own heart and household when he hacked the pretty statues. And made a great tragic actress out of my mother.

Alas, poor England, as divided over religion as my father and mother, and they're murdering people over religion in France, and burning people in Spain.

If it were not for our doughty Queen they'd have lighted all the fires of pious hatred here. May God prevail on His servants to give us peace.

I wonder if Robin came back what would happen. Would she cease loving children and worthless boys like me, and follow him this time wherever he goes?

To the scaffold, he thought, hearing the larks high in the air, following their voices until they were out of sight. But still the merry cries rang in the sky.

He came to a rude cottage by a stream, under aged oaks. The flock was standing, all facing the barnyard door from which the shepherd would come. Or shepherdess, he thought, creeping low along a hedge.

He waited there in the tall grass, which was full of the busy sounds of amorous creatures seeking one another, or hungry creatures, also seeking.

No shepherdess appeared. But old Tom Whittington came out and let the sheep into the pasture.

After awhile Willy wandered down to the stream, beginning to get hungry for breakfast. There was a small clump of willows here, and beneath them a spring-house where Anne's Aunt Kate would keep milk and butter, perhaps some few tasty dishes cold.

Then he forgot about breakfast, for Anne Hathaway was seated on the mossy bank, forlornly gazing down at a spider-web as if it were the tangled skein of her own life.

Some weary thought was making her sigh and shake her

head; and then she looked up at him. He saw the light come into her grey eyes.

"Willy!" she whispered, and then she was in his arms, laughing and crying. "Oh, my golden boy, I thought you were dead."

In the ruins of the priory they met many a night after that, whispering together of his hopes and dreams, and also of his morbid woes and despairs.

"I'm feared for thee, Willy. You say everything is wonderful one day, and then it's all black and horrible the next. Which do you believe?"

"Both," he said.

"How hurt you get! You must not let yourself brood on those things, or it will make you mad."

"You are a woman. I am a man."

"But all the raving, Willy! And the look you get in your eyes!"

"I'll hide my eyes, and sew up my lips."

"Willy —"

"Yes, no, and maybe."

"John has your future all settled."

He laughed and laughed. She had to grapple with him, and hold her hand over his mouth.

"Ah, Willy, with all your mad brightness and not a penny in your pocket. How are you going to jingle your way through life?"

"I'll serve Earl Ambrose."

"John's whole heart is set on your being a gentleman."

"With a hog's cheek on my shield."

"And who will you marry, Willy?"

"Oh, some girl somewhere."

Sometimes Anne would laugh at him. Sometimes she would be silent. Sometimes he would find an excuse to be over Bidford way and meet her at some market. They would go round sampling the vegetables together or following the Lord of Misrule through the village with vine leaves in their hair, surrounded by singing children. Sometimes a whole crowd of children would be following them down the street, laughing and shrieking like wild things, he had got them so excited. He would be any old thing out of history or the ragbag, and nobody had ever seen anything like it. But the children recognized it instantly, and adored him. Other times he would have them grave and quiet while he murmured to them in a little voice, like the breeze gentle, the night dark, until all at once he would horrify them with a whooping and hallooing that meant murder, blood, slaughter, and crime! crime! He would have them screaming and hiding under the market barrows while he leaped up on some old horse's back and yelled "Revenge! Revenge! Murder most foul! Blood! Blood!"

Anne did not know whether to sing, dance, laugh, cry, or run away and hide herself.

"Oh, Willy, how art thou going to last through life? When is thy kettle ever going to simmer down?"

Mr. Cottam, the schoolmaster in Stratford, who was a secret Catholic and whose brother was a priest with Robin Debdale in Rome, said that if William was going to frighten the children anyhow it would be better to frighten them in Latin, and give them some education out of it. This set him off on a whole new track that lasted as long as the schoolmaster's patience. Poor little Cottam was new here, only just arrived from Oxford, and had the shining innocence of scholarship upon him.

This was raw meat for William the Hungry. Refused any nibbles at the nipples of those great soul mothers Oxford and Cambridge, condemned to steal such titbits of knowledge as he could from stray glimpses at the books of gentlemen who were kind, snatched out of the grammar school and put to work at the pickling-vats and the scraping-benches, he now flung himself for a season into the heady game of assisting the innocent schoolmaster with the boys' declamations and spectacles.

Three months later, the exhausted scholar locked himself up in his lodgings until he should learn how to sleep again without the constant companionship of at least three overwhelming women, that is to say Melpomene, Thalia, and Calliope, the muses of Tragedy, Comedy, and Heroic Poems.

As for his assistant in scaring people with old Latin murders, rapes, tortures, and revenges out of Seneca, or romping comedies out of Plautus that were even more frightening to the ladies, he was feeling wonderful, and could not understand why they should not do five or six more complete plays between Michaelmas and Advent. As a slight consolation, he was allowed to lead the boys of Holy Trinity choir. In a few weeks he had them so beautifully sensitive that they were bursting into tears at the sound of their voices among the arches, and telling their fathers that they were all going to join Willy Shakspere's players as soon as he got permission from Earl Ambrose to form a company.

This could not last long. But what a sight it was to see him at rehearsal!

He would come strolling in late, with hay in his hair, his hose ungartered, and with cockle-burs, coloured stones, or perhaps a pigeon sticking out its idiot head and cooing from his pocket.

He would release it and it would go flapping off to the woods.

The wild yells of the boys would die down, finally, and they would be ready for music and amazement.

Under the dismal yews of the vicar's garden they would assemble, while the tender and fading light of afternoon, like the smile of a bemused mother, investigated their faces.

Willy would find an apple in his pocket and begin eating it.

Townspeople would be gathering in Sanctity Lane, as if they smelt music.

He would take a large bite out of the apple, spit out a seed, raise his right hand, still holding the bitten apple, and a high, sweet, piercing note would immediately ring from the boys' throats. Delicately he would flutter the fingers of his drooping left hand.

"God!" he yelled.

"Go-o-od," softly chanted the boys.

"My heart," whispered their leader, shaking his fist.

"My-ee heart!" clamoured the boys, bouncing the tones, soprano and alto, against the garden wall.

"My heart is ready; I will sing, and give praise with the best member that I have," shouted the young man, and threw the apple at the head of a twittering boy. "Stop!" he cried, and holding his belly with both hands he writhed and groaned, limping all over the orchard. The boys relaxed and waited until he should be done indicating to them that there was something which displeased him. They all knew Willy Shakspere. So did everybody in town.

But the rehearsal was always better than the performance, and anyhow he tired of all those well-dressed people coming to church and went out looking for gypsies, rogues, vagabonds, wanderers, in order to begin feeling like a Christian again.

Time enough for godly conformity later, when it would pay money.

But now he needed to get an education. This education was conducted in country inns and courtrooms, at market fairs and musterings, anywhere and everywhere there were happy people, wretched people, laughing people, suffering people, and all of them with some precious secret the son of the businessman was not happy until he had pried out of them. A party of tinkers would be muttering round a campfire and see someone with a high brow, auburn hair, and extraordinary eyes peering into their faces from the shadows. They came to know him, and made him welcome. Also he knew Abram men, Upright men, palliards, priggers of prancers, and had a laughing acquaintance with their walking morts and bawdy baskets, though he always refused to do the deed of darkness with them. Since he could run, leap, wrestle, and fight with their masters, there was nothing he needed to prove to the women.

"And who's your girl, lad?" the beer tipplers would ask him, when he sang heartbreakingly of the woes and miseries of love, and had them all crying.

"This one," he would explain, kissing the hostess, or the barmaid, whoever was nearer. "And twenty such, I care not."

"Ah, that's the only way. Laugh with 'em all."

He sang all the words in the song of love as if he had invented them. But he could do the same with words of hate and torment, and he was marvellous with curses of all kinds, so that it was a wonder how anyone so gentle could master such a heap of wrath, and masquerade as any horrible villain in history.

"That's what frightens me about you," Anne Hathaway said. "Even when you were a little boy, you could be a villain or a king. You could do anything, and knew everything before you needed to learn."

"Well, then it proves I'm just like everybody."

"Oh, no, Willy, never be like other people."

He was a farmer that week, because it was planting time, and other people were farmers. He became remarkable with seeds, and was very shrewd with worms. But he was so interested in everything that lived that one day it would be foxes, another day it would be hawks, at night it would be owls, on the ground it would be beetles or any other quick and gleaming fellows in the grass with the mystery and miracle of creation in them.

One day they found a baby fox in the woods. The huntsmen had murdered his mother.

"Look at his poor nose as sharp as a pen," he said, trembling almost as hard as the small creature itself. "This innocence of nature they would kill for their sport. Is it not monstrous of man? Who has commissioned him to make war upon his brothers? Who has empowered him to hunt down great Nature's equal children? What great goaler of the universe has given him the key to lock up the free and the wild?"

"I'll fetch the egg-basket," said Anne. "We'll keep him in the hut. Tom Whittington's bitch has puppies and will give him suck."

He looked at her with such fiery joy that she was afraid.

"Why, what is it, Willy?" she whispered.

He had tears in his eyes, and could not answer.

"What is it about you, darling? Are you all fire and air, and no earth at all?"

"Now wherever did you hear that? I thought it was just in books."

"Oh, Robin told me. I'll tell you a secret. Robin was so bad he had to be good. I fear for you both, but for him more. He had to be either a sinner or a great saint. Oh, there's fire in him too, beyond everything, and no earth at all."

"None at all, eh?" he said, feeling like his father, because he had sounded like him.

And he helped her with the milking that night. Any old humble task was as important to her as if it were a sacrament. She gave a dignity to things of the earth that seemed to him holy. Never had he seen her when she did not wear this simple dignity, like a garment of praise she had donned for the Lord. Surrounded by the peaceful crunching life of the good animals in the barn, with the rain pattering on the thatch and the swallows twittering to sleep, he knew such happiness that if he could have died then he would have been glad.

Sometimes in dreams he was wedded to her in death, and would wake sweating from the same old smothering darkness. They were in the tomb and would never get out. Help! Save the poor ghost!

He would fall out of bed and roll over the floor, struggling to get out of the tomb.

"Can't you sleep quiet?" Gilly would mumble, but little Dickie would be fascinated with his big brother's latest disaster, and sit there watching him with big eyes in the dark, like a cat.

People would look up at him sometimes of a morning, weighing his heavy thoughts again at the window, his chin upon his hand.

"What are you dreaming, Willy?"

Half the time he would not hear them at all.

Other times they would see him trailing off through the meadows, a book in his hand, more books in a bag, and would hear little Dickie's cry, "Wait for me!" Big brother would pause awhile, and then go on reading through the flowery fields until the neighbours could not see him any longer.

"What read you, Willy?" an old man would ask, winking at a comrade wag.

"Words, words, words," he would mumble, and go wandering away as if the very turf were the floor of dreams.

"There'll be no books left in the county," a deep thinker would point out. "Sir Fouck says he's read all his, Sir Richard is worried, and if he dared he'd go read all Earl Ambrose's too."

"Books are for gentlemen. Ought to be in the shop."

"Working hard."

"Our sons work."

"So did we."

"Father ought to send him off to war if he's no good here at home."

"Who'd want him for a soldier anyhow?"

"Aye, can you scare the Spanishers with books?"

One day they saw him reading some old dusty tome in the

window of Henry Rogers' office on Wood Street. The word went round, and all over Stratford people laughed.

"Helping the coroner!"

"He was always the one for graves!"

"Ghosts too, and gibberts!"

"The laziest man in town has the laziest clerk!"

"We'll never get buried now, neighbour."

"Nor written down dead in time for judgement."

But that did not last long either, and after attending a few inquests, and wandering in and out of the bone-house a few times, and going to sleep among a few graves, he gave up helping old Henry.

It was the inquest into the death of the poor little maiden of Tiddington that seemed to end all his love for the quillets and quiddities of country law. Just a poor girl, Kate Hamlet, drowned in the Avon. Whether she yearned for death or just fell in, who would know? The jurors believed it was as old Henry Rogers said: *per infortunium*, an accident.

But he woke up weeping and gnashing his teeth over the maimed rites for the poor little maiden, dug up again for the inquest, and hastily buried again with no rites at all. She just missed being thrown on a midden-heap at a crossroad, where the wanton passers-by could mock her, and throw trash upon her, for being a suicide.

"Is this the law?" he would cry, in the middle of the night. "Is this justice?"

"Ah, go to sleep," Gilly would growl.

When he went off to help Henry that day, the whole program of the coroner was to search the houses of all people suspected of being papists or plotting sedition.

"We might as well chase Squire Somerville for wanting to shoot the Queen," Willy said.

"Ah, he's mad," said Mr. Rogers.

"So are we all, and so am I, goodbye," said his disillusioned assistant, and was not seen again studying the law.

Old John Shakspere was patient for a whole season.

"I have been impatient, now I am being patient," he explained to his doubting wife.

"But what is the boy ever going to *be*?"

"Peace, woman, it is all decided."

"If only he could have gone to the university, like gentle-men's sons! Or to one of the inns of court, to study the law!"

"Ah, bah, I know law enough, he'll learn it from me."

"Your cousins the Greenes are sending their boys to study the law."

"Study dancing, and prancing, and fencing, and foining," grumbled the glove-maker.

There was a deep pool in the woods near the shepherd's cottage, and Anne would often find the wanderer there, look-ing down into the water.

"What see you in it, Willy?"

"You and me," he would say, and then, stooping down, and addling the water with his hand, he would dissolve their images together.

"We're drowned now," she would say.

"And we'll never awake. Or will we?"

"I've the sheep to shear anyhow."

He never told her that sometimes, when he had nothing better to do, he would write sonnets about this pool, and about their images lost in it together, or he would even make up some lamentatious story about hopeless love and false friendship, and put it in rime. Where else would anyone put it?

Why tell her he had written a sonnet about her?

"And what's a sonnet? I have to go milk the cows anyhow."

It was wonderfully hopeless, just like the imaginary ro-mances of the French and Italian sonneteers he had read at Sir Richard Moryson's or Sir Fouck Greville's. And never, never, never, never, would any of the cruel, cold, hard-hearted ladies do it.

I wonder if any of those fellows really desired those ladies made out of stars and globes and gold and alabaster anyhow, he would think. And I wonder why it is this one good woman I cannot get out of my dreams, when the whole county is teem-ing with eager giggling little girls.

Ugh.

Up in the counting-room was a good place to scratch off a few rimes while pretending to add up the alderman's ins and outs of the business.

"Ah, ah, good, good," John would say, seeing him scratching away.

But as soon as the old man had gone plodding down the stairs and out of the house to have a beer, the bogus clerk would bring the latest sonnet or *sesta rima* out of hiding and chop up a little more word-meat again.

Once Gilly caught him writing a poem about a horse, but he hid it safely afterwards, under a pile of hides. Lucky that his brother had not found the part about meeting the mare in the woods. Or about the master of the horse, young Adonis, who met grey-eyed Venus on a primrose bank.

Exactly the opposite of everything in real life, he thought. For in the ragged lines, mostly stolen from Ovid, he had the goddess glowing with passion for the reluctant boy. And then followed a scene in which the horse and the mare, and the goddess and the boy, either nayed their love, or spoke it, and there was the very devil to do after, to make a brother or a milkmaid blush, or a father roar.

So back beneath the pile of hides it went, to cool off.

No books did him any good after that. He returned to Sir Fouck's on a trumped-up errand and read a pile of them, but he was so miserable now that all he could find in the books was more evidence that sorrow was the whole end of man. Tortured spirits like his own spoke to him from these silent pages. A murmur, a thunder, a scream of horror rose. He looked with mad eyes at Sir Fouck, muttered his thanks, and went off to see Anne for the last time, the last time.

That day in the harvesting she wounded herself with the sickle, and he was right there to tear a strip from his shirt and bind up her bleeding wrist. Then over him came a fearful light, and he knew who it was had haunted him all these years, who had leaned down and kissed him out of a forgotten sky, and tied up his soul in her silken thongs. This face of wonder and sadness, gilded with heavenly light, had always been hovering just beyond the screen of sky and clouds, the deep banked lanes, the tall avenues of elms twittering with birds, and it was her voice that had been speaking to him beyond the roaring of water under the bridge by the mill, beyond the May meadows with the blackthorn blossoms spilling over the soaked grass, beyond everything of beauty in the world he knew. He wanted to kneel down and worship her there right in the rye-field. He stared into her wonderful eyes, and she bent down and kissed him. Her glorious hair came down and tumbled about them. Her eyes were all shiny, like the eyes of Venus in the fable of the goddess and the boy, and her lips were wonderful with that flame concealed beneath their silken touch. He stared at her as she looked down at him laughing, and his heart seemed to turn over like some troubled beast in a secret hiding place, never secret again now. Something had happened to destiny, it was as if great angels stood around him in the sunny and cloudy field and he heard their wings.

She went away laughing through the fields of rye as if nothing had happened.

Oh, what will I do? thought the son of the businessman, wandering dully through the woods hours, minutes, or days later. If only my father would awake from his mad dream of profit and let me go, I would run away, melt, fade, dissolve like smoke or a dream, before I am lost.

From an eventual seller of gloves, wool, and malt he became uneventual again, and went drooping and dragging about the woods and fields with straw in his hair and hayseed in his shoes, consorting with the woodcocks and the foxes, the deer and the doves. He was barked at by dogs and glared at by housewives, and spent many a misty morning trailing his fancies through the dim woods when he should have been helping his father at home.

"Look at the dew on him," John Shakspere would say. "Look at the straw on him. Did I go mooning among the flocks and herds? Was I ungartered? Was I unhouselled, frowselled and tousled? Was I a disgrace to my father?"

"Ah, let the boy alone, you were the same at his age," said Mrs. Shakspere, who was always kind to her eldest when the old man began doubting whether he had really begat him or not. This was a problem that fascinated the alderman.

Where did he come from? Who the devil had begat him? "Do I wear horns on my head?" John would ask in his amazement at having such a son in the midst of these steady, oaken English.

His eldest son would stand there sorrowfully glowing with golden light, his eyes speckled gold and green, his hair like a scoured copper pot, and all the light in the room would seem to be coming from him.

But the problem was that he glowed with everything. If he was happy, he glowed. If he was angry, he glowed. If he was sorrowful at being such a bad son he glowed with his sorrow. And always gentler with everybody, in spite of his fire and brimstone, than any of the girls.

"Look at him there," John would say. "Look at him like something that came out of the woods. Is he mine? Did I get him betwixt the lawful sheets? Eh, woman? Eh?"

And at last, at last, glory of glories, the son and his mother would be happy and united in this fearful wrong, and would defy the alderman with flashing looks, scornful drooping of lips, haughty upraised chins, until even the gib-cat on the hearth knew *they* were of the one blood and pride, whatever this mocking man had to say to them.

"Ha!" the alderman would cry, pointing. "All the damned Arden pride all over again. And who are the Ardens? Who are the Ardens?"

"Let the whole world hear," Mrs. Shakspere would answer, her magnificent eyes flashing.

But Mr. Shakspere dared not go into that because everybody in town knew the Ardens were everything in the whole county and the Shagsbeards were nothing. "How are you going to run a glove business?" he would roar, as if that were the problem.

"Oh, it will be easy, father, I'll do it in my spare time," the defiant son of Mary Arden said, which was wrong, and made the old man so mad that he ordered him right into the glove-shop, and he had to stay in there, twiddling with dividers and slicers and stitchers, until he had learned that his destiny lay here among all these pointing fingers, and nowhere else.

When he was allowed finally to come out he was so sorrow-ful, with his long golden eyelashes making exasperating sha-dows along his cheeks, he was more like some wild musical instrument than anything human and profitable to business. The words he spoke came out all mixed with music. He had been singing songs in there, drawing a whole flock of girls to the door, who had no money to buy gloves.

The next day he had a lute with him, borrowed from some tavern, and he was singing and playing to the girls. Each time he began a new song the girls would begin screaming.

"Away, wenches!" roared John, barging into the narrow shop.

And off went the girls, screaming and laughing, with his wanton son at their head, dancing down the street of respectable business, and into the meadows.

"The time has come to plight him!" said the baffled father.

"Not a one of them is good enough," said his wife.

One day when Mrs. Shakspere had been especially kind to him and correspondingly curst to his father, it seemed to Willy as if a great dark cloud had melted away from the world, and as if the warm tender light of love had broken through.

Why, there is no more need of war, he thought.

The man is right. Life is a grim business, so let's be about it.

He strode into the glove-shop, where the old man was gloomily sitting at his bench, staring at the rude whitewashed wall as if he were reading the whole doom of his life in the scrawls and scratches on it.

"I will do it, father," said the loving and repentant son, putting his arm around the alderman's shoulder.

Old John rolled an eye suspiciously round at him.

"I'll ask the dish-faced Lizzie with the fat ankles."

Another suspicious look from the glove-seller.

"You are right in saying we must marry the family with the most manure piles, and I'm off to the onion bed to plight my troth with the heiress."

"Let us have no more jests, let us have no more quips or quiddities."

"I mean it, father. I would want the same if I had a son."

A deep sigh came from the worried businessman. "I am a patient man. Thy mother is to bear a new one next May."

"All the more reason for me to begin building new bones, then."

"The more we sell, the more we are in debt."

"Trust me, father. I am about the business," said his son, and marched out of the glove-shop and through the orchard toward the onion beds between Swine Lane and the gild pits.

Lizzie Fisher was sadly weeding onions, her eyes red, her nose also. Who would have taken her to be the most desirable parcel a shrewd young businessman of this town could acquire? But her father owned the best house on the High Street, and her grandfather was the most greedy land-grabber in Warwick.

Here I go on my life of deeds and mortgages, William the Dutiful thought, approaching the freckle-faced girl.

An alarming vision of Anne Hathaway, all honey-brown and glistening in Aunt Kate Whittington's pool, suddenly burned before his eyes.

"Good day, Lizzie," he said gently.

She stuck out her tongue at him.

"I am glad to see thee yet living, anyhow," he told the dish-faced girl.

"I'd rather hear a dog bark than you speak," snapped Lizzie.

"Indeed, girl?"

"Oh, never mind thy mad airs, thou'rt just Willy Snagspatch and no better than any other yeoman's son."

"Indeed."

What shadings one could give that word! I must use it sometime, when I write plays, he decided.

Plays? They'd never play 'em anyhow.

"Oh, I'm so sick and lonely and miserable ever since Dickie went to London, we always went to Harvest Fair together," said Lizzie, beginning to weep.

A twinge of conscience twangled upon his heartstrings. My fault, no doubt. Ah, the poor wench, what is she if you stripped her but a poor forked radish out of the weedy garden of God? I must be kinder to her, somehow.

"I'm sorry for thee, Lizzie," he said gently.

"Oh, he's been gone so long, so long!"

"I miss him too."

"You did it, Willy Shackbag."

"He's well out of it."

"He is not, Willy Jacksbeer, I love him I will always love him and I hate you, Willy Sagsp —"

"Can we just get my name right?"

"Jakespear, Makespear, Breakspear, I hate thee, Willy Snakesmear, so there!"

Nobody was looking. Ah, ah, he saw the tip of the alderman's nose through the counting-room window. He sidled by the defiant girl, swept her into his strong arms, and began kissing her. She moaned, muttered, squealed, giggled, gulped, stammered, squirmed, wiggled, jumped, stamped, struggled, and gave up. Tighter and tighter clung her pudgy arms around his neck. He saw her avid eyes, big as lamps of doom, staring wildly straight into his brain. He let her go, and she sank down in the onion bed like an old sack from which the wool was gone. A blissful smile was on her face.

Well, that's done anyway, thought Willy, brushing his hands briskly together and turning away. He walked quickly back into his father's orchard.

John Shakyspear stood before him, his eyes popping, his mouth open.

"Give thee good day, father," his son said, bowing.

"Come with me," said his father.

"Yes sir, very good, sir."

When John had got him into the shop he hugged him. "Good, good, that is the way to do it," he whispered gleefully, rubbing his hands.

His son stared at the old man sadly. Alas, my plot is moving too well already, he thought.

"At last thou'rt a proper son of thy sire," said old John, clapping him on the back. "And was I not such another when I was full of sap? Mad Jack of Temple Grafton — of Snitterfield, I mean to say, that's what all the girls called me. Ah, what days, lad! What golden days!"

"Is this my father? Mad Jack, the girl grabber?"

"Thou canst say as much, go to," said the alderman, grinning and chuckling.

The false lover of Lizzie Fisher looked suspiciously at the bragging alderman.

"Dost love her, lad? Wilt have the wench?"

"Oh, madly, badly."

"Good, excellent, thou hast picked the best box of 'em all, the best manured land, and the best farms and houses. To it, lad, take her, capture her, and remember, when thou art bussing her, we'll get all old John Fisher's lands and properties. Ah, we'll wax, we'll grow fat. My son has his wits about him at last."

"Ugh."

"Did I not do the same? Did I not go to Master Arden himself when I was tenant farmer on the old Moryson Manor, and say, 'Master Arden, you have a daughter. She is your favourite, I believe.' 'She is, lad,' said Master Arden. A proud squire too, his nose always north-by-northeast, sniffing the air to see if it was rare enough. 'What then?' he said. 'What then, sir? Why, I'll marry her, Master Arden sir,' I said. And with her lands and pastures, it was but one step up to find a good flourishing business with an old man in it who needed an heir . . . ."

The boy looked gloomily at the bragging alderman. What depths, or heights, was he suddenly revealing? True friendship with his father was almost as alarming as the roaring, thwacking discipline of childhood. But John Shakspere was all passion and thunder, and life with him was one long dangerous and exciting journey through storm and darkness.

I wonder if there will be light at the end, the boy thought, looking at his mighty father with new interest. All the worthy citizens on the Council loved and feared the man. What if many a jealous Catholic mocked his wretched shaggy name? It was but a way to warn him not to rise again against them, or there would be bloodier wounds. It is little enough from them, but I wish we had some name they could not mock, he thought. Anyhow, whether he goes to the monthly meetings in the gildhall or whether he stays grumbling and growling at home because he's at war with the Bishop of Worcester and in fear of attachment, he's my father and I love him. And nobody in Stratford ever thinks of him as anyone but Master when they use his name straight, whatever in the name of Beelzebub it is. He should have his coat of arms like Squire Arden, he should, that's what he wants, that's what we must get for him. Why, you can buy your arms nowadays for twenty or thirty pounds. I must move the business with him. Arms over his door and on his saddle might quiet him nobly. And then we'll have an end of this madness over Lizzie Fishbait, whom I never should have kissed.

"Ah, ah, and I'll have fair fat grandchildren soon," chuckled the alderman, rubbing his big hands again.

"I am surprised at my own father. I have not bedded the wench yet. Give me some free years yet, in God's name."

"You can marry sooner than twenty-one. What! We must nail the business to our mast. I must mortgage thy mother's old land of Asbies this month, or the bishop will gobble it up.

I need the money anyhow, and Ned Lambert will lend me forty pounds."

"She'll never allow it, father."

"She has no choice in the matter, for am I not her master?" muttered John, his eyes glowing.

His son looked away in shame for him. Master indeed! Master of the jakes only.

"When thou hast five or six sons of thy own, my boy, as soon as possible, for so many die in infancy anyhow, then thou wilt understand. Business is business, remember that."

"I will remember it. I will remember it until the last whimper, and beyond that, and beyond that. I will remember —"

"What a business we'll have together, now that thou hast begun to grow out of thy wanton ways! And we'll grow too, we'll grow. With old John Fisher's bottom lands and herds and that nice lay of hillside by Chesterton pastures, we —"

"What if Lizzie will not have me? What if no one will have me but some poor spinster, some pauper, some milkmaid? What if no one but Anne Hathaway will take me? Where will our great lands and manure piles be then?"

"Thou art a jester," said his father.

"Indeed."

"Anne Hathaway, forsooth! She's still dreaming of the priest. Look, boy. Who did the Queen dine with in Warwick?"

"Earl Ambrose. And there is a matter concerning his household of which I wish to sp —"

"And who in Lower Itchington? Edward Fisher. Boy, use thy wits. We have a name to couple with lands and manors —"

"*We* have a name! Ha!"

"Aye, a name, a name, I said a name."

"And what is this name? What is this name?"

Old John looked at him darkly. "What mean you now? What mean you now?"

"What is our name? What is our name?"

Mr. Shakspere set his hat more firmly on his head. He arose from the cutting-bench, upon which various skins of dead animals lay, ready to become forests of fingers. "You are my son, I believe," observed the alderman in a polite tone.

"Indeed, sir."

"And not a bastard?"

"I doubt that, sir, for Mad Jack of Snitterfield is too much the man for that."

"I thank thee for thy good opinion," said his father, taking off his hat and bowing.

"It is a pleasure to consider myself thy true begotten issue, sir," replied his son, also lifting his hat and bowing. "But if we are to believe thy wife and my mother that I am truly the hope and heir to all the stinks and miseries of the glove business, what are we to put up on our sign for all the boobies of the town to see? Are we Jakesbeers? Shagbeards? Wagstaffs? Sagstaffs? Fallstaffs? Sadbirds? Madbirds?"

"Thou art Madbird's bastard son, belike," quickly put in the alderman.

"If I am a bastard begot then it's all one," said his son politely. "But begot in a boot, and my name Jackboot? Begot in a sack, and called Sackbutt? Begot in the jakes —"

"God forbid," said his father piously.

"Then sir, may I ask you a question?"

"You may, sir."

"What are we, sir? What are we?"

"I have a suggestion," said John, clamping his hat on very firmly.

"Good, good," said his son, clamping on his.

"And it is this," said the old man, shaking his fist at him. "You are a scholar! You are a studier! Study it then! Comb the bloody country! Hop over gravestones! Converse with clerks! Brood over books! And when thou hast discovered the true ancestor and inventor of this our scurvy name, I tell thee what to do with it then! Write it fair and large upon a wreath of our colours —"

"And what are those, sir?"

"Sable," said Mr. Shakspere, slapping his black doublet. "Gold!" he cried, whacking his sword. "Combe's got his arms. Quiney's got his gules. Greene's got his. Why not me, eh?"

"I'll do it, father."

"Then to it! Away!" roared the old man, bringing down his fist on the cutting-bench so that all his cutters and dividers danced like little people.

"I will, father," said his son, the fire of ambition lighting up in his eyes. "But if we are to be gentlemen, then I must have a steed. A good steed."

"Take Crispin! Take Crispin! But keep him upon the road and off the tails of mares!" said his father loudly.

"It shall be done, sir."

"And then we'll see if these Ardens are the only birds that can fly high in the country!"

So off went young Willy the Spearshaker on black Crispin to dig up some ancestors, or at least to sneeze over their names in some mouldy old parish registry.

## CHAPTER EIGHT

**H**E was gone for a week. When he came back, it was with glowing countenance, shining eyes, and a totally new outfit of orange-tawny, which he had won from a commercial traveller in Lower Clopton.

"I've found him, father!" he cried, dashing into the glove-shop.

The alderman looked up from his cutting-bench.

"Ah, ah," he said. He bowed to the three or four customers in the shop, which was a great many for that dark little place, and asked them very quietly if they would care to examine the new tassel-faced gloves for a moment while he stepped into the orchard with his son, whom he did not see very much nowadays.

"Well, well, well?" he demanded, trembling, behind the barn.

His son held out a parchment upon which was a drawing with some lettering below it.

John gazed eagerly at the drawing. It showed a gallows. Hanging from it was a man in a sack, still holding a spear.

"What is this jest?" muttered John, his hand shaking.

"It is our true coat, father, after much leaping over tombs and much sniffing over old parchments. I have discovered our ancestor."

And taking the parchment from his father's trembling hands he read the legend:

> "Will^um Sakspere of Clopton was thys daye
> hanged by hys neck until hee was dead ffor
> roberie uppon y^e publick highwaye . . . In Yeere
> of Our Lord 1248 & of Kyng Henry ye Turde xxxij."

He finished reading the legend. He looked up at his father,

and dropped the parchment. Old John had put his hands to his face, and the tears were running down his cheeks.

"Forgive me, father, it was but a scurvy jape."

A muffled cry came from the old man, then a howl of rage. Snatching up a pair of shears from the crotch of a peach-tree he sprang menacingly toward his son and might have well sheared him too if Willy had not leaped aside and taken to his heels.

The roaring of his maddened father echoed after him as he scudded over the ground, taking the quickest direction to the woods.

Three times he came tiptoeing back, all contrition, and each time the old man cried, "Away!" But the fourth time he had an old board he had found somewhere, a whitewashed board, and he held it before him as a shield.

"Away, jacksnape! Away, sop o' the moonshine!"

"Father. A word with you, dear father."

"Out, tickle-brain!"

"Behold our arms, father."

"Away, pint-pot!"

"Our true arms! Our true arms!" cried the repentant William, backing from him around the orchard.

"I'll arms ye!" said the old man, snatching up a bean-pole. "Ah, ye pagan rascal, have ye no respect for anything? Art thou mine, thou whoreson cullionly scarecrow? Did I beget thee betwixt the lawful sheets? Eh?"

"I know not, Mad Jack," sorrowfully replied the retreating youth, defending himself against the bean-pole. "But thou hast a damnable sneaking thrust there with thy spear, Master Jakes."

"Out, wastrel! Out, sprout! I am sorry I begat thee, if I did."

"Alas, Mr. Shake-pole, those be very bitter words," mildly observed the true-begotten son of the alderman, dodging so neatly that old John slipped in the wet grass and went down with an awful thud.

Willy looked contritely down at him. "Alas, to see thee fallen, Mad Jack. Well, go to, it was a good lad enough, and made the girls merry in his time."

"Silence!" groaned the fallen bean-shaker.

"Known throughout the length and breadth of Snitterfield

for a sad snatcher at maidenheads," more loudly proclaimed the returning wanderer, and re-returner, yea, and doubled, and tripled.

"Peace, pint-pot. Silence."

"Look up, father. See your arms."

"I am old, and have no good son, only a brawler, and dicer, and hayseed barn-swallow rogue."

"Arms, father." And pointing to the wobbly device he had scrawled on the old whitewashed board, stolen from a jakes, he explained each detail to the groaning alderman.

Round-eyed children and a lamenting wife were beginning to appear out of the house, and their time was limited.

"This is thy shield," Willy said rapidly. "A gold spear, on a bend sable. Thy crest, a falcon, a silver falcon, father. She is shaking a spear of gold. Do you like it, father? Your proper arms as soon as I can steal some paint and emblazon them."

Old John arose painfully and muttered, "Come with me to Bob Bratt's beer house. Too many people here."

"Directly," said young Willy, and they both retreated from their affectionate or at least interested kinfolk as expeditiously as they could.

"What a pox are we doing?" muttered John, regarding his bean-pole when they had got out into Henley Street.

"We need but a horse or two, and we might be true knights."

"What art about with that privy seat, bearing it through the town?"

"Alas, father, I have been disowned by my own progenitor, and must find what seat I can."

"Some day my patience will be exhausted."

"Father, I will never jest again in my whole life. I swear it."

"Bah. A shag-haired rogue, and his shoes full of hayseed."

But when they had thrown away their arms and had drunk the first two or three beers they felt better, and once they began laughing they could hardly stop. It was between one shout of laughter and another that his son William explained to the alderman that he had indeed truly found an ancestor they could be proud of, one William Shakespear of Lower Clopton, who had fought so bravely for King Harry the Seventh against Richard the Third that his Majesty had granted him lands as a reward.

"And his name, father, was not Sack, Jack, or Jakes. It was Shakespear, and it was spelled S-H-A-K-E-S-P-E-A-R, a noble name, a martial name, a proud name, O Lord, a lovely name to put upon a sign."

"Ah, ah, good, good," said old John, calling for two more beers.

"Shall we add an *e*, father? When I make the sign?"

"A whoreson *e*?"

"Aye, for elegance. So it will be S-H-A-K-E-S-P-E-A-R-E, a good rolling and resounding name."

"Enough! Thou art sure he is our ancestor?"

"I swear it, father. For he begat Henry, and Henry begat another William, and William begat Dick, and Dick begat thee."

"We were always fruitful, it is true," observed the alderman, blowing the foam off the beer. "Ah, and I tell thee this, when thou shalt make our sign, and put up our name, make it *Shakespeare & Son*. And let 'em mock that, eh? Let 'em mock that!"

# BOOK TWO

# SCANDAL
## IN STRATFORD

CHAPTER NINE

THE tenth of August in 1582 was a noisy day in Stratford. Not only was it St. Susanna's Eve, festival of virgins, but it was market day too, and that meant crowds of countrymen wanting to buy things.

All up and down Rother Street the merchants and their apprentices stood at their booths, hallooing and praising their wares. Asses were braying too, cattle were mooing, dogs were barking, and old Alfred, the town bear, was defending himself against ten snapping curs.

It was a hot and dusty day, and all the winking windows of the town were open.

Perched on a high stool before one of these windows, that excellent imitation of a businessman, young Willy Shakespeare, was totting up the year's transactions to see if the firm of Shakespeare & Son had made any money.

This took brains. Not even his father knew.

Where was the slim Adonis of three years ago? Where was Worthless Willy, with straw in his hair and hayseed in his shoes? This was a puffed and padded young man, addicted to neatness. Beer and food, in three years, had given him the look of any young clerk in the country: a stout fellow with goose-quills and ledgers, who dreamed of shillings and pounds, and would sit up for a penny.

Yet there was something about him: a drooping of the nether lip, of the eyelids circled with melancholy darkness. And did he sleep well?

Indeed now he yawned, and rubbed his forehead and the back of his neck.

Had Shakespeare & Son gained a fat profit this year? Or any profit at all?

The mind of Mr. W$^m$ the S$^h$ was dusty, and he had a great thirst.

Insinuating suggestions were being made by certain birds

in the trees outside the counting-room window. These he ignored.

All the pink and gold young virgins for twenty miles around were in Stratford for the day. Lazy punts floated upon the river, with young lovers in them. A lute was playing somewhere.

Alas! No love for Shakespeare & Son today.

A twinge hit the imitation businessman at the thought of his last quarrel with Lizzie Fisher.

What had they quarreled about? It depended on the time of year. Subjects were inexhaustible.

Is this love? he thought.

The fashionable Italian poets wrote sonnets about their sufferings.

Yea, but they wrote only of ladies who would not.

And Lizzie?

Some scribbler should write a book of sonnets about a real mistress, not a dream one. With a breath reeking of onions, and a hide like untanned leather.

Many years ago, he thought, when he was young, he should have finished those careless sonnets, before it had become necessary to be careful, and correct. *Love and Curses*, he would have called the little book. All about the Woman who Would.

I'll never have the time to write anything but accounts now. Under a pile of hides he had stowed away such idle papers as he had written in these three years of business: stray bits of fancy, scraps of monologue, a witty fool imagined, a dream of death or passion, and gleanings of wisdom from books. All dead, he thought.

He took up his quill again.

*Item, paid to the Court of Queens Bench in Westminster, xxxx li.*

Forty pounds! The price old John had got from Ned Lambert of Barton Heath for Mrs. Shakespeare's estate of Asbies in Wilmecote.

Alas for my baronial manor, and my mother's dreams! thought the ex-heir of the Ardens with a twisted smile. These days, like a cautious clerk, he smiled only with half his face.

That forty pounds had gone for the enormous fine his father

had paid for his failure to appear before the Court of Queen's Bench, where he had been summoned for attempting to evade, exceed, and outstep the laws limiting the incorporating of tradesmen who would not go to church.

It seems that all nature is against us, thought $W^m$ the $S^h$. Or can it be that we are against it?

For we owe everybody we can, and everybody owes us, so that throughout the whole broad valley of the Avon, from the heights of noble Clopton to the vale of Evesham, from the uplands of Ingon to the wild moors of Drayton, toiling up Bredon Hill or falling in the mill-pond at Bidford with the sippers and topers, or dancing on Shottery meadows or robbing the rabbits of their skins in Snitterfield, this whole mean scramble of trade and gain has us treading on our own heels all over the country to keep up with ourselves, and we only find profit by losing, and tot up our gains by the monstrousness of our debts in nature's infinite book of secrecy.

And that is very discouraging, and not to be thought of.

What then shall I think of?

I could think on peace, for we have that.

So he thought about peace, uneasy peace, timorous dove, still cooing over England in this the twenty-fourth year of Our Lady Elizabeth's Peace, as Abe Sturley or Henry Rogers would be writing it in the Council Book of the Stratford Corporation this Michaelmas.

If England were not at peace, I might be at some bloody ambuscade this very moment, hacking my way to glory.

His nostrils dilated, and he sniffed the gentle breeze. No trumpets yet, though people had been waiting for the Spaniards to come howling through the peaceful fields for years. Even though there had been scouring of swords and mending of calivers every June now for five years, and the mustered men from all the towns and hamlets in Warwickshire had paraded and practiced up and down every country green, there was no shooting yet, no slaughter.

All this frustration was owed, of course, to the brilliant Queen, who had diddled the bottle-nosed Frenchman into fighting her war for her against the Spaniards in the Low Countries, and now had the Scottish Queen shut up in Sheffield Castle, plotting busily to turn over England to the Catholics

just as soon as she could get her hands on it. And sailing into
and out of every seaport went the conspirators who were plotting to help her. Spies and priest-hunters scoured the country,
and the madness of Squire Somerville was a madness no longer:
in every shire there were young men planning to rise up and
liberate the happy kingdom, or to do something desperate
about it anyhow. Many innocent people got in the way, like
poor Robin Debdale, who no sooner arrived back in England
to say Masses and hear confessions than he was thrown into
prison, and tortured to make his own confession of treason.

Alas, poor Robin, who only wanted to do good.

*I fear for you both*, said Anne, *but I fear for him more.*

And I wonder if the torturers ever let him go, and he comes
home to Shottery, will the priest and the milkmaid meet again?

Two years now, over two years, and poor Cottam's brother
hanged at Tyburn, and the little schoolmaster hounded out of
our parish.

The imitation book-keeper sighed deeply, and looked
around at his own prison walls. Like a nutshell, he thought,
and I an industrious worm.

Arrows were shining in the air from the archery practice on
Mile End Green, and he could hear the distant sound of cannon
being fired. The voice of Tom Miller the sergeant howling at the
sixteen members of the town militia as they performed their
drill for the protection of England rose in notes of baffled frenzy
and was gone again on the warm air.

The son of the glove-maker stretched, and looked at the
cobwebs in the four corners of the ceiling, where a few trapped
flies remained uneaten by Milady Spider.

And how long will it be until I am one of their number? he
wondered.

Down in old Dick Hornby's shop he heard Willy Evans
scraping and scouring the harness and guns for the mustered
men. These scratchings and scourings made an undertone to
the happy noises of buying, selling, and bear-baiting. And a
clinking of big bottles and a clanking of little casks came from
the yawning cellar of Rafe Cawdrey's house, where the successful butcher and proprietor of the Angel was bringing out the
drink for the lords and gentlemen at the general muster this
afternoon.

Ah yes, peace, peace.

Just then a raucous voice brayed into his ear. "The Spaniards are coming!"

Young Willy the Peaceful shot straight up into the air. "Where?" he cried, coming down on all fours at a pile of mouldy hides and scrabbling in it for his father's second-best sword, which he had illegally appropriated and hidden here.

"From Spain, of course," the hoarse voice said, and there was an explosion of vulgar laughter. His brother Gilly had crept up the stairs and was standing there snorting with uncouth joy.

In three years he had become the fat boy of all England. Desperate at never being able to overtake his brother, he had launched himself upon a career of eating. He was eating now. Down upon the desk he set a pigeon pie, a sucket tart, and a bowl of cream all clotted.

"How much did we lose?" he asked.

William the Patient arose from the ignoble floor, shoving the old hacked and rusty sword back under the hides. The last time his father had used it had been to hack the saints and angels in the gild chapel, and smash the coloured glass in the windows.

"What art hunting there? Some poems to scare the Spanishers?" inquired his brother, between mouthfuls.

William the Dependable sat down upon his stool.

"I can tell thee just what we lost, and why," said Gilly, his large popping eyes glittering with stupidity and low cunning. "Buying from Tom Whittington over Temple Grafton way put us in the hole four pound nine and nine. Ever since Muster Field begun selling his best calfskins to that Frenchman in London we've been falling behind. We ought to start our own tannery. Those trips you took to Warwick and Coventry Fairs put us in the hole four pound ten for all that mad mummery, and your verses with the gloves weren't worth the time it took to wrap 'em. We're not doing half so good as he did afore he took you in the business, and what I told him is, he ought to set me up in a haberdashery and give me my share, I'd show him. What art spilling ink for?"

William the Patient arose from his stool, breathed deep, and sat down again. "We shall know where we are when I have finished my arithmetic," he said gently.

"Aye, seven and eleven," Gilly said, chomping at a pigeon breast. "Dice and primero, and your newfangled game of chess, that's where all your arithmetic goes."

A shudder came from the imitation businessman. It was true that in place of all his old vices he had acquired a passion for games of chance, and was beginning to win most alarmingly. As for the great and noble game of skill with queens, bishops, knights, pawns, and little peaceful kings, he could sit for hours over a chessboard with some other imitation businessman in a tavern, and never mind the time at all.

"And all the money too," added the fat boy, craunching some pigeon bones.

"I win more in a week than we make in a year," said his elder brother.

"Aye? Where's the money?" inquired Gilly.

His gentle brother smiled dreamily and waved him away. "That is the question," he said amiably. "And now, why not go downstairs and have your dessert?"

"Mother's got some quodling tarts," Gilly said, dutifully going to the stairs. But his round eyes peered from corner to corner, heap to heap, and he was still muttering about money as the first board creaked under his heavy feet.

Downstairs little Edmund, whom they all called Ned, was banging a spoon on a pan and pretending to be playing a tabor, like one of the clowns in Lord Harry Berkeley's company of players, who had been in Stratford last June.

This new addition to the Shakespeare family was only two, but full of the devil already, and promising to be even worse than Dependable William was in his youth.

A pleasing goodness, however, radiated from the other two children, sweet Joan and happy Dick, who knew their duty by heart. Joan was thirteen now, and Dick was eight: they never made any trouble.

No more do I, thought the faithful clerk, getting off his stool and hunting for his cap. All dutiful apprentices to a trade wore these custards on their costards, because the wool-dealers' guild had diddled a statute through Privy Council requiring them to, on pain of being snatched by any lawful recruiter and thrown into the Army.

A flickering light winked for an instant in the dull brain of the bookkeeper.

Wander forth into the world without my accursed cap. Escape. Away. France . . .

He sighed deeply, picked up the cap, and placed it upon that dome of buried hopes, his head, or, more exactly, his bolting-hutch of profits and losses.

Cautiously down the creaking stairs he went, hoping to escape at least the sermon for today from his mother.

Alas! She confronted him at the kitchen door.

"Willy, speak to your brother!"

"But why I, mother?"

"Is it not you he apes, until I know not what to do with him?"

Stamping, rolling, kicking upon the great hearth, his little brother Ned, cursed with the Arden pride and the Shakespeare temper, was screaming with rage so fierce it was joy.

"H'm," said his elder brother, intrigued by the Dionysian frenzy.

"Oh, stop him, Willy! It does no good throwing water on him. And thy father! Stamps out of the house and off to Bob Bratt's Beer House again! This one should never have been born."

The splendid old tragic note was throbbing in her voice.

"I think if we could bottle it, we could sell it at a profit," said her thoughtful son, beginning to make horrible faces and noises. "*Aqua shacra*, should we call it?"

"No, Willy! We have players enough in this house! Do not spoil a helpless child!"

But it worked. Little Ned suddenly stopped screaming and lay there with big eyes, a dreamy smile on his pretty lips.

"Oh, Willy," Mary said hopelessly. Her eldest son kissed her and smiled half a smile.

"Would it have troubled thee much, sweet mother, if I had run off and joined Earl Ambrose's boys?"

His mother immediately became logical. "The Fat Knight is

too much the Puritan to keep players any more, and anyhow they left him for the Earl of Oxford."

"Ah, true," mumbled her eldest son, taking a pickled quince to suck, waving farewell to little Ned, and starting out of the house by the front door.

"Do it again!" he heard his little brother calling, as he hastily went out under the large gilded sign now creaking over the glove-shop. Alas, no arms for the alderman yet, although he had applied thirteen years ago.

No hope of ever winning them for the old man now, thought the number-mumbler, wandering toward the booths on Rother Street.

Thus dies another dream. So die they all, not with a blare of trumpets on some bloody field, but in the mumble of creeping clerks on a street.

Oh, what has become of me? he thought.

The bawling of pre-slaughtered cows made the wind hideous. Praise be to God anyhow, thought the weary wanderer, that he has never opened his own shambles.

I would rather die than kill deer, and as for cows . . . .

The thought reminded him of his duly betrothed love, the amorous Lizzie, heiress to the best bottoms in the county.

Mostly all stolen from Johnny Somerville and the Ardens, he thought. But what madness made me rush unto the breach?

What's done is done, what's stolen is stolen.

He tiptoed past Lizzie's house. Fortunately they were not speaking this week.

"Hey, Worthless William!" cried a voice he had not heard for three years.

How interesting my midden-heap of mentality is, he thought. I hear voices, which are not voices. But what is, which is not? And what is not, which truly is?

"Hey there, Willy the Cat!" cried the voice loudly.

He spun round on his heel. There before the shop of Hamlet Sadler stood Dick Field, inhaling the perfume of the dreamer's tarts and pies, and waving a lace handkerchief at him.

Is this another of these idle fancies I have been having lately? mused W$^m$ the S$^h$.

Shall I talk to it?

Is it a good devil or a devil flown hither to convey me to hell?

That at least might be a change. Or would it?

"Through what window of eternity didst thou come, O shadow?" he inquired politely.

"From de hind parts of hell," answered the elegant shadow, bowing and fluttering its fingers like a fop in one of the bawdy plays. "And oo is these I ave de honour to be speakings?"

"Jaques of the Jakes," said the book-keeper.

"Ah, Monsieur Jaques!"

"I believe I know thee, little Richard."

And in amazement and some mortification they continued their inspection of each other.

"And what is this dish upon thy head, Bloody Richard?"

"A trifle," said the elegant et cetera, waving his handkerchief.

"Is it a pie?"

"A nothing, from France," said Dick.

"May I nibble it?"

"Still the clown, eh, Catbird?" said Dick, taking his arm and beginning to amble along down Dead Lane toward the Water Side, where the taverns and beer-houses were.

"You smell different too. Your own?"

"Plague on you country wits," said Dick fretfully. "My French mistress gave it me."

"A French mistress!" The eyes of the dutiful son opened wide, and his long upper lip looked almost goatish again, as in his lost youth.

"My French master's wife," said Dick. But judging from the look of modesty on the face of his friend, the explanation had not been adequate.

"Damn thee, Willy, hast become a hymn-singer too? I work for old Tom Vautrolier, and live with his wife and daughter."

Pious godliness beamed from the eyes of the totter-up of profits, or losses, and at any moment he was going to preach.

"Oh, Catbird, how I have missed thee!" said Dick, embracing him. "That face! That face! How I miss laughter! And only three years? How we are all translated! Me into French, Nick into Latin, and thee into round figures!"

"Well, I am content," said the book-keeper calmly.

"Is it possible?"

"As any mouse in a cheese, my boy. Fret not over me. But what of Nick? Is he a player, or a keeper of a bawdy-house, or has he joined the men of the moon?"

"Worse, Willy, worse."

"Hanged? Oh, poor Bottom!"

"Not yet, but wait a little."

"What, then? Out with it, man! I can take it."

"The Enterprise," said Dick in a whisper.

But his friend looked at him without comprehension.

"Met a priest in prison, and in fear of hellfire confessed his sins and bound himself to ride for them wherever they send him."

The dutiful book-keeper shook his head and put his finger to his lips.

"Old Billy Bott was always in league with 'em, or he'd never have acted as agent for the Underhills," Dick prattled on.

"Shhh! Let's talk of thy French mistress. Is she dark or fair? What weight? What gait?"

"Has the bloody plot spread even here?"

"How bears she her course, what breezes blow her?"

"Well, she has a pretty daughter," Dick said. "Come live with us, and she'll teach thee French by anatomizing it, arm, elbow, nose, leg, et cetera."

"I fear me for her et cetera, with thee in the house. No, I am content in my corner, my life goes smoothly in its groove, and look what happens to all the brave, all the best, when they fly too high. Why, poor Nick was the best of us all. A younger son, that was his only taint, but that tainted all. Well, I am the principal heir of a good business. My place is here."

"Damn thee, wilt thou die here?" cried Dick.

"Better men than I have. Poor Dick Hathaway last Michael-mas."

"Dick Hathaway! He died every day!"

Now the fashionable visitor began to see light. He shot a quizzical look at his reformed friend. "And how does his dearest daughter, sweet Anne Page-boy? Didst ever return her petticoat?"

Silence from William the Worthy.

"How such a leg would look in our French hose!"

A brooding, melancholy, dark, and dangerous glare began to glow in the goat-green eyes of the glove-maker's son.

"I spied her in Webb's horsepond once, mother-naked and

nut-brown like an Egyptian. Upon what lovely tree of Eden did ever such apples grow?"

A powerful fist, white at the knuckles, stained with ink at the thumb, suddenly quivered before Dick's fashionable nose. He choked. No more words came out of him until they reached the Swan Inn, at the Western end of Middle Row.

"Willy."

His friend glared with such passionate intensity into his face that the young apprentice to the French printer clacked his teeth against his tongue. "Ah!" he cried in anguish.

"Come in here." They entered the common-room.

A company of loud and handsome young men had nearly conquered the normal dullness of this gathering place for seemly businessmen. Lolling upon the padded benches, singing bawdy songs, with a fair young boy among them strumming a lute, they glowed, they gleamed, their brightness arched like a fair rainbow above the honest kersey clods who ordinarily peopled the place. O music, O love and laughter, O fleeting joy that tears the heart with memory, O tears of things, O hell! Young $W^m$ the $S^h$ recognized these wild young fellows at once, and shuddered as if they had risen up together, singing, from the mouldy grave of his hopes, to mock him. He sprang backward, landing upon the toes of Troublesome Richard.

"Ah!" screamed Dick, beginning to hop.

"Out, out, out," muttered the glove-maker's dependable heir, tugging him back into Bridge Street.

"But the players!" stammered Dick.

"Go back and join 'em then," said his friend savagely, shoving him once more toward the lattice of the Swan. And he started off at a run toward Henley Street and his father's glove-shop.

"They're Leicester's men! Don't you remember?" called Dick.

"I have to see my father."

"They rode down with me from the George in Chipping Norton! And one of 'em asked if you were dead yet!"

"No time!" called back Willy, breaking into a trot. But Dick came dashing after him. They streaked past the last butcher shop in the Chure, a narrow passageway crowded with tradesmen's lairs and taverns, and came clattering out among crowded countrymen grouped round a puppet-show in the Market Square.

"Come back, Willy! See the players!"

"No time! No time!"

Staring country girls called after them, as they had license to do on St. Susanna's Eve, and catch them too, if they could. One freckle-faced daughter in green silk reached out for Willy, and only succeeded in getting Dick. To him, however, she hung on, with the screams of virgins cheering her on.

"Will-ie!" wailed Dick.

It was his unlucky day again, as it had been three years ago. Lizzie Fisher had got him, and this time she did not mean to let him get away.

"Oh, Dickie! What luck!"

*"Pardonnez moi, je suis étranger."*

"Oh, la, hear him talk so *pretty*!"

Screaming girls began dancing around the captive, while Lizzie, in the middle, kissed him soundly, for forfeit number one, two, three, four, and the first dozen. Then the other girls began to close in, to collect theirs.

Dazed by his sudden escape, William the Speedy plunged straight into the belly of Alexander Aspinall, the new schoolmaster who had just come from Brasenose to replace Cottam the Catholic.

"Ugh!" said the schoolmaster, sitting hard on the pavement. He was a spindly Lancashire man, wearing yellow stockings, cross-gartered.

"I have hit *terra*," he groaned as the glove-seller helped him to his feet.

"But risen again, sir. *Statarius*," said Willy, bowing.

"Ah, *statarius*, yes, yes, good, good," stammered the schoolmaster, returning his bow.

"God save your worship," said Willy, bowing again.

And may he comfort your capicity, sir," replied Mr. Aspinall, bowing and waving.

Willy was still smiling his imitation smile and waving to the schoolmaster when he heard a rude snort. His old friend Bloody Richard had escaped the importunate Lizzie and had returned to laugh at him.

"O Lord," gasped Dick, staggering around. "O gracious

saints of glory, and a few more, and a few more! Oh, I never thought I would live to see the day! Oh, oh, help, help!"

Willy regarded him with some disgust.

"What's taken thee? What has got thee? Speak, speak."

"Oh, that monster, oh, that beautiful mountain of guts in the yellow stockings!" wheezed Dick, falling against a wall. "Oh, and cross-gartered too! Oh, I have lived! Oh, oh, goodbye, all my friends! I have seen the power and the glory and I am ready to depart. Goodbye, William. Goodbye, sir. *Statarius*, sir. Which end of you shall I kiss, sir? Oh, oh, oh," said Dick, taking off his elegant cap and waving it at a tethered horse. "God save your worship, sir. To hell with this stinking town. I am going away. You are an ass. Goodbye."

The imitation businessman walked humbly in step with him, away from the round-eyed girls and back to the Swan.

"I see what you mean," he said in a voice of such sweet Christian charity that his friend retched.

"Damn thee, Willy, I have lost all my hopes in life if they have got thee too. All my life I have admired one single solitary human being. I have remembered thee. I have patterned myself on thee. I have done all that I have done because of thee. And here I see thee in this sickening comedy, bowing and scraping to a whoreson puffed-up maltworm, an ordinary creeping schoolmaster, the lowest grovelling worm on the earth. Thee! Thee! The golden god of my youth, the image and excellence of all our dreaming, the very pattern of revolt, the true hue of rebellion, the utter form of resistance to all horrible things as they were, who used to eat little schoolmasters for dinner! Oh, Willy, I am sick, I am sick, give me to drink, help, help!"

And staggering into the taproom of the Swan he waved feebly to the vintner, Mr. Dickson, to fill him up a tall tankard and another for his humble friend now standing beside him and glowing with repentance for being such a disappointment.

"It is true, Dick, I recognize, that I have in some measure changed," he was saying gently and reasonably, while his hand, resting on the back of a bench, trembled alarmingly. "But must we not remember that there is a world of things as they are, not as they ought to be, and in this world of things as they are it is necessary for us to conf —"

"No more, no more," said Dick hopelessly, waving his hand. He raised the foaming tankard of ale and lifted it to his lips.

"You see," the imitation businessman went on patiently, "Mr. Aspinall, though a Brasenose scholar, is yet a very good businessman and is entering into some dealings with us in wool and malt, and we have every expectation that with his good will, he may favour us with some business which —"

Dick choked, and spat forth a shower of ale. "Stop! Stop!" he shouted.

And in a quivering silence the two old friends proceeded to gulp at their ale until it was all swallowed.

Meanwhile from the padded benches in the center of the taproom some loud young players were laughing and rolling themselves about. The voices of these loud young fellows were very musical indeed, and full of authority, moreover.

To these loud young players the son of the glove-seller paid no more attention than if they had been so many trusses of straw.

And this was very strange, for he knew them all.

They did not, of course, recognize him.

Why should they? At the time they had met three years ago in the yard of the Crown Inn in Warwick he had been a girl.

Now I am a man, he thought. Well, those childish dreams are forever dead.

If the votes go as they should, I may even be elected to Council this year. And that will be very good for business. I will speak to Dick Quiney about it after church on Sunday.

He awoke from his reverie to see his old friend Bloody Richard strolling over and greeting the gaudy handsome players. Laughing gaily among them was the beautiful boy who had played the girls' parts — the manager's son, he remembered, named Dick like his friend. Or ex-friend.

How fair, slim, lively, and beautiful this boy was now! A golden light streamed from his face and his long curling hair. And his voice was like violin music.

The players were slapping their thighs and laughing harder than before. And Dick Field was bending over the boy and whispering to him. Their faces turned toward the imitation businessman.

Dick Field said something to Dick What's-His-Name. Then the golden boy laughed so loudly that all the players looked where he was looking. He was looking at Willy, and he was pointing. Now they all laughed. And everyone in the taproom was turning to look.

Through a red mist, the imitation businessman heard everybody laughing at him now.

Hot, weak, dizzy, and sick, he fumbled for a coin and threw it down on the bar. With the mocking laughter still in his ears he strode out of the taproom and out into the heat of afternoon. Faces floated on the sunlit air, voices spoke. He rushed by all these unreal people, faster and faster.

The mustered men were marching up and down on the Green. "Hold!" shouted Tom Miller, the sergeant. "Traverse!" he yelled. "Come you in! Stand! Aim your pieces! Fire!"

A mad dream blazed up in the reeling mind of the imitation businessman.

Down the High Street came riding the great Earl Ambrose with a dozen or so retainers, and Sir Fouck Greville and Sir Richard Moryson riding beside him.

They will choose some more soldiers today.

Willy dashed into the glove-shop and saluted his father.

"Hail, Sir John of the Sack and Staff!" he cried.

Old John's large eyes opened wide in astonishment. His son had not addressed him so in years.

"Where hast thou been, eh?"

"Totting up our profits, father."

"Profits!"

"Just finished the mighty work, O Spearshaker."

"Let us have no jests, let us have no jests. This is man's work, man's work."

"Indeed."

Into this splendid word Willy put all the expression possible.

"Well, well, how much, how much?"

"To answer twice, sir, in two words —"

"Answer me once, answer me once!"

"Yes sir, it shall be done, sir. Our profits are, so to speak, not, *modo et forma*, as you would say, profits at all. *De nihilo nihil*, as Mr. Aspinall would say."

"Pox on Mr. Ass-All. How much?"

"Yes, father. Well, father, I have been thinking of my future today, and I have one little request before we face the figures. How would you like it, sir, if I —"

"How much? How much? How much?"

"In three words, sir —"

"How much?"

"Well, father, it has not been such a good year as last year. And last year was not such a good year as the year before."

"How much? How much? How much?"

"But orders will be coming from the Cotswolds, and the fringed gloves do well."

Bang! went John's fist on the cutting-bench. The dividers danced, the fingers flapped.

"Yes sir, I will tell you our profit, sir. It is an upsy-downsy, or minus decretal of some let me see . . ."

"Let me see! Let me see! Let me see! I already know what it is, I already know what it is. We have lost four pounds."

"Three pound nine, sir, less a few moys. A trifle. *Cum minus, menos,* as the schoolmaster might say."

"A pox on the schoolmaster, and all your mums and moys! I've made up my mind. We'll open our own slaughter-house. We'll start our own tannery. We'll rent Gybbs' barn. We'll take over your Uncle Henry's sheep and cows. He's in debt too. And Gilly will mind the shop."

"Yes sir, very good."

"And you'll run the slaughter-house. Have a good arm with the pole-ax."

Willy swallowed hard.

"I would rather go on the road, sir."

"You'll be the butcher! What's that arm for? What are those shoulders for? Enough, I have decided."

"But I cannot kill cows, sir."

Old John was beginning to work himself up. "Why not? Why not? Thou didst it at hockday, and made a speech."

"That was but a play, sir. I cannot kill any real cows. Their eyes would look at me."

"Thou hast talked of murther and blood and crime since thou first heard it from the harlotry players, and wilt thou now say, like any weak girl, 'I cannot kill cows? Their eyes would look at me'?"

"Sir, let me go on the road. I know how to make money, but in my own way."

"Thou canst not even keep thy hand from gaming, and from

dicing, and will this hand bring money to me? To the shambles thou wilt go."

"I ask you to let me go on the road, sir, or by heaven I swear —"

"Silence! I am master here!"

The approaching footsteps of Gilly broke the throbbing silence. In plodded the fat boy, munching at marchpane and pickled walnuts.

"Eat!" cried his baffled father, springing up from his arm-chair and clapping on his hat. "Great God, look at him eat!"

"Well, I'm off, sir," Willy said quickly.

"One gambler, and one guzzler! Is this what thou hast given me, woman?" shouted the glove-maker, seeing his wife approaching with a new housemaid following her, armed with mop and bucket. This last year Mrs. Shakespeare had acquired a marvellous passion for pursuing all dust, dirt, or disorder in the three old smoky houses the family now owned, sitting sill to sill, and eave to eave, and slowly sinking into the marshy ground, an inch every century.

"Ah, you were just the same at their age, let the boys do their growing," said their mother.

"But where are they growing to?" cried their father, beginning to wave his arms.

"Out of the house, I shouldn't wonder," said the good woman, motioning to the girl to set her bucket down. "I'll have the shelves scoured first, Maryann. Heap everything here. What, art thou not gone, Gilly? Take thy brother to the mustering, Willy, we are too many in here."

"I will, mother. And I'll join the Army today."

"That's good, and now begone," said Mrs. Shakespeare, waving them out.

Neither father nor mother heard his boast, or his promise, whichever it was. They were too busy with their own quarrel, which followed the two sons a little way along Henley Street, the one eating peacefully, the other thinking quite hard about doing just what he had said.

At the first market barrow young Gilly stopped to dream over the food, and there his elder brother left him, to think out this new thought, and see where it led him.

CHAPTER TEN

LAZILY riding their horses, the Earl of Leicester's players were showing themselves through the town with a whole crowd of children following them, wild with excitement. Up in front rode Dick Burbage, the glowing boy, elegant in silks and fair colours, and after him the uncommonly bold and handsome men of the company. Down before the gildhall they leaped and went jingling in to get their license for the performances today and tomorrow. The imitation businessman went right by, and he did not look back. The sergeant was still howling at the weary pikemen on the Green, the feeble forcible men, the shadows and scraps of soldiers whose fathers had not wanted them, whose masters had not bought them off, whose mothers probably did not love them, and whose country now had to use them in default of better.

O England! thought Will Shakespeare, staring with hot eyes at the heroes dragging up and down. However has the bloody country lived so long with such shadows to defend her? God bless the Queen for keeping out of war. And again before his mind shimmered the vision of the gorgeous lady he had seen so many years ago, when he was young and hopeful. So gold and pale she was, gleaming like pearl, with those strange golden eyes looking straight at him as he reached up and grabbed old Betsy's bridle rein, and saved the whole company of lords and ladies from the runaway mare. All his life he had remembered the Queen's wonderful eyes, and the light dancing in them as she broke into laughter. And then the golden moment was broken, and the procession went on over the hill toward where the people were waiting. The silver trumpets were ringing over the hills.

But the ears of Willy Shagspear were ringing with the music of history, and all its wonderful life and awful death, even as he listened to the drums and tabors of the players now before

112

the gildhall, and the howls of Tom Miller, the sergeant, at the feeble soldiers.

O England, he thought, his throat aching with the pain. O bloody and wonderful island, O shield of Mars, O golden land set in the silver sea, O semi-heaven, where the brood of um, the seed of ah, the let me see ...

He was fading away into poetry again, when the sound of loud voices woke him from the golden vision. Old Earl Ambrose of Warwick was limping painfully toward the armchair under the great elm, and Sir Fouck Greville and a crowd of eager clerks were clustering around him to be of service.

The howling of Tom Miller reached frenzy now, and he ordered the dragging pikemen to do everything.

But the old Earl waved his hand benignly. "Enough! Let 'em rest. Let 'em lie down."

As the Queen's Master of Ordnance and Lord Lieutenant of Warwickshire, as well as Member of the Privy Council, it was Earl Ambrose's duty to find, enlist, train, arm, equip, feed, clothe and furnish soldiers for the glory of England whenever she needed more glory. Unluckily, with all the bribing and buying off of men, it was the rogues, it was the vagabonds, it was the masterless men who were caught and pressed into service.

I might be an officer though, thought the son of the alderman. Earl Ambrose has noticed me more than once. All I need do is come to his attention brightly enough.

Visions of saving England flamed before him as this whole glimmering world of shapes and shadows spun round the sun, and his heart thundered in the prison of his ribs.

Nearer he drew to the group under the elm, hearing their voices gravely mumbling together. The tethered horses swished their tails at the flies, munching the delicious grass. Rather a large crowd of people had followed the Earl to the Green and were standing respectfully at proper distance.

Suddenly there was a diversion. A tall and rather stout young man in plain mud-brown had come forward and fallen on his knees before Earl Ambrose.

A murmur rose among the people. A clear young voice spoke. "My Lord, I would serve you."

The gentlemen around the Earl stared in alarm at this bold youth here. What, an ordinary yeoman, an apprentice without his cap, a mere cutter of gloves, a scratcher of numbers!

"Now then, Willy, be off," said Mr. Aglionby, the little clerk from Warwick who had read that long speech to the Queen about Caesar and Alexander, for which she had thanked him in a voice so cheerful, so fresh, so lively, and had smiled with such gay kindness that the little recorder had stammered and fumbled and dropped the hand she had held out to him to kiss. "It was told me," the Queen had said gaily, "that you would be afraid to look upon me or to speak so boldly. But you were not so fraid of me as I was of you."

How the people had laughed and cheered at that! Willy felt his heart leap with courage and delight at the recollection of it, and he smiled patiently and kindly at Mr. Aglionby now, though Sir Richard Moryson looked stern, Sir Thomas Lucy looked glum, and Sir William Catesby looked as if he had had too much to drink. As for Sir Fouck, who loved books, and had often been kind to the son of the alderman, he just looked amused at the whole business.

"It's Willy again!" called out someone at the edge of the circle. People were jumping up to see what he was doing *now*.

"It's Alderman Shakespeare's son," said Sir Fouck. "A very fine fellow, my Lord, and has read many of my books. And writes poetry."

"Poetry?" mumbled the good old Earl, trying to focus his eyes upon this powerful young man kneeling before him. "Let me see, let me see. Where have I seen thee, lad?"

"William Shakespeare, my Lord, who desires service in your army, and will ride into the jaws of hell and back for you and her Majesty."

The sad old eyes of the Earl looked straight at him for one blinding moment.

"By gad, the lad who stole my horse!" he said.

Someone laughed, like the twitter of a bird. Then a few other people laughed.

"The same rogue who saved the Queen from the romping mare!" added the Earl, and slapped his thigh. More people laughed now. The laughter was rising among the trees, into the air.

"Thou hast been eating well, my boy, thou art well-fed, and would make a better soldier than these shadows here. Well, thou canst ride well enough. Get me thy father's permission and have it signed and sworn to by two propertied witnesses and I will take thee into my household company. God bless thee."

His heart thudding louder, the son of the alderman rose from his knees and bowed himself backward away from the Earl even as he heard the old man ask Mr. Buffin, "Where is Mr. Shagsbye? I have not seen Mr. Shagsbye at the bench in a long time."

"My Lord, he stays at home," answered Mr. Fenton.

"It is business, my Lord," explained Sir Fouck quickly, though everybody knew the alderman had quarrelled so bitterly in Council that he never went any more, and was so deep in debt he stayed away from his creditors.

"Well, gentlemen, business is business, I always say," remarked the old Earl after a pause.

And a murmur of agreement ran round the whole company. "Business is business, ah, very true, business is business."

In his thundering ears, as he wandered away on a black cloud of despair, young $W^m$ heard the idiotic syllables repeated and repeated to the crack of doom.

No, it was hopeless, it could never be, the old man would never let him go, he was cursed forever, he could not escape, and to hell with all harlotry players, he thought, as he passed the gaudy young men posturing and slashing their swords together in imitation of courage, of slaughter.

Someone waved frantically to him from the doorway of the Bear. It was Dick Field, slim and elegant, brilliantly garbed, and full of ale. A great thirst surged up in William the Pen-Pusher. Ah, who cares what I do? What will it all matter three hundred and eighty-five years from now?

And feeling as dry, gutless, bloodless as a scarecrow flapping among crows, mocked and pecked at by everything beaked and winged, he shook his head at his old friend Bloody Richard and started rapidly away.

He had gone only half a block when he heard hasty footsteps coming after him. A heavy hand clapped him on the shoulder. "Sir, a word with you!" said a maddeningly vibrant voice.

He shuddered, then turned and glared into the merry, sparkling eyes of a handsome young player.

This handsome young player was clad in extravagant costume, all pinkings and paddings and slashings, with a little French cape, absurd in this hot weather, with puffed-up trunkhose of saffron and purple, with gold filigree-work and a codpiece like a lady's velvet purse, laughable, a bold Italian emphasis of what in Puritan England was severely subtracted from all sartorial consideration, with turned-up Venetian slippers of crimson velvet and copper lace, and on top of his hennaed curls such a hat as the glove-maker's dutiful clerk had not yet seen in his dusty life.

Was it a gravy-dish? A cockle-boat? A custard-coffin? A silken pie?

William the Shaking concentrated all his fading wits upon this hat.

"Will you not drink a thimbleful or two with us, O Proteus of Avon?" piped the handsome player, giving him a sweeping bow and waving the silken bauble like an ape at a fair.

He shuddered again. He looked up and down the street of respectable tipplers, topers, and tapsters. This gaudy player exhibited all the deplorable moral stigmata that any good businessman in the parish would be reluctantly forced to point out in Council before voting against allowing any further bawdy players to pollute the nice purities of the town. Item, he was painted like a punk. Item, he was perfumed. Item, he wore a lovelock, with a little scarlet ribbon tied in a bow around it. Item, he was as sinuous, as silky, as devilishly graceful as an Italian macaroni, one of those traveling acrobats or aping players you saw at Coventry Fair.

My mind is made up forever, thought William the Conquered. I will strangle this evil taste for plays if it chokes me to death. Everything they say about players is true, and I hate the sight of 'em.

An awful pain stabbed his chest. Muttering thickly, his head down, he started out blindly for the house and shop of his father. After he had got away from the fantastic player, whose name, he remembered somewhere in this choking haze, was Bob Wilson, he began walking faster, faster.

I am safe, thou art safe, he is safe, we are safe, you are safe, they are safe, he thought.

I wonder what language they use to conjugate their verbs in hell.

And then the blinding vision came of all life on earth in a dance of folly, a pageant of absurdity and horror. And these people on this laughably neat and idiotic street, these forked nothings, these eyed radishes, all were players on the monstrous stage of hell. The bright screen of time no longer hid the mockery from his eyes: he saw beyond the veil, beyond the monstrous hither-and-yonder scrambling of shrouded dancers, of solemn, staring, hollow masks in the streets, of shambling, slately, wooden-footed forms. What are these faces? he thought, the blinding vision aching in his eyes. Images of God, or apes out of the horrible belly of nature? Something has happened to me, but what is it?

The blinding light had faded, and he was there in the same busy street, among his kin.

"Willy! You're hopeless!" cried the voice of his old friend Dick Field, now the toy of another man's wife.

Ah, they'll all do it, the dazed son of the businessman was thinking. Stench and corruption, is it no more than this?

"Willy, art thou dead? The players want thee for sport!"

Aye, to mock me, he thought, as the gods mock men, or as wanton boys mock dancing flies, before tearing their wings off.

"What ails thee, Worthless? Have three short years done this to my idol?" Dick was saying in an aggrieved tone.

Aye, idol of idiot-worshippers, thought the bookkeeper. "I will riddle thee," he answered, nodding his head up and down. "Who is master o' the tiger?"

"Hell's fire, is this a time for riddles? Come on, Worthless, and clown awhile for the players. Rare sport, boy! They are still laughing at thee as a queen in Warwick. Would I had seen it!"

"A queen to 'em, and a quoin too," answered the imitation businessman. How is it I am killing the very joy I most wanted? he wondered, even as he was doing it.

"They want you to play the fool for 'em in the Bear yard! They had a boy die of plague, and you'd be perfect as the fool —"

"Away! And take the fool with you!"

Dick's amiable pink countenance showed very deep hurt. "You were always gentle with me all these years, I believed you were gentle, the girls all said so too," said Dick in a slow puzzled way. Tears stood in his blue eyes. His nether lip drooped.

"That friend who is gentle, my friend," said Willy with mad intensity, glaring into those unseeing blue eyes, unseeing as heaven, "it is that friend who is master o' the tiger. Beware of him, lest the tiger leap at thy throat."

Then he turned and walked away from his friend, straight home. His mind was working at last, after three years in the dust, it was working coolly, clearly, and cruelly. Before him, mocking him, went awful visions of the inexplicable horror of the universe, and small unwitting man on his ball of dung in the midst, dreaming of angels and demons, heaven and hell — and all the time his own heaven and hell within him.

And mine too, mine too, he thought. Why, for all my soft voice and womanly pity, for all my endurance of shame and blame, I am one of the greatest villains of history, in my teeming mind. And if my poor mother knew, she would be quiet for once, I think. She would know her own son.

A sudden squeezing pain gripped his gullet. He tried to swallow and could not swallow.

He began to choke, exactly like his father at some imitation tragedy by his mother.

God forgive me, thought Willy, staggering into the glove-shop, choking, believing his last minute had come.

The alderman, still trying to solve the aching puzzle of worry and debt, was bent over his $x$'s and $d$'s, muttering to himself and cursing.

His son was trying to speak. His voice rattled in his strangling throat: "For ... give ..."

Sorrowing faces looked down at him. He lay on the lumpy stone floor of the glove-shop, which in the old days had been a shambles, for murdering sheep.

His beautiful love, his darling, looked down at him. She looks like Our Lady before he hacked her with his sword, the fallen son of the alderman was dreamily thinking.

Well, mother, I'll be dead awhile now, and food for worms.

"Send for the doctor," he heard his darling mother say, who had always been so cruel to him.

Or was she? Let me think, he thought.

She is always kind when I am dying, he remembered. That time Anne leaped into the pool in her smock, and saved me, my mother was kind as Our Lady to her Child.

But ah, it was good in the pool with the shepherd's daughter, I could feel her thighs wrapped about mine, and she breathed deep, deep, as we came to surface, and so I lived again.

"Drink, my darling," murmured his beautiful mother, still beautiful, and with such mournful dark eyes.

This potion, this brew she wanted him to keep drinking, was bitter, bitter as wormwood. Bitter as the wormfood of life.

How do I know wormfood is bitter? he wondered, trying to drink from the cup as she asked him to do.

"Oh, drink, my darling," she said, in her voice like beautiful music. How sad to be leaving her when at last they were one in pain and love! Mothers and sons are forever united in pain, he thought, and we only know it now.

What was that roaring and rushing of wings?

"Drink, sweet boy," she said. "It's belladona, and will cure thee."

The cup was bitter, but he drank. *Bella Donna, Madonna, I see all clear now, when I'm entering death's dark kingdom,* he thought.

Out of the darkness he awoke and heard an owl hooting in the orchard.

Dry mouth, burning eyes, aching head, and rapidly beating heart — but the awful pain was gone. He felt dizzy, and dry as ashes. He seemed to remember a night of maniacal excitement, in which he had solved all the problems of the world, killed them with words. He remembered his whole family, living and dead, their eyes and faces, the three living brothers, the three dead sisters, and his mother, not yet dead, holding the bitter cup.

Bella donna, beautiful lady. An old brew of Anne's. Witch's brew.

All the windows of his mind were wide open. He saw everything and knew everything and was interested in all of it, all of it.

The owl hooted again in the orchard.

He floated up from his pallet of straw and went to the window. On such a night, he thought, stood Dido on the bank and saw the moonlight. Leander swam the Hellespont on a night like this. I think he would have lived many a year if it had not been for a hot summer night, and the affliction of a cramp.

He looked down into the orchard, and hooted in answer. Then he climbed up on the window-sill and reached for the old apple-tree branch. He dropped through spangled darkness, over the dovecote roof, and went rolling and laughing over the wet grass.

An elegant shape came tripping into the moonlight. It was Dick Field, in sea-water green and silver, with a French ruff like a platter upon which rode his head. He was all dressed up for return to the big city, and his horse whickered at the orchard gate.

"Well, I've come to hoot goodbye, Willy."

"A fond farewell, man o' the moon."

"Forgive me, Willy. I just wanted you to escape this place somehow, anyhow. Bob Wilson's chief of the players now, old Burbage stays in London and collects the money and fights the Puritans who want to close his houses. And Bob said to tell you, if you can get your father's permission, he'll hire you for his company."

"Wilson said that?"

"He said you're the perfect clown, but could play the rumbustious parts later too."

"Wilson said he'd hire me?"

"By the moon I swear he did."

"He was not mocking me?"

"You beetle-headed finger-peddler, how long must you be blind? The world of golden joys awaits you. Come live with me and my mistress, and her daughter. Her husband is in Scotland. Oh, Willy, the fops and fair ladies that swarm to our door!"

"He said he would take me into his company?"

"He did, he did."

"It is hopeless. I cannot go."

And bowing his head and shrugging his shoulders he began walking aimlessly out of the rustling orchard and into the muddy alley which led to the gild pits and the fields.

Dick strode after him and caught him by the arm. "Why not? Say why not?"

In the moonlight the son of the glove-seller looked glumly at his friend.

"All dead and rotten," he explained.

"What is rotten? What is rotten?"

"All, all, everything. No, it is impossible."

"You lily-livered, puke-stockinged, nott-pated patch of nothing, why is it so? It is only thy vanity makes it so."

"Ha!"

"Thou art a snivelling coward, afraid of thy father. What, man, he is but a country clown."

"Away! Tempt me not, thou mere et cetera, thou."

"Coward, coward, to commit the sin against the Holy Ghost. Murderer!"

"Ha, ha, ha."

"The gift of heaven was given you, and what did you commit? Murder, sneaking, snivelling murder. Will you come to London with me?"

"No."

"Will you join the players then?"

"Never."

"I have done with you! I give you up! I abandon you! Farewell!"

"Good night, good night, good night."

And they went off in different directions, muttering, cursing, and waving their arms in the moonlight.

A little boat glided out over the broad bosom of the river and floated along past the sleeping town. It glided by Holy Trinity, floating like a heavenly dream of itself over the water, and on toward Luddington and Weston. When the moon went out in the mist the little boat was swallowed up in the mist too.

At the pool in the woods, deep in the vale of Temple Grafton, a silent figure crouched a long time looking down into the dark water. Sometimes he would toss a pebble in, and the mocking face reflected dimly there would shiver, shake, and be gone in ripples flowing to the rim.

He came awake out of a haunted dream, hearing a rustle among the leaves.

"Art thou here, mad ape?" whispered Anne.

"A piece of me."

"And what is it this time, Willy?"

He shook his head and stared into the water. "What if we had drowned together, that time?"

"Oh, Willy, let's not be blue so early in the morning. Had your breakfast? Come, I have to feed my lambs."

"What if we were dead? Would we sleep well, and have no dreams?"

"Oh, I'd dream of you and you'd dream of me, come now and have some breakfast."

"There is an undiscovered country, and it waits for us."

"That's good, darling. Come along! I'll find you something from the spring-house. Poor Aunt Kate would pull you in by the heels if she saw you, hoping it was a man to marry me."

He sighed more deeply than ever, got wearily to his feet, and began dragging off after her into the woods toward the hut where she had kept the baby fox until he was set free, and where there was always a sick cat, or a wounded bird, or some other suffering creature of the forest to be nursed and mended.

"One of thy simples saved my life last night," he said glumly.

"That's good, honey-boy. Come in softly, don't make a sound."

"What a fine physician you'd have made, if women had any hope in this world," he said.

"Shhh!"

He waited while she inspected her wounded swan, a young one, arching his neck at the intruder and hissing.

"If they'd give me more of it I might have lain with you tonight in my dreams."

Silence from the straw where she knelt to feed the swan.

"Or with some ancestor's skeleton, in my lonely grave," said her gloomy visitor.

"Oh, Willy, have done with forever speaking of graves and bones. You have a fine life now in his counting-room and will be married to Lizzie soon. What ails thee anyhow?"

She stood up, as angry as he had ever seen her, and taking firm hold of his arm pulled him out of the hut. They stood facing each other in the misty wood, their breath coming fast and hard.

"You too," he whispered. "Like them all."

"When will you ever be a man?" she cried, stamping her foot in the moss.

"A witch has cast her spell on me," he said, staring at her with hot accusing eyes.

"You were always a mocker, a catbird, an ape. Be a man, Willy, and have done with these womanish vapours."

He caught her roughly in his arms and pressed his burning lips to hers.

"No, no, no, fool!" she gasped, shuddering hard. She tore herself out of his arms.

"It is you who spoiled me for any girl. I know you now, you witch. A potion brewed of hell —"

A choked cry came from Anne, and then laughter. "Be off with you, mocker!"

He fell to his knees before her. "I love you," he sobbed. "I worship you."

"Be off, I say! Mocker! Counterfeiter! Echo! There is no truth or manhood in thee! Away, schoolboy!"

"No, no, no, no," he moaned, clasping her knees and burying his face in the folds of her rough skirt.

"I will never speak to you as long as I live," said Anne, and struck him with her fist. Then she tore herself out of his grasp and ran from the woods.

## CHAPTER ELEVEN

"WELL, did you have enough sleep to last you for this week?" asked Mr. Shakespeare at dinner.

Unfortunately, now Willy was cured of the choking sickness, the family treated him like a dying hero no longer. The children, seated obediently at the table, waited for their father to give them permission to eat.

"Come, we have a hot venison pasty," John said. "Sit thee down, lad. Much business we have today, and I'm off to the Cotswolds as soon as we've made our inventory. Well, I've waited patiently, and now you've had enough sleep to be one of the dead. What is that limp? Lame again, boy? And what are these linen cheeks? How now, where is thy tongue?"

"Faith, I'll eat nothing, I thank you as much as though I did."

"Sit thee down, I say!"

"I had rather halt awhile, up and down," he said wildly, parading before the smoke-blackened chimney. "I must have bruised my shin playing at sword and dagger with one of Davy Jones's boys. Why do the dogs still bark? Has Alfred got out?"

"Come, sit down," said his mother, all compassion gone as soon as he was well again.

My life were better ended, he thought Who would these fardels bear? I had done better to be gone.

Lame, poor, despised, he felt the whole burden of this weary life upon his back as he came haltingly to the table, and sat down among these faces.

He bowed his head, not listening to the long Puritan grace his father declaimed, as if he were at a church feast. A plague on both their churches, William the Weary thought. We are of neither one nor t'other, and both are mured in hate that should be open to love. From now on, I shall be no Christian, but a Greek.

Mr. Shakespeare wound up his godly and garrulous prayer,

124

Mrs. Shakespeare made the sign of the cross, the children took up their knives, and William the Pagan looked at his father so scornfully the old man dropped his carving-knife.

"What a pox! Art a ghost?"

"I hope so," came mournfully the dry, old, grey, feeble voice of his eldest son and fondest hope for the future.

"Stick thy tongue out!" said Mr. Shakespeare.

"I would much rather not."

"Stick it out!"

"I assure you it is green, sir, green as grass."

"Am I to be obeyed in this house, or are my sons to make a monkey of me?"

"God forbid, father."

"Oogh, his tongue *is* green! Look at that, Gilly! Is it not horrible?"

An expression of gloomy disdain darkened the countenance of the former hero. As the fat boy leaned grinning forward to peer at his tongue, Willy stuck out his leg. Down went Gilly, rolling over the floor.

"What clownery is this? Art thou a knave in a scurvy play?" cried John.

"Would I were, and out of this bolting-hutch of beastliness!" suddenly howled William the Aching.

"What? What?"

The eyes of the family were all looking at him again, not a dying hero now, but a living villain. Something seemed to have gone off in his brain, and a red haze blinded his eyes.

"Venison!" he cried. "Eat, ye dead elms, eat! Fatten on life, ye living dead! A butcher-shop for me, to feed ye? I'll starve, beg, steal, murder, first! And you, fat-guts!" he yelled, dragging his bloated brother up by the collar and seating him with a thump at the table. "Gobble thy fill, ye swollen parcel of dropsies! And you may have all my share of gloves to wear for asses' ears!"

The ringing and chiming of all his buried, smothered, throttled, and strangled passions resounded in his voice, rolled into the orchard, startled the neighbours, and brought Dick Hornby to the door.

William the Revolting heard him knocking and shouting, and off went another explosion in his ringing head. Beginning to reach for earthen pots, wooden trenchers, copper pans, and anything else he could toss, he sprang to the door and roared into Hornby's face: "Dost thou hear me, Mr. Clanker?"

"In the name of the Father, and of the Son, and of the Holy Ghost," whispered Mr. Shakespeare, forgetting that he was not a Catholic any more. "My poor son is mad."

"I think he is drunk," said his wife.

"Aye, on the poison brew of a witch!" cried their eldest son, seizing the center of the stage, that is to say kitchen, from his mother. "I'll speak my speech before a crew of fiends carries me off, and let the end o' the world come, who cares?"

"I think thou hast forgotten thy place, boy," said Dick Hornby sternly.

"Horrible villain!" yelled the son of the glove-maker, seizing one of the blacksmith's ears in each powerful hand.

"Yow! Yow! Help!" screamed Mr. Hornby. "A madman!"

"Like old Diccon Shakeshaft, the shame of Snitterfield, wandering the heath in the storm, and wailing the wind and rain!" declaimed Mrs. Shakespeare, but her son was the leading actor now, and the family hardly listened to her.

"Give me thy hammer, thou weed of affliction!" cried Willy to the blacksmith, snatching it up. "Away, cacodemon! To dusty death! The way of all fools, and I'll gallop there before ye!"

He dashed out into the orchard, waving the hammer.

"Save him! He has run frantic!" cried his mother.

"The boy has been too gentle, he has bottled his passions like a spider," said Mr. Shakespeare. "Do I not know what he feels? Am I not his damned, doomed, and hell-blasted father?" And he went stumbling out after his maddened son, who had now entered the smithy and was making polite speeches to a groom in there, waiting for his horse to be shod.

"I trust I see you well, sir, and how blows the wind in your corner?"

"Eh?" said the groom.

"Art strong? Well-nourished? Vigorous?"

"Eh?" said the groom.

"Take this nutcracker," said William the Noisy. "And now," he requested politely, getting upon his knees and holding his bright head in an inviting position, "knock me upon this noggin and see if anyone's at home."

"Eh?" said the groom.

"This egg of inspiration," explained young Shakespeare as Lizzie Fisher, Polly Plumly, and Betty King came to the door and peeked in. "This well of wisdom. This sea of dreams in a skull the size of a pot."

More girls came staring into the smithy, but he paid no attention to them or to the worried Lizzie.

"Oh, my poor lover has strained his brains, I thought he would," Lizzie sobbed. The girls all shrieked with excitement and sorrow.

"This shell of shame," went on the raving heir to all the stinks and miseries of the glove business, "this bucket of despair, this case of memory, this basket of grief, this grinning death, this whittled cabbage, this p —"

A withered elder came to the door, spat, and mumbled, "It's Willy," and went away.

"Let's all go down the river with him, and he can take his lute, and we'll sing songs," said Betty King, whose father was an alderman in Warwick.

"And have a picnic," said Polly Plumly, who liked to eat.

"Away, you globes of sinful continents!" howled the son of the glove-maker, suddenly springing out from behind the forge. "Detested parasites! Affable wolves! Meek bears! Time's flies! Away, ye fools of fortune! I'll none of ye!"

Shrieking with enjoyment, all the girls went away to the door of the smithy and waited to see what would happen next. As for Lizzie Fisher, who was not sure she wanted to marry this dizzy speech-maker after all, she put her arms around Mr. Shakespeare's neck and kissed him a few times and wept in his ear.

"Be easy, be calm, I know just what the matter is," said the alderman, trembling all over. And patting the amorous girl a few times upon such portions of her anatomy as were in reach, he went up to his son, kissed him, and took him in his arms. "Come with me, my poor boy," he said gently.

"That fellow's mad," said the groom.

"Ah, he's like that from time to time," Dick Hornby said,

picking up his hammer and beginning to clink and clank again.

Lizzie followed Mr. Shakespeare into the orchard, but he waved her away.

"Oh, father, farewell, and forgive," said William the Penitent, weeping on his father's neck.

"I know just what is the matter with thee, poor lad," said John. "I remember how it was with me in the power of the blood. Strong as a bull I was, and fiery."

"Father, father, I want to die and be rotten," his son sobbed.

"All in good time, be of good cheer, we must get thee married with no further delay. What! You're more a man than ten of 'em, and don't gentlemen marry at eighteen? I'll go beard old John in his den and get our dowry in my pocket."

"Too late, father. Too late."

"You'll see, my boy, marriage will quiet thee down something wonderful, and with some new good bottom land we'll wax again and grow fat and prosperous."

"Late! Late! Too late!"

"Come, my boy, come, come, we'll soothe thee with a little drink," said his father kindly and thirstily, leading the dizzy, weak, and exhausted youth out the back way toward the Bear Inn, where nobody would bother them except possibly a wench or two, which was customary in country inns.

The first two mugs of ale did not do much, but with the third the secret hero and runner-off to glory had progressed into a state of pure clarity and appreciation of the pickle into which he had got. If I had never emblazoned those accursed arms, he thought, the old man never would have made me a partner in his misery, and I would have escaped by now, maybe be dead on some bloody field.

Well, I have not such a bad father anyhow, he thought, looking at the large congested countenance of the man who had begat him, the rather popping eyes of clear innocent English blue, the thick red beard which betrayed the Welsh in him, with a great many streaks of grey, which proved that he was getting old, or had suffered. As for the shining bald crown, it was a *memento mori*, a sign of what would happen to himself in good time, unless he died in France or the Low Countries first. He had to have another draught of foamy ale at the thought of how he would look in a few years, all brow and cheeks, with big mournful eyes staring out at the end of the world.

Ah yes, the end of the world. The thought heartened him. Everybody knew the end of the world was coming in 1588. Six more years, thought William the Thoughtful gloomily. Can I live?

He had another helping of redshank, with good Tewksbury mustard, also some spiced gherkins, and a loaf and some cheese.

Quite a few friendly businessmen stopped by their table to shake hands and talk of malt, wool, hides, sheep, hay, manure, and other excellent commodities. The fog in the bar was becoming thicker. Old John's eyes gleamed through this fog while he talked of the great days ahead for the glove business.

I love the man, thought Willy. It is that which makes me a coward. Tell him I must, and tell him I will.

"Ah, and all my business, and all my houses, and all my lands too, when I'm dead," old John was saying. "My eldest son gets the whole lot of 'em, with legal provision for the other boys and my girl, of course. Ah, but they're none of 'em like you. I know this age of sudden humours, of wild springs and starts. I was such another at your age. I've often said, alone and in secret, many a time laughing at thy mad jests, 'There's never such another boy in all England as I've got for a son. There's the boy that is the apple of my eye. There's the son where my pride is tenanted. There's the son I dream about. And he'll have my name and my business and my dignity to carry on and add to, intact and secure, in the good old English way, not all split up and spent after I'm gone.' What! Gilly can go into the haberdashery business with old Smith, he'll take him. Dickie I'll make a hatter. Little Ned? We'll see. Hold our property together, Willy, that's the only way. And marry property, bottle it up, tie it in good legal language and manure it well. Remember what I've told you when I'm dead and you come to die."

"Speaking of dying, father, I have a plan —"

"Now, you're educated. I was patient. I let you stay in school a mortal long time. But I had my plans. I had my dreams. Why, I'd hear you at your mad doings in the quad and hear the boys laughing and I'd say, 'Just like myself at his age. A boy wants a little of the devil in him to chasten. He'll be all the better for it.' And I'd say to myself, hearing thee at thy Latin, 'That's my son up there, the maddest and wildest, but the wisest too. Ha, listen to him! Some day that boy's going to be a gentleman. Some day he's going to be an esquire. Some day he'll have my business, and I'll lie quiet in my grave, knowing he has the wit to hold it together and make it grow'."

"We're not dead yet, father, but there is something I —"

"That's what I've worked for, Willy. I was the son of a poor shepherd, and look how far we've come. You'll be elected to Council one of these days. These times will not endure forever. We'll have our day. And when it comes, my boy I begat can stand up and look any English lord and gentleman in the eye and say, 'I'm as good as you are.' And he'll remember his father sometimes, and how I worked to put him there, and he'll say, 'Well, he wasn't such a bloody old bastard after all'."

Another party of businessmen came into the Bear and stopped to speak to Mr. Shakespeare.

"We do not see you out, John. Is Willy still with you?"

This from Mr. Dabridgecoat, a windy old meddler.

"Your eyes see him, sir," said the alderman.

"Oh, there you are, lad," said Mr. Dabridgecoat. "I thought you had gone into the Earl's service. When is it to be?"

Old John's eyes opened wider. His son gulped, stammered, and would have had to tell him then if the players had not all come piling into the Bear at once. They were hot and tired now from their appearances all over town and went immediately to the taproom, calling for ale.

As for the hope of the alderman, he rose hastily, muttered that he must get back to his accounts, and started out.

"Now, what's taken thee?" called his father after him.

"Anon, anon, father," said William the Hasty, and dashed out of the Bear before any of the players could speak to him.

That afternoon Sir Fouck Greville had a visitor at Beauchamp Court, the dusty old manor-house in which this amiable gentleman lived rather carelessly, surrounded by books and dogs, a few birds and bottles, a loaf or two, a cheese and the stuffed heads and carcasses of a few wild beasts he had killed from time to time.

"Sir Fouck, it's that boy to see you," his steward said.

"Boy? Boy?" said the good gentleman, who had been reading deeply in one of his dusty volumes and was still far away. "Not my son home from Jesus College, is it? Nothing to eat in the house."

"We have venison, sir, and a very good pie," answered the steward stiffly.

"Only me again, sir," said someone with bright hair and eager eyes, advancing into the cluttered hall.

"Ah?" said the vague gentleman. He kept the book ready while he spoke. "Glad to see you, Willy. Quite a speech you made before the Earl, eh?"

"That's what I came to see you about, sir," said Willy, out of breath. He waited. The vague gentleman was reading again.

"Ah yes," remarked Sir Fouck, after turning a page. "H'm. Fond of books still, Willy?"

"I love 'em sir, but time is galloping. I want to know how I can get my father to let me enter the Earl's household before all his friends tell him I'm doing it anyhow."

Sir Fouck put down the book and regarded the wretched sinner before him.

"Written any more poetry lately?"

"In secret, sir, a little."

"Ah, did you bring any? My boy writes fair verses, fair verses, but then he's getting all that education. How do you do it, Willy?"

"I can't stop it, sir."

"Bring any? Let me see."

"I did a few lines about Venus and Adonis, sir. And the stallion and the mare. But I hid it so well I've forgotten where I put it."

"Ovid's old story again? Want a book?"

"I've no more time, sir. The devil is breathing on the back of my neck. Will you help me enter the Earl's service? Could we do it before *he* finds out any more about it?"

Sir Fouck scratched his head, got up to take a turn around the hall, and came back. "Why do you desire to serve Earl Ambrose? He's poor now. Sick all the time. Old. Unhappy."

"I like him, sir."

"Very good. But you're the eldest son of your father. And he needs you more."

"He has three other sons."

"The eldest inherits the property and business. That's English."

"I do not want property and business," Will said with sudden passion.

"Ah, there you're wrong, Willy. Always inherit all property and business you can. Whole secret of the good English life. Throw it all away to enter the service of the Earl?"

"Yes sir, and see France."

"Why? Never saw such a boy in my life."

"History, sir."

Sir Fouck looked at him sadly, and shook his head.

"So I brought this, sir."

"Eh? What is it?"

"The permission from my father, sir."

Sir Fouck delicately took the document between thumb and finger of each hand.

> WHEREAS my Son Will<sup>m</sup> desires to enter the sarvice of my lord Ambrose Erl of Warwick ffrom thys daye forthe I do Freely Graunt my Permission for the sayd Will<sup>m</sup> to do so.
>
> John Shakespeare
> Hys Mark
>
> Wytnes, Hys Mark
> Wytness, Hys Mark

When he had finished reading the document, Sir Fouck sighed deeply.

"And what do you hope to do with this?" he asked.

"I thought you would give it to my father and persuade him to see the logic of it, sir. Since he does not read as well as we do I thought you could read it to him, sir."

"Ah, ah," said Sir Fouck gloomily.

"And then I thought you could get him to make his mark, sir, since —"

"Since he does not write as well as we do?"

"You have hit it, sir."

Sir Fouck placed the sheet of paper on a table. "How long can you wait before the sky falls on you?" he asked.

"I think it is beginning to sag already, sir."

The amiable gentleman put his arm around the powerful shoulders of the hasty soldier and walked him to the door. "While my son's away at Jesus I get a little lonely for some disorder and astonishment in this dusty life of mine. Come see us again, and meanwhile —"

The expressive face of young Will^m struggled with so many expressions that Sir Fouck smiled, shook his hand, and clapped him on the back.

"Meanwhile, how about a book, Willy?"

"Thank you, sir, but I may not have time," Willy said, and went away from there as if all hell were after him and catching up fast.

It caught up with him later that afternoon. Old John, black as a thundercloud, beckoned him into the shop. He followed with his heart thumping.

The good Gilbert was working at the cutting-bench.

"Go away," said his father. The obedient boy instantly put down the dividers and left the shop.

John Shakespeare sat down in his armchair behind the bench. "Now," he said. The first warning snarl and crackle of thunder and lightning was in his voice. "What is this Sir Fouck tells me?"

His son swallowed hard, and breathed deep.

"I will tell you, sir."

"Do so."

"Very well, sir." He swallowed again.

"What a pox are we waiting for? Begin! Begin!"

"Yes sir. I will, sir. Well, we talked about it, and we both agreed that —"

"We both agreed," said John. His voice died to a whisper. "We both agreed," he said.

"That is so, father. And Sir Fouck said —"

"Sir Fouck! Sir Fouck!"

"He said that if I — he said that if you —"

"Silence!" said the alderman, holding up his hand. The tears were streaming down his cheeks. His lips were shaking. He stood up from his armchair, looked desperately round at his dark little shop, and cried out in a sobbing voice, "Why didst shame me before the Earl? Answer! Answer!"

His son looked dumbly round the shop, and saw all the thumbs and fingers pointing at him. All his unshriven sins came twittering at him from the dark and bloody hell of his conscience, and he wished for dusty death, or for a wet one, and the warm, strong, loving arms of Anne Hathaway. The sound of his father's heavy breathing returned him to this dark doom, this low ceiling, these mean and grovelling ways from which he would never escape.

"Answer!" gasped old John Shakespeare, staggering toward him with glaring eyes.

"It was a whim," Willy said.

His father choked. His face was turning purple. "Boy, look at this shop," he said. "Use your brains. Think of thy grandfather, a poor witless tenant farmer, working all day on land not his own. Look back into history. See how far we have come."

"It is history, father, that Sir Fouck and I —"

"Sir Fouck! Sir Fouck!" the alderman yelled. He took off his hat and flapped it against the bench. Then he snatched up a keen knife and waved it in the air. "Let us hear no more about Sir Fouck!" he groaned.

"It is history, sir, that I must —"

Old John interrupted to say that by blood and oons Sir Fouck was no father of his sons however great a Fouck he was otherwise, and consequently —

He gasped, panted, and declared that he he might might be the son of a shepherd but he had, he had, he had risen above his origins even if his wife and children did not care. He had become an ale-taster, a constable, an affeeror, collected fees for two years, kept order in the town, gone into the chapel and hacked the statues with his sword, dragged out all the copes and vestments, whitewashed the walls, so that true worshipping Englishmen could stand up and sing their godly hymns with no Popish gewgaws and trumperies like free men, free men —

"I liked the statues, father. And the devils on the walls, and the angels. I think —"

"Free men!" his father shouted. "Free men who can hold up their heads in any company! But this son here, this son, is unmindful of that dignity for which generations fought, and wishes to become a base knee-crooking slave and groom. This son would undo centuries of glorious English history. This son —"

"It is history, father, I must study in the Earl's household. Wherever he leads I will go, France, Flanders, Spain —"

"You will not! I forbid it!"

Willy felt the devil rising in him now.

"With your gracious permission, sir, I will be in the household of a gentleman —"

"What? A gentleman?"

"The servant of a gentleman, a great gentleman, whom I love."

"Love! Love! Would you be a pantler? A bread-chipper? A groom?"

"No sir."

"A scullion? A snivelling, knee-crooking slave who art the son of an *alderman*?"

"Not that neither, sir."

"Then what? Then what?"

"Father, I would learn about the great world."

"The —" Mr. Shakespeare choked.

"Among gentle people, who —"

"*Gentle* people?"

"Ever since I saw the Queen, father, my mind has been away."

Old John glared at him savagely. "Ha! That's the truth."

"I have been studying history, father, I have a terrible thirst for it that will not be denied. I must learn all of it, all of it, and the only way I can do it is in a great house, where there are books, and if we march against the Spanish, why then I'll gladly go —"

"And is my house not great enough? Are not my lands endowment enough?"

"This house is dark and low, and weighs on me. And your lands are lost to a money-lender."

"Aye, yea, mock me, thou son of thy mother, who went to Masses with her in secret, who could be hanged for it, who could be hanged —"

"Then let 'em hang me now, I care not for life if it holds no more than this —"

"Silence! Silence! Great people, he says. Is thy *mother* not great people enough? Are the *Ardens* not great people enough? Is not my office, my office — that I wear the fur and chain, that I am preceded by, that I am preceded by —"

Willy's eyes suddenly grew brighter. Was he going to laugh at his father, or cry over him with shame?

Mr. Shakespeare was becoming dizzy. He reached out for the arm of his chair.

"Forgive me, father," he heard his son saying through the roaring in his ears.

"Away!" he shouted. "Away!" he whispered.

"Will you sign that permission for me to serve the Earl?"

"Never!" said Mr. Shakespeare. He stood with his head down, holding onto his chair, until his eldest son had turned from him and rushed out of the shop.

Then, looking all round his shop in a lost way, he shook his head dazedly, got down on his knees and hunted for his hat, managed to rise, took down his black robe, and went out of his shop and straight to Holy Trinity Church, past the church and past the graveyard and the charnel-house, until he came to the house of Dr. Haycroft, the vicar.

## CHAPTER TWELVE

**T**HAT evening Dr. Haycroft sent for W<sup>m</sup> S<sup>h</sup> all through the town until a couple of boys found him, lying by a bonfire with a company of beggars, kinching coves, and priggers of prancers, who were horse thieves.

The boys knew him for his bright eyes. "Hey, Willy, the vicar wants thee."

The friend of the ragged brotherhood sighed and arose from the bonfire. "Down with tom pats!" he said: meaning, parsons.

"Down with tom pats!" answered two or three evil-looking fellows from the shadows.

"Lead on, O fusty nuts with no kernels," said the son of the alderman.

"He's mad, Willy," one of the boys said, who was named Arthur, after the king.

"He's full of choler, Willy," said the other, who was named Mosley, and was called *Mouldy.*

"Then hang him for a scurvy-valiant ass," said the reluctant follower, coming out of the woods and crossing the orchard beyond Bull Lane. The boys went with him up to the vicar's door. Then, grinning with enjoyment of the new pickle Willy was in, they ran and hid under the vicar's study window.

Lame Margaret ushered the culprit in. "Ah, hast been up to more merry games, lad?" she chuckled, digging him in the ribs with a bony elbow: she had a bastard wench of her own.

"All I can, mother."

Lame Margaret limped mumbling and chuckling away, and he went decently, gravely, and respectfully into the vicar's study.

The good man was seated there at his desk, surrounded by proper books. He had a good round dish-face and raisin eyes; and a little fluff of white hair decorated the back of his neck.

He eyed young W<sup>m</sup> suspiciously, then seeing him grave and respectful, eyed him sadly.

137

"Good evening, William."

"Good evening, sir."

"How I miss your beautiful singing and leading of the choir, William! There has never been a voice like yours in my whole ministry, in which I have served these thirteen years, ever since our good Earl Ambrose presented me in '69. Ah, long years, William, long years. I miss that voice at the service."

"I am grown, sir, and it is gone."

"Some rumours have come to me, my dear boy —"

"Would you believe them, sir? Rumour is full of tongues."

"Ah, William. You love the Queen?"

"Yes sir."

"And you would serve her?"

"You have it exactly, sir. Ever since I saw her eleven years ago, I have dreamed of one day —"

Dr. Haycroft sighed. He was a good minister of the new religion, or rather of the old religion combined, altered, cut, spliced, modified, and fitted to the new, as prescribed by that artful Majesty, the Queen, to keep both angry Catholics and stubborn Puritans from destroying one another. But the heavy task of steering the mended ship through these forever troubled waters had made him old and tired.

"We all dream, my dear fellow. We all dream. However —"

Willy stood waiting, the hope beginning to die out of him again. For a moment the vicar had sounded like a vicar of hope and joy. Now he had become again a vicar of dull conformity.

"We must all learn to stifle our erring desires, William. In a word, I must counsel you, before it is too late, to be good for the sake of the Queen."

"How good is that, sir?"

"We must learn godly conformity to that station in life for which it has pleased Providence to fit us."

For a wild moment Willy thought of explaining to the preacher, pleading with the preacher, engulfing the preacher in this torrent of wild winged words that were thronging to his lips. But he shrugged his shoulders and said politely, "Aye, sir." He could not keep the mockery out of his voice, though he liked the old man well enough, even if his fellows had plundered the monasteries, burned down the nunneries, robbed the churches, stolen the lands and castles of the gentry, and filled the ancient cathedrals and churches with villainous hymns, which, more-over, they sang through their noses.

Dr. Haycroft turned red and quivered a little. He had a bad temper, and sometimes thrashed the boys in choir practice. It was for this reason, chiefly, that Willy had given up leading them in the plainsong, for he did not enjoy hearing the sobs and curses of the boys in between the measures, very low so that the vicar would not hear.

Dr. Haycroft shook his finger. "I know you, William. I know your mocking ways."

"Indeed, sir."

"And I say to you that our gracious Queen has desired that there shall be no disobedience among her people, and her godly bishops have decreed it. Our own bishop has issued his orders, and you have received them in this parish. Have you not? Answer!"

"Aye aye, sir."

What made it hopeless was that face, that dish of innocence, that countenance of a risen devil or a fallen angel, not to speak of that voice, which was as musical and rich as the tone of a *viola da gamba*, and could do anything.

Old Dr. Haycroft was discouraged.

"William, look at me."

"Aye, sir," said William, doing so.

For a giddy moment, laughter struggled in the throat of the preacher, and he was almost lost. But he got hold of himself.

Glowing with golden light, that face was turned to him with a look of such decency, such goodness, such angel sweetness and conformity that it was enough to make a cat laugh.

"Mocker!" shouted the preacher.

"If it please you, sir —"

"A harlotry player!" shouted the preacher. "At last I see it! At last I understand! Oh, idle! Oh, unnatural! It is that toward which all thy unmannerly and horrible ways have been leading thee! Oh, draw back from the brink, my son, before it is too late! Oh, repent, my son! Repent, and be a good son to thy father! Our bishop has spoken against these ungodly shows and incitements to lust and all manner of lecheries!"

"We could get a new bishop," murmured Willy thought-fully, his chin upon his hand. Glowing in the firelight of the preacher's study, his hair was like a flame, a dark-gold flame. As for his eyes, they gleamed with devil's light.

It was exactly the coming of a new bishop which was distressing the preacher that year, and this utter and indignant boy must have known it. How did he know it? The preacher began to lose his head, which had never been pinned on very well to begin with.

"The son of a respected father! An example! A shame! Turn back! Turn back!"

With polite interest the boy regarded this exhibition of middle-aged wisdom. The preacher lowered his voice to a thrilling whisper, or at least it was thrilling to him. He leaned forward, his fat face shook, his eyes watered. "Shalt thou be one with the dust of our roads, the scum of our cities, the forbidden and inhibited strolling players, the very brothel companies and wanton ruffians with their open shameless behaviour, those inciters to intolerable lust and all filthiness, who go clad in false feathers and trumpery taffeta, and do strut and prance about the bawdy stage the better to inflame, solicit, and cozen the customers into unnatural execrable uncleanness, the which I shudder, oh, I tremble, oh, I utterly abhor to think of? Wilt thou? Wilt thou?"

Willy answered gravely, calmly, and thoughtfully, resting his chin upon his hand, and with all the seriousness befitting the answer to so fundamental a question, "Well, I had not thought about it much until you mentioned it, sir, but I will consider it."

He then bowed to the preacher, who was taking another breath, stepped quickly to the door, bowed again, and got out as fast as he could.

CHAPTER THIRTEEN

LATE that night the alderman woke
and heard his son Gilly whispering to him. "He's doing it now,
father."

"Where?"

"The counting-room."

"Ssshh!"

But Mrs. Shakespeare had not awakened. Tiptoeing out of
the bedroom in his robe, the old man followed the eager Gilly
along the passage, down the stairs, out into the orchard, around
into the western house and up the back stairs to the counting-
room.

A candle was burning inside. Motioning to Gilly to be gone,
old John opened the door to the counting-room.

Laughter was coming from in there. His eldest son and heir,
dressed in a buff jerkin like a shepherd, was leering and grinning into a mirror, and wagging his head up and down as if he
had gone quite mad. A fiendish look was on his face.

Then, leaping from the mirror to his stool, he took up a quill
and began writing feverishly on some paper that looked as if it
had been torn out of the account book.

"Ha!" said the alderman.

His son gave a start, and dropped his pen.

"What art about at this hour? What are these scratchings?"

Willy got up from his stool, smiled sadly at his father, sighed
deeply, squared his shoulders, and said, "I will explain, father."

Perhaps he might have been able to do so even then, if the
eager Gilly had not come in and snatched up the paper from
the desk. "Oh, listen to this, father!" he said, beginning to
giggle. "All hail, Sir John Sack-and-Sugar! All hail, Fatguts!
Thou damnable misleader of youth, thou old, abhominable
belly-man! Thou vile trunk of p —"

"Stop!" yelled John, snatching the paper from the fat boy
and tearing it into many pieces. "Away!" he roared, shaking

141

his fist. Gilly stumbled back, knocking over the stool, and ducked out of the counting-room. From the apartment over the orchard came mutters and groans from Old Billy Burbage, the bitter tenant who did not like anything about the house.

"Now!" whispered John, staring at this son of his in the candlelight. "Tell me what is in thy twisted brain that impels thee to this scratching when thou shouldst be thinking of business? What are these murthers? What are these stabbings, these drownings? What have you to do with these kings and villains, when we have money to make, debts to pay, good honest man's work to do? Explain me that! Explain me that!"

"I will do so, father."

The hands of his son were trembling alarmingly. What was this lowly garment he had on? From what clothes-line had he stolen these trunk-hose, from what midden-heap this beehive hat?

"What is this jest? Art thou never to have done with jests and become a man?"

But his son was not listening to him. With a sudden cry, as if someone had stabbed him, he knelt before one of the many heaps of hides and began hunting through them. "My papers! He has stolen my papers!"

"Dost thou hear me?" said John, grabbing his shoulder and digging his powerful fingers in.

"Where are my papers?" muttered his son thickly, struggling to his feet. "Give me my papers!"

"To bed! To bed! Not one word more, or I'll not answer for what I do!"

"Give me my papers, I say!" whispered Willy, his hands about the throat of the alderman.

"Out! Out! To bed! To bed!"

"I'll have my papers of you, or I swear —"

"Away!" wheezed John, striking him with his fist so hard that he heard his jaws snap. "We'll see who swears in this house! Get thee to bed!"

"Father, one word, at last —"

"Enough of words! Enough of scratchings! Begone!"

Old Billy Burbage poked his sharp nose in the doorway and snarled, "Is there never to be any peace in this house?"

"Go to bed!" roared the alderman, barging toward him.

"No man tells me when to go to bed!" squeaked old Billy.

Willy tapped his father on the shoulder. "Come with me to the orchard, father, and I will explain everything."

"Speak to me not!" said his father. "Shame me not one more scurvy filthy scurvy day!"

"I have an explanation, father, that explains everything in history."

"Explain my mortgages!" yelled his father. "Explain my debts that I entattled myself into for thee and thy mother and thy sisters and thy brothers!" He began tearing his hair and beard and stamping.

"And explain the debt you owe me too," said old Billy, poking his withered face between them.

"Out, thou dead elm!" cried John.

"Pull out the last hairs from thy head, bald man!" snarled Billy. "Where's my money?"

With the roar of a maddened bull, old John rushed out of the counting-room and down the stairs. His son followed him out into the orchard.

"I have everything as clear and sharp in my brain as crystal and pasticcio," said young Willy, pursuing him among the apple trees.

The old man waved his arms, and his eyes glittered in the moonlight seeping among the trees. "Money!" he shouted. "Money! Money! Money!"

Other businessmen awoke from such dreams as they had been having and began muttering in houses.

Uncontrollable laughter surged up in the heir to all the stinks and miseries of the glove business. Yelling with laughter, holding his sides with both hands, he went staggering around after his father, back and forth across the orchard. Picking up a few apples and crunching them as he had an opportunity, he attempted to explain to the raving businessman that he understood everything he was thinking, everything he had ever thought, everything he was going to think, and that he sympathized with all of it, all of it, and that he loved him and the whole unhappy race of man with their suffering tripes and rebellious blood, their teeming brains and grieving hearts, the whole wonderful and terrible machine of sin and glory they all shared together. This shouting and ridiculous man had once been a boy, had once had dreams of beauty and truth, may even have slept in the rainy woods and wept for the human race, the whole awful swarm of man doomed to this prison of flesh from the beginning to the end of time. It was a jest of God, he desired to point out to his yelling father, and they must endure it with dignity and grace, even to the sound of heavenly laughter and while they knew they had been abandoned. The theatre was empty, and God had gone, taking the angels all with him. Unfortunately, young Shakespeare was alone, explaining to the trees.

Now where had his father vanished to? Was he hiding beneath this elm? Was he in the privy?

"Art thou there, Sir Shakes of the Jakes?" his son inquired, rapping upon the privy wall.

But the house of duty was empty, and so was the dove-cote, so was the smokehouse.

"I'll find him, I think I could explain anything tonight," said Willy, and was hit square in the face by some soft, squashy object. Other objects began falling round him.

"Go to bed! Are we never to have peace from these Shake-beers?" cried Mr. Wedgwood from his bedroom window.

"Ho ho ho ho ha ha ha!" went young Willy, staggering around the orchard, falling to the muddy ground and jumping up to laugh again. Was he mad at last? Mad still? Had he always been mad?

The swearing businessmen at their windows threw a few more articles at him there in the moonlight and heavy shadow, slammed their windows, and left him laughing at the far end of the orchard. Or was he crying?

His walking motions were indeed unsteady, and the wavings of his arms were wild. From a leather bottle at his side he took a very long swallow, or series of swallows, gasped, snorted, sighed, began laughing again, and then went dizzily out of his father's orchard, still vaguely looking for the old man, talking to him once in awhile, peeking behind midden-heaps and manure piles, looking up into trees, until he came to the gild pits, where he lay down to rest awhile. Then he crawled to his hands and knees, got hold of a tree and hung onto it until the sweetness and peace of that living wonder streamed into him, and after that, with the help of a few trees, he got down to the river and went to sleep in the bushes.

When he awoke the world was going steadily on. The trees, the stars, the sky, the clouds, all were doing splendidly. The water went chuckling by in the river over an old jest or no jest at all, the wind wrinkled the surface of the dim and misty river with messages or meaningless patterns of inconceivable ingenuity or accident, the moon came out gleaming from behind a cloud for some reason or for no reason at all, and a small moonlit rabbit sat up on a bank and watched William Shakespeare for quite awhile and made nothing or something of him, it was impossible to tell which. The world was virgin or hag, mother or enemy, illusion or dream, but as he lay there with the laughter all gone now he decided that the time had come to be free of this prison, or die in it.

He went first to his mother, and found her on her knees with her rosary.

"Give me your blessing, mother. I'm off to make buckets of money."

"He is your father," Mary Shakespeare said.

"I never doubted it, sweet mother. Sometimes it is all I can do to throttle the old man in my nature."

"Oh, my boy, we have so little time." She looked so pale and wan, and her eyes looked enormous. "They've hanged John Cottam at Tyburn, and who will be next? Poor Robin Debdale was thrown in prison as soon as he returned to England. Oh, Willy, if you'd been a priest they'd have hanged you too."

"Then thank the good Lord I have decided to be a sinner. Will you give me your blessing and let me go?"

"What will your father say? Oh, my boy, my boy!"

"I think he has said it all, mother."

"Poor Mr. Cottam had to leave the school because his brother was hanged. It might be one of us the next time."

"Oh, mother, who would it be? I must be off on the roads, and I need your blessing if I cannot have his."

He knelt before her and waited for his honourable discharge from this little dark row of houses they both had served in for these long, long, weary, aching years.

Mary Shakespeare was abstractedly feeling his head. "What is that lump? You did not use to have it."

"Bless me, mother, for I have sinned. Kiss me goodbye. I'll bring you hoops of gold, as soon as I discover where they are."

"Take your cloak, and your good suit. And your smocks need mending."

"Your blessing, mother, my knees are knobbled from kneeling."

"There's one thing you could do to please me, Willy."

"Name it, mother."

"You've never been kind or gentle to poor Squire Somerville. After all, he is of the gentry, and he did marry your cousin."

He groaned with impatience.

"I'm too old to hate anyone now, Willy. You will be some day. Make your peace with him? He could do so much for you, an Oxford scholar. I wanted your father to send you to Oxford, and be a gentleman. And Asbies gone."

"Very well, sweetheart. I'll offer him any love he'll take if ever we meet again."

"You were so gentle as a little boy. What has happened?"

"Oh, I'll be gentle again, mother, when I'm a lean and slippered pantaloon by some old goodwife's fire, and my teeth and hair are gone."

"Yet do I fear thy nature," murmured his mother with a heavy sigh. "Well, it is thy father's, of course. Take thy good boots. I'll fill a pannier with food."

"I've eaten too much for years. Well, mother, I'll have no knees to bend to Earl Ambrose."

Pressing her hands firmly down on his impatient head, Mary Shakespeare gave him her blessing in Latin, and then kissed him anxiously before going down to the kitchen to rattle up everything eatable and drinkable she could spare from her sleeping family.

With rations enough for a campaign to the Low Countries, he embarked in his little boat a little before one in the morning by the Market House clock. Out into the misty stream he paddled and went gliding down past Holy Trinity's dreaming spire. The river was alive with little boats, from which came the sleepy voices of young lovers.

Three miles down the river, at the long wide turn it made below Weston, he hid the well-provisioned boat in some reeds, then climbed the bank and struck out for the Bidford road. He crossed it, running, and plunged into the furze and thickets between here and the vale of Temple Grafton.

All around him bustled the busy life of creatures seeking one another in the dark. The winged and the armoured, the feathered and the furred, each to its mate and wedded to death. The clouds were heavy, the moon was gone, the mist was deep. A cat crept over his feet and went creeping into a bush. A mouse squeaked and was silent. He came to the cottage of Anne's nagging aunt. Even this early the old woman was up, making her speeches about ingratitude.

He crept up under a hedge and stood staring up at Anne's window. A pale form appeared, looking out into the dark.

"Why wilt thou not find a husband? Why didst not catch thee one tonight, as any respectable wench would do? Think of me, slaving and digging, and no gratitude for all I've done. If old Harry had not closed all the nunneries I'd put thee in one."

He heard a sigh from Anne. That heart was sorely charged.

"Oh, ungrateful! Oh, hard-hearted! No thought for her own flesh and blood. If my poor sister knew what a trial I have she'd turn in her grave."

He could see Anne's long hair, whose silky warmth and perfume he knew so well. An icy shiver went through him.

"What is it she wants? What is it she waits for? Her priest is in gaol, and every lusty farmer for miles around has given her up. And still she will not wed! Still she is too proud!"

"I would I were wedded to my grave," said Anne, and he heard her weeping.

"Go forth, I say!" croaked the old woman. "Go forth like any decent girl and take the first lusty farmer to cross thy path, with hay-cocks and barns enough, and bottoms too. Tell him thy dowry is six pound ten."

"Six pound thirteen and six," said Anne.

"Then tell him, tell him, what is she waiting for? Her own flesh and blood, slaving and digging, and no gratitude! Oh, if I were young! Ah, if I had my lustful flesh and appetites again! Ah, where is a husband? Where is a husband will take this girl off my hands tonight? The whole night full of love, love, and she is weeping for a man in a cassock!"

"I weep for no one, no one," said Anne.

The old woman's voice went muttering away into some other part of the cottage.

Time passed. He saw a candle go flickering from bedroom to kitchen.

Then Anne came out, in her nightgown.

He felt a stir of the very hairs on his head. To drown herself, like that poor milkmaid in Tiddington?

He followed her, among the dark trees.

That pale form moved deeper into the woods, appearing to float rather than walk.

Before she reached the pool he caught up with her and took her by the arm.

She was trembling, but he was trembling more.

"I'm the first man to cross thy path," he said. "And I'll plight my troth with thee."

"Are you mad?" said Anne. Her voice was cold.

"Not yet."

"Twenty-six does not plight her troth to eighteen. Would you be mocked through the streets? Would you be laughed at through life?"

"I have been well-mocked ere now, and lived."

"I told you to run away, go, go, while there was time. The whole wide world was before you. And what did you do? Became a little clerk, and grew fat on conformity."

"I've said farewell to them both, Anne. And my mother gave her blessing."

"And John?" she said, stopping quite still.

"His last words were, 'To bed.' Will you come to bed with me? Not for tonight, but for life?"

"You called me a witch, a witch, as if I cast a spell on you. Stay not for the witch's curse."

"Is it because you still love the priest that you will not marry any man?"

She stood glaring into his face. "You dare to speak of him!"

"Oh, I dare anything, before the end of the world. We have six years, the men who know things say. Come, I'll get my sack and my bottles from the boat, and we'll fare into the kind world together. I'll make thee the lustiest husband in the county."

"Oh, will God save me from this mocker?" she cried.

"If you'll not have me then, go to my father's house, they love thee," he said in desperation.

"Love me!" said Anne, and began laughing, or crying.

"They do, they do, and you saved my father's life more than once. Why not return to them? I'm leaving anyhow. I've said my last farewell. I'm going to join the Army."

"Leave me, leave me," she panted. "Tell me no more jests."

"I swear it's true. The first sergeant I meet, I'll let him take me in. Who cares? I'll be killed as well in Ireland or France as here, by a wench's cold eye."

"Willy, hear one word of sense," she said, stopping again. "Wilt thou stay thy clapper and hear it?"

"I will, for certain, and say yes. Is it yes?"

"I cannot go to his house. I cannot go to his house."

"But why not? The children love thee too."

"Willy, you fool, I left his house. I left it."

"But why? Why did you leave?"

Anne laughed wearily, and stood there looking straight at him. "Ask your father," she said.

He felt the horrible squeezing pain in his chest, and began to choke.

"Marry me then," he said. "Come away with me."

"Oh, fool, fool, fool," she moaned. "Hear this fool, how he mocks me!"

"You said you wanted me to be free. You told me a hundred times to go away and be something, not to die in a dust heap."

"A bitter fool, a weary fool, who knows not even what day it is or what's o'clock, and he will go forth to conquer the world."

"It is the last crack of St. Susanna's Day, a very good time for a fool and a witch to say farewell."

And he turned and left her there stamping and gasping at him among the ruins, the naked choirs, the dark trees stirring with amorous life.

He heard running footsteps and felt her arms twining around his neck, and her legs twining about his. She was shivering and moaning, and her face was wet with tears.

"Oh, you mad, blind, impossible, beautiful fool!" she sobbed, and dragged him down to the mossy bank. Her teeth stung his lips, her panting breath, her moans, her cries of passion or despair sounded in his ears, while a great whirling dream of joy flamed and beat in him, like a fiery flood, like the wild heart of the whole living night, at last.

The moon was down, the pale morning was coming in mist and leafy murmurs among the feathery trees. In grey stillness before dawn they whispered together, and kissed, and then he rose from among the leaves and went away quickly. The first streak of dirty white peeped under the blanket of the English clouds, and he heard the first lark following his morning salutations into the sky.

When he reached the bend in the river where he had hidden his boat the sun was palely gleaming through smoky mist. The day was beginning, all lovers had gone to bed, and even the bird-killers and rabbit-killers had gone home from the marshes and meadows. Another day of business was beginning.

He hunted and hunted among the reeds. Somebody had stolen his boat.

All the better reason for me to stop by at home again, he thought. Pray God he has not left for the Cotswolds yet.

"Father," he said, catching the old man in the stable just as he was about to mount with a cloak-bag full of gloves to sell in the Cotswolds, "I've come for your blessing, father."

John stared at him. He was all in black, with a black cloak in case of rain. "What is it *now*?"

"I ask your permission to marry Anne Hathaway."

"What? What? Are you mad?"

"Not now, father. I'm sane, father, and happy."

"Happy!" roared the old man. He sighed deeply, squinted at this son of his, gave it up, and climbed heavily into the saddle. The horse, good stolid Tom, prepared to start trotting away.

"Wait, father, wait! Give me your permission, and I'll be on my way to make some money."

"Thou hast it. Get thee to Lizzie Fisher and make thy betrothal vows before Sir Henry. So, so, there, there, now, now,

I have spoken. I'll hear no more jests."

"Father, I will not have the dish-faced Lizzie with the fat ankles."

"Speak not, I say thou wilt."

"Father, in one word —"

"Speak not, I say, reply not, do not answer me. My fingers itch. Out of my way!"

"Sir, it is impossible. Anne Hathaway shall be my bride, and no other in all history."

"Anne Hathaway, forsooth! Ha, ha, ha, ha."

"Father, it must be and shall be."

"Ho, ho, ho! Mad yesterday, and an idiot today! Anne Hathaway! A housemaid and a drudge, too old for any man in the parish! A poor creeping thing with a broom, a mother to no children of her own, a nurse to the cats and foxes! And now this fool would marry the nurse! Oh, I will split myself with laughing!"

"Ancient damnation, keep me from murder," said his pale and trembling son. With one powerful sweep of his arm he pulled the old man from the saddle and shook him like a rat. "Speak not of splitting, ye fatguts, or I'll crack thy dry bones and beat thy skull in. Your permission, I say!"

John glared steadily into the wild green eyes of his son. "Never in this world," he said. "And you would be the last I'd give her to in hell, whichever one reaches there first."

"Father, I beg you."

"Out, I say! Out of my stable! My house! My orchard! Take thyself away, or it will be the worse for thee! Go, I say! Out to the roads! Yesterday it was thy wish, and today thou hast it! To the roads, I say, be one with the vagabonds, the scum of the cities, go beg, starve, die in the streets, and be hanged! Thou art no son of mine!"

"Give me your permission to marry her, father."

"Marry the gutter! Marry the gibbet! Go hang, thou wilt never have license from me to do anything but starve and beg through life! Out, I say! Away!"

His son dropped his hands and turned away from the raving glove-seller.

"Thank you for your leave to starve, father. I will take it for my patrimony, and freely bestow all else upon your legitimate sons."

And with a cold brightness in his eyes, he strolled past the man, the horse, went out through the doorway into the green and golden light of day, bowed respectfully to a goose leading her family waddling across the orchard, and went off whistling through the gate and into Swine Lane.

He turned up that afternoon in the hut where Anne kept her family of ailing creatures. He was quiet, amiable, and seemed peaceful.

Anne started up as soon as he came in. A little whirl of ashes rose from the dead hearth and sprinkled down on her face and hair. An overwhelming sense of beauty and the sureness of death swept through him. It was as though a door in eternity had opened, and then had closed. He felt that all things were possible, and that all things were vain.

"Here's one more for your flock," he said, a gay smile lighting up his face.

She began to tremble. "He would not have me?"

"How could you know?" he stammered, the light fading right out of his eyes. "I was rehearsing the greatest lie in history, and now it is forever wasted."

"Oh, I'm glad," she said, with a sigh as of a great burden suddenly gone. "Now you can go on and be free. That's good, Willy."

"Free!"

She became even gayer than he had pretended to be.

"Is it possible?"

"Oh, I'd given up all hope for you, angel, and now it will be wonderful, wonderful! Hurry and kiss me goodbye."

"Goodbye! Are my ears hearing this?"

"Oh, Willy darling, what a life you'll have now! The whole world open! Run now, hurry, lose not a moment, hurry and be something, and remember me."

"Remember thee!"

"Oh, try, anyhow, darling, try," she said, and like a fond mother, or admiring sister, she patted his stout buff jerkin, smoothed his hair, kissed him with great cheerfulness, and pushed him toward the door.

"Off now, darling, begin!"

"Begin!" he groaned.

"Begin thy wonderful, wonderful free life at last," Anne

said, and pushed him firmly out of the hut, and closed the door after him.

He stood there for quite some time, listening and hearing nothing. All imitation gayety was gone from him now, and the old dark gloom was settling down for a long stay.

He looked all around at the peaceful trees, shook his head three or four times, and started away. When he had gone a few steps he turned, looked at the hut plaintively, as if it had eyes, and said, "They call *me* mad!"

Then he started off into the woods and kept on going, on a perfectly straight course, over hill, over dale, through bush and through briar, as if his whole future depended on it.

Between Red Hill and Burman he leaped a ditch, cleared a hedge like a hunter, and galloped into a barnyard on Sir Richard Moryson's old manor farm, now leased by Mr. Hales to his Uncle Henry Shakspur, who cared not a prune how anyone spelled his name, and was a sturdy tenant farmer like his father. On this, the principal manor of Snitterfield, old Diccon Shakeshaft had lived out his life as an honest yeoman, respected by all who knew him, even in his last foggy days when he had become so troubled over the mad ways of the world that he had gone out wandering the heath in a storm with cuckoo buds and darnel in his hair, predicting the end of the world.

The same mad passion was in him too, thought the son of the son who had risen in the world.

Over by the mill lived Old Sly of the Wold, as they called Billy Bott, the money-lender, who would lend, and squeeze, and haggle, and grab any bit of property in the county, from old New Place to Tommy Atkyns's breeches. He hated all Shakespeares, for it was John Shakespeare who had been made alderman in his stead when old Billy had been expelled from the Council.

No wonder poor Nick and I must be wanderers, thought Willy as he slowed down for the pigs and chickens in the stable-yard. I wonder where he rides now, and if we'll ever meet again.

Just then Uncle Henry came out of the shaggy barn.

"Hey!" said his nephew.

"Is it thee, lad?" inquired Uncle Henry calmly.

"It is me, uncle. And is Old Sly about?"

"Not since last Whitsuntide, damn his liver and lights. Who wants him, besides the devil?"

"Oh, I might want to buy a house of him, uncle."

"Well, he's stolen enough hereabouts."

"I thought I might buy New Place."

"New Place! And marry the ghost?"

"Well, uncle, I thought I would buy the best house in town while I was about it."

"It was a fine house, right enough, in better times than these," Uncle Henry said. "And art thou hungry, lad?"

"A little."

"Come in then, for God's sake," said his uncle, leading him into the old kitchen, with its great blackened fireplace, and the same old copper pots and pans hung up on the rude walls, the same rough table, the same old bench by the hearth.

It was here my father crawled before he could walk, thought the son of the alderman. And walked right away as soon as he could.

His Aunt Maggie came up to him and kissed him a hearty smack, then immediately began giving him things to eat. A jolly buxom woman, who had no children of her own, and should have had troops of them. But she adopted cats, puppies, ducks, all peepers and squeakers, barkers, mooers; whoever and whatever was living and hungry, she loved them all.

"Ah, honey-boy, it is beautiful to see thee eat," Aunt Maggie said, beaming.

And looking up at her he saw a heavenly glow all round this heavy and earth-coloured woman, and shining round her head a nimbus of radiant light.

When he had eaten well, and drunk even better, he kissed them goodbye and went off up the road to Warwick. Ahead of him went his lively imagination, in such a hurry to gallop into the future that he was already a hero on a vasty battlefield, with bleeding bodies all around him, horses screaming, soldiers groaning, ghosts getting ready to rise. Cheers rose over the fields, amidst the chirping of crickets.

His mind made up, the hero approached three sergeants between Snitterfield and Warwick and bravely offered his body to the Queen.

"Five shillings," said the first sergeant.

"What for?" asked the volunteer.

"To buy thy way out," the sergeant explained.

"But I wish to be in!"

"Off! Off! Away!"

The second sergeant was a fat old rascal with a white beard.

"I'm ready to go to Spain, sir, and kill Spanish soldiers."

"Go to, go to," said the sergeant with a wink.

"Aye, sir. Ready to go."

"Do not start before thou art pricked," said the sergeant.

"I care not when or how, sir. A man can die but once."

"Do not die here, do not die here," muttered the sergeant. "Away, boy! Thou art too soon for death."

The third sergeant, like the first, immediately wanted money.

"Sir, I have no money, take me in for nothing."

The sergeant, a lean and hungry fellow with a nose like a pomegranate, looked at him with sad reproach.

"I love the Queen, sir, and have an itch for battle."

A windy sigh came from the sergeant, and he shook his head mournfully. "What's to become of the country, when sturdy fellows haven't the money to pay their way?"

"I will march free, sir, and hack the heads from the base trunks of every enemy I meet. Let us go onward, dear friends, and fling ourselves upon the foe. War! War! St. George for England! To the fire-eyed maid of smoky war, a toast, a toast, in the wine of battle! And —"

"Peace, tickle-brain," muttered the sergeant. "On your way, pint-pot."

"Hail to the armed camp, and the big war! Onward, dear friends, to the breach! To the breach!"

"Thou art no soldier, thou art a cullionly rogue of a player. Now be off!" growled the sergeant. "Or I'll have thee arrested for disturbing the peace."

Deeply hurt, the patriot withdrew from the immediate vicinity of the military exercises.

It would serve them all right, he thought, if I gave up trying to do my duty and followed the players after all. And that night, a long, long, itching night in a hay-barn, he dreamed he was a bragging captain striding the London stage, and making ghosts of a large number of imaginary enemies, while the galleries cheered.

## CHAPTER FOURTEEN

JOHN Shakespeare sat up all night waiting for his son to come home. But he did not come home.

"Alas, this is no ordinary going," said his wife. "I fear we have lost our golden boy forever."

"What gold did he ever bring to the business?" growled John.

"It is you, you, who drove my poor beautiful boy out of this mouldy house!"

"Woman, have peace! Peace!"

"It was you, you, who lost my father's estate of Asbies to Ned Lambert, with your mortgages! Ned always wanted it, married my sister in hopes to get it, and my father left it to me anyhow! Ah, to play into his hands, and was to have been my son's inheritance, to be a gentleman of the country!"

"Peace, I say! Peace!"

"Where will he go now, without his rightful inheritance? What has he in this poor world but a blind man for a father, who could not see he had a child of light in this dark house, and who threw away the gift of heavenly grace?"

"Give me peace, woman. Peace!"

"I see him lying stark and stripped, the frightful ravens knocking their bills upon his bones," said Mrs. Shakespeare, sweeping to the center of the stage, or, rather, smoky old kitchen. "I see him taken by the brutal press-men and dragged all bloody, my poor golden boy, to make more food for powder on some crimson field. Oh, oh, I see him slaughtered by the horrible executioner, true to his faith to the end, his poor beautiful head rolling across the bloody boards, while the mob howls! O England, England, what will you do to my boy, my boy? I see him —"

"Now plague take these old scurvy plays that fill the heads of our women with nothing but murther, blood, crime, and corpses!" roared the alderman, snatching up his black hat and cloak.

The sounds of horrible tragedy still throbbed like the wail of an insatiable violin through the house as he stamped out to the stable.

"Where to now, John?" inquired old Dick Hornby, stopping his clanking for long enough to look out of his smithy.

"I'll find that boy before nightfall. We'll see who is blind or not."

"Follow the players, John, follow the players."

"Pox on the players! They should be hounded out of our parishes and never permitted to return. Drive our wives mad, they will."

"Oh, John, you always liked the plays. I remember when you were the lad's own age you could not get enough of murther, and ghosts, and queens, and that."

"Queens!" said John, and rode off toward the gildhall for help. It took him longer to round up the constables than he had expected, for Tom Rogers, Jack Gybbs, and Hugh Pyggin were all busy counting trees, and Tom Roberts and Arthur Boyce were up on a roof of Anthony Wolston's tenement counting the tiles needing to be replaced. Whenever the good burghers of Stratford were worried over war, treason, or invasion, it was their custom to go out and count all the elm trees of the best sort and of the small sort, also the third sort, and to add up all the money they would bring in, even though timber was cheap; and to count all the tiles that needed to be mended; and to inspect the backsides of all the barns to see if the sills needed to be repaired; and then to go all together, at the completion of their survey, to dine at the Bear and take plenty of sack and sugar.

Ah, were these fools ever to see anything beyond their noses?

"Where go you now, John?" called out Ad Quiney, who had charge of all the surveying, and nearly everything else in Stratford, this year.

"A little business, a little business," said John.

"Buying green apples?" said Quiney, at which three or four nott-heads laughed.

When he left the Bear he had Henry Rogers with him anyhow, even though he was three-quarters useless. Now that Abe Sturley was leaving to become a solicitor for Sir Thomas Lucy, there might be a good place in his law office for a promising lad who could write long words.

"Aye, aye, I could have used the boy," said Henry, as they went hunting for the constables. "He used to help me, a little, years ago, for nothing."

"He'd make a good assistant coroner now, Henry. Was always interested in the dead, and fair loved skulls and skeletons."

"Good, good, but we must have John Sadler for bailiff, we must have John Sadler for bailiff, I could never have thy boy in my office with Cawdrey or Quiney, John."

"I'll go to Council and vote for John, Henry. There, I've broke my vow never to come back till these mad days are mended. Will you take the boy if we get John Sadler in?"

"Send him to me, send him to me. If I like him well —"

"Henry, you'll love him, you'll love him, Henry, I promise you. What! He must marry and make a home."

"Aye, aye, a home. A home?"

"Anon, anon, we'll go into that in good time, Henry, I must up to Warwick now, on business."

It was nearly three when he rode off with Hal Wilson and Hugh Pyggin to hunt for the future assistant to the coroner, and they were not even constables, they were ale-tasters, and had been well-tasting ale too, moreover.

They hunted till evening, stopping at each tavern on the way for refreshment and information. Had anybody seen a boy with green eyes, red hair, clad in a buff jerkin and red hose (unless he had traded these garments for better ones in some game of dice or primero), and talking of mad things out of books?

"No, sir. No, your worship."

"The devil!" said John to Hal and Hugh. They all had a drink before going on to the next place.

"There's caves over by Guy's Cliff 'a might ha' fancied," said Hal, who was a very poetic man, and given to singing after the first drink. He was singing now.

"He's a great 'un for castles, and might be with the Earl," said Hugh.

"He is forbidden! He is forbidden!" said John.

Throbbing with silence, they rode on to the George, in Lower Fulbrook.

"Aye, there was such a fellow here," said the hostess. "La!"

"Aye, and where'd he go? Where'd he go? Speak, woman, speak!"

"I'll not be called so, in my own house, and was not never called so in my time," began the hostess, swelling up at him. Hal and Hugh had to buy drinks all round to cool off the host, the hostess, the father, and the daughter of the hostess, who was hot for some reason.

That house was hopeless anyway, for nobody in it would talk, so at last the hunters rode away into the fog.

After they had gone, a ruddy young fellow in buff jerkin crawled out from under the hostess's bed and kissed her and the daughter goodbye. Then he strolled off to the Three Jolly Friars, in Hampton Hill, where he paid for his supper by twangling upon the lute and singing some bawdy songs to a company of godly Puritans on their way to Bristol, where they would take ship for Ireland, to tame the wild men there.

"And the women?" asked the singer.

The women would be no problem. The godly men were still explaining why they would be no problem when a clattering of horses and a shouting of certain riders interrupted the explanation.

"In here, in here!" cried the hostess.

"In here, in here," said the tavern wench.

For a moment he hesitated, then dove for the pantry and the wench.

## CHAPTER FIFTEEN

ONE last throw of the dice, and then let Fortune take me, the wandering minstrel was thinking as he strolled up and down the streets of Warwick.

But he avoided the Crown Inn, where his cousins were.

There was still the Cross, and even better, the Sign of the Unicorn, where members of the brotherhood of rogues sometimes met.

I might as well join them, as join any provincial companies of players, he thought. There's only one left in England now that's any good. And I've lost my chance with them.

If I had the permission of the man of wrath I would yet run after 'em wherever they wander, and beg Bob Wilson to take me as his butt.

For Tarleton is their fool, a great fool too.

And with this halting tread of mine, from all my falling out of trees, and gypsy-fighting, who would want me for the young lover or the hero?

I think I was not meant for a player, but an ape of all players. Any of them mouth their parts better than I.

What then? How then? And when?

Meanwhile he wandered nearer to the castle of dread, where lived the man he loved, who was so stern and yet so kind, and had such a passion for order, because there had been so little in his life, poor old man. Two wives died on him already, the third one childless, his only son long laid in his cold tomb. Old ghosts haunting Earl Ambrose too, especially his father's, who had persecuted the Catholics with savage fury, scattered the great Oxford library, debased the coinage, drained the Treasury, marched against the people, tried to get Lady Jane, his daughter-in-law, made Queen, and was executed immediately after sneaking back into the Catholic Church.

"He's had too much history, while I have not had enough," said the yearning wanderer, strolling along the road by the eastern side of the ancient town, passing through a gateway, and now on a broad winding road cut through the rock, deeply garlanded with ivy and overgrown with moss. And suddenly, there, the mighty Tower of Caesar, so ancient it was a dream in stone, not real any longer, too old to believe. He went as far as Ethelfrieda's Mound, leaving the Tower of Guy of Warwick behind, and he was standing in a dream on the rich greensward, staring up at the mossy legends of history written all over the great court, when he was challenged by a burly warder with a steel breastplate and a halberd.

"Stand, fellow, and give the countersign!"

"I think is was *St. Ethelfrieda* Tuesday before next, I have a mouldy memory," he answered. "Does Earl Ambrose need any gloves today, captain?"

"No, he does not need any gloves. Be off with ye, fellow, or there'll be rare whipping of thy carcass."

"Any songs, or shows, or slight pageants for the ladies?"

"No, they do not want any low songs from such as thee," said the burly fellow.

"I'll play the lute free, and —"

"Off! Off! Out! I'll sing ye!"

The unwelcome son of the yeoman limped away, and was nearly run down by a jolly troop of hunters cantering home, waving the bloody brush of a fox. Among these people rode young ladies too, beautiful and laughing. Clinging to the old mossy wall, the singer of songs too low for such as them watched the rumps of their horses dancing past and away into the green sunny courtyard. Beyond the courtyard, the pleasure gardens, and beyond them the river, and beyond that the ancient Forest of Arden, said by Mary Shakespeare to have belonged to her ancestors, who were kings.

I should have worn my good suit, thought her son.

Then he went on back to Warwick, thinking of how some day he would be received in castles like that one, if he could only decide how to do it.

Made lame by fortune's dearest spite, he thought. Poor and despised. I could write a sonnet about that, if I had the time.

## CHAPTER SIXTEEN

**A** weary company of players lolled upon padded benches at the George, in Leamington.

Not men, these players — brawny and evil-looking boys, with two quarrelling masters.

Ah, I know these fellows, thought the wanderer, limping into the taproom and ordering brown ale, to be warmed at the hob, with spices.

After he had drunk it off, savouring it slowly, for it might be the last, he walked up to the two quarrelling boy-quellers and asked gently, "May I speak to you, gentlemen?"

"You seem to be doing it," said the hawk-beaked one, a weary old player named Dutton, who had been put out of Earl Ambrose's company years ago, before it had been disbanded.

"My name is Wagstaff, sir. Would you need a man in your company?"

Mr. Dutton looked at him resentfully. "Me a man? Why?"

"I though you just might, sir."

"And my brother needs no men either."

"Who said I did?" piped up the dumpy man beside him.

"You said so," snarled Hawk-beak, and they began quarrelling again.

After waiting politely, Willy said, "Perhaps in the future, sir?"

"No future in it," said the dumpy Dutton.

"And never was, only a past," said his brother.

"It's about time you admit it," said the dumpy Dutton.

"I've been trying to get *you* to admit it," said Hawk-beak. "We never should have left Earl Ambrose and gone with Oxford in the first place. *He* only wants someone to write his plays, not us to act them."

"Did you say someone to write his plays, sir?" asked the young visitor with interest.

"That's right, wants to be known as one of the best for

162

comedy, and has no more comedy in him than an apple," said Hawk-beak.

"You talk too much, Larry," said the dumpy Dutton, turning suddenly and sticking out a finger at young Wagstaff. "What my brother means is that times have changed, and playing isn't the great profession it once was. Everybody's against us, including ourselves. People so afraid of what they might see, hear, or feel they can't bear to look at us. No, the golden times are gone."

"Perhaps they will come again, sir. I believe it."

But old Hawk-beak interrupted impatiently. "Are you trying to tell us our business, fellow? Who cares what you believe?"

His dumpy brother patted Shakespeare on the cheek. "Don't mind Larry. He's high-strung, you know, like an instrument all made of wires, a virginal perhaps. Come along with me, dear."

And he led the intruder out of the taproom and into the shabby innyard. Here the boy who had driven the players' cart was unloading a frowsy collection of old swords, cloaks, daggers, petticoats, bodices, wigs, copper lace, and the usual extra heads, including one bloody one with tongue out and eyes that rolled each time it was moved a little. Leaning down from an upstairs gallery, a few commercial travellers were uttering a gibe or two from time to time, waiting for the players to become victims of their boredom, or their outraged Puritan morality.

Two of the brawny boys now come striding out of the common room, snatched up a sword and dagger each from the rusty collection in the wagon, and began sadly carving at the air around each other, as if they hated it.

"Come, come, get killed, boys," said dumpy Dutton, whose name, he told Willy affectionately, squeezing his arm, was Jackie. "You foin, do you, sweetheart?"

"Um, yes sir. Fence, that is."

"Oh how darling of you! Box? Wrestle? Dance? Ride?"

"Yes sir."

"Do call me Jackie. Declaim Seneca I suppose."

"Oh yes, Jackie, I do that, sir."

"All you lovely fellows do," said Jackie. "Could have played a princess, five or six years ago, h'm?"

"Well, I might have, yes."

"Anything you can't do?"

"Sell gloves, malt, wool, timber, and hides, sir. Or kill cows. Or be content with s —"

"With selling all that umble-mumble and killing cows, I suppose," said Jackie discontentedly. "Pity you are aging so fast, poor fellow. If you were a ravishing boy of thirteen, now, I'd snap you up just like that. Our boy Tommy left us to go to bed. Would you do that, dear? What's your name again?"

"Wagshaft, sir."

"Ah yes, darling name. His death-bed, you know. Died of plague."

"I'm sorry, sir."

"Oh, we'll get another, we'll get more than another, if we have to take one up from the roads, as Giles does for the Queen's Chapel, you know. Interesting custom. See that pretty lady up there. Would you like silly ladies like that to flirt with you, do you think?"

"Not the *silly* ladies, sir."

"H'm," said Jackie. "Wouldn't like them to meet you after the play, I suppose, and buy you a supper, and kiss you, and fondle you, and take you into their beds for the night?"

"It leaves not very much for me to do, does it, sir?"

"And then they'd leave their husbands for you, and there'd be the devil to pay, and we couldn't pay him, for we have no money, and we'd have to get rid of you, and hire somebody repulsive. What a catastrophe."

"Oh yes, awful."

The dumpy Jackie sighed fretfully and said, "Did you know my brother Larry and I are by ancient charter entitled to have dominion over all the players in Chester for as long as our name shall live?"

"I'm glad to know it, indeed."

"Duttons of Chester frightened the wild Welshmen away over three hundred years ago. Did it with fiddles and flutes. Everybody in Chester terribly grateful. Isn't that splendid?"

"Excellent well fiddled and fluted, yes."

"And for our reward," Jackie said, "they call us the lewd people. Been nothing but lewd people for three hundred years. You look as wild as a Welshman."

"I feel like one too, sir."

"Not as gentle as people think, are you?"

"I eat Englishmen for breakfast sometimes."

"Splendid. Ought to come up to Chester, might have some good times there. People don't appreciate lewd people like us in this damned Protestant part of the country. In a few years they'll run us into our graves. Would you like the silly men to make love to you, do you think?"

The fugitive from Stratford looked regretfully at Mr. Dutton.

"They will do it, you know, especially the inns of court men, and the fops, and people who've read all those sickening Greek poets. We deny it, of course. Would you deny it?"

"Nature has pricked me out for other pleasures, I believe," said young Shakespeare thoughtfully.

"By God, that's good," said Jackie with a short yelp of laughter. "Damned if you mightn't do. Nice leg you have. Handsome, well-shaped, full of sap, and what a voice! Gives you the shivers. Can't make out what's wrong with you. Let's see you walk."

Shakespeare braced himself, gritted his teeth, and walked across the innyard and back. When he stood before the dumpy Dutton again he had beads of sweat on his face.

"What a pity," said Jackie. "Can't have the young hero with a limp already, before he's gone to war, or to bed, or wherever he is going."

"I'm sorry, sir."

"Born with it?"

"Oh no, sir. Fell out of an apple tree too many times. I look on my lameness as temporary, my poverty even more so."

"Splendid attitude, excellent. Look at all the abuse you'll never need to endure. People hate us more every year, and we are doomed."

"If you have any old plays, I could mend and patch them for you. You said the Earl of Oxford might want —"

"Mum as to that, Waggystaff. Has a fellow to do it all now, name of Lyly, after the flower that grows in swamps you know. University man, M.A. and everything."

"I might hold the prompt-book, and sing and play the lute, and —"

"And play the old men's parts, and ghosts, and offstage noises," said Jackie petulantly. "Then too, there was that lame king, that fellow at Bosworth Field — who was it again?"

"Richard III."

"My advice to you, Wagstaff, is to go right away from here, never speak to players again. Meet a man in the business who collects the money, and make friends with him. We haven't any money. Go to London, meet Mr. Burbage, he has the right mystery, owns two playhouses, and takes all the money. Good-bye, my dear, God bless you."

And patting him on the cheek again, and smiling alarmingly, rather like the decapitated head lying there in the innyard, the dumpy Mr. Dutton trotted across to the two jaded players who had been idly lunging at each other with swords, and somnolently thrusting at each other with daggers, and dreamily tangling each other up in cloaks, without doing each other any harm at all.

Snatching up a sword and dagger from the heap of properties, Mr. Dutton made for the two sleepy fencers with such frightful yells, and such dangerous slashings and clashings, that they both took to their heels, and went running round and round the innyard.

"I'll kill you all some day!" he screamed.

Shakespeare watched him pensively for some time, sighed, shook his head, and went hopelessly back into the taproom.

That man is not real at all, he decided. And neither am I, nor is any man. We are all shadows in a world of dreams.

The taproom was beginning to fill up now with commercial travellers and a few young men whispering together at a table in the far corner. There was something familiar about one of these young men, but his back was turned, and he wore a hat with a pull-down brim, and a starched pull-up collar, so that there would not be much of his face to see anyhow.

Leaning against the wainscoting beside the young men were some fat saddlebags, which travellers these days no longer trusted to the ostlers who rubbed down their horses and gave them food and water.

There was a lute by the door, and Shakespeare took it up and sat down on a joint-stool, facing the young men.

After tuning the lute against his ear, and twanging it a little, he struck up a song, and began singing it, as follows:

"A quart of ale's a dish for a king,
 And worms for birds, to make them sing.
A sheet's for a wench, to roll her in,
 And my shirt's a sheet, with four holes in.

But shall I go mourn for that, my dear?
 The pale moon shines by night.
And when I wander here and there,
 I then do most go right.

If tinkers may have leave to live,
 And bear the sow-skin bucket,
Then my account I well may give,
 And in the stocks I'll cuck it."

By this time the young man with the big hat and the high collar had turned round, jumped up, and run over.

"Hey, Catbird!" he cried.

"Bottom the Spider!"

"And hast thou taken any more maidenheads, Worthless William?" asked Nick Bott, giving a loud twangle to the lute-strings.

"No more than thou hast taken deer, old friend."

"I've better game than that. Come over and drink with the lads. Why, how thou art shrunken, Willy! I heard thou wert fat and prosperous."

"A cold wind is coming, Nick."

"Aye, that's God's truth," said his old friend, coughing.

"Well met, anyhow."

"I had hoped to free thee from some gaol, to pay my debt," said Bott. "How's the justice?"

"There's no justice in nature, nor know I none."

"What? What? Out in the cold world?"

"I'm my own man, Nick."

"Ah, just in time for something good, Catbird."

"My time is in the yellow leaf, old friend," said Shakespeare in mournful tones. "And soon the leaves will be falling."

"Here's an old cat from Stratford, boys," said Nick, leading him over to his companions. One was an evil-looking fellow with a bulbous nose and a bad eye, the other a squatty man in a dyed red wig.

"Not a boy-lover is he?" asked the evil-looking fellow, winking the good eye. "Saw him with the Duttons. Bad company."

"Hang all mouldy players, I say," remarked the squatty man, who looked rather mouldy himself.

"No, no, Willy's a wencher from Wenchborough, has rolled the best of 'em in the hay, eh? You dog," said Nick, digging him in the ribs. "How's Anne Hathaway, eh?"

"Still fairest and best of all friends I have," said Willy with a steady stare.

They sat down at the table, and the squatty man passed a wine-pitcher. It seemed that his name was Nick too, Nick Skeres, and he spoke more thieves' cant than English. The other one had a voice almost as musical as Shakespeare's, and seemed to be a decayed scholar, on the outs with himself, desperate enough to do anything. His name was Poley, Bob Poley, and he had the greyness of gaol about him. He was richly dressed, however, and wore both sword and dagger, as the others did.

"Nick was one of the best players in Warwickshire, in my time," Shakespeare said, "and we always said we'd run away and found our own company. I'd play the old men's parts, and the ghosts."

"We've a quicker way to make you a ghost, Catbird," said Nick Bott. "Lend thy big ears to us, and we'll pour in a tale to freeze thy young blood, if there's any left."

"I think I'll travel, gentlemen. How is it in Italy?"

"That's the best place, these days," said the squatty man. "Like to ride fast horses, Mr. Catbird?"

"Oh, Willy's the best in Warwickshire," said Nick. "Should see him ride, Bob."

And it became clear that this dubious trio wanted another rider in their business. What was their business? He pretended so successfully not to know that finally Nick Bottom had to explain, in spite of the menacing looks of the other two.

"Catbird is one of us," Nick said. "There's Squire Somerville, he's ready to dispatch the red harlot any day. There's young Babington, and there's the Habingtons too, and the Underhills. All the Ardens, my boy, especially your cousin at Park Hall. And there's money in it too. Come in with us?"

"Tell no more names, Bottom, and these I have not heard. My road is elsewhere."

"Why, Robin said you'd be one," Nick grumbled, looking surprised.

But Willy was already on his way, only pausing to ask, "What, Robin has spoken with you, Nick? Wert thou in gaol again?"

"He's out, Cat, he's out, dressed as a country squire, like us. We all go in gentle apparel, and no questions asked."

"Where is he?"

"Oh, there may be a wench back home, in Shottery or Temple Grafton," said Nick with a mean light in his eyes.

Willy made no answer, only smiled briefly at the three masqueraders.

"If you change your mind, we'll give you post-horses to ride as far as Sheffield Castle," said Nick, following him to the tap-room door. "Hell and death, Willy, this is opportunity."

"But not for me, Nick. Forget you ever said anything at all, and I will."

"What, hast gone over to the hymn-singers? This is impossible," said Nick, looking puzzled.

"In four words, I love the Queen," Shakespeare answered, looking at him with such burning candour that Nick flinched.

"Then our ways lie apart, Catbird."

"May we meet again in happier times, Nick."

And he went quickly out of the taproom and was on his way somewhere, anywhere, he did not very much care. He felt very tired, as if the last hope had gone out of him. Indeed, he had lost that lovely faith in himself, which had been unconquerable until today, and he seemed to have lost considerable faith in a grey-eyed goddess who had been kind to a boy.

She was only waiting till Robin would return, he thought. And why should I sorrow over so ripe a virgin, who was not a virgin anyhow? Or a friend I loved, and thought him holy?

Are not priests men, and has he not already sold his honour to the Enterprise, with none left to pawn?

And what is that honour but a word, and what is that word but air?

I am sorry, though, that Nick should have told me so much, or that he spoke any names. Those two rogues looked at me as if they would kill me.

## CHAPTER SEVENTEEN

SHAKING their heads over the Shakespeares was the big thing among neighbours that autumn. They had expected the alderman's worthless son to run off for good some time, but it was a sad thing for the old man, all the same.

He never went to Council any more. He never went to church either, though he was fined for it by the stern new bishop, who persecuted Puritans by the Queen's orders now just as shrewdly as the old bishop had persecuted Catholics.

John stayed mostly in his counting-room, puzzling over all the queer papers and tablets confiscated from his son, bewildered by these murdering kings, these howling madmen, these philosophizing fools, a whole world of strange people he had never heard of and could not get out of his head. And these mad lists of everything under heaven, from antiquity all the way to the present, and beyond the seas, and in hell also, these goddesses and all their several charms, these battles, these murders of all kinds, done by stabbing, choking, disembowelling, drowning, beheading, hanging, throat-slitting, these catalogues of weeds, flowers, animals, jewels, and the strange speeches that caused a squeezing up of his heart and a burning of his eyes, and filled his head with thunder and lightning.

There were also some lecherous verses about Venus and the boy Adonis, which troubled the alderman when he got some educated fellow in a tavern to read them to him, especially the part about the coupling of the stallion and the mare.

No, no, it could not be the Hathaway mare.

It could not be Anne....

He would stare gloomily into the faces of commercial travellers in country inns, and forget all about trying to sell them any gloves.

When he was alone with a harmless drinker again, he would take a few pages out of his doublet and ask him to read them. "I can read well enough," he would say, "but you can read better."

Sometimes he would listen to some story told by a babbling fool like old Hugh Pyggin or Ananias Nason, and yet different, as if these babblings were spoken on the moon, or beyond it.

"Where got you these pages, sir? Who has written them?"

But old John would shake his head and sigh, and after buying the accommodating stranger a cup or two of sack he would thank him for his good reading of this slight matter, and go barging off into the woods and fields again.

"Who are these people?" a tavern-keeper asked him.

"Who are they not?" said John.

But when he was alone in the night and the dark, and no one could hear, John Shakespeare would cry aloud to the un-listening sky, "I have wronged the boy. I have wronged my son. He was mine and I never knew him. He speaks what is in my heart and I never knew how to speak. Oh, come home, my son, come home. . . ."

The old dark house was too small for the alderman now, the ceiling too low, the walls too narrow for his woes. Off he would go again across the pastures and into the woods, a dog or two at his heels. He would stop at every inn to inquire if anyone had seen a tall lad with hair the colour of a ruddy apple, a fellow all madness and jests, who could ape a king or a clown, and could keep a whole room in a roar.

"There was such a fellow last week," one innkeeper said. "But this was a wandering rogue, and he was followed by thieves."

"Which way did they go?" asked John.

"So long as they swagger elsewhere, I care not," said the hostess. "I'll have no swaggerers here, I can't abide 'em."

So off old John would go again, hunting for the wanderer.

One time he thought he saw him among a troop of mounted men in the Queen's service, but this fellow rode off on some errand before he could reach them, and the captain said he had no man in his company named Will Shake-anything.

If I had not been taken that night with the falling sickness all would be well, John would think. What! We've seen the seven stars together, we are men. He told Hugh Pyggin and the watchmen to be alert for any sight of his runaway son, and to prevail upon him to return; and the old men promised that they would, yea, and constrain him too, and subdue him.

If it had not been for Gilly, the business would have gone to ruin. It was this fine boy, with a dish of pickled oysters in one hand, a dish of anchovies in the other, who went into the glove-shop that unhappy morning after they found the old man stiff and staring under a thorn-bush, his mouth gone slack, unable to speak and his right arm paralyzed. While Dick Hornby and the Cawdreys carried the old man to his bed, it was good Gilbert who began selling gloves with passion, yea, with poetry, so that the citizens of Stratford marvelled, and said they had never seen such an inspired glove-seller in their lives. He soon made important changes in the business too, setting up a trade in French gloves and taking in a line of Norwich hats. Still the old man was not comforted, and the first words he spoke when his sickness was mended and he could move his arm a little, were, "Look at him eat! Great God, look at him eat!"

And as soon as he was on his feet again he employed them to take him away from the house and into the woods and fields.

The Council never fined him for staying away from his duties. All the grave aldermen, even his former enemies, forgave him and maintained his chair vacant for him, although this had never been done before in Stratford.

But had any man in memory been so sorely tried with a disobedient son, a lamentatious wife, and such fits and starts of nature as this Shakespeare?

What noble thunder and lightning he had created in Council in his good old obstreperous and shouting days! Without him in the chamber the grave men discovered themselves to be very dull fellows.

No more noise from John. All quiet now, all brooding and darkness, his mind busy, turning over all of it, his whole life, all nothing now, a striving after wind. A curse on him, something he had done wrong somewhere, a curse from heaven.

"A curse," he would whisper, and began turning it all over again.

One day he went to see Anne Hathaway at the cottage of Tom Whittington the shepherd, who had married her Aunt Kate.

"Will you tell me where he has gone?" he asked.

But she turned away from him and would not answer.

## CHAPTER EIGHTEEN

$S$EPTEMBER shimmered into October, and golden October faded to dank November. More vagabonds on the roads now then ever before: it was peace that was the problem. Without any war to send them to, the Queen's representatives in every parish merely sent them to the devil now. Homeless wanderers and broken soldiers, discontented farm boys and discharged servants, rogues whipped at cart's tail, and a whole new brotherhood of sturdy beggars springing up in every county — it was no longer safe for honest tradesmen to travel the roads these days.

Too many snafflers, too many pickpurses, too many cutthroat robbers, too many thieves. In every parish the worried tradesmen appointed surveyors to assist the frightened constables in driving out the haggard wanderers.

With the old monasteries gone, the alms were gone too. With the old farms broken up into pastures, the little farmers were broken too. With the old noble houses humbled, their servants were humbled too.

The angry Queen, cheated of marrying the bottle-nosed Frenchman, took revenge upon her people. They had not been going to church enough, or paying taxes enough. They had been listening to false prophecies, they had been uttering seditious speeches, they had been going to bawdy plays. It was true the Queen liked these same licentious entertainments herself; but the players were the servants of those stubborn earls who had dared to stand up and tell her she could not have the bottle-nosed Frenchman, when she had not wanted him anyway.

Since Leicester had spoken loudest against the lady and her little French lover, her wrath hit his players hardest of all.

Sheriffs pursued them; beadles bullied them; headboroughs harried them; the Puritan justices and the godly money-lenders hounded them out of their London playhouses and drove them to the provinces. Now on every street corner the preachers of doom and brimstone bawled against the bawdy players; in every town the virtuous tradesmen decreed that these licentious rascals should quickly betake themselves out of the parish and back onto the roads again. On, on, out, out, away!

And a certain stubborn fellow with bright eyes went with them, and the cold wind followed them all. This wind was a shrewd wind. It searched his garments with icy fingers, it whined and muttered through his dreams in haybarns, it whipped him on from the campfires of tinkers and other homeless knaves who were his friends that autumn.

But his best friend was the fair boy of the Earl of Leicester's players. How this great affection happened to come about nobody in the company knew; one day, the wanderer was with them, and young Dick was laughing with him all over the innyard.

Soon after that, they had a free helper, who fed horses, opened up play wagons, hung curtains, held prompt-books in the yawning pit of Hell Mouth, or mounted the ramparts of heavenly castles to sing like an angel.

"We'll stir up more trouble with the justices, if they find you at work for us," said Laneham, one of the players.

"It's not work, sir, at all," the wanderer assured him. From the day he had discovered them in Bristol they had not been able to shake him.

"Let him play or work, who cares? We're doomed anyhow," Bob Wilson said. He had about decided to give up being a player and singer, and go into the play-writing business himself. No money in it if you signed your own, but there were lazy noblemen who wanted helpful spirits to beget heirs for them.

Wilson was about ready to resign, too, as nurse and comforter for Mr. Burbage's boy, who played the nymphs and princesses so perfectly that he was becoming as spoiled as any pampered princess in real life. When he was painted and powdered and wigged, when he was padded and laced and gowned, and was mincing about on his pattens as Diana or Cleopatra, it must be admitted the boy was wonderful. Between performances, though, what to do with him? The manager's son, the rich man's pride and joy, who would some day be the greatest player of manly parts in the country. But now! Coyness and tears, vixenish starts and hoydenish romps, and nobody could restrain him but this gentle vagabond, who seemed to know everything in the boy's nature before it became manifest, and to be ready with a word of grace, and patience.

They had no boy this season for the comic parts, and Wilson wept tears of rage to think that it was only one stubborn alderman in a country town who kept them from having the best for comedy they had ever seen.

But Tarleton was with them, and that was more than enough comedy, and sometimes too much, for he never willingly kept within the bounds of modesty and chastity, and had the stinkards roaring and whistling with his mad jests right in the middle of some more important loving, or dying.

"You keep Dick down, I'll tame Tarleton," said Wilson to the new free helper, after the first week.

And that was the bargain, before everything fell to pieces in Coventry, where they should never have risked going at all.

Things went well enough for awhile, though, until the brawls began in one town after another. It seemed almost as though some devilish arranger of discord went before them, to stir up the citizens against the Earl of Leicester's players.

"We carry our own hell with us anyhow, in our wagon," said Wilson, "without our enemies preparing any for us."

Mostly they went back to the old pageants the people had always loved, and gave up trying any new things. The promptbooks were falling apart from age and use, and the players knew all the old lines so well they could almost run through them in their sleep. And their free prompter would always wake them.

"But why not try something new?" he would ask Bob Wilson, when he thought the man would be in a good mood.

"Pox, we played *Pompey the Great* in Bristol."

"Mmm..."

"We played *Catiline's Conspiracies* in Worcester and Kidderminster."

"Um..."

"For a country clerk thou art damned queasy over these plays that have pleased the general and the particular, at court and in the suburbs."

"Well, but something *new*, something..."

"We played *The Blacksmith's Daughter* in Birmingham."

"Ugh."

"*The Play of Plays* is new, the country clown does not like that either, it is only by our best university man, Tom Lodge himself. Hear him, ye gods!"

"Um, aye, but ... something *new* ..."

"I'll write a new play myself then, will that satisfy thee?"

But the country clerk still looked strangely unsatisfied. At last, after some weeks of wandering about the Cotswold country, the whole secret came out.

The country clerk had been writing verses himself, scraps anyhow, a scene here, a scene there, and had inserted them into the prompt-books so that somebody would stumble upon them, and be amazed, no doubt, at his genius.

Imagine such effrontery!

The whole company laughed. Let the mocker, the counterfeiter, the clown, be satisfied with his imitations, and not aspire to the stern work of scholars and masters.

But he was not satisfied. Frustrated from improving any of the scenes the players already knew in their sleep, and could run off without coming more than half awake, he began scribbling sonnets.

Sonnets, in the name of all that's wonderful!

Courtly stuff, imitations of the great Ronsard, the great Tasso, the great Aretino, and the great, great Petrarch.

The country clerk's imitations of constables and shepherds made the players howl, but the day they discovered his imitations of the courtly sonneteers the whole company laughed.

How it came out was that the boy Dick showed some of the fanciful quartorzains to the players, swearing them to secrecy.

There were jests in rime on the players' painting and wig-wearing, on their posturing before mirrors, and on their riding up and down the country making themselves the butt of rural wits, there were punning sonnets on the scribbler's name *Will*, and one or two, perhaps more, ardent sonnets on friendship.

"Ho ho!"

"Ha ha!"

"Says his verse will endure when he's compounded of clay!"

"Will outlive the very brass of funeral monuments!"

Bob Wilson began to be a little sorry for the country scribbler. "Well, well, the lad thinks nothing of it, and it's all a fashion he's read about in books somewhere, though how he ever managed to learn so much in the country I can't imagine. Say nothing to him, boys. Let him dream."

So the players contained themselves, and anyhow they liked the young fellow, he was so gentle, so hard-working, and his imitations were truly remarkable. For instance, he was a teacher tonight, drilling a skittish scholar, who was named William.

"What? What? What are you reading?" cried the schoolmaster, who seemed to be a Welshman with an Oxford education, so that his natural wildness of mouth, full of fritters and whistles, came sideways, as it were, as through a flute.

"Words, sir," answered William.

"Then read them as words! Read them as worrds!"

So the boy began again, trying to be dull and ordinary and good, but then some dark power would get hold of him and he would be worse again, with the laughter of everybody in the taproom ho-hoing all around him.

"Boy, boy, shtop! It is not *adfistuitwitter tui*, it is no twitter at all. Shay after me, *adfuistine concione sacrae hodie.*"

"Adfuishtine twitter towhit tuwhoo concontwitter sac —"

"It ish not twitter at all! It ish not twitter at all!"

"It is twitter to me, sir," said William.

"Where got you these intonations?"

"From some bird in my throat, sir, I do believe."

"Now then, boy, boy! Attend to me, boy! Art thou attending?"

"I am, sir. Yes."

"Shay after me some common English word. Shay *blood.*"

"Bblleuhhdd."

"No! No!"

"Neuhhw! Neheuww!"

Roaring laughter swept the taproom, bringing in people from off the street, even the sick, even the lame and poor and despised, and the dogs and tabby-cats too. They all came in that night to hear this clown who was better than Tarleton himself, some people said, and not even permitted to play except in taprooms, for a free supper, and a few cups of sack.

He imitated everything in the taproom that night, systematically, as if determined to compass everything around him
before it melted away forever, and then he imitated a few
country people, out of his head, including a timid constable,
a shrewish wife, a modest maid, and a shambling, shuffling
assistant to a skinker who had flat feet, numb hands, ringing
ears, and a queasy stomach. He did the seven ages of man after
that, starting as an infant, idiotically hungry, always after his
nurse, so that the barmaid suddenly shieked and the commercial travelers at the best table roared, and then he let the poor
girl alone until he was at the next age, and the next, progressing
to the awful cousin of the skull at the end, when she began
screaming with fear, and he and all the players had to kiss her
to bring her back to Christian hope and confidence again.
Young Dick laughed and laughed, and promised that when he
owned his father's playhouses his beloved Will should be his
partner, and they would both be rich.

Another night, at the George in Coventry, he was a cowardly
soldier sneaking off to war. And when the banging and sticking began, he was such a cringing and whimpering mockery
of a soldier that they all were relieved to see him crawl out of
the battle, stumble away from the last empty vessel of honour
lying on the battlefield, and come skipping home. O England,
O wonderful bloody country, where got you such a soldier?

"O Willy, where saw you such a lovely soldier?"

But he seemed to know everything about all sad, sweet,
awful, wonderful people.

He was the devil at painting his face with wrinkles too, and
all the blights and corruptions of the lazar house and the plague,
scaring even the tricky Dick into screaming and whooping all
round the innyard. This was an art he had learned from the
palliards, or clapperdudgeons, a brotherhood of rogues who
painted themselves with false sores, or burned them in with
arsenic or ratsbane, to frighten countrywomen into giving them
food and money, before they should infect the children.

Another thing he did was steal any scraps of paper from
cooks' pies in the inn-kitchens, and begin scribbling on them.

"Another sonnet, Willy?"

It was these sonnets that undid him.

They were rehearsing *A Greek Maid* in a big stone tithe-barn just outside ancient Coventry one afternoon. The weather had turned colder and wetter than ever, and they had driven the tall wagon in through the big west door and set up the stages inside. Right in the middle of rehearsal who should come ambling in but Hawk-beak himself, with his dumpy brother after him.

"Hey, boys! We've come to join ye!" called out Larry Dutton.

"About time too!" said his brother.

All rehearsing stopped while the players flocked around them. The Queen had called all their boys back to the Chapel for the winter, and now they had no company. But their talents were offered to the Earl of Leicester's men, free and clear.

Bob Wilson huddled with Laneham, Perkin, and Johnson, talking it over. Meanwhile the dumpy Dutton embraced Dick Burbage and patted Shakespeare on the cheek.

"How good to see you! Waggyback isn't it?"

"Shakebag is more like it, sir."

"Call me Jackie, dear. What a lovely companion you have, Shakebag!"

"See what he's just written me," said Dick in all innocence, handing the dumpy Dutton the latest sonnet.

"My friend and I are one!" whooped Jackie, skimming it like some obscene carrion-bird. "Oh, delicious! How fortunate for you, Shakecheek!" And he went skipping off to read the gentle sonnet to the other players, then pass it from hand to hand, with many chuckles and whispers. But Wilson looked annoyed, and then alarmed.

"Why, I'm sure the lad had no such design," they heard him say quite distinctly, looking over at them.

More whispering and chuckling from the dumpy Dutton. Shakespeare felt a chill not from the rain and cold.

Wilson took him aside later that afternoon.

"I've worked long and hard to keep this company going, Willy. But I fear our days are numbered. No use planning great triumphs in London. Put that right out of your mind."

"Will the Duttons be joining us, Bob?"

"Those two buzzards? No, I've told 'em no, and they'll hate

us all now, doubtless. They think you're playing on Dick to get part of his money."

"His *money*?"

"Why, when he and Cuthbert inherit old Burbage's playhouses. The boy is as loving as any I've had, and as gullible too. Perhaps his head is addled with so much attention. Poems and all."

"I see," said Shakespeare, feeling hot, and then cold again.

"The world esteems as vile what may be most innocent, Willy. Sometimes I think you know the whole heart of man, but other times you seem as virgin-pure as any nun. But please, no more sonnets to the boy, as long as he's under my protection. He'll think he's something between Lord of Misrule and Queen o' the May, with such passionate praise and heart's love poured out to him. And then too, Willy, the wise world may look into your heart, and mock you with him — eh?"

Wilson looked compassionately into his eyes, clapped him on the shoulder, and smiled. "Well, on with our Greek maid, pox take her! I feel in my bones some trouble before morning."

The Duttons went off in a little while, braying out false friendship even while looking most bitter. They finished the rehearsal with no further interruption. But the spell of the Duttons seemed to have twisted a good many meanings awry, and exacerbated many old rivalries, and some newer ones.

The old tithe-barn stood outside the ancient wall of Coventry, but not too far to expect some company the next afternoon. Only, the rough young fellows with the clubs began gathering very early, and they stirred up trouble even before the play began. Quarrels broke out here and there among the penny stinkards almost as soon as Wilson and Dick began their first love scene. Then someone began playing a flute, and someone else started sawing on a fiddle. This was the signal for a general uproar. Turnips and rotten apples began flying through the air. The players gave up trying to entertain such people and barricaded themselves behind the wagon, but the club-swingers found them, and their feeble swords and leaden daggers were no defense. Still there was no blood flowing until one of the roughs yanked out Dick Burbage from among the ambuscaded players and stripped off his gown. "To the stocks with the sodomite!"

That was when Shakespeare, with a howl of rage, threw himself upon the rough and began knocking his head upon the stone floor.

The constables closed in, with their elbows and knees getting in everybody's way, but there was time enough for a few roughs to beat Shakespeare bloody, and knock the players into submission.

"Away, ye sinners! Away, ye sodomites! Out of our city! To the roads!"

"Here's a fellow with no badge," said a constable.

"A sturdy vagabond among the players! To the stocks with him!"

"To the gaol!"

"Whip him awake! We'll have no thieving knaves here!"

The last thing Shakespeare remembered before he woke up in a stinking gaol was Dick's wild yelling as the constables closed in and began thumping everybody with their official clubs. He was alone in this gaol, except for a few thieves and homeless vagabonds. There were two pocky whores also.

"The players," he groaned, feeling the raw pain begin to beat in his head.

"Damn all players," snarled one of the thieves, and he heard screeching laughter from the whores.

"The players! Send for the players!" he cried.

"Hang 'em, scurvy rogues," growled a palliard with big sores on his naked arms. "I'll not steal in their company."

"The players! I'm a friend of Earl Robert's players!" he moaned.

"We'll be your players, sweetheart," screeched the whores. He tried to get away from them, but when he stood up he knew why his arms and legs ached so. He was in irons, with a heavy weight of chain.

"Water," he muttered, and fell. Two or three thieves came and kicked him, and they all cursed him, for being so proud in their company, which had its own rules of order.

It was this order that marched up and down in his aching

head through the long hours afterwards: The bee, the flea, the fly, the ant, marched rank on rank across his twittering nerves, and he heard the morning and evening stars singing together in strict harmony. An army of justices, led by thieves, marched bravely upon a navy of priests, commanded by pirates. And all great nature teemed with order, order among the tigers, who ate tabby-cats, order among the mice, who ate cheese, order among the dogs, who bayed the moon, order among the women, who were arrayed against the men, order among the fiddlers, who fought the fluters, a marvelous universe of marching orders, all killing, slaughtering, gnawing, gobbling one another, life eating death, death swallowing life, and upstairs, in the wanton tops of the clouds, rolled and tumbled the rosy gods and goddesses, laughing gloriously.

"The Duttons! The Duttons did it!" he moaned, waking out of this nightmare. "It was Hawk-beak, it was Hawk-beak set on the fiddlers and fluters! Send for Earl Robert! Send for Earl Ambrose!"

Now it was the gentle skies and dreaming fields of home that shimmered before his burning eyes. Everybody he had ever known in his life paraded before him in orderly file — Lame Margaret, Ananias Nason, Lewis ap Williams, Humffrey Plumley; Betty King, all pink and gold, who wanted to sail down the river and sing; Lizzie Fisher, who wanted to quarrel fiercely in order to kiss and make up even more fiercely; Uncle Henry, in the Clink again for defying gouty John Fisher of Warwick; Aunt Maggie, with a bowl of good soup; and he loved them all now, even those menacing people at the end of the file, his father and mother, who had grown to the size of giants.

"Forgive me, mother," he moaned, remembering how she had stolen into the little dark room under the low-hanging beams after another beating by his father, and had held him in her darling arms, and wept real tears over her unconquerable son. "He means it not, he loves thee dearly," she whispered.

Ah, those were the happy days, with nothing but regular beatings from his father and from one schoolmaster after another: Master Hunt, gone off to be a priest, taking poor Robin Debdale with him; Master Jenkins, with his Oxford stutterings and terrible restrained temper, which made him shake; Master

Cottam, whose brother was hanged for religion; Master Aspinall, with his yellow garters. What excellent teachers I had, thought the dreaming prisoner. How was it that I became worthless then?

But the two people who haunted him most were Anne Hathaway and Debdale the priest. He could not shut out the horrible visions of the two lovers together.

"Water, for the love of Christ!" he whispered, into some pock-marked face.

Yes, they were lovers, and that was why she could love a boy, with no design to marry in this life. So I had the priest's blessing.

My father loved her too, and many another godly citizen lusted for sweet Anne. My father's thunder and lightning and my mother's rainy tears came from that source, I think. They quarrelled not over religion at all.

"Anne!" he cried, to the whore who pawed at him.

"Call me Doll," cackled the whore.

"Away, ye secret, black, and midnight hag!" he croaked, with his last bit of strength.

"Hang thee, mouldy boy!" she screeched, and spat in his face.

"Oh, he'll hang soon enough," said an Abram man, or false madman, creeping up to be the first snatcher-off of his doublet and hose, when he would be too weak to defend his wardrobe.

But two cursing gaolers plodded in to take the new criminal before the magistrate, and he was dragged between them into a vagabonds' court, which was held in a cellar, before a small hairy fellow in scarlet.

"Strike off his irons!" said this minion of justice.

But the turnkey explained that the criminal had not paid his sixpence for irons and so was not eligible for such mercy.

It was all a mumbling and muttering anyhow. No complainant had troubled to come to this ignoble court; therefore no one could lawfully accuse the prisoner.

"The players' boy? Where is the players' boy? He stands accused of stealing the purse of the players' boy."

"The players have disbanded, your worship, and gone off to seek honest employment."

"And the boy? Fetch hither the boy."

"They've taken the boy too, your worship."

Alas, my fair friend, thought the prisoner. When shall we meet again? And he lost all interest in the proceedings, so that his answers to the magistrate's questions were a dreamy mumbling of to-whits and to-whats, and he thought he was back in school, and the beating would begin soon, which it did.

"Have you any friends, fellow?"

The prisoner was heard to stammer that all friendship was foining, all loving was leaving, and he kept falling to the floor and going to sleep again.

"Water," he explained dully, when they raised him up.

"Is it an idiot?" inquired the magistrate. "Hast thou a father, fellow?"

A gleam of strange light glowed in the eyes of the dreaming prisoner. "My father's an owl, my mother's a falcon, and I am a most magnanimous mouse," he told the magistrate earnestly, just before the first of the many blows which constituted his orderly and official beating.

They seemed to have taken off his irons anyhow, and that was a great improvement, but now he was in the pillory, right in the great square of the ancient city of Coventry, a very convenient place for the people to mark him and mock him, also to throw any rotten turnips at him, or other tokens of lawful disapproval.

After twelve hours in the stocks, the constables came and whipped him round the market square, and he heard the great bells of the cathedral tolling for some saint's death or birthday as they whipped him out of town.

"And never return, or ye'll hang next time!"

"Water," he said as they threw him bleeding into a ditch.

Delirium burned away his pain. He dreamed Coventry was burning, all the crooked cobbled ways, all the beetle-browed houses, all the shining spires. The flaming houses roared and glowed, and even the old tithe-barns fell into Hell Mouth among black devils with pitchforks.

All the people in Coventry were burned in the great fire, and he heard them howl. Lady Godiva burned with them, which was a great pity.

They were dragging Anne Hathaway to the fire when a tall priest disguised as an apple-squire snatched her in his arms and made off with her.

Well, I'm glad they're together at last, he thought. If any were happy in this burning world it's their turn.

His mother and father were singing in the kitchen, and all his brothers and little dead sisters were laughing. The lovely firelight glowed on their beautiful laughing faces.

# CHAPTER NINETEEN

**H**OW long he lay in the ditch he never knew. He woke from delirium aching and cold.

Will I die here then?

The bitterness of despair surged in his heart as he stared up at the deaf and unheeding sky.

Now the son of the justice has equal whipping with the son of the thief.

And to find a cave in a storm, a philosopher might share the straw with a fool.

Oh, to die, to sleep, never to ache again! To be one with Caesar and Alexander and all other sons of dusty death! For who knows which passion now is compounded all of clay? Is not this the great equality of man, that Caesar's dust might end stopping a bung-hole?

So are we players all, done to death and gone to bed. The godly men will send us all to death.

But he did not die, no matter how he longed for death. I must be living, he decided, for I am in pain.

But where am I now? And what are these fields where I seem to be wandering?

And what is this river? And would its waters bring back my memory, or forgetfulness?

But he knew the river, even as he staggered and fell upon its muddy bank, and he wept as he lay among the reeds.

When he woke this time from a feverish dream there was music in the misty air. The horns of the hunters, and then the voices of the hounds like a choir, the deep voices, the middle and high chiming whoops of the small singing beagles, until it was like bells among the aisles of the trees.

It was there the keepers and constables found him, his arm

around the neck of a dead stag. Both wounded creatures had found their way to the river, yet neither had been able to reach it, and drink.

"These damned poachers are getting bolder and bolder," said one of the keepers.

"Fellow would have eaten the quarry, if he'd not been drunk," said another.

"I think he's mad," said a constable, bending low to listen to the babble of words that came from the human creature's lips.

"You spoke truth there, Tom," said the other constable. "I know this fellow. He's Willy Shagspear, and he's wanted in Stratford."

"Take him then, for God's sake," said the head keeper. "These poachers will be the death of me."

And this rage, this murder in my heart must be the death of me, unless I conquer it, thought the prisoner as they lifted him like a cloak-bag full of old fardels and flung him over the withers of the chief constable's horse.

His mind was very clear now, exactly as it had been that night he had wanted to explain the universe to his father, and had only succeeded in driving the old man mad over money.

And how does Sir John of the Sack and Spear now, I wonder, thought his son, as he felt the plodding motions of the horse in his painful belly.

And my poor mother, doomed to that smoky house, who should have been a queen of Egypt?

Would the old man have damned me for being such a lover of plays if his wife had not been the greatest unknown player in England?

"Where are you taking me?" he asked the man who rode with him, as soon as he could speak clearly enough to be understood.

"To Stratford, my boy."

"No, no!" he groaned. "Do not take me to Stratford! I do not want to go to Stratford!"

But the constable laughed, and one of the other fellows called out that they could whip a poacher as well in Stratford as any other place, for all that.

"They'll not whip this one," said the constable. "It's his

father has combed the country round for him, and has given us
our orders to bring him home."

A struggle suddenly ensued across the withers of the lead
horse. The prisoner was grappling with the constable.

So they had to beat him on the head with their truncheons
until he was still.

A yellow and sullen moon was up over the little town by
the shining river.

"Alas, this is an unlucky night," said Humffrey Brace, who
was chief constable in Stratford that year.

"I would rather they had brought us a hedgehog," said
Ananias Nason, who was keeper of the Cage, and did not like
the duty.

"Hold fast, do not let him scape this time," said Hugh
Pyggin, who did not like any duty at all.

All three little old men finally succeeded in dragging the
prisoner into the Cage.

"Well, we must whip him the first thing in the morning,"
said Mr. Brace, as Ananias Nason locked the door. They went
away into the heavy shadows lying along Wood Street.

From the bear pit in the Market Square, Alfred lifted up his
snout and sniffed.

Then he began to growl, and he even roared a little, as well
as he could in old age, with all his wounds.

The prisoner in the straw awoke finally, hearing this peculiar roaring.

"What, is it thee, Alfred?" he managed to mutter. And
moving carefully, so as not to break anything he still had, he
crawled to the bars of the Cage and peered out into the moonlit square.

"It seems we have not escaped yet, old friend," he said.
"But look, the miracle! For who among the millions can speak
like us?"

Alfred stopped his grunting, growling, and roaring, and
made a small whimpering sound.

"We are not here to whine, Alfred. Let us die bravely, and
take as many dogs with us as come within reach of our fangs
and claws."

Alfred yawned, and then began gnawing the bars of his prison.

As for the other prisoner, he carefully emptied out his pockets to see what tools he had that might be of use in gaining such freedom as was possible.

Only a stick of madder, given him by Dick Burbage, and another of *caput mortuum*.

H'm, what can I do with these? he thought.

While he was thinking, he became aware of a stirring and muttering in the straw back in the dark corner where no moonlight could leak.

"Who's there?" called out a hoarse voice.

The aching prisoner felt the hairs rise on his head. "What, is it thee, Uncle Henry?"

"Is it thou, dear boy?"

"What a pleasure it is to be with thee, uncle!"

"Alas, what hast thou done, lad?"

"Nothing, uncle. And thee?"

"Old Foxy Fisher is after the Moryson land again, and has taken me for debt."

"What, the old manor of the Ardens?"

"Just my part of it, and who's to pay this time? I'm fair desperate, I am."

"Why, my father, he'll pay, I'm sure of that."

Uncle Henry laughed, and then began coughing.

"How does Aunt Maggie, dear uncle?"

"Goes cold to bed," said Uncle Henry, crawling over and embracing him. "What hast done anyhow, Willy? I fear thou hast not listened to me in thy youth."

"Never fear, uncle, and marked thee too."

"Hast any little bottle about thee, dear lad?"

"Alas, no, and I'm beyond thirst anyhow." By now he dared to ask the important question. "How are my father and mother?"

"Oh, you know her, lad. But John's not so well."

Uncle Henry began coughing again. "Why do they not give us to drink?" he grumbled.

"Tell me, uncle. Is it the choking sickness?"

"Worse, boy, worse. The man is not what he was."

"Tell me then."

"Do you not know already?"

"Only that I've disobeyed him all my life, or half of it, and now I've gone about living it."

"As to that, Willy, who can blame thee? I've always had a taste for freedom, myself. I think he grieves over Anne Hathaway."

Uncle Henry's nephew felt a chill of fear.

"Poor soul, I'll not condemn her. A modest maid she was, and good-hearted too. No, I'll not laugh, or mock her."

"In God's name, uncle, tell me without further ado."

"They say it was thee, Willy, without a doubt. Tried to drown herself, she did, and only saved by the shepherd. Well, women have fallen afore, and will again, most likely. Three months gone with child, and who's to marry her? A bad business, and her father dead."

"Where is she?" His voice was dry.

"Still in Tom Whittington's cottage in Temple Grafton. And run half mad with her burden, poor girl. People are cruel, Willy, and love sorrow. They'll drag her to the cucking stool now her trouble is known, and whip her round the town."

"Have you spoken with my —"

"Who, Willy?"

"With my father?"

"The man's not what he was. Dark and troubled, boy, and gets no contentment out of the business. Can't bear the sight of Gilly, and won't even answer thy mother's complaints. Hangs his head down and lets her bait him. No, he's not the same since he was sick."

"Sick?"

"Ever since you ran away he's not been the same. The apple of his eye, my boy. The one hope of his life."

"I want to get out of here," said Willy, taking hold of two bars and trying to tear them out of the stones.

"So do I, lad," said Uncle Henry, beginning to cough again.

A little after three o'clock in the morning, a sturdy vagabond came strolling past the narrow window of the Cage.

He paused to peer in at the prisoners and growl, "What, little cuckoos!"

With a cry of joy, the son of the alderman sprang up from

the straw. "Hey, Tom! Is it thee?"

"Aye, my lad, and who art thou?" asked the sturdy vagabond.

"Remember me? Remember learning me the tricks of palliards, and the gypsies' holds in wrestling?"

"What, Jakes of Arden?"

"Me, old man of the moon."

"The aper of players, and of kings too? To what hast thou
come?"

Uncle Henry could be heard coughing.

"Who's the dad?" inquired the vagabond.

"My uncle Henry, Tom. Hey, Uncle Henry, here's an old
friend, Tom Tiddler of the Glen."

"Well met, Mr. Tiddler," croaked Uncle Henry.

"It is an honour, dad, to flip the famble of one who has such
a fine lad in the litter," said Mr. Tiddler, reaching in through
the bars of the Cage to shake hands with Uncle Henry. "In all
my travels I've never seen a finer hand with the dice, no, nor
with the cards, neither. What a pile of money he could make!"

"I'm glad to meet one of my nephew's friends of the forest,"
croaked Uncle Henry, for truly his cough was very bad.

"Allow me, sir, to give you something for that whoreson
rheum," said the friendly vagabond. And from his well-padded
garments he produced a fat leather bottle and passed it in
through the bars of the Cage.

There followed a grateful gurgling from within.

"God bless you, sir," said Uncle Henry in a fine clear voice,
passing the bottle to his nephew.

"He looks after me, dad. But why is your nephew here?"

"Gone and got a good woman with child, Mr. Tiddler. I
fear he did not listen to his father."

"Well, what son ever does?" said Tom. "None of mine ever
did. Leastways, them as I knew was mine."

"It is the way of youth, Mr. Tiddler. No son of my own."

"Have hope, dad, have hope. Try, try again."

"This nephew of mine has better luck. I fear me there'll
be a bastard kicking the air come spring."

The conversation of the uncle and the vagabond was becoming too mellow to please the nephew.

"Well, it has happened afore, from time to time, the women

being the weaker vessels, and made to bear our mad humours,"
said Mr. Tiddler. "What! They can only hang us once. But 'a
was a fellow of merry jests."

The subject of the philosophical discourse now interposed
a more practical remark. "And now I have the merriest jest of
all," he said.

"I'd like to hear it, mad wag," said the vagabond.

"Is your horse anywhere near, uncle?" asked Willy.

"Penned up at old Ananias's, and that's flat burglary,"
Uncle Henry answered.

"And will you lend him to me for a little business?"

"He's yours for the riding, lad, just as old Betsy his mother
was when you rode off to see the Queen ten whole years agone."

"Then come closer, Tom, and we'll hatch our jest."

There followed considerable whispering, and then a few
hoarse chuckles.

But the feeble old men of the Watch were coming down the
High Street, tapping their long staves upon the stones to warn
all evil-doers to escape, or it might go hard with them.

"Away, Tom, away!"

"Good night, friend and uncle, and give you a fair good
morning," whispered the vagabond, and melted away into the
black shadows reaching out from Wood Street, as if it were a
street of deep woods indeed.

There followed a little while, during which the old men of
the Watch paused to inspect the prisoners in the Cage and wish
them good amendment of conscience, and the prisoners
thanked them for their pains, and hoped they would have a
good sleep before the sun rose. Then all said good night and
the watchmen tottered on down the High Street, calling out to
anyone waking to guard his latches, guard his fires, and God
bless her Majesty, and might she live long.

A horse whinnied from Hog Lane, and was suddenly quiet,
so that anyone listening could almost see, and feel, the strong
fingers clamped down over nostrils. A gentle clopping sounded
over cobblestones. A rider trotted off into Back Bridge Street.
Then came the sweet sound of hoofs cantering across the bridge.

And in the Cage Uncle Henry and his nephew exhaled, and
whacked each other on the back, and then they finished the
bottle.

CHAPTER TWENTY

€ARLY in the morning, before any dutiful citizens had come out of their smoky houses into the foggy streets, Mr. Brace and Mr. Nason opened the door of the Clink, or as it was beginning to be called lately, the Cage, because so many birds had a habit of flying out of it.

But not this rare one they had now, they were determined he should not fly out from among their fumbling fingers.

"Have a care now, Ananias, we must keep our five wits togather," old Mr. Brace was saying as the little men, in their long cloaks and heavy bonnets, with clumsy halberds for their only weapons, began clattering at the door.

"Go to, I have handled offenders afore, in my time, and accused them too, beside our fat knight himself, God help him to a good death, poor old man," mumbled Mr. Nason, dropping the key.

"Amen," answered the offender within the Cage, patiently waiting for the grave men to accomplish their duties. "There it is, by thy right toe, Master Constabull, God save your good bones."

"Now, now, which is the offender to be whipped? Is it thee, Willy? It is a long time since I have seen thee here. What a misfortune for thy father!"

"Well, we must bear it with a good grace, and so make it easier for him, masters," gently remarked the offender, who well knew what the law was for such malefactors as himself. The first penalty for getting a wench with child was whipping, the second was dragging at cart's tail, the third was public interrogation, the fourth was public sentencing, and the fifth was to marry the wench.

"Now, Henry, lend a hand here, thou knowest the lad well, we must bind him straight," said Ananias, dropping the key.

"Permit me, sir, it does keep falling, the naughty engine," said the recreant, stooping to recover the key and handing it politely to Mr. Nason.

Uncle Henry strolled out of the Cage and stood beside his nephew, yawning and shaking his head like Alfred, who, his chin on one paw, was sleepily regarding the lawful procedures of these citizens.

"Thou wert always gentle, Willy. What a pity to be so inflicted with fits of nature!" said Ananias, tripping over his long halberd but keeping hold of the key anyhow.

"It has been my cross, sir, I do admit it."

"Well, I was such a one in my time, go to," said Mr. Nason, chuckling and digging him in the ribs. "Now, let me see, let me see. Where are the whips?"

While they had been fumbling, and stumbling, and stooping, and stopping, and starting, a small group of young men on ragged horses had ridden into the square and now sat lazily in their saddles, interestedly watching and waiting for what was going to happen.

"Let us have no strangers here," said Mr. Brace. "We want no strangers here, putting your duty aside, in the Queen's work."

"Aye, no, on your way, strangers, if ye are true men," piped Mr. Nason.

"Directly, masters, directly," said the man who appeared to be the leader of the rather ill-looking troupe. He was mounted upon Uncle Henry's horse, who was named James, after the King of Scotland, and was a rather handsome red roan, of the same colouring as his Majesty, and rather spindly in the shanks too, like that same rickety gentleman.

Indeed it was the recreant himself who had named the animal, when he was first foaled by old Betsy. He now waved to young James, and the friendly horse wrinkled up his nose and uttered a slight whicker.

"Are you on your way, strangers? We all fear God here, I hope," said Mr. Brace, who had always been an officious fellow, ever since he had been passed over for High Bailiff twenty-five years ago.

"But before we go, masters," said Mr. Tiddler, nodding to his companions, "look at these poor men's faces. No, no, I mean the prisoners, the prisoners. Ye're not going to whip a poor boy with the spotted plague, masters?"

"What, what, where?" croaked Mr. Brace, dropping his halberd.

"On his face, on his face, master, and his uncle's too," called out Mr. Tiddler helpfully, pointing.

"Mother of God!" cried Mr. Nason, in the way of good Puritans when surprised by trouble, for, truly, they would forget from time to time that they had reformed the religion at all, and would be back there with their mothers again.

And indeed, now they came to look at them, the prisoners, who were in truth not prisoners any more, since they were standing free and without irons, helpfully turning their countenances toward the dim English dawn now creeping like dirty water under a blanket, these same two naughty prisoners looked worse than any horrible imaginings it was legally permitted, God save two old men, to have.

All over their smiling countenances were the most hideous sores, pure madder and *caput mortuum* in colour.

"The plague!" screamed old Ananias, tripping over Mr. Brace's halberd.

"A mercy on thy old bones," said the gentle offender, picking him up.

"Oh, help, help, away, Willy! Come not near me! Hence with thee, poor boy, in the name of the Father, and of the Son, and of the Holy Ghost, Amen."

"Keep thy good distance, neighbours! Keep thy reverend good distances, we are Queen's men!" stammered Humffrey Brace.

Meanwhile the strangers on horseback had quietly dismounted from two of their steeds and had led up Uncle Henry's horse James, and a ragged Irish hobby such as could be bought in any horse market for three pounds, or stolen for nothing but a slight leap or a few twitches, or so. Mr. Tiddler then mounted a Spanish jenny, Uncle Henry mounted the hobby, and calling out to his frightful-looking nephew to leap upon James, wished the trembling keepers of the Cage a very good morning.

"Oh, alas, we must go home and burn strong herbs, or we are dead men," whimpered Mr. Nason.

"And our poor wives also, the pretty fools," moaned Mr. Brace, who was married to Giant Nell, as she was called, behind her broad back.

"What will we say to the justices?" asked Mr. Nason, as they tottered away.

"Bid them farewell, gentle **friends**, as I **do!**" called out young Willy from the saddle of young James.

"Then off to the greenmans, ride!" shouted the leader of the ragged company. And off to the fields and woods they went, at a good gallop.

"You know, uncle, I always like that place," Willy observed, as they cantered along toward where they were going.

"What place, dear boy?" asked Uncle Henry.

"The Cage," Willy said. "I like the way the first story sits up fatter than the basement, and the second chapter sits up fatter than the first, and the third chapter, or story, I mean to say, sits up on top fatter than all of 'em. So I'm going to buy it, when I come back. And I'm going to buy New Place too, and have the best house in Stratford."

"Thou art such another as thy father, boy, with thy mad ambitions for houses and properties, before thou hast full ownership to the shirt on thy back, God save thee."

"Wait and see, uncle, wait and see."

"Let us not wait any longer, let us get thee married, let us get thee married," said Uncle Henry.

# CHAPTER TWENTY-ONE

T HAT was the last time Willy
Shakespeare was seen around Stratford by daylight that year,
but he made a quick stop at Temple Grafton.

Out of the fog surrounding the cottage of Tom Whittington
appeared a party of young riders. The youngest, in a buff jerkin,
with wild flaming hair, and a face all staring with plague-sores,
leaped down and ran straight into the kitchen.

A few moments of silence, then cries of joy, followed by
cries of horror, then of rage, and then of fear.

"The plague! Help! Help!" shrieked Aunt Kate Whittington.

Then out came running the young fellow in the buff jerkin,
carrying a weeping and wailing young woman whose long
chestnut hair streamed after them in the wind as they galloped
away on the red roan, with the party of riders after them,
hallooing like hunters.

When they came to a little stream that went darkly shining
over the cold stones the party reined in and passed a bottle all
round, after which Uncle Henry and his nephew leaped down
and washed the horrible plague-sores from their faces.

"See?" Willy said to Anne.

"Would you mark your own helpless child?" she cried, so
angry he stepped aside just in time to avoid the crack of her
strong right hand.

"I never thought of that," he said, looking confused.

"I'll not have you anyway, with a clean face or a foul one,"
she said, stamping upon the ground, her grey eyes glittering
and full of danger.

"What? After all I have suffered, and overcome, and before
all I mean to do? What is this we've got anyhow, a shrew?" he
inquired of the grinning young men, all attentively earing the
quarrel, and having a good time of it.

"Ah, they will be curst, in their time," said Mr. Tiddler
reminiscently. "I mind me of how my wench Long Meg would

197

stamp, and rail, and be curst, and curst, afore when she foaled, as would daunt any Christom man, and put him in doubt of his salvation, ah, and —"

"Let me comprehend this, I had not planned this, let us all hear again, whether you will have me or no," said the angry young rider who, moreover, was dismounted, and disconcerted, and distracted.

"Never, never, I'd rather die," said Anne, again stamping upon the ground, and starting to run.

"Why then, she's a shrew, let her run mad," said one of the company, a small, shrunken fellow with sore eyes and a swollen nose.

"And marvellous ill-spoken, after all our pains," said a fat one, who looked like a horse thief well-known in those parts, who thus far had avoided the gallows.

"This is ingratitude," stated the son of the alderman flatly, adding that it was besotted, base, unkind, and marble-hearted, and he would have none of it now or hereafter, and there was an end.

Then he stood with folded arms, glaring after her as she ran along the bank of the stream, toward the pool in the woods.

"There she goes, stop her, stop her, she'll drown herself again!" shouted Uncle Henry, dashing into the woods.

"And I'll drown myself too!" cried his nephew, springing off after them.

Tom Tiddler and his companions winked at one another, yawned, for it was still early in the morning, and passed the little time that followed in deciding where they would do some good stealing today. They had about decided on Fidwell Forest when the young lovers came strolling out of the woods, their arms about each other, stopping to embrace passionately two or three times, while Uncle Henry came briskly along and nodded to Mr. Tiddler & Company.

"The business is all clear now, lads, so we'll wish you a pleasant journey, and go on to Worcester," he said, mounting his shaggy hobby.

"Clear till the next rainstorm," said Mr. Tiddler, leaning over to shake hands with him.

"Ah, they'll have their storms, and their thunders, and their lightnings, it is but nature, and the ready weather of marriage,"

SHAKESPEARE & SON 199

Uncle Henry said, as Anne and Willy came lovingly toward them, with misty eyes, and smiling lips, and dreaming motions, as if they were a merman and mermaid, peacefully afloat upon the bosom of their mother, the sea.

They were still dreaming, and smiling, and sighing, when the company of horsemen waved farewell from the crown of the hill, and they mounted the red roan together, she in the saddle, because of her excellent and ancient condition, though still new to her and exceedingly new to him, and he behind her, so that he could enjoy the pleasure of his strong arms around her, and could look over her comely shoulder into the future, as well as ahead on the road to Worcester.

"All clear now, nephew?" inquired Uncle Henry patiently.

"Clear as crystal and pasticcio," said Willy, and they rode on at a good clip-clop toward the bishop's palace, and whatever was before them.

"How did you do it, Willy?" muttered Uncle Henry, at one turn in the road.

"Oh, I explained clearly what my methods would be to make heaps and hoops of money out of playing, and how we were going to live in the best house in Stratford, as soon as we could buy it," his nephew informed him.

"Money in playing?" Uncle Henry inquired doubtfully. "Not what I heared, in my time, man and boy these forty years."

"Aye, uncle, aye, not for the players but for the managers, and owners, and sharers, for I had it all explained to me how, last August, by a man who knew how the world wags, and so I intend to be a sharer, and we'll live on money, money!"

"Oh, Henry, is he not sweet, after all?" murmured Anne, a look of bliss upon her face, quite altering its ordinary expression of good sense and intelligence.

## CHAPTER TWENTY-TWO

SO at last they stood dreaming in line at the Bishop of Worcester's Consistory Court, waiting to make their application for lawful marriage, hearing the voice of the little man up front droning on, and his pen scratching entries into the big register before him.

He got to them by noon or so, and immediately began scolding them for their ignorance.

"Know you not this is the holy season of Advent and therefore forbidden?"

The two loving people only smiled mistily, and murmured dimly, so that Uncle Henry had to go forward, clear his throat politely, and whisper in the ear of the gentleman, who was a very high churchman, who was named Cosin, or Cozen.

"Ah, why did they not say that before?"

"Bridegroom unfortunately far away, and did not know, sir," respectfully answered Uncle Henry, beginning to sweat more than a little.

"It is his duty to know! I'm tired of you young fellows coming into this court with your troth-plights, and your sweethearts, and expecting His Grace to put you all right in two shakes, when it is illegal, this is illegal!" said Dr. Cosin, shaking his finger at them. "His Grace likes it not, and I like it not."

"This is no troth-plight, your honour," said Anne dreamily, smiling as though she were basking in the glow of some fire.

"No troth-plight? Then what is it?" barked Dr. Cosin.

"Why, I'm with child by him, for I love him," said the young woman, standing up straight and looking him in the eye. "And he's come to you in all honesty to make it a right marriage, so do it, good man, and let us be about having our baby in peace, and no more scratchings and nonsense."

"You're a proud woman, are you?" said Dr. Cosin, staring back at her.

"I am, and I'll be treated so in this place and all places," said Anne, folding her strong arms and throwing back her magnificent shoulders.

A small cheer went up from the humble petitioners waiting in line behind them.

"Order! Order in the court!" shouted Dr. Cosin, looking nearly as warm as Anne.

"The woman's right, so give her the license, o' God's name!" spoke up a countryman from the rear of the room.

"Aye, aye, a good stout speaker for the right o' freeborn Englishmen!" said another.

The bishop's court was not liked at all anywhere in the county, with its constant spyings, and fines, and penalties, and petty nigglings and naggings of the stubborn English people, and they all had various ways of outwitting it anyhow.

Dr. Cosin sniffed, and snorted, and fretted awhile, and told one or two low fellows to watch out there, or the constables and beadles, aye, and the sextons too, would have them by the heels, and by the ears too, but he had lost heart already, and was no match for the strong young woman with the glowing righteousness about her, as if she had done something wonderful, and deserved praise for it.

"With no troth-plight, I know not rightly just what to do," said Dr. Cosin. "Sure there was no troth-plight? It seems to be customary among you country people."

"A troth-plight with him? He's too young!" cried Anne indignantly, and everybody but Dr. Cosin laughed.

"Order, order, we can do nothing without strict order in this court and in this diocese, and His Grace will have it too, and know the reason why not, too, and now come up here and tell me your names slowly and in good countenance, and where your parish is, and the boy will have to give me the signed permission from his father, he's too young, the girl says so herself."

"But his father cannot sign any permission, the man is sick, the man is dying!" muttered Uncle Henry.

"What?" cried the bridegroom, seizing his uncle in his arms and staring into his face. "You did not tell me! Is it the truth?"

"The truth of God, so help me," Uncle Henry said.

So between the new tragedy and the old trouble, not to

speak of the new laws, it began to look as if there would be no marriage after all, there were so many obstacles.

Finally they decided what they would do, after they had gone out into the courtyard and cooled off at the little well, which had a bucket, for the watering of horses.

"But Maggie'll be heartburned, waiting for me," Uncle Henry said.

"Oh, I'll send one of my brothers off to tell her the whole story, she'll love thee all the better for a few nights' absence, and perhaps you'll get yourselves a baby at long last," Willy said.

"Well, he won't be named William, that I can tell you now," Uncle Henry grumbled. "Too much fitting and starting for fair, in one o' that name, I could name."

"Name him James then, after thy good horse," Willy said, mounting again. "And take good care of my bride. I am beginning to like her all over again."

"Be sure and bring a cloak-bag full of good clothes," said Anne as he prepared to ride away. "And my dowry from Henry Rogers' office, he's had it locked up long enough to be mouldy."

"And if Maggie has any nightgowns for the bride, throw 'em in, she'll need warmth this winter!" called Uncle Henry after him.

"She'll be warm with me, and I'll see you tomorrow!"

Then Willy rode off in a hurry, to do all that had to be done, in good order, or at least in whatever order he would be able.

When he dismounted in the Henley Street stable-yard his brother Gilly was there, meditatively eating a potato pie.

"How's father?" cried Willy, springing from the saddle.

"Eh?" said Gilly, staring.

"Does he live? Does he breathe? Is he not choking?"

"Eh? Where'd you come from?"

"I came to see father, you fool!" said Willy, rushing into the house.

Confused noises began echoing in there, from kitchen to parlour, from bedroom to bedroom. Gilly went on peacefully eating, though once in awhile shrugging up his fat shoulders and shaking his fat head. And James, the red roan, looked all around at the orchard, sniffed and snuffed at the grass and trees,

and then began eating little old apple-johns out of a basket
somebody had forgotten to put away in the pantry, or in the
cellar.

"Father! Father! Forgive me! It's me!" cried the returned
wanderer, rushing into the bedroom where people sat looking
sad.

"Oh, Willy! Home at last!" cried his mother, clasping her
hands and raising them toward the old, low, heavy ceiling.

"Home to put on my good suit, mother, and pack all my
things, and to be married, but how's father?" he said, embracing her and all his family and cousins that were there, which
was not many, for the room was small.

Will Smith, his godfather, was there though, and Tom
Greene from Warwick, and the Webbs from Bearley.

Old John's heavy breathing filled the room with its long,
slow, struggling sound. He was busily talking to himself, in
a dry, grey murmur.

"Mother, mother, I did not know," said the weeping son,
kneeling by the second-best bed and kissing her hands.

"Thou art so thin, poor boy, where hast thou laid thy head
all these bitter nights?"

"Oh, that's nothing, mother, nothing at all," he said, hearing
the wandering voice of the old man babbling on. "What does
he say, mother?"

"Oh, one thing and another thing, darling, and ever the
same. A puzzle to him, like a web, and he's never out of it long.
Thou hast been out in the rain and cold, poor fool, and thy good
clothes wasted all at home."

"Oh, I'll take 'em along, mother," he said impatiently.

Someone tall and in black came into the low room and all
the people stood up.

"Pax vobiscum," said a low, deep voice that sent a shiver
along Willy's spine. He sprang to his feet and stared as his old
friend Debdale came up to the bed and made the sign of the
cross over the babbling alderman.

"No change?" whispered Debdale, and then held out his
arms to embrace this eldest son who was so startled at the sight
of him.

"But Robin, how did you — how did he — I do not comprehend anything."

"Seek not to question it then," said Debdale, kissing him on the forehead. "It is a miracle for more than one of us to be living at all. God be praised for sending thee back, Willy."

"Ask him for his blessing, darling," whispered Mary.

"Give me your blessing, Robin, Father, that is to say, but I do not understand how my father, who is the stubbornest Puritan of them all, would find the road back to —"

"And who among us can understand the wonderful ways of God?" inquired Father Debdale of the awe-stricken or at least dumb-stricken people in the room, and there was a respectful murmur from at least two of them.

"Well, perhaps there is a book about it somewhere, there ought to be anyhow," said Willy hopelessly, kneeling down for his old friend's blessing, just in case there might be some good in it. "But I warn thee, Robin, I'm not even a Christian this year, I've given up on both sides of your argument and gone back to the Greeks, so perhaps it will not take."

"Have no fear, old friend, it is strong enough to take even thee," said Father Debdale, taking strong hold of his head and stating firmly in Latin that this son of God was to be accorded special attention and watched closely by the most trustworthy angels.

"Well, thank you, Father, it was a good blessing and I may need it. Anne and I are to be married as soon as I can get my father's permission. Is that possible?"

And he looked at his old friend with a weird light in his eyes, whether jealousy, or mischief, or the devil, could not be determined in that dim light.

"Oh, darling, poor Anne! What could you have been thinking of?" cried his mother, wringing her hands.

"Thinking of something else, mother, I promise thee that," said her son, while his two little brothers kept on staring at him, and young Joan just wept, and smiled whenever his goat-eye looked at her.

"She has told me all about it, and you have my blessing for your journey together, God grant it may begin soon," said Debdale, with something of a glint in his own eye by now. Not for nothing had he whipped and beaten his lusty nature into this vessel of grace, if he had really attained grace yet. His friend wondered, eyeing him suspiciously from time to time as they all waited for some sign of change in the hard-breathing and babbling alderman.

"How long?" whispered Willy.

"Oh, some days he's very bad, and then others, he knows us and is almost himself," answered his mother.

"He looks thirsty to me. Can he have any wine? He likes the malmsey best."

"Dr. Ward has forbidden it, lamb, and the poor man has tried everything, with his cuppings, purgings, bleedings, possets, infusions, and all."

"If Anne could be here, she might cure him."

"We've done everything human," said his mother, her fine eyes beginning to glow with dangerous fire.

"Oh, I believe it, mother," he said, but his restless eyes showed his doubt, and distrust, and discontent. He began prowling round the house, opening cupboards, highboys, lowboys, taking out things, putting things in a huge cloak-bag and two saddlebags. The house was already too small for him, just as it had been before. Not even give him wine! he thought.

"What do doctors know?" he barked at Gilly, just plodding in for something to eat.

"Eh?"

"It is his mind, his mind, and who can minister to a mind?"

"Eh? Where'd thou come from anyhow, Willy?"

"Ask the doctor," his brother said, giving up on the people in this house. After awhile he went out into the town to attend to all the business that had to be done before Anne could get her dowry, and he could get his license, and Dr. Cosin could get his bond, which would be for the horrible sum of forty pounds. What householder, shop-keeper, or farmer would sign such a bond before tomorrow?

"Why, Willy, I thought thou wert in the Cage!"

"Aye, old Ananias said he had thee there, and then thou wert dead of the plague."

"Well, well, old men have fancies," he told them, smiling madly, because his heart pained him and his stomach felt reluctant and stubborn, over all these scratchings and scribblings and quidlicets and whereas's of asses in offices.

He was blazing with the old impatience again before he returned to the old smoky house. Now his mind was made up.

They've not cured the old man in all these months or weeks, whatever it has been, and now it's my turn, he decided, and he strode into the establishment with his head high and his eyes bright, as eldest son and legal heir to the whole basket if he wanted it, and he did not want it, at least not yet.

"Joan, bring out two bottles of his ancient malmsey from Spain, the ones those traveling leathermen smuggled in," he told his sister. "And he likes pickled herring with it, and if you have any good redshank, or rare beef, we'll have it on a big platter, with a loaf and cheese."

"Oh, Willy, *mother!*" said his gentle sister, sighing with fear and fatigue.

"Mother is a woman, go," he said, kissing her a hearty smack, and whacking her upon the seat.

"Oh!" said the girl, and began laughing, the first sound of honest life in that house he had heard yet, on this hasty visit.

Ah, it feels good to be a married man, almost, he thought. One can cope better with 'em, I suppose.

Yet he still wondered a little bit, thinking of Anne's forthright and stubborn speeches before the mighty representative of Bishop Whitgift, that pursuer of stubborn Puritans, as his predecessor, old blind Grindal, had been a chaser of Catholics. Well, it may all come out even in the end, but what an end, he thought. And so will we, before we're through, I hope.

And he went briskly up the stairs with his dutiful sister Joan, as soon as she had the wine and the other things ready.

"Now, friends, I would be alone with my father, I'll see you all anon," he said, standing masterfully at the door of the bedroom.

It was not long before he had cleared them all out. His friend or rival, or ex-rival the priest, had been gone since early afternoon.

"Fetch hither my lute," he said to little Dick.

"It's broke," said the freckled boy sadly.

"Fetch it hither, it will have strings enough."

"Oh, lamb, have you any hope? Singing, eating, drinking?"

"Just like Jesus, mother, with his friends from the byways, I'm all blessed now and know all about it."

"Alas, alas, the doctor said —"

"He came eating and drinking, mother, and the doctors did

not like him either. Now go sleep and rest awhile, or vice versa. I think my father is lonely for sweet music, and his little blood left by the doctor needs red wine to make more. I know all about it, mother, I've studied medicine in books. Trust me, good night."

So at last he was alone with the old man with whom he had fought the long, long, tedious and impossible war, and he felt nothing stirring in him but doubt, and disgust at doctors, and hunger and thirst too, for that matter.

People in the house, and out in the street, heard him singing and playing old songs half the night. Many neighbours stopped and listened and murmured, and shook their heads, but the end of it was they all went to bed, and he still went on playing and singing. And drinking and eating too, his weary mother supposed, listening at the door at about three o'clock in the morning.

She heard voices singing, not one voice singing, but voices. She uttered a loud cry.

"Oh, darling, darling," she sobbed, going trembling into the bedroom from which she had been routed by this utterly grown-up son. Alas, where was the lovely boy he had been? All gone now in this stern and masterful man, with his kingly orders and his voice like that of some ancient Welshman off the moors, enough to bring pity to hearts of stone.

Her husband opened his eyes and looked at her in the candlelight.

"John, John, wert thou singing with our boy?" she sobbed. "Was it thee, John?"

"Woman, did it sound like the cat on the wall?" inquired her husband.

"Oh, John," she whispered, and there was no play-acting at all, she was too tired, she just sat down by the bed and waited for what was going to happen next, since there was now a man in the house who decided such things.

When the bread, cheese, beef, and wine were all gone, and old Willy Smith and Tom Greene were rousted out again to witness the deed of parental permission to get married without delay, there was now little more to do than kiss everybody all round, and be off again to Worcester.

As for the matter of two property-holders to sign the bond against impediments, Willy had found two old neighbours of Dick Hathaway in Shottery who would do that — Fulke Sandells and John Richardson, good steady farmers, not startled by anything, and waiting by now at the old mill on the road to Worcester, if they kept their promise.

"Give it me, give it me, lads, I want to write it large and fair, I can do it boldly, like a smug bridgegroom," said John, who was now sitting up in bed, looking still a little waxy and wan, but with uncommonly bright eyes, and two spots of red, one on either side of his nose.

"Now, John, do not tire thyself, man, make thy old mark of thy dividers, it is good enough for the business," said his cousin Tom Greene.

"Bah, I've read so many scribbles by the boy, I can write as fair as he can, aye, and jest as foul too," said the stubborn alderman, holding out his trembling hand for the goose-quill and frowning at the paper they had put before him, on a trencher. "What, shall I eat it? That's illegal, or has the bishop begun a new rule on it too?"

"Only scratch our name down, father, any old way, and I'll be off on Uncle Henry's horse."

"What's amiss with Crispin? Take Crispin," growled old John. "The son of a Stratford yeoman ought to have a horse for himself. Let thy wife have the roan."

Willy looked down at the old cracked floor, feeling sudden shame at the long war he had fought with this man. I am already beginning to forget why, he thought. Well, I will have time to study it later.

"And my sword," said John, scratching away at the paper. "A young man needs a good sword on the roads these days. Fetch my sword, Gilly, be quick about it, prance!"

"O Lord, father," said his eldest son, beginning to choke.

"With a whoreson *e*," his father remarked, holding up the paper. "And let 'em mock that in the bishop's court, eh? Let 'em mock that!"

Then with a long sigh he put his head back on the pillow, smacked his lips a few times, muttered something about hearing chimes in his ears, playing the tune of *Greensleeves*, and fell asleep.

Early on Wednesday morning, which was the feast of St. James and a cold rainy one, young Willy and two companions rode into the courtyard of the Bishop of Worcester's palace, with Uncle Henry's horse James clopping after them on a lead rein, bearing two fat panniers and a big cloak-bag for burden so far, until there was a bride to ride him.

Willy wore his good suit, his warm cloak, a new Norwich hat with a falcon feather. His father's Sheffield sword clanked proudly at his side, he had boots of good Spanish morocco, and what made him beam with joy was his detailed recollection of all the gifts his mother and Joan and Mrs. Bassett and the wives of his two companions had put into the cloak-bag for the bride.

But where was the bride?

"Well, well, boy, the girl would not be standing in the rain all night, look inside the castle," said Mr. Sandells, who knew her extremely well.

"There, lad, she's waited long enough for thee, now do a little seeking thyself," said Mr. Richardson, as the two large and substantial farmers climbed ponderously down from their sturdy plough-horses and led them to the well for a drink.

"I hope nothing has happened to her," said Willy, disguising the fact that he was disappointed because she had not seen his entrance into the courtyard, with that falcon feather, that hat, riding black Crispin, the pride of the whole Shakespeare family, almost never ridden by anyone but his father, and O beautiful, this bright sword, tenderly shielded in its scabbard from the heavy dew of this important morning.

"Has anyone seen a handsome young woman about, in blue gown and hood, with eyes as clear as the shield of Mars before the battle?" he inquired politely of the first acolyte he met in the long hallway of the bishop's palace, which led to the kitchens.

"Sounds delightful sort of girl, try the kitchen, good many people work there," muttered the acolyte, hurrying on to chapel, or consistory court, with a swishing of long flapping skirts.

Kitchen indeed! thought the bridegroom.

He hunted around and around inside the palace, going nearly everywhere he could without challenge, or scandal. No Anne, no Uncle Henry.

"Hey, Willy, where art thou?" called Mr. Richardson, coming fast round a corner. "Anne's been waiting all this time at the front gate of the palace, and she's a bit angry."

"*She* is angry!" said the bridegroom, but he quickly recovered his marvellous new manly pride and confidence, and with long sword clanking bravely against his thigh he strode after his bondsman, who so recklessly would soon be signing an agreement to forfeit twenty pounds, and his neighbour the same, if some other girl turned up and proved a troth-plight, and demanded marriage to the bridegroom.

O Lord, Lizzie! he thought all of a sudden. And he broke into a brisk trot. "Let us make haste, Mr. Richardson, for we have a long ride ahead of us, and should be in Evesham before noon."

"Thou shouldst have hurried afore now, Willy. Contain thy patience, all will be well," said Mr. Richardson.

Out they came into the misty morning, the rain pretty much all dribbled down now, only dropping off a few naked limbs of trees, and the bride and bridegroom met with happy cries.

"Wait till I show thee the presents!"

"Oh, lamb, how beautiful you look in all those clothes! But no haircut!"

"Time enough for that, time enough for that, let us all go in now and sign the bond against impediments, take our license and gallop away."

"Oh, but angel — can't we stay at the inn and be wed at St. Martin's in the Corn Market? Uncle Henry wants to sell his new ewes at the fair."

"No, no, straight on to London, not a minute to lose," he muttered, propelling her along toward the courtroom where the line was gathering again. Then into her shadowy hood he whispered, "Lizzie!"

"O Lord, I forgot all about her," said Anne, and started hurrying faster than he was.

Uncle Henry and Mr. Sandells managed to reach them in the line of petitioners, suitors, bondsmen, and plain old sinners, and they had a good, long, impatient, simmering wait until they stood again before Dr. Cosin at his haughty bench.

But the fussy clerical gentleman was delighted to see them this morning, and smiled three whole times at Anne, during his swearing them, and spelling their names, and re-spelling them, until he finally got it approximately right, William Shagspere on thone partie, and Anne Hathwey of Stratford in the Dioces of Worcester maiden, although their names were scrambled up into Willelmum Shaxpere and Annam Whateley of Temple Grafton, in the license.

"And now, dear friends, in case no other bride appears with prior claim —"

The two young people looked alarmingly innocent, and the bondsmen and the uncle looked grim.

"— either expectedly or unexpectedly," continued Dr. Cosin, with a dry smile at Anne, and a suspicious look at the bridegroom, "or in case the groom should be imprisoned —"

The innocent expression of the bridegroom at this point would have made a cat laugh, whether it knew him or not.

"— or should um ah suddenly quit the country, as has happened before, unfortunately, I think there will now be no obstacles to a good marriage to a good woman and now I shall kiss the bride," concluded Dr. Cosin, bounding up from his armchair and coming round smiling a little hungrily.

The kissing went off all smoothly, with everybody friendly and calm-looking, though the long sword clattered quite a bit, before the whole party got out into the courtyard again, and could hug one another, and kiss again all round, and shake any old hand over and over again.

"Oh, I thought we'd never do it," gasped Anne, leaning against the fat cloak-bag.

"Have a care, have a care to thy presents, some of them break!" cried out the bridegroom.

It was like a celebration already, round the well and the bucket.

"There's one thing I regret," said Willy with a sad look on his clean, handsome face.

"Is it Lizzie?" whispered Anne.

"O Lord, I forgot her again," he said. "No, the size of the

bond. He was in such a good humour I should have got him to knock off ten pounds."

"Well, we can go for it, and now let's to the Corn Market, Henry, and peddle thy new ewes, and I've some barley they might have a taste for, went good and long in the grain this year."

So saying, after having a bit of a wash at the well, and combing the uncle's hair, which looked rather wild, Mr. Sandells assisted the bride to her saddle between the panniers, so that she had the cloak-bag behind her, and was disposed marvellously comfortable for a good journey.

"Well, Willy, and what are thy prospects, eh, lad?" asked Mr. Richardson, as they all mounted.

"Look, we've two good horses already, have we not, Uncle Henry? Or shall you take James back to eat up oats in the barn all winter?"

"He's yours, he's yours, did I not say it afore?"

"And with two fine horses then, we can let 'em out for hire when we get to London, and Crispin will fetch a good price at stud —"

"Aye, but, never mind the breeding, never mind the breeding, we all understand that, but what is it thou art after in London, Willy, in one word?"

The young bridegroom, taking up his reins and speaking authoritatively to Crispin, took the head of the procession. As the handsome black animal stepped gracefully forward, Willy took off his new hat with the falcon feather and waved it in the air.

"Money!" he said.

Anne, Uncle Henry, and the two farmers followed him, looking convinced.